Pathways to Career Success for Women

A Resource Guide to Colleges, Financial Aid, and Work

Ferguson Publishing Company, Chicago, Illinois

Editor: Laurie Sabol
Writers: Sherry Powley, Laurie Sabol
Proofreader: Bonnie Needham
Cover Design: Robert Howard Graphic Design

Library of Congress Cataloging-in-Publication Data

Pathways to career success for women: a resource guide to colleges, financial aid, and work
    p. cm.--(The pathways to career success series)

Includes index

ISBN 0-89434-281-9
    1. Vocational guidance for women--United States. 2. Women--Employment--United
States. 3. Vocational guidance for women--United States--Directories. I. Series.

HF5382.65 .P38 2000
650.14'082'0973--dc21   00-021892

Copyright 2000 by Ferguson Publishing Company

Published and Distributed by
Ferguson Publishing Company
200 West Jackson, Suite 700
Chicago, Illinois 60606
800-306-9941
http://www.fergpubco.com

Printed in the United States of America

X-4

Table of Contents

SECTION D: INDEXES

Introduction

It's an exciting time to be a woman! Though some inequities still exist, women have gained entry to virtually every existing career field and girls enjoy wider educational opportunities. Women are excelling in physically and intellectually challenging disciplines traditionally dominated by men and are breaking "weaker sex" stereotypes. They are starting new firms at twice the rate of all other businesses and own nearly 40 percent of all firms in the United States, according to the Small Business Administration. Having seen the opportunities that await them, more women are earning college degrees every year than men are. Several forces have galvanized the movement for equal opportunity, not the least of which is the united front presented when women organize to make their voices a collective force for change. Women's professional organizations provide the framework for equal opportunity and are the heart of this directory.

Pathways to Career Success for Women: A Resource Guide to Colleges, Financial Aid, and Work is a directory of tools to help women get started or take their career to the next level—professional and trade organizations, financial assistance, publications, Internet resources, women's colleges, internships, and mentoring programs. All are a means for women to network with each other and to learn from and be inspired by successful women in their field. Women in virtually every discipline will find at least one organization that specializes in their line of work; most will find many. This directory is primarily a compilation of opportunities for individuals, though organizations may also benefit from much of the information. Program directors and career guidance counselors will find resources to assist their target groups and employers may find ways to create a fairer workplace.

This directory is for women of all ages and all professional levels, from students to women returning to the workforce after an absence to experienced professionals. It is for women who work with their hands in various skilled trades, and women who conduct highly specialized scientific research, and the thousands of women who work in more traditional careers such as teaching, child care, and clerical work.

How to Use This Book

Pathways to Career Success for Women is organized to allow readers to quickly locate resources in their particular career area. Those looking for financial aid can browse through Section A for fellowships, grants, loans, and scholarships organized alphabetically by the funder's name. Section B lists contact information for professional organizations and a brief description of membership benefits. Section C includes free publications, internships, Internet resources, women's research centers, and academic camps for girls. Since many professional and trade organizations offer financial assistance as well as other programs, these organizations are listed more than once in different sections. Readers will benefit from checking these duplicate entries because they contain different information, depending upon the section in which they are found.

Introduction

Section A: Financial Aid

For the purposes of this directory, there are five types of financial aid: fellowships, grants, scholarships, awards, and loans. This directory lists only financial aid that is available to women in general. Financial aid that requires membership in an organization is not listed in this section, but is noted in Section B under membership benefits of organizations. Students and working women who are not currently members may still be interested in the members-only information, because in many cases they are immediately eligible for financial assistance upon joining an organization. Other organizations require members to be in good standing for a year or more before they are eligible for financial aid. Readers should check with the organization regarding eligibility before applying for membership or financial aid.

Fellowships generally are offered at the graduate, postgraduate, or doctoral level, often for research projects or dissertation assistance.

Grants are similar to fellowships, although they may be given at any level, and are generally given for work on a specific project, such as research or for travel expenses to a professional conference.

Scholarships are offered at all levels, from high school through postdoctoral to working women.

Awards are generally given in recognition of achievement, either to a promising young woman moving up in her career field or to an experienced professional for a lifetime of achievement. Many awards include a monetary stipend; others don't grant any money at all but are valuable recognition by one's peers and excellent resume-builders.

Loans for women-only and women and minority-friendly loans are available from lenders around the country. Your local Small Business Administration office can get you connected with specialized lenders.

Section B: Organizations

A wide range of organizations make up Section B. All work on behalf of women, but their structure, goals, services, and activities vary greatly. In addition to being women-oriented, organizations selected for listing in this directory also were required to have a career or educational focus. This section is broken down as follows:

In this directory, professional organizations cover a range of groups working on behalf of women. Most included here are trade and professional associations that recruit members, hold meetings, and offer training. Also listed are organizations that advocate on behalf of women without offering specific membership activities, but instead keep women apprised of developments in the field and women's rights in general. Many organizations listed here also accept men, but maintain a primary focus of advancing and recognizing women in the field.

Members of the Women's College Coalition, an organization of 79 women's colleges in the U.S. and Canada are listed with contact information for each college.

Greek-letter societies, including sororities, honorary societies, and service organizations offer social, philanthropic, and personal development opportunities to women. Contact information only is listed for sororities and service organizations. Although there are sororities in specific career fields, most list sisterhood and service in general as their main objectives. This list is certainly not a comprehensive list of all sororities in the United States. Rather, the national offices of large sororities and service organizations with a presence on several campuses are listed here. Honorary societies for professionals and college alumnae are also listed here.

A number of women's athletic organizations are listed, including governing organizations for various sports and contacts for coaching organizations and athletic scholarship information.

Commissions are created by government to improve the status of women and to work toward equality and justice for all women. The National Association of Commissions for Women is an umbrella organization for government-sanctioned regional, state, county, and local commissions across the United States. These commissions have been created by law and are service delivery organizations with a grassroots network of volunteers. Commissions act as information and referral resources for women in employment and education, as well as domestic violence, health, and child care. The National Association of Commissions for Women (NACW) can be reached at 8630 Fenton Street, Silver Spring, MD 20910-3808. Telephone: 301/585-8101. Internet: http://www.nacw.org.

The federal government's Small Business Administration coordinates a network of more than 60 Women's Business Centers in 36 states, the District of Columbia, and Puerto Rico. These centers provide a wide range of services to women entrepreneurs at all levels of business development. WBCs teach women the principles of finance, management, and marketing, as well as specialized topics such as how to get a government contract or how to start a home-based business. The SBA Web site also offers online information, such as articles on starting and growing a business, technology, and procurement. Further information on SBA services for women can be found in Section B under its organizational listing and in Section A under loans.

Section C: Additional Information

A variety of career aids can be found in this section.

Publications. There are many publications offered free or for a nominal fee that contain career-specific information not found elsewhere. Professional journals keep women up- to-date on developments in the field and provide an outlet for research conducted by and about women. Newsletters that are membership benefits of an organization are listed under organizational entries in Section B. Publications listed in this section are available to the general public upon request or by subscription. Membership in an organization is not necessary to obtain the publications listed in this section.

Online Resources. The Internet provides a wealth of information for working women and students, all free! The Web sites listed in this section vary from informal discussion forums for women in a particular field to detailed articles with professional advice from women who have experience working in a certain area. Web sites compiled as free information resources by organizations are included here, as well as some Web sites compiled by individuals. Please note that the information found on Web sites created by an individual may not be as reliable as that posted by an organization. Every effort has been taken to include only Web sites with reliable, accurate information, but readers will be well-served to consider the source of any information they find on the Internet.

Internships are a great way to gain valuable work experience and develop contacts that may help you find a job later. Many internships are unpaid; others offer assistance with lodging. Most will work with the schools to allow the intern to receive college credit. The internships listed in this section are geared toward women. Many state that they are

Introduction

women-only; others are for organizations that generally attract women, such as feminist, reproductive health, and women's research organizations.

Work-at-home resources are included in this directory because working at home or other alternative work arrangements are attractive options for many women trying to balance professional and family responsibilities. Many of the organizations listed in this section are not expressly for women.

Many U.S. colleges and other institutions now offer Women's History/Research programs and resources. Umbrella organizations such the National Women's History Project, National Council for Research on Women, and National Women's Studies Association maintain lists of member organizations across the country and can direct you to resources in your area; there are women's history/research resources in all 50 states. Contact information for members' programs are listed in this section.

There are a number of excellent academic and career programs to help girls get interested in and explore science, math, technology, and other careers. Girls' programs such as weekend workshops, academic camps, career workshops, mentoring arrangements, and competitions are also listed. Of course, many programs operate on a small scale at the local level. Included here are programs that are nationally available or duplicated locally.

Part I

Essays on Women's Topics

Legal Pathways to Success for Women: Equal Education and Equal Employment

Pathways to Career Success for Women is about helping girls and women find resources to be successful in their life endeavors. It reflects an underlying belief that advancing the status of women will improve the quality of life for women, their families and communities, the nation, and the planet.

During the last four decades of the twentieth century, the U.S. government enacted important laws that established legal pathways women can follow to attain gender equity—equitable treatment of women and men—in school and in the workplace. These laws prohibit discrimination in education and in employment on the basis of gender.

Equal Education

Education provides the basis upon which an individual builds career choices, life choices, and economic independence. The United States has one of the highest standards of education in the world, and its goal is to offer equal educational opportunity to all. The number of girls completing high school, those entering and graduating from college, and women completing advanced degrees has been increasing steadily.

However, gender bias is still evident in our educational system. Many school administrators and teachers unconsciously communicate and reinforce stereotypes regarding girls' capabilities. Females are underrepresented in critical subject areas such as math and science. In addition, girls' and women's athletics receive less attention and funding than athletics for boys and men.

Girls, women, educators, and parents need to be aware of gender equity laws and the right to equal education opportunities. They must also know about school grievance procedures and the legal steps to follow in case those rights are violated.

Title IX of the Education Amendments of 1972

A major step forward for women occurred when President Nixon signed into law Title IX of the Education Amendments of 1972 (Title IX). This law prohibits discrimination on the basis of sex in educational programs and activities that receive any federal funding. Since the federal government is the largest single source of financial aid to education in the United States, Title IX applies to most public schools, colleges, and universities, and even affects some private schools.

Title IX specifically prohibits discrimination on the basis of gender—from school admission, to financial aid, to athletics, and everything in between. It also protects against

3

discrimination on the basis of marital and parental status. In addition, it protects against sexual harassment.

Title IX holds every educational institution that receives federal funds responsible for complying with its requirements. Every institution must designate a Title IX Coordinator who must establish and make public its nondiscrimination policies and its grievance procedures. It is important that females learn about their educational institution's policies and know the grievance procedures and how to follow them, if necessary.

When prompt, appropriate action is not taken by an educational institution to resolve a discrimination issue, legal action may be necessary. More and more cases of sexual harassment in schools has been reaching the courts. For information on Title IX, its regulations, and strategies for dealing with sexual harassment, visit the Equity Online Web site (http://www.edc.org/WomensEquity/).

Women's Educational Equity Act of 1974

Title IX's protection of women's rights in education was expanded in 1974 when the U.S. Department of Education initiated the Women's Educational Equity Act (WEEA) to reduce the educational disparity between men and women. This act awards grants to schools, universities, community organizations, and individuals, and it encourages gender-fair programs in math and science. Equity Online (http://www.edc.org/WomensEquity/) is a resource center maintained by WEEA and includes extensive information on gender equity and on Title IX. This Web site contains comprehensive information on Title IX sexual harassment issues, and includes constructive ways for educational institutions and individuals to deal with sexual harassment.

Higher Education Act Amendments of 1998

Another act that helps make postsecondary education available to women is the Higher Education Act Amendments of 1998. This act makes grants available to educational institutions in order to help provide campus-based child care services to low-income students. According to the act, a low-income student is defined as any student who qualifies for a federal Pell Grant. Women who are interested in applying for these child care services should verify that the schools they are considering participate in the Pell Grant program and that child care services are available. For more information on Pell Grants and other financial aid, see the Financial Aid section in this book.

Progress Report

Women's access to education has increased; however, equal educational opportunities have not always resulted in equity for females. Studies of the federal government's efforts to increase gender equity in schools show that the results have been mixed. False beliefs about differences in aptitudes and abilities between boys and girls that are held by parents, professionals, and students often perpetuate unfair treatment and unequal educational opportunities. Gender bias in standardized tests continues to limit women's access to educational institutions, financial aid, and career opportunities. Women of color and women with disabilities encounter even greater obstacles.

Recognizing and overcoming gender inequities in education is crucial to raising the educational level and improving the quality of life of women in the United States. Advancing the status of women means improving the quality of life not only for them, but for their children, families, and communities as well. The references at the end of this article include programs that will help females and those who care about them find the resources needed to overcome gender barriers in education and to achieve career success.

Equal Employment

Positive advances in educational equality will help pave the way toward greater employment equality for women. Progress toward gender equity in the workplace has been increasing, but it is still slow. Civil rights and employment legislation enacted in the last half of the twentieth century have give women important rights in the workplace.

Regardless of these strides, however, women are still underrepresented in many critical careers. Helping girls and women build their self-esteem and their confidence in their abilities to succeed in math, science, and technology can help fill the nation's need for trained workers, and subsequently increase the standard of living for many women and their families. The United States has a growing need for technicians, scientists, and skilled workers. Most of these occupations are still considered nontraditional careers for women; that is, jobs in which women comprise less than 25 percent of the workers. Many jobs that are considered nontraditional for women pay higher wages than those that are considered "women's work." For more information on nontraditional careers and how to pursue them, see the essay "Excellent Opportunities for Women: Nontraditional Career."

In career fields that are more traditional for women, few women have broken through the so-called glass ceiling—the invisible barrier to advancement that keeps women from attaining the top positions in the workplace. The salary gap between women's and men's incomes still exists. Studies showed that in 1996 women only earned 74 cents for every dollar men earned. Women also hold fewer jobs that offer good benefits such as insurance, profit sharing, and retirement plans. See the essay "Overcoming Roadblocks in a Woman's Pathway to Success: The Wage Gap, the Glass Ceiling, and Sexual Harassment" for more information on these and other employment issues facing women today.

Clearly, gender bias continues to exist in the workplace and in society. To attain gender equity for themselves, their daughters, and all women, individuals need to be aware of the laws that protect women's employment rights. They must also learn how to address grievances in the workplace, and how to seek legal remedies when necessary.

Title VII of the Civil Rights Act of 1964

Title VII of the Civil Rights Act of 1964 (Title VII) prohibits employment discrimination based on race, color, religion, sex, or national origin. It applies to all businesses that employ at least 15 workers.

Under Title VII, employers are not allowed to

• discriminate against women when hiring

• base employment decisions on stereotypes

• pay women less than men for similar work

• deny women training opportunities that they offer to men

• refuse to consider women for higher positions

• establish lower wages for "women's jobs" than for "men's jobs" that require equal skills

- tolerate sexual harassment in the workplace

- discriminate against women on the basis of pregnancy

Title VII greatly improves employment equity and opportunities for women who work for larger employers, but it does not offer protection to women who work for employers with fewer than 15 employees.

Equal Pay Act of 1963

The Equal Pay Act of 1963 (EPA) requires all employers to pay equal wages and benefits to women and men who perform "substantially equal" work in the same establishment. In some cases, that affords more protection for women who work for smaller employers. However, over half of the women in the workforce are employed in "women's jobs" where no men work. Where there are no men's wages to serve as a comparison, the EPA does not protect women's wages from remaining artificially low.

Age Discrimination in Employment Act of 1967

The Age Discrimination in Employment Act of 1967 (ADEA) prohibits employers who have at least 20 employees from discriminating on the basis of age against people who are over 40.

The ADEA prevents employers from

- recruiting or hiring only younger applicants

- withholding training opportunities from workers on the basis of age

- firing or forcing an employee to retire due to age (a few occupations, such as high-level executives and policy makers, are exceptions)

- denying older workers advantageous schedules or work options, such as flexible schedules or telecommuting, that are made available to younger workers

The ADEA is of great importance to women. Our society particularly focuses on women's youth and physical attractiveness to the exclusion of other attributes and talents. As a result, discrimination against older women is more likely. In addition, since many women earn less and have fewer benefits than many men, they may need to work longer. Women also generally tend to live longer than men do and, therefore, are in the workforce longer.

Pregnancy Discrimination Act of 1978

The Pregnancy Discrimination Act of 1978 (PDA) is an amendment to Title VII. The PDA makes clear that pregnancy discrimination is illegal sex discrimination. An employer cannot fire or deny a job or promotion to a worker because she is, or may become, pregnant.

Americans with Disabilities Act of 1990

Women with disabilities have additional protection under the Americans with Disabilities Act of 1990 (ADA).

Civil Rights Act of 1991

The Civil Rights Act of 1991 gives additional force to the other federal laws prohibiting employment discrimination. It authorizes the award of compensatory and punitive damages where discrimination is found to be intentional. It also provides for the payment of attorneys' fees and the possibility of jury trials.

Family and Medical Leave Act of 1993

The Family and Medical Leave Act of 1993 gives employees the right to take unpaid leave from work under certain circumstances. This act applies to companies that have at least 50 employees. Smaller companies are exempt. Those who work in larger organizations must meet certain requirements to be eligible.

For employees who qualify, the Family and Medical Leave Act provides for up to 12 weeks of unpaid leave to

- have or care for a new baby
- adopt a child
- become a foster parent
- care for the employee's illness
- care for a child, spouse, or parent who is very ill

The benefits of the Family and Medical Leave Act apply to both women and men. Since women are more frequently caregivers to children, the sick, and the aged, this law particularly helps them. It affords women the opportunity to take time from work when they need it. The Family and Medical Leave Act protects the employee's job, status, insurance, and other benefits during the leave. The leave is unpaid, however, and the loss of income can present a hardship.

Grievances in the Workplace

If you believe an employer has violated your employment rights, write down what happened as soon as possible. As time passes, remembering all the details may be difficult. Include the date, time, place, names of people involved, and the names of any witnesses. Keep a copy of your notes at home.

The first place to look for a remedy for your grievances is within the workplace. If you belong to a union, the union representative can help file a grievance. Contact the human resources department or check the employee handbook to learn your company's procedures for filing grievances.

The Women's Bureau of the U.S. Department of Labor offers information and guidance in many areas of employment discrimination. They have practical brochures in print and online detailing how to deal with wage discrimination, sexual harassment, pregnancy discrimination, age discrimination, and family and medical leave. The national office of the Women's Bureau listed below can direct you to the regional office nearest you.

Women's Bureau
U.S. Department of Labor
Washington, DC 20210
800-827-5335
http://www.dol.gov/dol/wb

If the issue cannot be satisfactorily addressed within the workplace, file a complaint with the appropriate government agency. Time restrictions apply to filing complaints, so once you decide to take that step, file as soon as possible. Once the regulation time has passed, the regulating agency can no longer help.

For complaints involving the Family and Medical Leave Act, contact the nearest office of the Wage and Hour Division, Employment Standards Administration, U.S. Department of Labor. Complaints must generally be filed within two years of the event. The Women's Bureau of the Department of Labor can supply the location of the nearest office.

The U.S. Equal Employment Opportunity Commission (EEOC) handles all other employment discrimination complaints. The EEOC generally requires that a charge be filed within 180 days of the alleged violation. The agency tries to resolve the discrimination charges to the satisfaction of both parties. If that cannot be accomplished, the EEOC will decide whether to bring suit in federal court. If it decides not to bring suit, the charging party usually has 90 days to file a lawsuit. To file a discrimination charge with the EEOC call 800-669-4000 (TTY: 800-669-6820).

U.S. Equal Employment Opportunity Commission
Publications Distribution Center
PO Box 12549
Cincinnati, OH 44212-0549
800-669-3362
http://www.eeoc.gov

Progress Report

United States laws prohibiting employment discrimination against women have improved the lives of many women and families over the past 40 years. Much work remains to be done. Women of color, women with disabilities, and women on welfare still face enormous discrimination in the workplace. Women in all career fields continue to experience sexual harassment and unequal pay.

Working toward equal pay and equal employment is essential to raise the standard of living of American women and their families. Women must be aware of their legal rights and take the necessary actions to defend them. Recognizing and overcoming gender inequities in education and employment in the United States will ultimately help improve the quality of life for women, men, children, families, and communities around the world.

For More Information

The Alliance for Justice is a national association of environmental, civil rights, mental health, women's, children's, and consumer advocacy organizations. Its Web site links to the Web pages of its members, which provide a wealth of legal resources.

Alliance for Justice
2000 P Street, NW, Suite 712
Washington, DC 20036
202-822-6070
http://www.afj.org/

Resources for Women's Success: Role Models, Networks, and Mentors

Achieving success in education and work can often be more challenging for women than it is for men. Educational systems, business, and industry were originally the domains of men. Although U.S. laws now prohibit discrimination on the basis of gender in education and employment, the systems underlying our economy have not yet made a full transition to gender equity—the equal treatment of women and men. Most women still encounter more obstacles to career success than men do. The playing field is not yet level. However, women now make up over half of the U.S. workforce, and they have begun to develop some of the resources for success that traditionally were only available to men. Three powerful resources females can use to advance toward success in all aspects of their lives are role models, networks, and mentors.

Role Models

Positive role models for success have been readily available to men in many career fields for a long time. Until recently, educational materials, the media, and many forms of popular culture, including movies and television shows, were not gender fair—they generally portrayed men in leadership roles and women in supportive roles, both at home and in the workplace. As a result, girls have had more difficulty finding female role models who have succeeded in careers outside of those considered traditional for women, such as nursing and clerical work.

Areas in which women have been particularly discouraged are science, technology, and mathematics. Cultural stereotypes have perpetuated the myth that girls and women cannot, or should not, excel in math, science, or technical fields. Studies show that giving girls positive female role models who have succeeded in these areas, and in other nontraditional careers, is an important way to build self-confidence and overcome negative stereotypes. Federal, state, and local governments, as well as educators and parents, are involved in developing programs to help females have more confidence in their capabilities. Programs are also being developed to encourage success in a wider variety of careers. The essay, Nontraditional Career Options, gives suggestions for pursuing a variety of careers.

The resources listed at the end of this article include role model programs for girls and women of all ages. Some of the resources offer ideas for parents and educators about how to develop role model programs for students from kindergarten through high school.

Networks and Networking

One way for women to find positive role models is through networking. The use of the term "networking" began in the 1960s. It means the exchange of information and development of contacts between individuals or groups. The function of networking is to help others and share resources with people who have similar interests and goals. This concept of exchanging, or sharing information and help is fundamental to the success of networking.

Networks are important resources that women can use to help achieve their goals. They have helped many women learn and advance in their profession by allowing them to find the resources and develop the contacts they have needed.

Many of us are accustomed to thinking of networks in terms of "the old boys' network," which effectively excluded women and minorities from upper-level positions in business and industry. Unfortunately, some "new girls' networks" have also become exclusive and elitist and have done little to change the status quo. They have only created new groups that include a few successful women at the top of their fields, but they still exclude the rest of the world.

However, many networks now exist for the purpose of helping girls and women gain access to the skills, experience, and contacts they need to succeed in all areas of life—not just at work. Networks help individuals realize that they are not alone in whatever endeavors they undertake. Networks allow those who are new to a field a way to reach out for support and encouragement from others who have had similar experiences.

Networks fall into three general categories: formal, informal, and Internet.

Formal Networks

Professional associations exist in nearly every career field. Associations are organizations of people who have a common interest or purpose. Many associations provide excellent opportunities for men and women to network, and some have special interest groups designed to give women an opportunity to network on their own. See the "Professional Organizations" section for more information.

Informal Networks

Some networks are informal. Although many networks are career related, anyone can set up a network to further any goal or shared purpose. Members of networks may share information, experiences, and contacts related to anything—schools, gardening, single parenting, travel, or careers, to name a few examples. If you do not find a network that meets your interests or needs, locate a few people who have similar needs and interests, and form your own informal networks.

Internet Networks

The Internet is a rich source for networking. Many interesting, creative sites already exist that encourage girls and women to share their thoughts and experiences with each other through professional networks, chat rooms, and bulletin boards. The possibilities are growing daily for those who have access to the World Wide Web. Visit some of the Web sites listed at the end of this article to discover some of the women's networks on the Internet. Each site can link you to other sites, and you are quite likely to find a network that will help you.

Networking is a skill that you can easily develop. Find and join a formal, informal, or Internet networking group, or create a network that meets your own needs. Practice your networking skills. Just as with exercising, the more you do it, the better you will become.

Networking Tips

You can be a great networker and be successful at finding what you want and need if you keep a few simple principles in mind.

Share. The first key to successful networking is remembering to share help and information. Sharing means giving as well as receiving. You look for a network because you need something, but remember that you also have something to give. Even if you are new to a field, you have something to offer others. You can volunteer to help make telephone calls, plan a meeting, or work at a registration table at an event or workshop. Contribute whatever you can. Be willing to share the knowledge and skills you have, and you will be surprised what you will receive in return.

Help others. Try to help others find what they need. If you are able to help others make the connections they need, they will remember your help, and they just might reciprocate.

Be considerate. Remember that people who attend a meeting want to enjoy themselves and achieve their goals, too. If a person you really want to get to know is at a gathering, introduce yourself, express your interest, and ask if you may contact her later. Exchange contact information or business cards, and then move on. Few people appreciate having their time monopolized at a meeting.

Follow up. Make the most of the contacts you develop. Use the contact information you receive to follow up later and get to know people better. Let them know your interests without making demands. Relax and enjoy the people you meet.

You will find many excellent books on developing networking skills at the library or bookstore. Networking does not need to be complicated or mysterious. Just follow these tips, and networking can be enjoyable, easy, and productive. Your networking skills can increase your chances of success in any endeavor, and they can be especially helpful when you look for a mentor.

Mentors and Mentoring

Mentoring is a one-to-one form of sharing in which a more experienced person helps a less experienced person. It is a cooperative, nurturing relationship. Mentoring can help girls learn needed skills, and it can help women progress in their careers. A mentor shares her experiences and insights regarding a particular area of knowledge or career field with a protégé (sometimes called a partner or a mentee). The mentor often helps the protégé learn important business concepts, make essential contacts, find needed resources, and learn networking skills.

Importance of Mentors

Studies show that having a mentor or mentors is highly related to career success. Having a mentor can be an important factor in helping girls and women overcome the barriers that traditionally have kept them from excelling in math and science, or reaching top career positions and obtaining equal pay and benefits. Although not having a mentor will not necessarily doom you to failure, having a mentor can be a great help along the path to success.

Finding a Mentor

A mentor usually is a role model you choose for yourself. Some schools and organizations assign mentors to new individuals, but most successful women who have had mentors agree that you are better off finding your own.

The best way to find a mentor is to seek out a person you admire in your school, job, or field. Finding a person with whom you can be comfortable is important because mentoring is an ongoing relationship. Ask to speak with that person at a convenient time. When you meet with him or her, ask if the person would be willing to spend a little time each week or month helping you develop the qualities you admire. Most people will be flattered by your interest. Even very busy, successful people usually are willing to spend a small amount of time mentoring because they understand how vital these relationships are.

If you are unable to find a mentor immediately, continue looking. Many of the professional associations listed in this book are good sources for mentors. Some professional association Web sites offer electronic mentoring opportunities. Check out the Web sites of associations that interest you to see if such opportunities are available. A number of women's Web sites are designed to be electronic networking and support systems for women, and some even offer mentoring. Several outstanding Web sites for women and girls are listed below.

Whatever your age, your interests, and your goals and dreams, it is important to find an inspiring role model. It is also vital to join networking groups and to learn networking skills. Make every effort to develop a relationship with a mentor who can help you along your path to success.

For More Information

All of the resources listed below offer a variety of important topics for women and girls. They are presented according to the age group they address, but the information they contain can be useful to women of all ages and backgrounds.

Resources for Girls

The Role Model Project for Girls (http://womenswork.org/girls/) is based on the belief that girls can grow up to be almost anything—in a wide variety of professional careers. The site offers excellent references and resources for women and girls. It includes links to sites for or by girls, mentoring and other role model projects, and information regarding the status of women in the United States.

TAP Junior (http://www.cs.yale.edu/~tap/tap-junior.html) includes information and issues relating to K-12 girls and computing. It offers software, games, activities, and programs for girls, and information and resources for parents and educators.

Donna L. Woodka's book, *The Internet for Girls: Connecting Girls with Math, Science and Technology,* is available on the Internet (http://www.sdsc.edu/~woodka/donna.html). It has fun resources for girls, ideas for parents and teachers, and a wealth of links to other Internet resources.

The Backyard Project (http://www.backyard.org/index.html) is devoted to high school girls. While its focus is to encourage young women to explore careers in computer science, it shows girls how they might be able to use their talents in a variety of careers.

Resources for Women

Advancing Women (http://www.advancingwomen.com) is a Web site designed as an electronic networking and support system for women. It contains a wealth of information on networking, mentoring, business, careers, and money matters.

Equity Online (http://www.edc.org/WomensEquity/) is the resource center for the national Women's Educational Equity Act (WEEA). It provides extensive information on gender equity; Title IX; sexual harassment; a free science, engineering, and mathematics CD-ROM; and extensive links to other equity sites.

W.I.N., the Women's Information Networking directory (http://edie.cprost.sfu.ca/~spiders/), is an online mentoring program. Successful women from all career fields and professions—from the arts to law to physics—are available to answer queries and offer advice via email.

Securing the Pathway: Financial Management for Women

If you are like some women, you may not feel comfortable or confident making financial decisions. Recently, hundreds of books have been written that address financial management issues for women. Instead of making the subject less threatening for many women, this abundance of information may be making it seem more confusing and somewhat overwhelming. Financial management is not mysterious or difficult. If you feel uneducated or insecure about money matters, this article may help you realize that you can manage finances and take control of money matters.

There are five basic steps to get you started on your way to successful money management.

Step One: Understand Women and Money

Managing money has traditionally been a mysterious, difficult topic for women. Until the twentieth century, most women worked in the home, did not earn a paycheck, and had little experience managing money. Women's education did not focus on mathematical skills. On the contrary, women were taught that being intelligent and successful was not "feminine." Money issues were considered the province of men. As a result of traditional women's education, women were at a great economic disadvantage if they did not have a father, brother, husband, or son on whom they could rely for financial support and money management.

Women and society changed drastically during the twentieth century. By the end of the century, women had become a major force in the economy of the United States. According to the U.S. Small Business Administration, women made up almost half of the workforce, owned nearly 50 percent of small businesses, and comprised 41 percent of the individuals who had a net worth of $500 thousand or more. Women also accounted for 80 percent of consumer spending and made 75 percent of health care decisions.

In spite of all the growth and change in women's educational achievements, employment opportunities, and financial status, statistics show that women generally still earn 20 to 30 percent less than men do. Some women earn less due to gender bias, which is the tendency of employers to give men higher wages, more benefits, and more promotions. Other women are paid less because they are employed in lower-paying clerical, retail, and support positions. Some women are underemployed or unemployed so they can care for their children, husbands, or aging parents. (Women provide 75 percent of the family caregiving in the United States.) Other women work for small employers who do not provide benefits.

Whatever the reasons for the lower wages and lower benefits women receive, those lower earnings have an impact on their financial status throughout their lives. Shorter careers, lower earnings, and fewer benefits during a woman's working years translate to lower Social Security benefits, smaller savings, and lower or nonexistent pension benefits when a woman retires.

The fact is that women tend to live longer than men and they need to save more than men do in preparation for a longer retirement. Yet the irony is that their limited incomes generally allow them to save much less. As a result, many older women live below the poverty level. In 1996, twice as many older women (13.6 percent) as men (6.8 percent) lived below the poverty level. The Women's Institute for a Secure Retirement (WISER) offers valuable information to help women plan for greater security in retirement.

Women's Institute for a Secure Retirement
1201 Pennsylvania Avenue, NW, Suite 619
Washington, DC 20004
http://www.wiser.heinz.org/

Women must learn to take control of their financial lives if they are to overcome the inequities that leave many of them struggling financially during their working years and living in poverty when they retire. Yet many women are still uncomfortable and insecure when it comes to managing money. If you are among them, don't despair. You can start today to overcome your fears about managing money, gain more knowledge and confidence, and get on the path toward sound financial management and a more secure financial future.

Step Two: Understand Your Relationship with Money

For most people, but especially for women, money is not just a financial issue, it is also an emotional one. Money—or actually what it can provide—can make people feel happy, sad, secure, or insecure, and it can elicit almost every emotion in between.

How do you feel about money? If your answer to that question is "knowledgeable" or "very secure," you already have a good relationship with money, and you can skip to Step Four. If your answer is not so positive, give that question some more thought. Consider why you feel negative, angry, overwhelmed, or insecure about money issues. How did your parents relate to money? How did you feel about mathematics as a student?

A unique Web site, WMoneytalk (http://www.wmoneytalk.com/home.htm), helps you explore your feelings about money. Dr. Anne-Marie Pollowy Toliver, the creator of WMoneytalk.com, suggests setting up a financial journal to track your feelings about money, your use of money, and your successes and failures. For those who are not online, Suze Orman's book *The 9 Steps to Financial Freedom* (Crown Publishers) also discusses overcoming financial anxieties.

The American Association of Retired Persons (AARP) offers a free publication, *A Primer on Personal Money Management* (publication D13183).

AARP/Fulfillment
601 E Street, NW
Washington, DC 20049
202-434-2277
http://www.aarp.org/

Many women may need different financial advice than men do because of the differences in their temperaments, feelings about money, and financial situations. Numerous financial management resources are designed expressly for women and choosing among them can be overwhelming. To help cut through all the clutter, First Union, a women-friendly financial institution, reviewed many of the books available and recommended three they found to contain particularly sound financial advice for women.

Ernst & Young's Financial Planning for Women (Wiley, $16.95), 241 pages.

It Takes Money, Honey, by Georgette Mosebacher (Regan books, $24), 272 pages.

The 9 Steps to Financial Freedom, by Suze Orman (Crown Publishers, $23), 290 pages.

First Union Corporation
One First Union Center
301 South College Street, Suite 4000
Charlotte, NC 28288
704-374-4880
http://www.firstunion.com/

Perhaps you already have discovered a book or Web site about finances you like. It doesn't matter which resource you use since most will give you the basic information you need. The important thing is to choose one or two resources that you are comfortable with and use them to help you change your relationship with money and take charge of your finances.

Step Three: Change How You Relate to Money

The most important ingredient in most successful relationships is a good attitude. The same is true of your relationship with money. Build a positive attitude toward money and your ability to manage it.

Be positive. Women have told themselves negative things about money for too long. "I'm not good at math." "I don't understand money management." "I don't understand investing." "My husband (father, brother, son) takes care of that." If you feel insecure about your math skills, read the essay "Resources for Women's Success," in this section of *Pathways to Career Success for Women*. It includes many ideas and resources that can help you overcome your fear of math. If you can learn to be confident in math, that confidence will help you manage your finances.

You will need financial confidence to take control of your life. Studies show that 90 percent of all women in the United States will live alone and have financial responsibility for themselves at some time in their lives. The number of single-parent families is increasing rapidly, and women head the majority of those families. Of all families in which a woman is the sole support, nearly one-third live below the poverty level.

Because of these statistics, women need to realize that they can no longer afford negative relationships with money. Many of today's women have what it takes to manage money. Many own businesses, work in high-paying jobs, and save and invest money well. You can, too. Start today to think and act positively about your money-managing ability and watch your confidence increase.

Start a financial journal. Use a small notebook that you can carry with you to write down everything you buy and how much you spend. Use Dr. Toliver's idea and also keep track of how you feel about your spending. Did you get a bargain on something you needed and feel good about it? Write that down. Did you make an impulse purchase and later regret it? Write that down. When you review your journal, you will see how much you have spent, and you will begin to get a better sense of how you use money and how you feel about that.

Talk to other women about your feelings regarding money and ask them about their successful financial strategies. The Internet has many helpful sites that offer chances to exchange ideas with other women. Advancing Women (http://www.advancingwomen.com) and WMoneytalk.com are two good places to start. Local community groups and banks frequently offer free or inexpensive seminars on money management for women.

Use the resources that are available to you. When you read, attend meetings, or talk to others, remember you do not have to know everything. If you knew everything, you would not be working on this issue. Ask questions, and if you do not understand the answer, ask for a clarification. You do not have to learn it all immediately. If you can learn one or two new ideas each time, you will be surprised how quickly your feelings about your knowledge and ability will change. Once you are beginning to feel more positive about your relationship with money, you can start to define your present financial position.

Step Four: Understand Your Present Financial Position

To know how your relationship to money changes, you must know and understand your current status. Gather and organize your financial records, determine your net worth, and determine your cash flow.

Gather your documents. The first step is to find and organize everything that relates to your financial situation. This includes bank books, pension plans, Social Security information, wills, directories of people who should be notified in case of emergencies—everything! Consult the financial management resources you have chosen for lists of what to gather, how to organize, and where to store everything.

Determine your net worth. Net worth is the result of subtracting your total liabilities (what you owe) from your total assets (what you own). (Total Assets - Total Liabilities = Net Worth) The resource you have chosen will contain lists of assets and liabilities. Use those lists to determine your net worth. The final figure may be positive, or it may be negative, which means that you owe more than you own. Don't worry if the net worth is negative! That has no effect on your value as an individual. That is just a starting point for measuring the improvement you will be making.

Determine your cash flow. Cash flow is a picture of your income and expenses. Income is all the money you earn or receive from sources such as interest, social security, alimony, etc. Expenses are everything you spend, including savings. The cash flow picture shows what came in and where it went. Since savings and other investments are included as part of your expenses, your total expenses should always equal your total income. (Total Income = Total Expenses)

Once you have gathered your documents, determined your net worth, and determined your cash flow, you will understand your present financial situation. Then you can begin to set objectives for improving your finances.

Step Five: Plan Your Financial Goals

The financial management guide you have chosen will give detailed ideas on defining short-term, medium-term, and long-term financial goals. Don't be overwhelmed. You don't have to do everything at once. The important thing is to start. Choose one or two goals and start to work on them right away.

Building new habits and gaining confidence are most important. Take small steps so you can experience immediate success. If your first goal is to start saving, do that—even if you can only save $5 a week. If your goal is to contribute to the pension plan at work, start at the highest amount that is comfortable for you. If you can only contribute the very minimum amount, start there.

Once you have made one or two improvements, the feeling of success will help you move forward. If you are keeping a financial journal, you may begin to see areas where you can save money. Use the money you save to work toward your financial goals. Perhaps now you will be able to save $10 a week or increase your contribution to the pension plan.

Managing your finances is an ongoing endeavor. Keep talking with other women and attending seminars or classes. The financial resources you have chosen to use will give you many ideas for budgeting, saving, and investing. The Web site of First Union (http://www.firstunion.com/), a women-friendly financial institution has a particularly clear presentation of financial planning in general and women's financial issues in particular. Use all the resources you can find to strengthen your knowledge of successful financial strategies.

As you see success in your efforts, your confidence in your ability will build. With your new, more positive relationship with money, you will be able to set and achieve financial goals that will put you on the pathway to a more secure financial future.

An Issue of the Heart: Child Care

Child Care in the United States

Employers and employees agree that few issues are more distracting to workers or cause more loss of productivity to employers than the powerful pull of the needs of children. Women have traditionally been the major caregivers to children. Throughout the twentieth century, the number of women working outside the home increased steadily. This has led to a corresponding increase in the need for child care services. The U.S. government, employers, and employees recognize child care as being among the most important issues facing the American workforce today.

During the final decade of the twentieth century, child care rose to the forefront of national issues. According to the U.S. Census Bureau, in 1970 only 30 percent of mothers of children under age six worked outside the home. By 1998, that number had increased to 66 percent. The statistics on school-age children are similar. One out of four mothers of children between the ages of six and 16 held jobs outside the home in 1965. That number jumped to three out of four in 1996.

The national norm for married couples in the United States is for both partners to work. Particularly among younger couples, today's fathers are taking a more active role in caring for children and in seeking out child care options than their fathers did. The increasing number of resources for working fathers testifies to that fact. A good resource for fathers is the Fatherhood Project (http://www.fatherhoodproject.org).

In spite of the encouraging increase in the involvement of fathers in child care, recent studies show that 75 percent of all caregivers are still women. This is partially due to the continuing traditional role of women as caregivers. Another important factor is the rapid increase in single-parent families headed by women. In 1975, single-parent families made up 16 percent of all families with children. By 1992, that number had increased to 27 percent. Increases in divorce, separation, and out-of-wedlock births leave millions of single mothers struggling to support themselves and their children.

Whatever your life situation, if you are a working mother, you need high-quality, affordable child care. This article outlines strategies you can use to identify quality child care and to afford the quality care you need.

Acquiring Quality Child Care

The task of finding the right care situation for one of the most precious people in your life can seem overwhelming. To make the process easier, you can break it down into five smaller steps:

1. Determine what type of care is appropriate

2. Identify possible caregivers

3. Screen potential caregivers

4. Assess the candidates

5. Choose the best caregiver for your child

Determine the Appropriate Type of Care

The first step in choosing quality child care is deciding which type of care is most appropriate for your child and your situation. There are three major types of child care: child care centers, family care, and in-home care (nanny/au pair).

Child care centers are specifically designed for the care of children. Individual states license child care centers. Licensing regulations usually specify the ratio of staff to children. Some states require centers to care for infants, toddlers, and preschoolers separately according to the staff-to-children ratios each state mandates for each age group. State health and social services frequently pay surprise visits to child care centers to ensure that they comply with state licensing regulations. The number of children who attend a center can range from a few to more than a hundred. Due to the size of child care centers, children usually have many opportunities to socialize with other children and to build friendships. Many centers accept children from birth to 12 years of age so children and parents may have the continuity of going to the same center for many years.

Family care takes place in the home of the caregiver. Many family care providers are parents. Like child care centers, family care providers must meet specific health and safety standards and be licensed by the individual states in which they operate. Most states license family care providers to care for a maximum of 12 children. Infants, toddlers, and preschool children may be grouped together in a family care setting. A child may have the same family care provider for years, and some children build close bonds with their providers.

In-home care is supplied by individual nannies or au pairs who care for children in the children's homes. Nannies are usually women who live in the home of the employing family and care for a child or children. Au pairs are often foreign exchange students. They care for a child or children in return for room and board and a stipend. Au pairs are regulated by the U.S. Information Agency through nongovernment agencies authorized to administer the au pair program.

Identify Possible Caregivers

Once you have decided on the type of child care that best suits your child and your circumstances, the next step is to find a quality child care center, family care provider, or individual. One of the best ways to find good care is to ask other parents for recommendations. Firsthand experience of others is perhaps the best indication of what you can expect from any caregiver. Also check community papers and the yellow pages. Contact state agencies that regulate child care for information on caregiving options and caregivers in your area. The National Child Care Information Center (http://ericps.ed.uiuc.edu/nccic/) has contact information for state agencies involved in child care. Check out the CareGuide.com (http://www.careguide.com), Child Care Aware (http://www.naccrra.net/childcareaware/index.htm), and Zero to Three (http://www.zerotothree.org) Web sites for searchable online databases of caregivers.

Screen Potential Caregivers

After you have identified caregivers that might be of interest to you, the real work begins. Finding the right care is essential to your child's well-being and to your peace of mind. Start by telephoning each potential caregiver. You may be able to save valuable time by eliminating some through telephone interviews.

Visit each of the homes or centers or interview each of the individuals you are seriously considering. Observe the way the caregivers interact with children. Ask about the caregivers' backgrounds and certifications. If you are visiting a child care center or family care home, notice whether the surroundings are safe and pleasant. Check the ratio of staff to children. The fewer children per adult, the more time the caregivers will have for your child. A low number of children per adult is particularly important for infants and toddlers.

Assess the Candidates

Books about child care and Web sites such as the three mentioned above supply questions to ask and detailed checklists to complete as you visit each potential caregiver. Checklists can help you remember to look at all the important details. Complete the same checklist for each caregiver so you can easily compare them.

Choose the Best Caregiver for Your Child

By the time you have carefully assessed each potential child care provider, you may already know which one you believe is best for your child. If you still have questions or doubts, revisit those you have not eliminated. Review the points you may have missed on your checklists and ask the questions you need to have answered. Then make your decision.

Affording Quality Child Care

Once you have decided which child care provider is best for your child, you can turn to determining how you can afford to pay for that care. The cost of child care can be enormous, but there are ways to reduce the cost. Most parents can use at least some strategies for reducing child care costs. These strategies fall into five general categories:

1. Cost reductions

2. Family-friendly employers

3. Tax-based subsidies

4. Public subsidies

5. Loans and scholarships

Consider which strategies might be available to you, and pursue all that apply.

Cost Reductions

Many women meet child care needs by combining paid care with the unpaid help of family and friends. Some trade child care services with other mothers who work different shifts.

Some child care providers offer discounts if more than one child from a family enrolls. Other providers have a reduced fee schedule for lower income families. Organizations such as the YWCA and religious-affiliated care centers may offer lower rates to members.

Family-Friendly Employers

The Office of Personnel Management (OPM) of the U.S. government has initiated a program of family-friendly workplace advocacy. The program is intended to serve as a model for, and an encouragement to U.S. businesses to develop more family-friendly work practices. The OPM program supports the use of flexible work schedules and work sites, leave programs, part-time employment, job sharing, telecommuting, and onsite child development centers.

U.S. Office of Personnel Management
1900 E Street, NW, Room 7315
Washington, DC 20415-2000
202-606-2011
http://www.opm.gov/wrkfam/

As women figure ever more prominently in the U.S. workforce, more employers in the private sector are following the lead of the OPM program and offering more family-friendly job options. These options allow mothers to make their work schedules more compatible with their children's schedules, thus reducing the amount of money they spend on child care.

When you are job hunting, look for family-friendly employers. *Working Mother* magazine publishes a list of top family-friendly companies.

Working Mother
135 West 50th Street
New York, NY 10020
212-445-6100
http://www.workingmother.com/

Encourage your employer to adopt more family-friendly employment practices. Visit the Work & Family Connection, Inc. Web site (http://www.workfamily.com/) for information on family-friendly workplace options, including setting up onsite daycare centers.

Many mothers start their own businesses at home so they can care for their children and work at the same time. Check out the essay, "Building a New pathway: Starting a Business," in this book for ideas about working at home.

Tax-Based Subsidies

The federal government offers two tax-based subsidies. The Child and Dependent Care Credit allows many parents to deduct a portion of their child care expenses from their federal income tax. The Earned Income Credit is available to taxpayers who have low or moderate incomes. Specific requirements and limitations apply to both credits. Check with the Internal Revenue Service to learn whether you are eligible for these credits.

Some states also offer tax credits based on child care expenses. Ask your state's child care information and referral agency for information about tax credit programs. Contact information for those agencies is available at the Web site of the National Child Care Information Center (http://ericps.ed.uiuc.edu/nccic/).

Public Subsidies

Public subsidies assist low-income families with child care expenses. Subsidies use a combination of federal, state, and local tax dollars. Programs and their eligibility requirements change frequently. Your local child care information and referral agency can give you current information on programs in your area.

Low-income parents attending institutions of higher education may be eligible for campus-based child care services. The Higher Education Act Amendments of 1998 provide grant opportunities to institutions of higher education to assist in providing such services. If you are a student at an institution of higher education, ask whether the campus-based child care program is available and whether you qualify.

Loans and Scholarships

When necessary, some parents take out loans to finance child care. A loan may make it possible for you to afford child care when you need it. However, this approach must be carefully evaluated like any other financial planning decision.

Some child care providers and some community programs offer scholarships for families that demonstrate financial need. Ask your child care provider and your local child care information and referral agency about the availability of such scholarships.

A variety of strategies are available to help you afford quality child care. Visit the Web site of CareGuide.com (http://www.careguide.com) for more suggestions on ways to reduce child care costs. Ask your child care provider. Talk to other mothers about what they do. Ask your employer about starting an onsite child care program.

Finding affordable, quality child care can improve the quality of life for you and your family, and it can increase your peace of mind while you work. Take advantage of the resources and strategies available to make finding and affording quality child care easier.

For More Information

CareGuide.com (http://www.careguide.com) is a Web site that provides directories to national child care agencies and organizations, a searchable database of child care providers, articles on choosing caregivers, and interview questions and checklists for evaluating child care providers.

Child Care Aware offers information about child care resource and referral agencies throughout the United States. Its mission is to ensure that parents have access to good information about finding quality child care and resources in their community.

Child Care Aware
1319 F Street, NW, Suite 810
Washington, DC 20004
800-424-2246
http://www.naccrra.net/childcareaware/index.htm

The Fatherhood Project (http://www.fatherhoodproject.org) is a national research and education project that is examining the future of fatherhood and developing ways to support men's involvement in child rearing. It offers materials to support fathers and mothers in their parenting roles and in balancing work and family.

Essays on Women's Topics

The National Child Care Information Center (http://ericps.ed.uiuc.edu/nccic) is supported by a contract from the U.S. Department of Health and Human Services. Its Web site provides demographic information on the numbers of children and status of child care in each state, child care licensing requirements, and contact information for state agencies involved in child care. The NCCIC Web site also contains extensive links to child care and education sites.

The Office of Personnel Management of the U.S. government has a family-friendly workplace advocacy program. Its Web site gives detailed information that could be useful for employers who wish to set up family-friendly programs and to employees who wish to encourage employers to do so.

U.S. Office of Personnel Management
1900 E Street, NW, Room 7315
Washington, DC 20415-2000
202-606-2011
http://www.opm.gov/wrkfam/

Work & Family Connection, Inc.'s Web site is devoted to work-life issues. It contains a wealth of free online information for employers and employees on work-life issues and setting up family-friendly workplace policies. Additional information is available on a fee basis.

Work & Family Connection, Inc.
5197 Beachside Drive
Minnetonka, MN 55343
800-487-7898
http://www.workfamily.com/

Working Mother magazine features sections on child care issues, workplace flexibility, finance, and health care for women. It periodically publishes lists of the best companies for working mothers.

Working Mother
135 West 50th Street
New York, NY 10020
212-445-6100
http://www.workingmother.com/

Zero to Three is dedicated to the healthy development of infants and toddlers through the first three years of life. Their Web site offers information for parents and professionals.

Zero to Three: National Center for Infants, Toddlers and Families
734 15th Street, NW, Suite 1000
Washington, DC 20005
202-638-1144
http://www.zerotothree.org

General Introduction to Financial Aid

The importance of higher education is increasing, and so is the cost of obtaining it. To find the pathway to personal and professional success, minorities must determine the education they need and find a way to get that education. College or graduate school costs can seem overwhelming, but don't lose heart. There are ways to find dollars for college. In fact, there are many options. This article will help you learn how to look for financial aid, where to look, and what kinds of aid are available.

Looking for financial aid can seem confusing, but take it a step at a time, and you'll soon be an expert. The steps outlined below will get you started.

Step 1: Determine Your Financial Need

First, determine whether you actually need financial aid. Use the formula that colleges and funding sources use to determine financial need: the Cost of Attendance minus the Expected Family Contribution (EFC). The cost of attendance includes the cost of schooling (tuition, fees, books, and supplies) plus living expenses (room and board, travel, and incidental expenses). Every school can supply an estimated average cost of attendance. The expected family contribution (EFC) is based on family income and expense information you provide. Subtract the EFC from the cost of attendance at a particular educational institution to determine what your financial need would be if you attended that school.

If the financial need formula shows that you do not need aid, you may just have saved yourself a lot of time and work. Even if you do not need financial aid, read the section below on scholarships and grants (financial aid that you do not have to repay). You may qualify for awards based on particular skills or interests. Read the section on tax credits, too, because you may be able to recover some of the money you spend on education.

Step 2: Contact Financial Aid Offices

If you determine that you do need financial aid, start looking right away. Finding the many kinds of aid that may be available to you takes time and energy. Starting early can improve your chances of obtaining aid. Get off to a good start by contacting the financial aid offices of the schools you are considering. The financial aid packages different colleges offer you may be a determining factor in your final selection. Each college or university has its own requirements, and failing to learn about them could slow down or jeopardize your financial aid. To learn as much as you can about each school's financial aid process, ask a financial aid officer these questions:

What types of financial aid do you offer?

What are your guidelines for requesting financial aid?

What application materials do you require?

What are the deadlines for submitting financial aid requests?

What effect will my request for financial aid have on my admission?

Will your school be able to cover my total financial need?

Will the school cover my financial need for four years?

When will you notify me of my eligibility for financial aid?

What other sources of aid should I know about?

Get to know the aid administrators. Tell them about any unusual circumstances or expenses you have. They may be able to help you. Each school has its own procedures and forms, but most of them also use the Free Application for Federal Student Aid (FAFSA).

Step 3: Complete the FAFSA

The Free Application for Federal Student Aid (FAFSA) is the form you must complete to apply for federal assistance of any kind. Complete the FAFSA first, and complete it as soon after January 1 as possible. Note that you will have to provide tax return information on your FAFSA, so complete your federal and state tax returns before you fill out your FAFSA. Applications are accepted as of January 1 each year, and the earlier you apply, the better your chances of receiving what you need. If you apply late, you will miss out on aid that has already been awarded. The government takes three to four weeks to process the application.

Experts suggest that students submit the FAFSA whether they think they qualify for aid or not. Many colleges and universities use it in their aid decisions. Some forms of private assistance only are available after you have been rejected for federal aid. The FAFSA form is available in high schools and colleges, by telephone (1-800-4-FEDAID), and online (http://www.fafsa.ed.gov).

Step 4: Learn about the Types of Financial Aid

Free information about student aid is available in the reference section of the library. Look under "financial aid" or "student aid." Many books on financial aid are available at the library or in bookstores. The Internet also has a wealth of financial aid information. Some excellent Web sites are mentioned at the end of this article. (If you do not have a computer, go to the library or your school. Most libraries and schools now have computers available at little or no cost.) All of these resources can help you learn more about the three basic kinds of financial aid:

1. Money you don't have to pay back (grants and scholarships)

2. Money you must pay back (loans)

3. Money you earn as you go (employer tuition reimbursement programs, military tuition assistance programs, work-study programs)

You may need to combine more than one type of financial aid to cover all of the costs of higher education, so learn about, consider, and apply for as many forms of aid as you can.

Money That Does Not Have to Be Paid Back

First, look for sources of funds you do not have to pay back. They fall into two categories: grants and scholarships.

Grants

Grants are monetary awards that do not have to be repaid. There are two kinds: grants based on financial need and grants that support a specific project.

Grants Based on Financial Need. The federal government sponsors two grants that are based entirely on financial need: the Pell Grant and the Federal Supplemental Educational Opportunity Grant (FSEOG). Both require that applicants submit the FAFSA in order to be considered.

Grants That Support a Specific Project. The federal government and other organizations offer funds to support research in specific areas. The sponsor generally requires that applicants submit grant proposals for evaluation. This type of grant is most common in applications for graduate study.

To apply for the Pell and FSEOG grants, consult *The Student Guide* of the U.S. Department of Education. (Ordering information is given on page 33.) The reference desk of the library has books that list grants and fellowships available through government agencies and other organizations throughout the United States. Also check the financial aid Web sites starting on page 32. Free Internet searches can supply the latest information on available grants.

Scholarships

Scholarships are usually short-term monetary awards. Like grants, they do not have to be repaid. Scholarships are offered by a variety of providers. Each scholarship provider sets the criteria for application. The criteria can range from financial need to special hobbies and interests to academic excellence. This is an area in which creative thinking and research can help you find dollars. Think of all of the kinds of scholarships for which you may be eligible.

First, consider your major and minor subjects. Some organizations offer scholarships especially for minorities who are entering certain fields. Learn about professional associations in your field and find out if they offer scholarships. The Organizations Section of this book contains contact information for many women's associations that may sponsor scholarships, and the Financial Aid Section lists many scholarships that are available to women.

Next think about your hobbies, talents, and interests. Your ability in sports, music, or creative writing or your interest in the environment or in helping others might help finance your education.

Find all the scholarships for which you might qualify and apply for as many as you can. A number of online resources feature free searches to help locate scholarships for which you qualify. Several are listed at the end of this article.

Beware of Scholarship Scams!

While most organizations offer bona fide scholarships, the Federal Trade Commission (FTC) warns that scholarship scams do exist. The FTC recently brought actions against several companies that collectively cheated over 175,000 consumers out of millions of dollars.

Keep in mind the old adage, "If it sounds too good to be true, it probably is!" Here are some warning signs of a potential scam:

Offers a scholarship or award for which you did not apply

Guarantees a scholarship in return for advance fees

Asks for credit card or bank account numbers

Charges an advance fee for a loan

Provides only a P.O. Box

Uses a hard-sell approach

If you suspect a scam, report it to

National Fraud Information Center
PO Box 65868
Washington, DC 20035
800-876-7060

or

Federal Trade Commission
Correspondence Branch
Federal Trade Commission, Room 200
6th Street & Pennsylvania Avenue, NW
Washington, DC 20580
877-382-4375

Money That Must Be Paid Back

Few individuals who need financial aid can put together enough scholarships to pay for school entirely with "free money." Most students also need loans. Whether loans are federal or private, they must be paid back.

Federal Loans

The largest sources of student financial aid in the United States are the government's Student Financial Assistance Programs. They account for 70 percent of all student financial aid. All federal loans require the completion of the Free Application for Federal Student Aid (FAFSA). The government makes loans to students and to parents.

Loans to Students. Stafford Loans are federal loans to students. Both undergraduate and graduate students may apply. The loan amounts vary. The loan amount can increase, based on years in school, up to as much as $5,500 after two years of study. Interest rates are variable, but they never exceed 8.25 percent.

Perkins Loans are available to both undergraduate and graduate students who have exceptional financial need. These loans are campus-based. Interested students should consult their school financial aid counselors about the availability of and requirements for Perkins Loans.

Loans to Parents. Parent Loan for Undergraduate Students (PLUS) Loans are federal loans available to parents. They must also be repaid. The interest rates are variable, but they never exceed 9 percent.

For current rates and application information for federal assistance programs and to complete the FAFSA online, visit FAFSA on the Web (http://www.fafsa.ed.gov) and the site of the Office of Student Financial Assistance Programs (OSFAP, see page 33). The OSFAP also sponsors "Help Lines for Students."

Private Loans

Many private financial institutions make loans to both students and their parents. Some of the federal financial aid Web sites referenced at the end of this article suggest preferred lenders.

Money That Is Paid While Attending School

Many colleges, universities, and other organizations offer alternate forms of financial aid. Some require students to work to earn the financial aid. Others give students credit on different bases.

Tuition Payment Plans

Many colleges and universities offer short-term installment plans. These plans frequently split the costs into equal monthly payments. Many plans are free of interest, but some have finance charges and/or fees. Ask the schools you are considering about the availability of tuition payment plans.

Employer Tuition Support

If you are working, ask whether your employer has an educational assistance program. Many employers recognize the importance of helping employees advance. An added advantage to employer-provided educational assistance is that money received for courses that begin before June 1, 2000, are exempt from taxes. To learn whether that tax credit will be extended beyond that date, see the Internal Revenue Service Web site (http://www.irs.ustreas.gov/hot/not97-60.html) for up-to-date information.

Military Service Benefits

Branches of the U.S. military offer a number of tuition assistance programs. The Web addresses for all five branches—Air Force, Army, Coast Guard, Marines, and Navy—are listed on page 54.

Work-Study Programs

Work-study programs allow you to earn money by working while you go to school. These programs may involve work on or off campus. Work-study programs are available through colleges and universities, private sources, and the Federal Work-Study Program. Ask financial aid counselors about opportunities at the schools you are considering. For information on the Federal Work-Study Program, see the current volume of *The Student Guide* of the U.S. Department of Education. Details are given at the end of this article.

National Service

The Corporation for National Service sponsors AmeriCorps, a service organization that helps people in need throughout the United States. AmeriCorps projects include tutoring children, building homes, creating health clinics, and hundreds of other projects. AmeriCorps offers living allowances, health insurance, student loans, and education awards to AmeriCorps members.

Corporation for National Service
1201 New York Avenue, NW
Washington, DC 20525
202-606-5000
http://www.americorps.org/

Tax Credit

The Taxpayer Relief Act of 1997 and subsequent tax legislation have made a number of tax credits available to students and their parents. These credits can be a great help to most families.

Hope Scholarship Credit. This credit is only available during the first two years of postsecondary education for students who are enrolled at least half time in a program leading to a recognized educational credential, such as a degree or certificate. The maximum credit per tax year is $1,500 per student.

Lifetime Learning Credit. Taxpayers may claim this credit for qualified tuition and related expenses of students of all ages who are enrolled in eligible educational institutions. The program does not have to lead to a degree or certificate. The maximum tax credit per year through 2002 is $1,000. After 2002, the maximum credit will be $2,000.

Student Loan Interest Deduction. Taxpayers who have taken loans to pay for the cost of attending an eligible educational institution may generally deduct the interest on the loans from their income taxes.

Ask the educational institutions that you are considering whether study with them will qualify for these tax deductions. Information on these and other tax credit programs that may help you and/or your family recover some of the costs of financing higher education can be obtained from the Internal Revenue Service. The Internal Revenue Service published "Notice 97-60: Administrative, Procedural, and Miscellaneous Education Tax Incentives" to explain the higher education tax incentives offered by the Taxpayer Relief Act of 1997. The IRS Web site includes up-to-date information on higher education tax incentive programs. To order IRS Notice 97-60, call 1-800-829-3676 or visit their Web site at (http://www.irs.ustreas.gov/hot/not97-60.html). Tax laws change frequently, so keep informed so you can take advantage of any credits that apply to you.

Higher education is indeed expensive, but financial aid is available to nearly everyone. By exploring the many sources of financial aid, you can find a way to finance your pathway to success.

For More Information

College Is Possible (http://www.collegeispossible.com), a Web site produced by a coalition of America's colleges and universities, recommends books, Web sites, and other resources and gives information on preparing for college, choosing a college, and paying for college.

The Educational Foundation of the American Association of University Women funds pioneering research on girls and education, community action projects, and fellowships and grants for outstanding women around the world.

The American Association of University Women
1111 16th Street, NW
Washington, DC 20036
800-326-AAUW
http://www.aauw.org

FastWeb (http://www.fastweb.com) is an excellent source of information for planning for college and beyond. It includes admissions, scholarships, financial aid, and tips on college life. It offers a free search of over 400,000 scholarships totaling more than $1 billion in financial aid and a college search to help match colleges to students' interests.

FinAid (http://www.finaid.org) is another excellent Web site that focuses on financial aid. It offers calculators to help determine total school costs and financial need and links to free financial aid searches. It also reviews many books on financial aid for undergraduates and for graduates.

The Student Guide (http://www.ed.gov/prog_info/SFA/StudentGuide/) from the U.S. Department of Education is the most comprehensive resource on all student financial aid available through the federal Student Financial Assistance Programs—grants, loans, and work-study. *The Student Guide* is updated each year. To request a free copy, call: 1-800-4-Fed-AID. The current guide is also available online.

Contact the Office of Student Financial Assistance Programs of the U.S. Department of Education for information on financial assistance and for help applying. The OSFAP sponsors several "Help Lines for Students":

General aid information or help applying for student aid: 800-433-3242

Help with software for applying electronically: 800-801-0576

Help consolidating student loans: 800-557-7394

Help with a defaulted student loan: 800-621-3115

The Internal Revenue Service (IRS) published "Notice 97-60: Administrative, Procedural, and Miscellaneous Education Tax Incentives" to explain the higher education tax incentives offered by the Taxpayer Relief Act of 1997. The IRS Web site includes up-to-date information on higher education tax incentive programs. To order IRS Notice 97-60, call 800-829-3676. Web: http://www.irs.ustreas.gov/hot/not97-60.html.

The Corporation for National Service offers education awards and student loans in return for national service to members of AmeriCorps.

Corporation for National Service
1201 New York Avenue, NW
Washington, DC 20525
202-606-5000
http://www.americorps.org/

A Woman's Head Start on the Pathway to Success: Women's Colleges and Women's Studies

Women make up more than 50 percent of the population of the United States. Logically, you would assume that women would account for 50 percent of our leaders, scientists, top executives, and elected officials. But they don't. Why? According to many leaders, educators, and psychologists, the lack of equal opportunities in education and the workplace are the major reasons.

Many believe that attending women's colleges and taking classes in women's studies can help females develop the leadership and critical thinking skills that can give them a head start toward career success in a male-dominated world.

Women's Colleges

Women's colleges first appeared in the United States as early as 1772, when Salem Academy was founded in North Carolina. In this country's early years, girls and women generally did not receive the formal education that males received. A few early forms of academic education offered some of the elements of education that boys received, and prepared some girls to be community leaders and benefactors. However, most of the education for females focused on preparing them for roles as wives and mothers. It was discovered in those early years that only by attending women's colleges could females obtain the higher education that had always been reserved for males.

In the mid-1800s, many women championed the abolition of slavery and strongly identified with these people whose rights were violated. As a result, women began to demand a greater role in society as well and, in response to that demand, many women's colleges were established.

In the 1960s women worked actively to obtain civil rights for minorities. Again women saw their own situations mirrored in the plight of minority groups. Increased activism for women's rights resulted. In response to demands for equal and better education for females, co-educational facilities became nearly universal in the United States by 1972, resulting in a declining enrollment in women's colleges.

Many more co-educational opportunities existed for women in the last half of the twentieth century than ever before. Today nearly half of all college students are women, yet women still hold far less than half of the leadership roles. Is this because of the education women receive in a co-educational environment? Can women's leadership success be linked to attending a woman's college or university?

Recent studies show that a disproportionately large percentage of women who do attain leadership positions have been educated in women's colleges. Although less than 4 percent of women who graduate from college have attended women's colleges, a 1997 survey shows that 20 percent of the 100 most powerful women in Washington, DC, came from women's colleges. More than twice as many women who graduate from women's colleges enter medical school or go on to receive doctoral degrees than do women who graduate from co-educational institutions. Students who attend women's colleges graduate with degrees in math and science 1.5 times as often as women who attend co-educational colleges.

What accounts for this difference? In women's colleges, young women do not encounter the gender bias—the stereotypical expectation that boys will achieve more than girls—that exists in co-educational schools. In single-sex schools, young women fill all the leadership roles. They are the class presidents, the team captains, and the ones chosen "most likely to succeed." They see women in leadership roles, and they have the opportunity to be leaders as well.

Not all people believe, however, that women's colleges are the answer to developing a woman's potential. Some individuals, including some very accomplished women, believe that the same-gender environment of women's colleges is too divorced from real-life situations. They point out that once women leave the college environment, they must compete with men.

On the other hand, prominent graduates of women's colleges maintain that their all-women experiences helped them gain self-confidence. They believe that this learning environment taught them to overcome stereotypes regarding women's capabilities, enabling them to compete better in the male-dominated workforce.

In the past, women's colleges were often attended only by the wealthy, and they were considered elite finishing schools. Today's women's colleges attract a wide variety of students from all socioeconomic, racial, and ethnic backgrounds. Forty-five to 70 percent of all students receive financial aid.

Diversity and tolerance are goals of all educational institutions, and this is especially true of women's colleges. National college surveys show that women's colleges are among the top U.S. colleges with the largest and most diverse international populations. Nine out of ten contemporary women's colleges have cross-registration with nearby men's colleges and universities. This arrangement offers opportunities for women to interact with men through co-ed classes, and social and sporting events.

For more information about women's colleges, check out the Web site of the Women's College Coalition (http://www.womenscolleges.org). There you will find details on life at women's colleges and contact information for women's colleges throughout the United States and Canada.

Attending a women's college is usually a two- or four-year commitment. For those who do not attend women's colleges, taking courses in women's studies offers many of the same advantages.

Women's Studies

The term "women's studies" refers to courses of study that focus on the social, political, and cultural experiences of women. These classes highlight women's achievements and contributions throughout history and in the present. As women contributed to the abolitionist movement in the mid-1800s and to the civil rights movement of the mid-1900s, they became increasingly aware of the parallels between the experiences of women and those of other groups of people oppressed by the political establishment of white male supremacy. Women's studies evolved out of the feminist movement of the 1960s. This feminist movement continues to seek to establish the political, economic, and social equality of both sexes.

Courses in women's studies are often offered in women's colleges and are being offered as part of the curriculum at co-educational institutions as well. Some women's studies programs are called "Women's and Gender Studies" in recognition of the diversity of life they consider. Some women's studies courses are individual classes offered as a small part of the curriculum within very diverse educational institutions. Some are isolated courses, while others lead to certificates, undergraduate minors and majors, and graduate degrees.

Women's studies courses encourage students to question traditional knowledge and to explore differences among individuals. They consider women's works and lives as well as the experiences of lesbians and gays. Women's studies teach an understanding of, sensitivity to, and respect for differences in gender, class, ability, race, age, ethnicity, religion, nationality, and sexual orientation. Men as well as women benefit from the increased understanding of diversity that is a product of women's studies.

Women's studies programs provide positive role models for women. These courses help them build their confidence and self-esteem, as well as encourage them to challenge the stereotypical male and female roles. Women's studies help women succeed in a male-dominated world. Graduates of women's studies programs have prospered in law, business, health care, public administration, government, journalism, nontraditional careers for women, and many other fields.

The pathway to career success is not the same for women as it is for men. Women's colleges and women's studies are two opportunities for women to get a head start toward career success. They allow and encourage females to develop their leadership skills, and they teach them an appreciation of diversity that helps prepare them for success. For more information on women's studies, contact the National Women's Studies Association (NWSA).

For More Information

Expect the Best from a Girl. That's What You'll Get (http://www.academic.org/) is a Web site sponsored by the Women's College Coalition in partnership with the Advertising Council. The goal of the project is to raise the expectations and aspirations of girls and women and to foster the creation of optimal learning environments for all girls and women. It includes suggestions for parents, teachers, and girls and has excellent links to other programs that promote gender equity.

The National Women's Studies Association (NWSA) supports and promotes feminist/womanist teaching, learning, research, and professional and community service at all educational levels. Its Web site includes links (organized by state) to more than 700 colleges and universities that teach women's studies.

National Women's Studies Association (NWSA)
University of Maryland
7100 Baltimore Boulevard, Suite 500
College Park, MD 20740
301-403-0525
http://www.nwsa.org/

Essays on Women's Topics

The Smith College Web site (http://www.smith.edu/wst/gradlinks.html) gives a list of graduate programs in women's studies. The programs are categorized according to Ph.D. stand-alone programs, M.A. programs, minors, certificates, and concentrations in women's studies.

The Women's College Coalition offers extensive information on the benefits of women's colleges. Its Web site includes a complete list of women's colleges in the United States and Canada as well as links to those that have Web sites. The site also includes sections on rankings of women's colleges, and myths and facts about women's colleges.

Women's College Coalition
125 Michigan Avenue, NE
Washington, DC 20017
202-234-0443
http://www.womenscolleges.org

Overcoming Roadblocks in a Woman's Pathway to Success: The Wage Gap, the Glass Ceiling, and Sexual Harassment

Nowhere is the importance of attaining gender equity—equitable treatment of women and men—more evident than in the workplace. Women make up about half of all U.S. workers. The number of women entering the workforce is increasing faster than the number of men. Even so, women earn less than men do for equal work. Women hold only 5 percent of top management positions, and women are often victims of sexual harassment on the job. This essay examines three major roadblocks to gender equity and women's career success and offers suggestions and resources for overcoming those obstacles. The roadblocks that are holding women back are the wage gap, the glass ceiling, and sexual harassment.

The Wage Gap

The wage gap is the difference between the incomes of women and men. The wage gap manifests itself in two ways. The first is lower pay for equal work and the second is a lower pay scale for "women's work."

Lower Pay for Equal Work

Equal pay for equal work has been the law since 1963. However, in 1998 women still earned only 76 cents for every dollar men earned. According to a joint report by the AFL-CIO and the Institute for Women's Policy Research (IWPR), that difference means that working American families lose $200 billion in income a year due to the wage gap. That translates to an average loss of $4,000 for each working woman's family.

Lower Pay for Women's Work

The other manifestation of the wage gap is the generally lower pay scale of traditionally female jobs. A major national survey conducted by the Women's Bureau of the U.S. Department of Labor in 1994 showed that over half of all women worked in traditionally female jobs. Most of those jobs, such as child care worker, clerical worker, and cleaning staff, were comparatively low paying. According to that study, nearly 60 percent of American women who worked full time earned less than $25,000 per year. Men who worked in female-dominated careers also earned less (although they still earned more than their female counterparts).

Effects of the Wage Gap

The wage gap hurts men, women, and children. Two-income families are the national norm among married couples. According to a 1997 AFL-CIO study, 52 percent of married women provided half, or more than half, of their households' incomes. The same study showed that 41 percent of working women headed their own households and 28 percent of women who were heads of households had dependent children. In families where women were the sole source of support, nearly one-third lived below the poverty level. Studies show that if women were paid as much as men doing comparable work, and if compensation for women's work were increased, the standard of living in the United States would improve immensely, and the poverty rates would drop dramatically.

Unequal pay has far-reaching effects. In addition to affecting a woman's present standard of living, it has significant consequences for her lifetime earning power. Lower pay in the present means lower benefits, lower savings, lower pensions, and lower retirement income in the future. For many working women and their families, the pay gap means a low standard of living in the present and a likelihood of living below the poverty level in old age. For more information on the wage gap, its implications, and ways to overcome it, contact the Women's Bureau of the U.S. Department of Labor and the AFL-CIO at the addresses listed at the end of this article.

The Glass Ceiling

A second major roadblock to women's career success is the glass ceiling—the invisible barrier that keeps women from advancing to higher levels of responsibility and higher pay. Although women may encounter the glass ceiling early in their careers, they more frequently encounter it in mid-career—once they have established themselves and begin to seek higher-level positions.

The glass ceiling was initially a product of the old boys' network, the tendency of men in positions of power to hire and promote white males to the exclusion of women and minorities. Antidiscrimination laws have helped women and minorities make major steps toward breaking through the old boys' network. However, women continue to be held back by what some have termed the "new glass ceiling"—gender bias at work and the responsibility for child care and elder care.

Gender Bias at Work

Gender bias at work, the first component of the new glass ceiling, is readily apparent in the numbers of women who reach (or do not reach) the top positions in large corporations. In 1999, only three of the Fortune 500 companies had women as chief executive officers.

Negative stereotypes are another manifestation of gender bias in the workplace. Women frequently encounter stereotypes that portray them as less qualified, less hard-working, less valuable, and less tough than men. The majority of upper-level managers who hold these biases are men, and they are more likely to promote other men into positions of authority. Studies show that men get promoted earlier in their careers, often while they are still learning skills needed for the next position. Women generally have to wait until they have proven they possess the skills needed for the next position before they are considered for promotion.

Care Giving at Home

The second component of the new glass ceiling is women's continuing role as the major caregivers at home. Women are much more likely than men to be involved in caring for children and the aged. Employers use this fact to discriminate against women based on the perception that women might not stay at a job as long, be as dependable, or be as willing to travel or work overtime as men. Studies of women employees have shown that this stereotypical perception of women workers is not true, but gender bias continues in the workplace. For more information on the glass ceiling, visit the Advancing Women (http://www.advancingwomen.com) and Shatter the Glass Ceiling (http://www.theglass-ceiling.com/) Web sites.

Strategies for Overcoming the Wage Gap and Breaking the Glass Ceiling

Closing the wage gap and breaking through the glass ceiling can help improve life for American women and their families. Both collective and individual strategies are available to help women overcome these roadblocks.

The government of the United States now recognizes the importance of equitable opportunity and pay for women. The government, educators, women's groups, labor unions, and employers are making efforts to increase the equitable treatment of women. Much has been accomplished, but even more remains to be done. Some programs aimed at overcoming barriers to women's success are described below.

Gender Equity in Education

The U.S. Department of Labor studies show a strong correlation between level of education and employment. Women who are more educated are less likely to be unemployed. Girls who have positive female role models are more likely to develop positive self-images and to be successful in their education, their careers, and their lives. The federal government has passed laws to increase gender equity in education. (For more information on gender equity in education, see the articles on women's legal rights and on role models in this section.)

Women and girls who study advanced science and math are more likely to succeed in careers that are considered nontraditional for women—jobs in which less than 25 percent of the workers are women. Many nontraditional careers offer higher pay, better benefits, and more chances for advancement. Programs that encourage gender equity in education also encourage girls and young women to develop the skills they need to succeed in nontraditional careers. (See the article on nontraditional careers in this section.)

Fair Pay Clearinghouse

The U.S. Department of Labor Women's Bureau maintains the Women's Bureau Fair Pay Clearinghouse to assist employers and employees who want to adapt wage-setting practices so that female-dominated jobs are more fairly paid. The Clearinghouse offers information on how to attain fair pay, how employers have changed their pay practices, and who is working to improve pay for "women's work." Contact information for the Fair Pay Clearinghouse is included in the Women's Bureau information at the end of this article.

Civil Service Jobs

According to the U.S. Department of Labor, greater progress toward gender equity is evident in jobs in the public sector. Wages paid by city, state, county, and federal governments are public information, so government bodies are often subject to more pressure to adjust their pay systems. Women may find that fair pay and equal advancement opportunities are more readily available in government jobs.

Unions

Union representation has proved to be a powerful force for raising women's wages and increasing their opportunities for advancement. According to an AFL-CIO study, female union members earn nearly 39 percent more per week than nonunion women workers. Women who work where union membership is an option would be wise to consider membership. Where no union is available, women should consider forming one. For more information on the benefits of union membership, see the AFL-CIO contact information on page 45.

In addition to learning about and taking advantage of collective strategies, every woman must develop her own tactics for closing the pay gap and breaking through the glass ceiling. As with any other journey, before you start on your pathway to success, you must decide where you want to go and how to get there. Build a personal career plan that includes a skills inventory, networks and mentors, openness to change, negotiation skills, family-friendly companies, proactivism, and self-reliance.

Skills Inventory

Take an inventory of your knowledge and skills. Identify your core talents and build strategies that will use your knowledge and skills to help you grow and advance. Add to the inventory as your skills increase. Look for jobs that will give you the best income and opportunity for advancement for your skills. Consider what capabilities you might need to acquire in order to move to the next level in your field. Libraries and bookstores have career development books that contain examples of skills inventories. You'll find a free online skills assessment at the University of Waterloo Web site (http://www.adm.uwaterloo.ca/infocecs/CRC/manual/introduction.html). Build your skills inventory now, and review it every few years for the rest of your life.

Networks and Mentors

Identify women's organizations and networks that relate to your goals and interests. Get to know other women who share your goals and discuss strategies for attaining those goals. Take every opportunity to develop networks and seek mentors who can help increase your skills and develop contacts. Many successful women credit strong networks and mentors with helping them build successful careers. See the article Resources for Women's Success: Role Models, Networks, and Mentors in this section for information on finding networks and mentors and for networking tips.

Openness to Change

Cultivate an openness to change. Given the fast pace of change in the world, women who have a positive attitude toward change will have the best chance to succeed. Continually add to your skills inventory. When change confronts you, examine how you can build on the knowledge and skills you have to benefit from that change. Take charge of your career—don't just let things happen! You may need to restructure your career and even change careers a number of times throughout your lifetime. Stay flexible and evaluate what new jobs fit your skills and strengths. The Women's Bureau of the U.S. Department of Labor and *Working Woman* magazine publish lists of "hot jobs" for the future. Their contact information is at the end of this article.

Negotiations

Learn to negotiate better jobs and better pay. Before you go to an interview or to a salary review, research the pay rates in your field and/or company. Know what other workers, both men and women, are paid for the work you do. Decide on your asking price. Decide on your minimum. Know the value of your skills and the work you do, and ask for what you should be paid. Women too often fail to negotiate and end up settling for less than they should. Read books on negotiating and take classes in negotiations.

Use your negotiating skills at home, too. Women must learn to demand that their partners help with work at home. In families where both partners work, many women have two full-time jobs: full-time work and full-time caregiving. Negotiate with your partner to assume half of the caregiving responsibilities so each of you will have a job and a half. Negotiate to hire out some of the domestic duties—housecleaning, delivery, laundry—to reduce the load on both of you. Visit Web sites such as the Monster.com (http://monster.com) to learn more about career development and negotiating for what you deserve.

Family-Friendly Companies

A great way to overcome both gender bias and caregiving issues is to work for companies that are family friendly and women friendly. Research companies to find out how many women they have in upper management and on their boards of directors. Check resources such as *Working Woman* (http://www.workingwoman.com/) and *Working Mother* (http://www.workingmother.com/) magazines for recent ratings of the best companies for working women and working mothers.

Proactivism

Take action on wage-gap and glass-ceiling issues. Vote for people who support legislation for fair pay and opportunities for advancement for women. Write letters to the editors of magazines and newspapers. Write to government representatives to ask their support for issues that affect women. Women's organizations such as the National Organization for Women (NOW) will help you keep informed about women's issues and legislation affecting women.

National Organization for Women (NOW)
1000 16th Street, NW, #700
Washington, DC 20036
202-785-8576
http://www.now.org

Self-Reliance

Many successful women say that no strategy has helped as much as being self-reliant. There is no denying women's pathway to success is strewn with roadblocks. Building inner resources and strength will help you navigate around the roadblocks and map out your personal career plan. Review your career plan frequently, and reevaluate the progress of your personal and professional growth. For an ongoing discussion on building self-reliance, visit Dr. Sarah Banda Purvis's Web site (http://www.insiderviews.com).

Both collective and individual strategies can help you overcome the first two major roadblocks in the pathway to success: the wage gap and the glass ceiling, The third road-block requires different strategies.

Sexual Harassment

A third major barrier to women's career success is sexual harassment. Although the Civil Rights Act of 1964 made sexual harassment in the workplace illegal, women and men still contend with this issue today. Sexual harassment affects both genders. However, women and girls experience it more frequently and report more negative psychological, emotional, and physical effects from it than men and boys do.

Sexual harassment is defined as "unwanted and unwelcome behavior of a sexual nature." If flirtatious behavior or sexual overtures or advances are welcome, the behavior is not sexual harassment.

If sexual overtures or advances in the workplace are not welcome, the behavior is sexual harassment, and it is illegal. Two types of sexual harassment on the job have been specifically defined: quid pro quo situations and hostile environment harassment.

A quid pro quo situation is one in which a person in authority, such as a supervisor or boss, links some aspect of an employee's job or advancement to that employee's response to sexual overtures. For example, a supervisor may suggest that an employee will receive a promotion in return for sexual favors or that a raise will be denied unless the person complies with sexual requests.

Hostile environment harassment exists when unwelcome verbal or physical conduct by supervisors or co-workers is sufficiently persistent or severe to cause a reasonable person to feel that the environment is abusive or hostile. Examples are persistent use of abusive or suggestive language, unwelcome physical contact, or displaying pornographic pictures.

Sexual harassment can cause low morale, low productivity, high employee turnover, and increased lawsuits. Recent court cases have made it clear that employers are liable for the actions of supervisors who engage in sexual harassment. Employers are also responsible for ensuring the absence of a hostile environment. Preventing and containing sexual harassment in the workplace is in the best interest of employers and employees.

Strategies for Dealing with Sexual Harassment

If you experience sexual harassment on the job, tell the harasser to stop. Always write down the facts of the incident. Record all of the details. Include all the elements of good reporting: who, what, when, where, why, and how.

Keep a copy of your notes at home. Always keep copies of your performance evaluations and any documents that show your good work record at home. If your harasser causes you to lose your job, you will need those records.

Talk to others at work. Find out if other women are experiencing the same behaviors. If you belong to a union, talk to the union representative. Talk to an authority in the personnel office at your job. Find out what procedures your employer has in place for making a complaint.

Try to work out the problem through your employer and union first, but be prepared to take further action if you do not get satisfaction. The Women's Bureau of the U.S. Department of Labor can give you more information about your rights. The Equal Employment Opportunity Commission (EEOC) handles discrimination complaints. The National Organization for Women is active in combating sexual harassment. You have a right to file a complaint, and you can win.

Although the pay gap, the glass ceiling, and sexual harassment still represent major roadblocks in the pathway to women's career success, laws and organizations exist to help you overcome them. Take advantage of the help that exists—you do not have to face the roadblocks alone. Other women have overcome these roadblocks, and you can, too.

For More Information

Advancing Women (http://www.advancingwomen.com) is a Web site designed as an electronic networking and support system for women. It contains a wealth of information on networking, mentoring, business, careers, and money matters.

The AFL-CIO represents more than 13 million working women and men. It is the largest national organization for working women with 5.5 million women members. Its Web site includes the results of the 1997 "Ask a Working Woman" survey, a calculator, "How Much Will the Pay Gap Cost YOU?," and information on closing the pay gap.

AFL-CIO
815 16th Street, NW
Washington, DC 20006
202-637-5000
http://www.aflcio.org/women

EEOC publications on employment rights and issues are available at no cost. To file a discrimination charge with the EEOC: 800-669-4000

U.S. Equal Employment Opportunity Commission (EEOC)
Publications Distribution Center
PO Box 12549
Cincinnati, OH 44212-0549
800-669-3362
http://www.eeoc.gov

Insider Views on Workplace Issues (http://www.insiderviews.com) is a Web site developed and maintained by Dr. Sarah Banda Purvis. It includes provocative thoughts and insights on issues that affect working women, a survey on workplace experiences, extensive and frequently updated links, and opportunities for ongoing dialogue with Dr. Purvis and other women in the workforce.

Monster.com (http://monster.com) is an enormous Web site that offers career development resources including how to interview and network, how to write resumes and letters, how to manage your career, and how to develop skills such as negotiation. The site lets you build and store a resume online, research companies, and search for jobs.

The National Organization for Women (NOW) has over 500,000 contributing members and is the largest feminist organization in the United States. Since it was founded in 1966, NOW has worked for justice and equality for women. It actively promotes legislation that will improve the lives of women.

National Organization for Women (NOW)
1000 16th Street, NW, #700
Washington, DC 20036
202-785-8576
http://www.now.org

Shatter the Glass Ceiling (http://www.theglassceiling.com/) is a Web site that includes information about succeeding in business, glass ceiling issues, family issues, health issues, and a legal center. Women (75 percent) and men (25 percent) who struggle with glass ceiling issues share their experiences.

The University of Waterloo Web site (http://www.adm.uwaterloo.ca/infocecs/CRC/manual/introduction.html) has an excellent section entitled, "Steps to Career/Life Planning Success." It includes a free online skills assessment and sound advice on life planning.

The Women's Bureau of the U.S. Department of Labor informs women and the public of, and advocates for, women's work rights and employment issues. The Women's Bureau Fair Pay Clearinghouse assists employees and employers who want to improve wage-setting practices. The toll free number to the Fair Pay Clearinghouse is 800-347-3741. For information on regional offices of the Women's Bureau, contact:

Women's Bureau
U.S. Department of Labor
Washington, DC 20210
800-827-5335
http://www.dol.gov/dol/wb

Working Mother magazine features sections on child care issues, workplace flexibility, finance, and health care for women. It periodically publishes lists of the best companies for working mothers.

Working Mother
135 West 50th Street
New York, NY 10020
212-445-6100
http://www.workingmother.com/

Working Woman magazine is one of the few national magazines that publishes the entire contents of the magazine on the Internet. In addition to many helpful articles for women who work, it publishes an annual salary survey that includes comparisons between women's and men's wages.

Working Woman
135 West 50th Street
New York, NY 10020
212-445-6100
http://www.workingwoman.com/

Smoothing the Pathway: Work-Life Balance

Does your job have you feeling stressed and pressed for time? That is certainly not unusual in this day and age. Stress and pressure are part of the bad news for workers in the United States today. The good news is that you can do something about it.

How did all of this job stress and pressure come about? In the late twentieth and early twenty-first centuries, the cumulative effects of industrialization in the United States—growth of large cities and corporations, suburban sprawl, consumerism, traffic jams, pollution, and seemingly endless commuting—combined to create a society in which people have less and less time for themselves and their families. Large companies merge to form even larger corporate giants in order to compete in an increasingly global economy. At the same time, companies reorganize or downsize to become more efficient and effective.

The good news is that all that growth, change, and competition have made finding, training, and keeping the best employees crucial to businesses of all sizes. Approximately one-half of today's workforce is made up of women, many of whom are single parents. In addition, nearly one-half of all U.S. workers are part of dual-income families. During the 1980s and 1990s, studies of workplace practices increasingly showed that helping employees balance the competing demands of work, life, and family improved the bottom line for corporations. As a result, many employers began to develop flexible work arrangements to attract and keep employees.

In the 1990s, the U.S. government took a leading role in developing a "family-friendly workplace" for their employees. This program was developed as a model for employers throughout the country. Information on the government's progress in its family-friendly workplace advocacy program is available from the United States Office of Personnel Management.

United States Office of Personnel Management
1900 East Street, NW
Washington, DC 20415-0001
202-606-1800
http://www.opm.gov/wrkfam/index.html-ssi

Employers give different names to their efforts to improve the balance of life for their workers. Some popular names are family-friendly, women-friendly, work-life, and lifestyle strategies. Whatever they are called, many of these new work options are especially beneficial for women who want to improve the balance between work and the rest of their lives.

Flexible Work Arrangements

Some of the most helpful work options for women are flexible work arrangements: flextime, part-time work, job sharing, and telecommuting.

Essays on Women's Topics

Flextime

Flextime (also called flexitime) is a flexible work arrangement that allows employees to adjust their work schedules to balance the demands of life and work. Surveys of employees show that flextime is among the most valued flexible job options. One survey of 3,000 employees showed that 60 percent of the workers found flextime to be of great importance.

Many approaches to flextime exist. Some companies allow employees to choose their starting and ending times. Employees may select the schedule that works best for them; however, they must stick with that schedule. Other employers give workers the option of varying their starting and ending times—sometimes even daily—as long as they work a certain number of hours. The feasibility of flextime plans varies according to the type of work performed.

A variation of flextime is a compressed workweek. That usually means working a 40-hour week in fewer days. The most usual arrangement is four 10-hour days a week, which gives workers an extra free day a week. Another version, called the 5-4/9 option, involves working five 9-hour days one week and four 9-hour days the next. The 5-4/9 arrangement gives employees one extra day off every two weeks.

Part-Time Work

A growing number of employers are offering part-time work options in which employees are hired for only two or three days a week. Women make up about 68 percent of part-time workers. Women most often decide to work part-time due to caregiving responsibilities for children, the infirmed, or the aged. A smaller number of women choose part-time work to reduce stress or to pursue personal interests. Men are more likely to choose part-time work as a preparation for retirement.

Women who have worked part-time caution that going part-time is not simply reducing the number of hours or days worked. Working part-time requires planning and good communication. Unless a change of responsibility to match the change in hours is carefully planned and agreed upon with superiors, part-timers may end up with full-time workloads to be accomplished during part-time hours. Communication with co-workers is also important to avoid co-worker jealousy and to be sure part-timers stay current on policy and project changes.

Another communication issue for part-time employees is letting their superiors know that they are still interested in career advancement. Unless they clearly communicate that they are interested in more challenging projects, part-timers may be overlooked.

Benefits can be an issue for part-time workers. Larger corporations usually offer benefits for part-timers. Some offer full benefits, while others give reduced benefits based on the time worked. Smaller organizations frequently do not offer benefits to part-time employees.

If you are thinking about working part-time, be sure to establish the terms of your employment, including benefits, in writing well before you make the change. For more details on the pros and cons of working part-time, visit the Women's Wire (http://www.womenswire.com/work/work.html) and the Work Options, Inc. (http://www.workoptions.com/) Web sites.

Job Sharing

Another flexible arrangement that is becoming increasingly popular among women is job sharing. Job sharing involves two people working at and being responsible for the same job. The time commitment is often similar to part-time work—with each job-sharing partner working two or three days a week.

Job sharing frequently begins when an individual who has a job wants to work part-time without giving up the job. Most companies that allow job sharing expect the employee who wants to share her job to find the appropriate partner. Special arrangements must be negotiated with the company concerning how the salary and benefits will be allotted.

Successful job-sharing partners point out that finding the right partner and establishing excellent communication are crucial to a successful working arrangement. Each partner must be very organized and able to keep the other informed of all details of the job.

If you are interested in job sharing, check out the Work Options, Inc. (http://www.workoptions.com/) and the Women's Wire (http://www.womenswire.com/work/work.html) Web sites.

Telecommuting

The term "telecommuting" is commonly used in two ways. Employers who offer telecommuting options define a telecommuter as someone who has already been employed by the company, has proven to be dependable, is capable of working with little supervision, and is willing and able to work from home or from a telecenter a few days a week.

The second type of telecommuting is discussed as "work-at-home" in the article, Building a New Pathway: Starting a New Business, in this section of *Pathways to Career Success for Women*. Many individuals who are not already employed by a company, who only want to work from home, and who look for work through the Internet, agencies, direct mail, and classified advertising also call their work telecommuting.

In this article, telecommuting is discussed as a flexible work arrangement offered by an employer. Organizations that offer telecommuting options may allow employees to work from their homes or they may set up telecenters, which are smaller office centers located away from the main corporate office to help reduce commuting distance and time for employees.

The federal government has taken a lead in promoting telecommuting because of its beneficial effects on the environment. Telecommuting reduces traffic, energy consumption, and pollution, and has life-work benefits for employees. In 1996, the President's Management Council endorsed a National Telecommuting Initiative to significantly increase the numbers of federal employees who telecommute. The outline of the government's telecommuting initiative, including reasons for telecommuting, steps to implementing a telecommuting program, and a sample telecommuting agreement for use between employer and telecommuter, are available from the Office of Personnel Management.

Of the flexible work arrangements discussed here, telecommuting demands the most employer cooperation and investment. Most large organizations pay the costs of setting up an employee's home office. In some instances that may be as simple as installing an extra telephone line; in others, the costs include computer hardware and software, phone lines, computer lines, and other business equipment such as copiers and faxes. The Web site of

Gil Gordon Associates (http://www.gilgordon.com/) is a great resource for new and sea-soned telecommuters and their managers.

Success in Flexible Work Arrangements

The key to the success of every flexible work arrangement is that it must truly be bene-ficial for both employer and employee. If your employer offers flexible work-life options, consider carefully whether they would be helpful and valuable to you before you apply for them.

If you like your present employer but would like to have more flexible work arrange-ments, ask your employer to consider those options. Before you make your proposal, know how your suggestion will benefit your employer. The Web site of the Minnesota Center for Corporate Responsibility (http://tigger.stthomas.edu/mccr/WL_Report.htm) contains an excellent article, "Creating High Performance Organizations . . . The Bottom Line Value of Work/Life Strategies," that details how business benefits from these strategies. Such infor-mation can help you determine the value of your proposal to your employer.

Once you know how your plan will benefit you and your employer, put your proposal in writing. Studies show that written proposals have a much greater chance of being accepted, and of being successful. Many books have excellent information on proposal writing. For user-friendly help on proposal writing, visit the Web site of Work Options, Inc. (http://www.workoptions.com/).

Once you have developed your written proposal, give careful thought to whom you should present it and when. You will definitely need the cooperation and support of your immediate supervisor. Consider that person's personality to determine the best timing. What time of day is best? When is your supervisor most receptive to new ideas? A thought-fully developed written proposal presented to the right person at the right time has the best chance of success.

If your employer is opposed to offering flexible job options, and they are important to you, consider finding a company that offers them. Many excellent resources are available to help you find companies that offer good work-life arrangements. *Working Woman* mag-azine publishes lists of women-friendly employers. *Working Mother* magazine offers lists that focus on family-friendly employers. Women's Wire, an online magazine devoted to women's issues, offers a list of women-friendly and family-friendly companies that is searchable both alphabetically and by city. Contact information for all three resources is given at the end of this article.

In addition to the flexible job options discussed in this article, many other types of flexible work arrangements and work-life balancing strategies exist. Work & Family Connection, Inc.'s Web site (http://www.workfamily.com/) acts as a clearinghouse for information on work-life options. The "Internet resources" section is particularly well organized and gives detailed descriptions of the contents of each link.

You can smooth your pathway to career success by balancing work with the rest of your life. You can get help balancing your life by working for companies that offer flexible job options or by convincing your employer to begin offering them.

For More Information

Gil Gordon Associates' Web site offers a wealth of resources for telecommuters and their managers. The site includes articles on setting up telecommuting programs, successful telecommuting, telecommuting tools, how-to resources, and worldwide resources.

Gil Gordon Associates
10 Donner Court
Monmouth Junction, NJ 08852
732-329-2266
http://www.gilgordon.com/

The Minnesota Center for Corporate Responsibility (MCCR) is affiliated with the University of St. Thomas in Minnesota. The MCCR report, "Creating High Performance Organizations...The Bottom Line Value of Work/Life Strategies," contains extensive information on these strategies and their value to corporations.

Minnesota Center for Corporate Responsibility
1000 LaSalle Avenue, Suite 153
Minneapolis, MN 55403-2005
651-962-4120
http://tigger.stthomas.edu/mccr/WL_Report.htm

The U.S. Office of Personnel Management (OPM), the federal government's human resources agency, operates a government-wide pilot project to develop and encourage family-friendly workplace advocacy. In addition to other family-friendly practices, its Web site details reasons for telecommuting, steps to implementing a telecommuting program, and a sample telecommuting agreement for use between employer and telecommuter.

United States Office of Personnel Management
1900 East Street, NW
Washington, DC 20415-0001
202-606-1800

Women's Wire (http://www.womenswire.com/work/work.html) is an online women's magazine that is part of the Women.com network. It offers information on money, work, and flexible work options. It also features a searchable database of women-friendly and family-friendly employers. Companies are included in the list based on salary, benefits, and opportunities for advancement.

Work & Family Connection, Inc.'s Web site is a clearinghouse devoted to work-life issues. It contains a wealth of free online information for employers and employees on work-life issues and on setting up family-friendly workplace policies. Well-organized links with excellent descriptions lead to over 80 other resources related to work-life issues. Additional information is available on a fee basis.

Work & Family Connection, Inc.
5197 Beachside Drive
Minnetonka, MN 55343
800-487-7898
http://www.workfamily.com/

Essays on Women's Topics

Working Mother magazine features sections on child care issues, workplace flexibility, finance, and health care for women. It periodically publishes lists of the best companies for working mothers.

Working Mother
135 West 50th Street
New York, NY 10020
212-445-6100
http://www.workingmother.com/

Working Woman magazine is one of the few national magazines that publishes the entire contents of the magazine on the Internet. In addition to many helpful articles for women who work, it publishes an annual salary survey that includes comparisons between women's and men's wages.

Working Woman
135 West 50th Street
New York, NY 10020
212-445-6100
http://www.workingwoman.com/

Work Options, Inc. is the home-based one-woman consulting firm of Pat Katepoo. Her Web site includes extensive free information on the advantages and disadvantages of flexible job options, on negotiating flexible work arrangements, and on writing proposals. She offers a time-saving proposal template for a modest fee.

Work Options, Inc.
47-370 Mawaena Street
Kaneohe, HI 96744-4721 USA
888-279-FLEX
http://www.workoptions.com/

Excellent Opportunities for Women: Nontraditional Careers

Nontraditional careers offer women particularly attractive opportunities to advance along the pathway to success. A nontraditional career for women is defined as one in which 25 percent or fewer of the workers are women. Women who choose nontraditional careers generally average 20 to 30 percent higher incomes and usually receive better benefits than those who work in more traditional female positions. The issue of gender equity—equal access to, and equal training and pay for all types of work —is of particular importance to women's success in nontraditional careers.

This article introduces some nontraditional careers (the skilled trades, the military, and science, mathematics, engineering, and technology fields) and discusses how women can prepare for and thrive in nontraditional careers.

Exploring Nontraditional Careers

A 1998 report by the U.S. Department of Labor lists nearly 100 nontraditional occupations for women. Many of the nontraditional jobs mentioned offer women excellent opportunities for advancement. Many of the jobs listed are in the skilled trades, the military, and scientific and technological careers.

Skilled Trades

Recent federal legislation has advanced the cause of gender equity in vocational and technical education. Federal programs have provided seed (start-up) money to state and local governments to develop programs that provide training for women and that offer them the opportunity to work and succeed in the skilled trades.

The Nontraditional Employment for Women Act of 1992, also known as the Women in Apprenticeship and Nontraditional Occupations Act, works to remedy the exclusion of women from the skilled trades—especially those that require apprenticeships for entry. (Apprenticeships are a type of training program to learn the skills of a specific trade. Many of the skills are taught on the job.) As a result of this legislation, federal and state governments, labor unions, and industry have initiated programs to help women enter into the skilled trades. State Bureaus of Apprenticeship and Training have information about apprenticeship opportunities. Contact the National Office of the Bureau of Apprenticeship and Training listed at the end of this article for addresses of state offices.

The School-to-Work Opportunities Act of 1994 encourages state and local partnerships of government, labor, business, education, and community organizations to develop programs to help students make the transition from high school to the workforce. While school-to-work programs are developed for all students, many focus on providing young women access to the same opportunities that young men receive. The federal portion of this program ends in 2001, but the programs established at the state and local levels may continue. To learn about school-to-work opportunities in your area, contact the National School-to-Work Learning and Information Center or Wider Opportunities for Women (WOW). Information on both of these organizations appears at the end of this article.

The Carl D. Perkins Vocational and Technical Education Act of 1998 (Perkins III) encourages preparation for nontraditional employment and addresses the needs of special populations, such as women. Every state is required to have a plan for vocational and technical education. Ask your school or career counselor about the programs available in your state.

Programs change frequently, but federal legislation encourages state and local governments, employers, and unions to work toward gender equity. Talk to unions and employers in the trades that interest you. Ask what programs are available and how you can become involved.

Military Careers

Although women have long served in the military, they still account for less than 25 percent of military personnel. All five branches of the U.S. armed forces (Air Force, Army, Coast Guard, Marines, and Navy) are open to women.

In response to civil rights laws, all branches of the military are working to increase the percentages of occupational specialties, and positions within those specialties that are open to women. According to a 1997 report by the U.S. Department of Defense, the Coast Guard leads the way with 100 percent of its occupations and positions open to women. The Air Force is a close second with 99 percent. The Navy, the Army, and the Marines follow, in that order.

The military careers still closed to women are associated with ground combat and submarine warfare. Congress passed significant changes to the combat restriction laws in the early 1990s. However, a study commissioned by the Department of Defense showed that many women did not take advantage of the newly available combat positions due to lack of training. The study also showed that some commanders still were reluctant to assign women to vacant combat positions despite the passage of new laws.

Each branch of the military has a specific function, so if you are considering a career in the military, you will want to consider the differences between the branches. The Air Force is responsible for space and air defense, while the Army is responsible for defense on land. The Navy is in charge of sea-based defense initiatives, and the Marines provide ground support for the Navy. The Coast Guard fills different roles in times of peace and in times of war. In peacetime, it works for the Department of Transportation and controls access to the shores of the United States. During a war, it works with the Navy. The Web sites of the five military branches are listed at the end of this article.

One important advantage of a military career is the access it provides to schooling, training, and travel. The five branches offer different benefits and incentives at different times. They sometimes offer attractive bonuses when they need people who possess particular skills. Talk to recruiters for the services that interest you. Ask them about their programs and what benefits they currently offer. Be aware that they do not offer the same incentives to everyone. Once a recruiter has told you about the incentives and benefits, ask, "What other incentives are available? Is this the best offer you can make?"

The Military Woman Web site listed at the end of this article offers a unique opportunity to learn about women's experiences in the military. Women candidly share their personal opinions (pro and con) about life in the military. This site is not affiliated with the Department of Defense.

Some military occupations train women for jobs in the skilled trades. Other military positions prepare them for nontraditional work in more scientific and technological fields.

Science, Mathematics, Engineering, and Technology Careers

The National Science Foundation (NSF) is responsible for ensuring the vitality of the nation's scientific, technological, and engineering enterprises. Women are still underrepresented in these fields, and the government considered this a national concern. In response, the Human Resources Development Department of the NSF has initiated programs to increase successful participation by women and girls in engineering, math, science, and technology.

The Human Resources Development Department of the National Science Foundation sponsors the Program for Gender Equity in Science, Mathematics, Engineering, and Technology. The Program for Gender Equity is "dedicated to changing factors that have discouraged the early, and continuing, interest in SMET (Science, Mathematics, Engineering, and Technology), and to developing interest, knowledge, and involvement of girls and young women in these fields." An annual budget of around $9 million became available in 1999, and grant proposals are scheduled at least through 2005. For more information, visit the Program for Gender Equity Web site listed below.

For women already involved in science and engineering, the Human Resources Development Department of the NSF sponsors the Professional Opportunities for Women in Research and Education (POWRE) program. This program awards one-time funding to enhance the professional advancement of women in science and engineering.

Many associations and organizations also provide opportunities for girls and women in science, math, engineering, and technology. Such organizations may offer networking, mentoring, scholarships, or career advancement services. The list at the end of this article is only a beginning. Check out the Organizations section of this book for more resources.

Preparing for a Nontraditional Career

When considering a nontraditional career, how do you know which one to choose? What can you do to prepare?

Assess Your Interests and Skills

Many general career guidance books include interest and skills assessments that are helpful in choosing a career path. You'll find a wealth of such books at the library or bookstore. Take time to evaluate your strengths and interests. Your likes and dislikes can give clues to whether a nontraditional career is right for you.

Consider the following questions. Do you like to work with your hands? Do you get bored listening to others talk about their problems? Do computers and other electronic equipment fascinate you? Do you like to be outdoors? Do you love to solve puzzles or technical problems? Do you hate being in one place all day?

The University of Missouri-Columbia has developed an online self-assessment survey with questions such as these that can help you explore your suitability for nontraditional careers (http://www.iml.coe.missouri.edu/services/Enter/survey.html).

Study Science, Math, and Computers

Fear of math and science has caused many women to give up pursuing the career of their dreams. Don't let math and science stand in your way. Check out the resources at the end of this article and throughout this book for opportunities to improve your confidence and your ability in math and science. Other women have succeeded in these areas, and you can, too. The programs are out there to help you. The opportunities exist. Go after them!

Take Continuing Education Classes

Sign up for the classes that relate to the work that interests you. If you like engineering, take a course in engineering technology. If computers attract you, take computer-aided design (CAD) or other computer courses. Look for courses in materials and processes if you want to work in a skilled trade. Take the courses that can lead you in the direction you want to go.

Talk to School or Job Counselors

Counselors may have resources that can help you learn about the jobs that interest you. However, if you sense that the counselor is steering you away from what you want, look for another counselor. Even professionals can be victims of unconscious stereotypes about women and nontraditional careers.

Network with Women in Nontraditional Careers

Many career fields have general associations and women's associations that can help you. Some associations have Web sites and opportunities for online discussions. Many offer workshops and scholarships. For more information on associations and networking, check out the references at the end of this article, see the article on role models, mentors, and networks in this section, and be sure to check the references in the Organizations section of this book.

Look for a Mentor

A mentor is a person who has experience in a particular field and is willing to share information and help you learn about that profession. Finding the right mentor can give you an enormous boost toward achieving your goals. Read the article, Resources for Women's Success: Role Models, Networks, and Mentors, for more information about how to find mentors and how they can help you meet your career goals.

Surviving in a Nontraditional Career

Nontraditional careers offer many potential benefits. They also give women opportunities to contribute to overcoming gender bias and building gender equity. If you choose a nontraditional career, you will be studying and working mostly among men, and you will encounter a variety of negative and positive responses to your presence. You'll need to develop some special tools to deal with the obstacles that may confront you. Taking the following actions can help you survive and become successful.

Cultivate Allies and Mentors

Use networking skills to develop allies and mentors in your school or work. Having solid, helping relationships with other students or co-workers, as well as mentors, will give you "strength in numbers." Trying to do everything alone is much tougher. Help others achieve their goals, and they are likely to help you as well.

Join Professional Associations and Women's Support Groups

You may be the only woman, or one of very few in your work setting. Join professional associations that are related to your field. They can give you opportunities to network with women who work in similar situations. Find out how they deal with issues that arise. Online networks and support groups can be particularly helpful because they are easily accessible. The Advancing Women and the Electra Pages Web sites are some of the references that can lead you to women's organizations and associations. Also read the Organizations section of this book for more information.

Learn to Respond Constructively to Peer Teasing

In nontraditional jobs, women frequently have to deal with teasing or condescending remarks from peers. These negative comments may come from women and men. Talking with mentors and other women in nontraditional roles can help you develop a constructive approach to dealing with these unpleasant situations.

Learn to Avoid or Diffuse Verbal or Physical Harassment

Women need this skill for life in general, but in nontraditional jobs where there are few women, diffusing both verbal and physical harassment becomes even more important. Equity Online, the resource center for the national Women's Educational Equity Act (WEEA), provides extensive information on ways to deal with sexual harassment. The contact information for Equity Online is listed at the end of this article.

Know Your Legal Rights

Be aware of your rights and know how to implement legal procedures when necessary. Seeking legal remedies is usually time-consuming, often unpleasant, and frequently disappointing, so this should truly be the last resort. However, in spite of the difficulties of pursuing legal resolutions, women can be successful in standing up for their rights. See the article in this directory on women's legal rights for more information.

Nontraditional careers offer women interesting challenges, excellent opportunities for growth, and increased income and benefits. Consider how a nontraditional career might advance you along your pathway to success.

For More Information

The resources below are listed according to their primary focus: gender equity; skilled trades; the military; or science, mathematics, engineering, and technology.

Essays on Women's Topics

Gender Equity

Advancing Women (http://www.advancingwomen.com) is an electronic networking and support system for women. It contains a wealth of information on networking, mentoring, business, careers, employment opportunities, and money matters.

The Electra Pages (http://electrapages.com), a Web site maintained by the Women's Information Exchange, contains a searchable directory of 9,000 women's organizations.

Equity Online (http://www.edc.org/WomensEquity/) is the resource center for the national Women's Educational Equity Act (WEEA). It offers extensive information on gender equity and sexual harassment as well as a free science, engineering, and mathematics CD-ROM. It also has good links to similar sites.

"Why Are There so Few Female Computer Scientists?" (http://www.ai.mit.edu/people/ellens/Gender/wom_and_min.html) by Ellen Spertus is a detailed study of the factors involved in the perpetuation of gender bias. The report includes accounts of creative ways women have dealt with sexual harassment.

Skilled Trades

The University of Missouri-Columbia's Project ENTER (Educating for NonTraditional Employment Roles) includes a free, online, self-assessment survey (http://www.iml.coe.missouri.edu/services/Enter/survey.html) that helps you explore whether a nontraditional career is for you.

The National School-to-Work Learning and Information Center gives information on finding, setting up, and running school-to-work programs. It includes a calendar of programs scheduled through the end of the year 2000.

The National School-to-Work Learning and Information Center
400 Virginia Avenue, Room 150
Washington, DC 20024
800-251-7236
http://www.stw.ed.gov

Wider Opportunities for Women (WOW), a nonprofit organization, works to achieve economic independence and equal opportunity for women and girls. It has employment programs and advocates in every state and the District of Columbia. Programs emphasize literacy, technical and nontraditional skills, welfare-to-work transition, and career development.

Wider Opportunities for Women (WOW)
815 15th Street, NW, Suite 916
Washington, DC 20005
202-638-3143
http://www.w-o-w.org

The National Office of the Bureau of Apprenticeship and Training has information on state apprenticeship offices and programs.

Employment and Training Administration/Bureau of Apprenticeship and Training
Frances Perkins Building, N4649
200 Constitution Avenue, NW
Washington, DC 20210
202-219-5921
http://www.doleta.gov/bat/

Military

The Military Woman Web site (http://www.militarywoman.org/) offers extensive information for women in the military, women contemplating military service, and women veterans. An outstanding feature is the open exchange of thoughts and experiences among women about their lives in the military. The site is not affiliated with the Department of Defense.

The Women's Research and Education Institute (http://wrei.org) has many sections of particular interest to women considering a military career, women in the military, and women veterans.

Air Force (http://www.airforce.com)

Army (http://www.goarmy.com)

Coast Guard (http://www.uscg.mil)

Marines (http://www.marines.com)

Navy (http://www.navyjobs.com)

Science, Mathematics, Engineering, and Technology

Program for Gender Equity in Science, Mathematics, Engineering, and Technology sponsored by the Human Resources Development Department of the National Science Foundation, offers grants and programs to increase women's opportunities in science, mathematics, engineering, and technology. The Web site contains many links to other gender equity programs.

Program for Gender Equity in Science, Mathematics, Engineering, and Technology
Human Resources Development Department
National Science Foundation
4201 Wilson Boulevard
Arlington, VA 22230
703-306-1234
http://www.ehr.nsf.gov/ehr/hrd/ge/ge-index.htm

The Institute for Women and Technology (http://www.iwt.org) works to increase the impact women make on technology, to increase the positive impact technology makes on the lives of women, and to help the world benefit from these increases.

The ACM-W (the women's division of the Association for Computing Machinery), the world's first education and scientific computing society, promotes more equal representation for women in computing. Some internships are available.

ACM-Association for Computing Machinery
1515 Broadway
New York, NY 10036
800-342-6626
http://www.acm.org/women/home.shtml

The Association for Women in Mathematics (http://www.awm-math.org/)encourages women in the mathematical sciences. The Web site offers educational resources and discussion groups. Some grants and awards are available.

Essays on Women's Topics

The Association of Women in Science promotes the achievement of equity and full participation of women in all areas of science and technology. It offers educational resources, scholarships, and internships.

Association for Women in Science
1200 New York Avenue, Suite 650
Washington, DC 20005
202-326-8940
http://www.awis.org/

The Society of Women Engineers offers student services, scholarships, career services, and career guidance.

Society of Women Engineers
120 Wall Street, 11th Floor
New York, NY 10005-3902
212-509-9577
http://www.swe.org/

Building a New Pathway: Starting a Business

Women-Owned Businesses

Have you ever considered starting your own business? If you have, you are in excellent company. Women started businesses at a phenomenal rate during the last decade of the twentieth century.

Studies show that women become entrepreneurs for a variety of reasons. High on the list are the opportunity to implement an idea, a desire for independence, a disenchantment with corporate culture and/or the glass ceiling, a desire to balance work-life issues, and an opportunity to make more money.

In 1999, the number of women-owned businesses in the United States rose to over 9 million—more than doubling in 12 years. According to *1999 Facts on Women-Owned Businesses: Trends in the U.S. and the 50 States,* a report by the National Foundation for Women Business Owners (NFWBO), the number of people employed in women-owned businesses quadrupled, and sales expanded five-fold from 1987 to 1999. Contact NFWBO or visit their Web site listed at the end of this article for the complete report.

According to the 1999 NFWBO report, women-owned businesses made up 30 percent of all U.S. businesses. They employed 27.5 million people, and they produced more than $3.6 trillion in annual sales. The largest number of women-owned businesses were in the service sector. The greatest growth in numbers of women-owned organizations was in occupations considered to be nontraditional for women, such as agriculture, construction, manufacturing, and communications.

Women-owned businesses are an important economic force in the United States, and this is an excellent time for women to become entrepreneurs. If you are considering starting a business, read on. This article will help you define what type of entrepreneur you might be, give you some insights into home-based business options, and give you an idea what it takes to start a business.

Types of Entrepreneurs

There are three basic types of entrepreneurs: moonlighters, independents, and chief executive officers (CEOs). Which type do you think you are?

Moonlighters

Moonlighters build their businesses in their spare time. Some have full-time jobs that provide a living until their businesses grow. Some are full-time mothers who supplement their families' incomes by working in the evenings or when the children are at school or napping.

Moonlighting can be a good way to start a new endeavor without giving up the security of a job. A part-time business that can be run from home generally requires only a small investment of time and money to get started.

Independents

Independents decide to go into business full-time. They set up offices in their homes or in rented office spaces. Independents may work totally alone, or they may have employees.

Setting up a full-time business requires a much greater commitment of time and money than moonlighting does, and involves a lot more risk.

CEOs

Chief executive officers think in bigger terms. They envision setting up large organizations and employing many people. They may buy existing businesses, or they may start new ones.

Buying a company or starting a new one requires a lot of money. CEOs often need to find partners, loans, or venture capital. They think big and take big risks.

Some women business owners start out as moonlighters, become independents, and later become CEOs. Other women entrepreneurs are drawn to one type of business and stay with that type. To explore further which type of entrepreneur you might be and what resources you will need to start the business that interests you, visit the Women.com Web site (http://www.womenswire.com/smallbiz/start/).

Home-Based Businesses

A special mention of home-based businesses is essential because so many women find working from home to be a logical starting point to business ownership. Moonlighting and independent businesses are frequently home-based businesses (also called work-at-home businesses). A number of large women-owned corporations have started out as home-based enterprises that have later grown into large organizations. Opportunities for home-based businesses have increased due to technological advances and demands for service-oriented businesses.

According to a 1995 study conducted by the National Foundation of Women Business Owners, there were more than 3.5 million women-owned, home-based businesses in the United States. Those businesses supplied full- or part-time employment for approximately 14 million workers.

The NFWBO study found that home-based women entrepreneurs were demographically very similar to women business owners who were not home based. The average number of children at home, the age distribution, and the racial composition of home-based women business owners were similar to the figures for women entrepreneurs who were not home based.

According to the NFWBO study, most home-based women entrepreneurs are technologically savvy. Their home offices contain computers, modems, fax machines, and copiers. In fact, many women-owned home offices are based on some aspect of information technology or e-commerce. Women increasingly use the Internet to overcome traditional work barriers, to network, and to build their businesses. Recent studies show that women are rapidly displacing men as the majority on the Internet.

Working from home has some special benefits as well as some special difficulties. Operating a business from home saves the cost of renting an office. A home office frequently qualifies the entrepreneur for partial tax write-offs of rent or mortgage, maintenance, and utilities. Working from home also saves the business owner commuting time and provides more freedom, flexibility, and control over her schedule. At the same time, a home-based business requires increased self-discipline. Setting boundaries between work and private life is one of the greatest challenges of working from home, especially for mothers with children at home. Home-based entrepreneurs may also experience a sense of isolation. Anyone considering working from home should carefully weigh the benefits and difficulties before beginning a home-based business.

If you are considering starting a home-based business, contact the Office of Women's Business Ownership within the U.S. Small Business Administration (SBA). Also check out the Web sites of the Online Women's Business Center (cosponsored by the SBA and the OWBO) and the Small Office Home Office (SOHO) resources listed among the references below. Visit Rosalind Mays's site for valuable information on how to identify and avoid work-at-home scams. Do your homework before you start to work at home!

Whichever type of entrepreneur you are, and whether you work at home, rent an office, or buy a company, going into business requires a lot of thought, planning, time, and work.

Starting a Business

Whatever your enterprise, the pathway to success starts with the same steps. You must first carefully assess yourself—your personality, determination, and skills. Then, you need to set personal goals, plan your business, and make a strategic business plan.

Assessing Yourself

Being honest with yourself is crucial. Do you have what it takes to be an entrepreneur? Women business owners need to be able to take risks, live with uncertainty, and learn from their experiences. They must believe in their ability to overcome adversity and be passionate enough about their work to put in long hours when necessary. Entrepreneurs need a variety of skills to succeed. In addition to having expertise in their fields, they must have business management, people management, sales, and marketing skills. Do you have the skills you need or can you find a way to make up for those you lack?

Libraries and bookstores have many resources on starting businesses. Find one that offers a good self-analysis. The Online Women's Business Center (http://www.onlinewbc.org) has an interactive self-evaluation that can help you determine whether you have the characteristics of an entrepreneur. Visit the Advancing Women's Web site (http://www.advancingwomen.com). Their Business Center includes an entire section devoted to becoming an entrepreneur.

Setting Personal Goals

You've done your self-evaluation, and you've decided you have what it takes to be an entrepreneur. The next step is reviewing your personal goals. What would you like your life to be like in five years? Ten years? Twenty years?

Setting personal goals is essential when you are thinking about starting a business. Your business will affect every other part of your life. You need to have a life plan in order to know how your business will fit into your life and whether it will help you reach your goals. For online help in setting goals, see the Personal Goal-Setting article in the Online Women's Business Center.

Planning Your Business

Once you have planned your life goals, you can plan how your business will fit into your life and help you achieve your personal goals. Take time to carefully research and plan where you are going. Remember the adage, "Failing to plan is planning to fail."

Excellent help is available in books and on the Internet. Contact the Office of Women's Business Ownership nearest you for help with your planning. The Online Women's Business Center (http://www.onlinewbc.org) places an enormous amount of business information at your fingertips. The Advancing Women (http://www.advancingwomen.com) Web site includes a section of forms that you can download free. The small business section at Women.com (http://www.womenswire.com/smallbiz/start/) includes an online calculator to help figure startup costs and monthly expenses. Take advantage of all the wonderful resources available to you.

Writing a Business Plan

After you plan your business, be sure to write a business plan. A business plan is a blueprint of your company written in a clear, organized format. It explains your company's vision. It helps you plan, make decisions, and measure performance. You need a business plan to get loans or attract investors.

Many entrepreneurs wait until they have already started their businesses and run into trouble, or need to get a loan, before they develop business plans. This often happens because they believe that writing a business plan is too difficult and takes too much time.

Writing a business plan does not have to be an enormous ordeal. Free online templates are available at the Women.com (http://www.womenswire.com/smallbiz/start/) small business site and the Money Hunt Web site (http://www.moneyhunter.com/). Use a template to get started. Then refine and improve it as your business develops.

Once you have carefully assessed yourself, set personal goals, planned your business, and written your business plan, you will be ready to actually start your business. Becoming an entrepreneur and building your own business takes time and work, but it can also offer many rewards. If you find that your pathway to career success has too many roadblocks or doesn't offer the opportunities you seek, consider starting your own business and building your own pathway to success.

For More Information

Advancing Women (http://www.advancingwomen.com) is an electronic networking and support system for women. It offers comprehensive information on networking, mentoring, business, careers, and money matters. Its Business Center includes sections on becoming an entrepreneur, a business owner's handbook, and free business forms.

Rosalind Mays maintains a Web site (http://members.aol.com/ siennapco/telecom.htm) for individuals who work from their homes via computer or otherwise. Her site shares her struggles to find viable work through the Internet and ways to recognize and avoid the many scams that are out there.

The Money Hunter Web site (http://www.moneyhunter.com/) is the online companion to the Money Hunt TV program. It offers a free download of award-winning business plan templates and an opportunity to apply for an audition for your company for the TV show.

The National Foundation for Women Business Owners (NFWBO) supports women business owners and their enterprises by conducting research to document the economic and social contributions of women-owned firms.

National Foundation for Women Business Owners
1100 Wayne Avenue, Suite 830
Silver Spring, MD 20910-5603
301-495-4975
http://www.nfwbo.org

The Office of Women's Business Ownership within the U.S. Small Business Administration (SBA) maintains a network of Women's Business Centers (WBCs) in 47 states, the District of Columbia, Puerto Rico, and the Virgin Islands. The WBCs teach women the principles of finance, management, and marketing. They help women put together loan packages and offer loan guaranty programs. The WBCs assist women in making the welfare-to-work transition. Contact the national office or visit their Web site for the address of the WBC nearest you.

U.S. Small Business Administration
Office of Women's Business Ownership
409 Third Street, SW, Fourth Floor
Washington, DC 20416
202-205-6673
http://www.sba.gov/womeninbusiness

The Online Women's Business Center (http://www.onlinewbc.org) is an amazing business resource designed particularly for women. It offers an enormous range of information for women business owners at all levels—from the dreaming and planning stage to the ongoing care and feeding of a successful business. Topics range from starting, growing, and expanding a business to managing, financing, and marketing the business. Interactive questionnaires allow women to assess their skills, strengths, weaknesses, and possibilities for success. Don't miss this one! (The Small Business Administration and the Office of Women's Business Ownership cosponsor the Online Women's Business Center.)

Small Office Home Office (SOHO) (http://www.soho.org/) America is a virtual community where you can exchange ideas and interact with small-office/home-office professionals. SOHO Online has information and resources for starting and succeeding at home-based business.

Essays on Women's Topics

The Women.com Web site (http://www.womenswire.com/smallbiz/start/), contains a small business section full of helpful information on starting a business. Topics include determining your business style and calculating how much money you will need. The site has useful cash calculators to help determine the worth of a business.

Part II

Directory

Section A
Financial Aid

For the purposes of this directory, there are five types of financial aid: fellowships, grants, scholarships, awards, and loans. This directory lists only financial aid that is available to women in general. Financial aid that requires membership in an organization is not listed in this section, but is noted in Section B under membership benefits of organizations. Students and working women who are not currently members may still be interested in the members-only information, because in many cases they are immediately eligible for financial assistance upon joining an organization. Other organizations require members to be in good standing for a year or more before they are eligible for financial aid. Readers should check with the organization regarding eligibility before applying for membership or financial aid.

Awards

Awards are generally given in recognition of achievement, either to a promising young woman moving up in her career field or to an experienced professional for a lifetime of achievement. Many awards include a monetary stipend; others don't grant any money at all but are valuable recognition by one's peers and excellent resume-builders.

American Association of Family and Consumer Sciences

Fellowships and Grants Program
1555 King Street
Alexandria, VA 22314
703-706-4600
http://www.aafcs.org

The **Gladys Branegan Chalkley Public Policy Visiting Scholar Award** is a $3,500 honorarium in support of a 10-week program in Washington, DC. Applicants must have a bachelor's degree in an area of family and consumer sciences.

The **Wiley-Berger Award for Volunteer Service** recognizes an individual who has demonstrated how family and consumer sciences can improve the community through volunteer efforts. Self-nomination or nomination by a local organization is accepted. These awards are not expressly for women, but most past recipients have been women.

American Association of Women Emergency Physicians

3020 Legacy Drive, Suite 100-102
Plano, TX 75023
972-208-4543
http://www.aawep.org

AAWEP is a national, professional organization for women emergency physicians. Each year, AAWEP presents awards to deserving women in a number of areas, such as leadership, research, education, and well-being. Not all awards are monetary. For nomination information, contact the association.

American Chemical Society

Women Chemists Committee
1155 16th Street, NW
Washington, DC 20036
202-872-4481
http://www.acs.org

The **Francis P. Garvan-John M. Olin Medal** is an award given to women chemists in recognition of distinguished service to chemistry. The award consists of a $5,000 cash prize, an inscribed gold medal, and a bronze replica of the medal. A $1,000 travel allowance is provided for travel to the meeting at which the award is presented.

American Congress on Surveying and Mapping

5410 Grosvenor Lane, Suite 100
Bethesda, MD 20814-2122
301-493-0200

The $1,000 **Porter McDonnell Memorial Award** is given annually to a woman working on an undergraduate degree in surveying who shows potential for leadership in the surveying and mapping profession. Recipients must join ACM.

American Historical Association

Joan Kelly Memorial Prize in Women's History
400 A Street, SE
Washington, DC 20003-3889
202-544-2422
http://www.theaha.org

The **Joan Kelly Memorial Prize in Women's History** is awarded annually by the AHA for the book in women's history or feminist theory that best reflects the high intellectual and scholarly ideals exemplified by the life and work of Joan Kelly. Books should address the interrelationship between women and the historical process.

American Medical Women's Association

Elizabeth Blackwell Medal
801 North Fairfax, Suite 400
Alexandria, VA 22314
703-838-0500
http://www.amwa-doc.org

AMWA addresses the challenges specific to women physicians and the needs particular to women patients. The AMWA **Elizabeth Blackwell Medal** is given annually to a woman physician who has made an outstanding contribution to the cause of women in the medical field.

American Nuclear Society

555 Kensington Avenue
LaGrange Park, IL 60526-5592
708-352-0499
http://www.ans.org

ANS offers the ANS **Women's Achievement Award** to recognize outstanding personal dedication and technical advancement by a woman in the fields of nuclear science, nuclear engineering, research, or education. This nonfinancial award consists of an inscribed plaque presented at the society's winter meeting. Nominations are solicited from ANS members, but nominees need not be members.

American Physical Society

1 Physics Ellipse
College Park, MD 20740
301-209-3100
http://www.aps.org

The **Maria Goeppert-Mayer Award** provides an opportunity for women physicists to share their achievements through public lectures. The award consists of $2,500 plus a $4,000 travel allowance for women of any nationality who are working in a field of physics and are in the early stages of their careers. They must have received their doctorate no more than 10 years ago. APS also has a program that provides funds to institutions that host women colloquium speakers.

American Vacuum Society

120 Wall Street, 32nd Floor
New York, NY 10005-3993
212-248-0200
http://www.vacuum.org

The **Nellie Yeoh Whetten Award** is awarded to women of any nationality accepted or enrolled in a graduate school in North America and studying vacuum science and technology. The stipend is $1,500 and additional travel reimbursement for travel to the society's international symposium.

Association for Women in Communications

1244 Ritchie Highway, Suite 6
Arnold, MD 21012-1887
410-544-7442
http://www.womcom.org

AWC, formerly Women in Communications, Inc., recognizes women working in all disciplines of communications, print, broadcast, and film with annual awards. Some awards are available to nonmembers; additional awards are available to members. **The Chair's Women in Communications Award** recognizes a professional communicator for groundbreaking accomplishments or original contributions to the field. The **Headliner Award** rewards recent national or international accomplishments. The **International Matrix Award** rewards a communications professional for achieving the highest level of professional excellence (Jane Pauley was a recent winner). The **Clarion Awards** are several awards recognizing excellence in thirteen communications categories. Entry fees are assessed for the Clarion Awards. Visit the Web site for information.

Association for Women in Computing

41 Sutter Street, Suite 1006
San Francisco, CA 94104
415-905-4663
http://www.awc-hq.org

AWC is a professional organization for individuals with an interest in information technology. It offers the annual **Augusta Ada Lovelace Award** to individuals who excelled in either outstanding scientific and technical achievement, or extraordinary service to the computing community through their accomplishments and contributions on behalf of women in the computing profession. The award doesn't specify women only, but all recipients to date have been women.

Association for Women in Mathematics

Schafer (or Hay) Award Selection Committee
4114 Computer & Space Sciences Building
University of Maryland
College Park, MD 20742-2461
301-405-7892
http://www.awm-math.org

AWM, a national organization that encourages women in the mathematical sciences, offers two annual awards to recognize achievements in the field of mathematics. Candidates must be nominated based on the quality of their performance in advanced mathematics courses, ability for independent work and real interest in mathematics, and performance in mathematical competitions. Anyone may submit a nomination. The **Alice T. Schafer Mathematics Prize** is awarded to undergraduate women for excellence in mathematics. The **Louise Hay Award for Contributions to Mathematics Education** recognizes outstanding achievements of those who teach in any area of mathematics education.

Association for Women Veterinarians

32205 Allison Drive
Union City, CA 94587
510-471-8379

The Association of Women Veterinarians promotes the role of women in veterinary medicine. It offers the **Outstanding Woman Veterinarian** and **Distinguished Service Award** for individuals who have worked toward supporting and promoting the role of women in veterinary medicine.

Association of American Medical Colleges

2450 N Street, NW
Washington, DC 20037-1126
202-828-0521
http://www.aamc.org

The Association of American Medical Colleges gives the **Women in Medicine Leadership Award** annually in recognition of an individual's efforts in advancing the cause of women in the field of medicine.

Financial Aid

Avon Latina Model of the Year

Rules Requests
1251 Sixth Avenue
New York, NY 10020-1196
800-FOR-AVON

Hispanic females between the ages of 17 and 25 are eligible for this annual competition. Winners receive up to $15,000 in educational awards and modeling fees and gifts. Send a SASE for application and official rules.

Barnum Festival Foundation

Jenny Lind Competition—Sopranos
1070 Main Street
Bridgeport, CT 06604
203-367-8495

The **Jenny Lind Competition** is held annually to present a $2,000 scholarship to a female singer who has not yet reached professional status. The winner is presented at a concert in Sweden. Second place wins $1,000; third place wins $500. Contact the foundation for details and application forms.

Biophysical Society

9650 Rockville Pike
Bethesda, MD 20814
301-530-7114
http://www.biophysics.org

The **Margaret Oakley Dayhoff Award** is presented each year at the annual meeting of the Biophysical Society to a junior woman scientist in a field within the range of interest of the Biophysical Society. The award honors a woman of high promise who has not yet gained recognition within the structures of academic society. The award consists of a $2,000 prize and is for U.S. citizens only. Self-nomination is not permitted.

Black Women Lawyers Association of Greater Chicago

321 South Plymouth Court, Sixth Floor
Chicago, IL 60604
312-554-2088

The BWLA is a professional organization of over 500 African American women lawyers in the Chicago area. It recognizes African American women who have demonstrated leadership in the community with the **Distinguished Service Award.** Past winners include a senator, a law professor, and several judges.

Carrie Chapman Catt Center for Women and Politics

Carrie Chapman Catt Prize for Research on Women and Politics
309 Carrie Chapman Catt Hall
Ames, IA 50011-1305
http://www.apsanet.org/PS/grants/catt.html

The annual **Carrie Chapman Catt Prize for Research on Women and Politics** is designed to encourage and reward scholars embarking on significant research in the area of women and politics. The prize includes a $1,000 cash award and travel expenses to the center's annual conference. Scholars at any level, including graduate students and junior faculty members may apply.

Center for the American Woman and Politics

Good Housekeeping Award for Women in Government
191 Ryders Lane
Rutgers University
New Brunswick, NJ 08901
732-932-9384
http://www.rci.rutgers.edu/~cawp

CAWP co-sponsors the **Good Housekeeping Award for Women in Government,** which celebrates the accomplishments of women in government. Any woman who works in government, from a school board member to a member of Congress, is eligible. The applicant should write about a specific achievement or solution to a problem. One award of $25,000 and nine awards of $2,500 each will be presented, and winners will be featured in an issue of *Good Housekeeping.* Nomination materials are available on the Web site or by calling.

Computing Research Association

1100 17th Street, NW, Suite 507
Washington, DC 20036-4632
202-234-2111
http;//cra.org/Activities/craw/

The **Computer Research Association Undergraduate Awards**is an annual competition recognizing exceptional female and male undergraduates in computer science and engineering. Nominations are submitted by computer science and engineering departments for Outstanding Female Undergraduate and Outstanding Male Undergraduate. Winners receive a cash prize of $1,000. The award seeks to recognize students who show outstanding research potential in an area of importance to computing.

Coordinating Council for Women in History

Berkshire Conference AwardsCommittee
Department of History
Pacific Lutheran University
Tacoma, WA 98447
http://www.plu.edu/~hamesgl/

The CCWH and Berkshire Conference of Women Historians offers two $500 graduate student awards. The applicant for the **CCWH/Berkshire Award** must be a woman graduate student historian in a history department at a U.S. college, and may specialize in any field of history. The applicant for the **CCWH/Ida B. Wells Award** must be a woman graduate student at a U.S. institution. She may specialize in any field, but must be working on an historical project. Contact the awards committee chair at the address listed or visit the Web site for an application form.

Denver Women's Chorus

Competition for Women Composers
PO Box 2638
Denver, CO 80202
303-274-4177
http://members.tde.com/dwc/index.htm

Women composers are eligible to compete for a prize of $1,000 for the composition of a six- to ten-minute piece making an affirmative state-ment about women. The competition is held every other year.

Erector Square Gallery

315 Peck Street 20
New Haven, CT 06513
203-865-5055

The gallery awards the **Women in the Visual Arts Award** in the amount of $1,500 to female artists over the age of 18. Works must have been completed in the past two years. Send a SASE for details.

Federal Women in Science and Engineering

c/o Joan Humphries
PO Box 310
Tarpon Springs, FL 34688-0310
http://www.fedwise.org

FedWise, a federal interagency committee of women scientists and engineers, recognizes three outstanding federal women scientists and engineers annually. Winners are nominated through the agency (civilian or non-civilian) in which they are employed. Winners receive a plaque and recognition at the annual awards luncheon.

FedWise also offers a challenge to young women students in the Washington, DC; Maryland; and Virginia metropolitan areas. To enter, ninth and tenth grade girls develop and display an original science or engineering project. Winners may be selected for one of four monetary awards (savings bonds) and a reception with women scientists and engineers and government officials. Visit the Web site for entry information and a list of past winners and examples of their projects.

Foundation of American Women in Radio and Television, Inc.

1650 Tysons Boulevard, Suite 200
McLean, VA 22102
703-506-3290
http://www.awrt.org

Financial Aid

The **Gracie Allen Awards** recognize current and future leaders in electronic media. Write or call for details. Award winners are recognized at an annual event in New York City.

Free Will Baptists

Women's National Auxiliary Convention
PO Box 5002
5233 Mt. View Road
Antioch, TN 37103

Members of local Free Will Baptists Women's Auxiliaries are eligible to submit entries for the **Creative Arts Contest** in five categories: art, articles, plays/skills, poetry, and programs. Three prizes are awarded in each of the five categories.

Friday Morning Music Club, Inc.

4925 MacArthur Boulevard, NW
Washington, DC 20007
202-333-2075

Young women singers under age 30 who are preparing for a professional career are eligible to compete for awards ranging from $2,000 to $7,000 as part of the triennial Washington International Competition for Singers. Competitions are scheduled for March 2001 and 2004. Write to national headquarters for information.

Friends of Lulu

4657 Cajon Way
San Diego, CA 92115
http://www.friends-lulu.org

Friends of Lulu, a national organization aimed at getting more women and girls involved in comic books, offers the annual **Lulu Awards,** which include **Women Cartoonist Hall of Fame Awards** and the **Kim Yale Award for Best New Talent.** Visit the Web site for current information or write to request information.

General Federation of Women's Clubs

Jane Cunningham Croly/GFWC Print Journalism Award
1734 N Street, NW
Washington, DC 20036-2990
202-347-3168
http://www.gfwc.org

Most GFWC scholarships are offered at state and local levels, with the exception of the **Jane Cunningham Croly Award.** The award, for excellence in covering women's issues, honors the print journalist whose writing best captures the courage, vision, and spirit of Jane Cunningham Croly, GFWC founder and pioneer journalist. Applicants should submit three stories published in a newspaper or magazine in the previous year. The contest is open to women and men, but winners have been primarily women. The winner is awarded $1,000. GFWC members are not eligible. Call or write the contest coordinator for information.

Glamour Top Ten College Women

Conde Nast Building
350 Madison Avenue
New York, NY 10017
800-244-GLAM

Any woman who is a junior and enrolled full-time in courses leading to an undergraduate degree at an accredited college or university is eligible to enter **Glamour's Top Ten College Women Competition.** Applicants must submit an essay describing their most meaningful achievements in their field of study and relating them to their life goals. Ten winners are selected annually for the $1,000 prize and trip to New York City.

Hobart and William Smith Colleges

Elizabeth Blackwell Award
315-781-3540
http://www.nws.edu/NEW/bwaward/index.html

Hobart and William Smith Colleges gives the **Elizabeth Blackwell Award** to a woman whose life exemplifies outstanding service to humanity. The award is not conferred at regular intervals, but may be presented whenever a candidate of sufficient stature and appropriate qualifications is identified. Past winners include Billie Jean King and Margaret Mead. Contact the college for nomination information.

Independent Means

126 Powers Avenue
Santa Barbara, CA 93103
800-350-1816
http://www.anincomeoftheirown.com

Independent Means is a national organization that seeks to instill in girls under 20 the desire and the means to attain financial independence and maintain it throughout adult life. It offers the annual **National Business Plan Competition** for girls 13 to 19 years of age. Winners receive an expenses-paid trip to Washington, DC, for the awards ceremony, $2,500 in cash, a business kit, and other gifts. Several winners are selected.

International Alliance for Women In Music

IAWM Administrative Office
Department of Music
422 South 11th Street, Room 209
Indiana University of Pennsylvania
Indiana, PA 15705-7918
724-357-7918
http://music.acu.edu/www.iawm/home.html

The IAWM sponsors the annual Search for New Music and Pauline Alderman Awards. Contestants must be IAWM members or willing to join at time of entry. **Search for New Music Awards** include the **Student Composer Prize** for women currently in school in any medium; the **Ellen Taaffe Zwilich Prize** for women under 21; and the **Miriam Gideon Prize** for women over 50 for voice and piano, or voice and small instrumental ensemble.

The Pauline Alderman Awards recognize new research on women in music. Past prizes have included books, articles, papers, essays, dissertations, and other published and unpublished materials. Visit IAWM's Web site for details.

Iota Sigma Pi

http://chem-faculty.ucsd.edu/sawrey/ISP/awards.html

Iota Sigma Pi, a national honorary society for women chemists, recognizes the achievements of women in chemistry. Membership in Iota Sigma Pi is not necessary. The **National**

Honorary Member Award is a triennial award and is the highest honor Iota Sigma Pi bestows on outstanding women chemists.

The **Award for Professional Excellence,** also a triennial award, is for outstanding contribution by a woman to chemistry and its allied fields. Both awards consist of $500 and a lifetime waiver of Iota Sigma Pi dues.

The **Agnes Fay Morgan Research Award** is awarded annually for research achievement by a woman chemist not over 40 years of age.

The **Anna Louise Hoffman Award for Outstanding Achievement in Graduate Research** is awarded annually to a full-time graduate student who was nominated by a faculty member. The award is $400.

The **Undergraduate Award for Excellence in Chemistry** is awarded annually to a woman undergraduate nominated by a faculty member.

League of Canadian Poets

54 Wolseley Street, Suite 203
Toronto, Ontario, M5T 1A5 Canada
416-504-1657
http://www.poets.ca

The league offers the **Pat Lowther Award** for the best book of poetry of at least 48 pages published in the previous calendar year. Applicants must be women who are Canadian citizens or landed immigrants. The award carries a $1,000 prize.

Lilla Jewel Fund for Women Artists

McKenzie River Gathering Foundation
3558 S. E. Hawthorne Boulevard
Portland, OR 97214
503-233-0271

Women artists in Oregon may apply for a $3,000 prize awarded annually in one of three rotating categories: Media and Multi-Arts; Visual Arts; or Music or Dance. Send SASE for application details.

Financial Aid

Margaret McNamara Memorial Fund

The World Bank Group
1818 H Street, NW Q5-080
Washington, DC 20433
202-473-8751

The Margaret McNamara Memorial Fund, administered by the World Bank Volunteer Services, seeks to strengthen the role of women in any aspect of their country's life. Awards are annual, up to $7,000 and are not renewable. Five are available annually. Applicants must be a citizen of a specified country (write or call for country eligibility list), a full-time student, at least 25 years old, have financial need and record of service to women and children of her home country, and plan to return to her home country within two years of the award. U.S. residents are not eligible.

National Association of Women in Education

1325 18th Street, NW, Suite 210
Washington, DC 20036
202-659-9330
http://www.nawe.org

NAWE seeks to advance and support women in higher education careers. The **Ruth Strang Research Awards** of $750 are designed to honor excellence in research by, for, and about women. Two awards will be presented annually; one is reserved for research by a graduate student and another is for research completed at any professional level. Up to six **Graduate Student Presentation Awards** will be given annually. Winners will give brief presentations at the annual conference. Presentations should relate to the theme "Advancing Women in Higher Education." Award winners will receive skill-building feedback from experienced presenters. Registration fees and hotel accommodations are paid.

National Council of Administrative Women in Education

1 Potbelly Beach Road
Aptos, CA 95003-3579
412-826-4771

The council awards a **Leadership Award** for recognition of superior research pertaining to women in educational administration. Awardee's travel expenses to the national conference are covered by the council.

National Federation of Music Clubs

1336 North Delaware
Indianapolis, IN 46202-2481
317-638-4003
http://www.NFMC-music.org

NFMC offers a number of awards to men and women, including several set aside for women specifically. Applicants must become members of NFMC before applying. The **Biennial Young Artist Awards** are awarded in four categories, including one for women's voice. The $10,000 prize is offered in odd-numbered years to women between 23 and 35 years of age. Other women's awards are offered, from $250 to $1,500. The Web site has detailed information on eligibility, which varies for each award, or call to request information.

National Federation of Press Women

PO Box 5556
Arlington, VA 22205
800-780-2715
http://www.nfpw.org

The NFPW sponsors an annual **High School Journalism Contest,** and awards cash prizes. Students may enter work in editorial, feature, review, news, sports, column, feature photo, cartooning, single page layout, or graphics categories. Awards consist of $100 cash for first place, and plaques for second and third place. Students compete at the state level, and may advance to the national contest. Visit the Web site or call for further details.

National Hispana Leadership Institute

1901 North Moore Street, Suite 206
Arlington, VA 22209
703-527-6007
http://www.nhli.org

The annual **Mujer Award** recognizes the sustained lifetime achievements of a Hispanic woman who has served her community and acted with justice, love, and pride in culture. NHLI honors the Mujer Award recipient at an annual gala event. Contact NHLI for nomination information.

National Women's Studies Association

University of Maryland
7100 Baltimore Avenue, Suite 500
College Park, MD 20740
301-403-0525
http://www.nwsa.org

Financial assistance is available to women whose scholarship will help expand the boundaries and possibilities of women's studies programs. The $250 **Pat Parker Poetry Award** is given for an outstanding narrative poem or dramatic monologue by a black, lesbian, feminist poet.The $250 **Audre Lorde Memorial Prose Prize** is awarded in two categories: fiction and nonfiction. This award is given to feminist writers who write fiction or prose. The winner is announced annually on Lorde's birthday (February 18).

Newswomen's Club of New York

National Arts Building
15 Gramercy Park South
New York, NY 10003
212-777-1610
http://www.newswomensclub.com

An award and U.S. savings bond are presented annually to women journalists in the New York City (tri-state) area who are recognized by the club for outstanding talent in the field. Awards are presented in several media categories.

Ninety-Nines

Box 965
7100 Terminal Drive
Oklahoma City, OK 73159-0965
800-994-1929
http://www.ninety-nines.org

Ninety-Nines is an international organization of licensed women pilots. Several scholarships and grants are offered for members and nonmembers. The **Ninety-Nines Awards of Merit** recognizes individuals or organizations outside the Ninety-Nines who have made significant contributions to aviation, aviation education, science, or aviation history. The **Award of Inspiration** is given by the board of directors to an individual or group whose activities have had a significant impact on the Ninety-Nines, the world aviation community, or the art and science of aviation or aerospace. The **Katherine B. Wright Memorial Trophy** is presented to a woman or group for the advancement of the art, sport, and science of aviation and space flight over an extended career.

Organization of American Historians

Lerner Scott Prize
112 North Bryan Avenue
Bloomington, IN 47408
812-855-9852
http://www.indianau.edu/~oah/

The **Lerner-Scott Prize** is awarded annually for the best doctoral dissertation in U.S. women's history. Each application must contain a letter of support from a faculty member, along with an abstract, table of contents, and sample chapter. The award is $1,000.

Pen and Brush Club

16 East 10th Street
New York, NY 10003
212-475-3669

Women artists, including sculptors, painters, musicians, and craftswomen are eligible for awards ranging from $50 to $500. Write for details.

Professional Women of Color

Awards Committee
PO Box 5196
New York, NY 10185
212-714-7190
http://www.pwconline.org

Professional Women of Color seeks to advance the careers of women of color in all professions. Annual awards offered are **Breaking the Mold Award,** which recognizes a woman of color for her ability to develop opportunities for other women of color in a particular industry and develop unique strategies for successs. The **PWC**

Financial Aid

Pioneer Award recognizes a woman of color for her unique contributions to her community. Contact the organization for further award and nomination information.

Society for Historians of American Foreign Relations

c/o Department of History
Wright State University
Dayton, OH 45435
937-873-3110
http://www.ohiou.edu/shafr/shafr.html

Books written by women on U.S. foreign relations, transnational history, international history, peace studies, cultural interchange, and defense studies published during the previous two years are eligible for the **Myrna Bernath Book Prize**. The $2,500 prize is offered every two years; apply in odd-numbered years.

Soroptimist International of the Americas

2 Penn Center Plaza, Suite 1000
Philadelphia, PA 19102-1883
215-557-9300
http://www.siahq.com

The **Women's Opportunity Program** assists women who, as head of their households, must enter or return to the workforce or upgrade their employment status. The program begins on the local level, after which recipients become eligible for region-level and national awards. Three recipients of each of SIA's 29 regions receive awards: one $5,000 award and two $3,000 awards. One finalist is chosen among the region winners to receive an additional $10,000. Applications are available from local Soroptimist clubs or by sending a SASE to the attention of Women's Opportunity Awards.

Southern Association for Women Historians

Department of History
Agnes Scott College
Decatur, GA 30030-3797
http://www.h-net.msu.edu/~sawh.html

The **Willie Lee Rose Publication Prize in Southern History** is awarded for books on southern history that were written by women. The award consists of $750 and a plaque. Apply in odd-numbered years.

Women Basketball Coaches Association

4646 Lawrenceville Highway
Lilburn, GA 30047-3620
770-279-8027
http://www.wbca.org

The WBCA recognizes coaches and players with numerous awards. The WBCA honors **Coaches of the Year** at a special banquet. Coaching accomplishments are also recognized with various other individual awards. Players are recognized through the **Rawlings/WBCA Players of the Year** and **Kodak All-America Awards.** The **WBCA Scholarship Award** is presented annually to two women's basketball players who have demonstrated outstanding commitment to the sport and academic excellence. Female basketball players in all five intercollegiate divisions are eligible for the $1,000 award.

The **Charles T. Stoner Law Scholarship** is a $500 award to a woman collegiate basketball player who intends to pursue a career in law. Female basketball players in all divisions are eligible.

Women in Cell Biology

American Society for Cell Biology
9650 Rockville Pike
Bethesda, MD 20814
301-530-7153

Women in Cell Biology is a committee of the American Society of Cell Biology. The WICB committee recognizes outstanding achievements in cell biology by presenting two Career Recognition Awards at the ACSB annual meeting. The **Junior Award** is given to a woman in an early stage of her career (assistant professor or equivalent). The **Senior Award** is given to a woman in a later career stage (full professor or equivalent). To submit a nomination, contact the ASCB National Office.

Women in Endocrinology

http://www.women-in-endo.org

The **Women in Endocrinology Mentor Award** is supported by a grant from the Women's Health Care Division of Parke-Davis. It is given annually to a woman, or a man, whose outstanding scientific achievements are coupled with a record of support for women in academics and of mentoring women in their scientific careers. The recipient receives an honorarium of $1,000 and travel expenses to the annual WE meeting.

Women in Production

347 Fifth Avenue
New York, NY 10016
212-481-7793
http://www.wip.org

Women in Production is a professional and educational organization for women in all aspects of the graphic arts industry. The **Luminaire Awards** recognize the outstanding achievements and dedication of women and men in the field.

Women Marines Association

9608 North May Avenue, Box 265
Oklahoma City, OK 73120-2798
http://www.womenmarines.org

The Women Marines Association presents the **Molly Marine Award** to the honor graduate of each female platoon that graduates from recruit training at Marine Corps Recruit Depot Parris Island, South Carolina. It also presents an award annually to the **Outstanding Marine Corps Junior ROTC Cadet** in high schools across the United States.

Women's Caucus for the Modern Languages

Florence Howe Award for Feminist Scholarship
c/o Magali Cornier Michael
Department of English, Duquesne University
Pittsburgh, PA 15282

The **Florence Howe Award for Feminist Scholarship** each year recognizes an outstanding essay by a feminist scholar. The recipient is announced at the annual Modern Language Association meeting. Essays may be published or unpublished works of 25-30 pages on a feminist topic or written from a feminist perspective. Contact WCML for submission information.

Women's Classical Caucus

http://weber.u.washington.edu/~wcc/WCC.html

The Women's Classical Caucus awards two prizes annually for outstanding scholarship relating to gender or race issues in classical antiquity, feminist analyses of aspects of classical antiquity, or the classical tradition, and women's history in classical antiquity. Nominees need not be members of WCC. Papers delivered to the American Philosophical Association or International Philosophical Association annual meeting are eligible.

Women's Sports Foundation

AQHA Female Equestrian Award
Eisenhower Park
East Meadow, NY 11554
800-227-3988
http://www.womenssportsfoundation.org

The **AQHA Female Equestrian Award** offers one $2,000 award annually to honor an outstanding female equestrian and reward her for her accomplishments as a horsewoman and as an athlete. Female equestrians with national ranking and competition who exhibit leadership, sportsmanship, and commitment to the sport are eligible.

Women's World Summit Foundation

Prize for Rural Women
PO Box 2001
1211 Geneva 1, Switzerland

WWSF, an international coalition for the future of women and children, annually presents awards to outstanding women and women's groups from around the world who exhibit exceptional creativity in improving life in rural communities. Thirty or more awards of $500 are given annually. The prize seeks to draw international attention to the winners' contributions to sustainable development and household food security. Candidates cannot be nominated by themselves, nor by members of their family.

Financial Aid

Nominations can be submitted by organizations or individuals who have direct knowledge of the candidate's work.

Zonta International Foundation

557 West Randolph Street
Chicago, IL 60661-2206
312-930-5848
http://www.zonta.org

The **Zonta International Young Women in Public Affairs Awards** were established to encourage young women to pursue careers and seek leadership positions in public policy, government, and volunteer organizations. The awards program operates at the club, district, and international levels. Each club selects a winner and submits her name to the district. The application of the district winner is forwarded to the international headquarters for international competition. International winners receive a $1,000 award. Application information is available on the Web site or from local clubs.

Fellowships

Fellowships are generally offered at the graduate, postgraduate, or doctoral level, often for research projects or dissertation assistance.

Alfred P. Sloan Foundation

Pre-Tenure Leave Fellowship Program
630 Fifth Avenue, Suite 2550
New York, NY 10111-0242
212-649-1649
http://www.sloan.org

The Alfred P. Sloan Foundation includes the interests of women as one of its major program areas. Financial assistance programs vary, but all seek to help women in the home and in their careers. A current program is the **Pre-Tenure**

Leave Fellowship, which provides funding to regular, untenured, tenure-track women faculty in the fields of mathematics, science, engineering, or technology who are faced with urgent family responsibilities. Funding enables fellows to take a leave with salary, or after a leave, resume research. Qualifying situations include pregnancy, childbirth, or response to an unexpected crisis requiring special care of a family member. Fellowships are up to $20,000. In addition, $5,000 is offered to the faculty member's department to be used to address work-family issues for other faculty. Visit the Web site for complete information, or call for information to be mailed.

American Agricultural Economics Association

Committee on Women in Agricultural Economics
415 S. Duff Ave., Suite C
Ames, IA 50010-6600
515-233-3202
http://www.aaea.org

The **Sylvia Lane Fellowship Fund** offers short-term (up to one year) grants for women conducting innovative research about food, agricultural, or natural resources issues. The grant defrays direct research costs, travel, and temporary relocation expenses for new research to work with an established expert. Applicants must have completed an academic year in an accredited graduate degree program in agricultural economics or closely related discipline and must have initiated a mentor association with an expert in the field. Women with recent Ph.D. degrees and advanced graduate students are also encouraged to apply. Mentors should have a Ph.D. Visit the Web site for contact information on the current chair of the Sylvia Lane Fellowship Committee or write the above address.

American Association of Family and Consumer Sciences

Fellowships and Grants Program
1555 King Street
Alexandria, VA 22314
703-706-4600
http://www.aafcs.org

The **Mary Josephine Cochran Fellowship** of $3,000 is available to a student with a strong academic record and potential to specialize in textiles and clothing while working on a master's degree. This award is not expressly for women, but most past recipients have been women.

American Association of University Women Educational Foundation

Department 60
2201 North Dodge Street
Ames, IA 52243-4030
319-337-1716
http://www.aauw.org

American Fellowships support women doctoral candidates completing dissertations and scholars seeking funds for postdoctoral research leave or preparing completed research for publication. Applicants must be U.S. citizens and may apply for one of the three awards.

The **Postdoctoral Research Leave Fellowship** offers one-year support to women who have earned doctoral degrees; 16 postdoctoral fellowships are available in the arts and humanities, social sciences, and natural sciences. One is designated for a woman from an underrepresented group in any field.

Dissertation Fellowships are available to women in the final year of a doctoral degree program. Fifty-one fellowships are available in any field of study except engineering.

Summer/Short-Term Research Publication Grants fund women college and university faculty and independent researchers to prepare research for publication. Funds cannot be used for undertaking research. Six publication grants are available.

Selected Professions Fellowships are awarded to women in the final year of graduate study in fields where women's participation has been low. Some are restricted to minority women. Fill out a request for an application at AAUW's Web site or call or write.

American Press Institute

Cissy Patterson Fellowship
11690 Sunrise Valley Drive
Reston, VA 20191-1498

The **Cissy Patterson Fellowship,** a memorial to the owner of the former Washington, DC, *Times-Herald,* is open to a female reporter or editor from a U.S. or Canadian newspaper with a daily circulation below 25,000. The fellowship funds tuition, room, meals, and travel. Request further information in writing.

American Water Works Association

Scholarship Committee
6666 West Quincy Avenue
Denver, CO 80235
303-347-6206
http://www.awwa.org/tande/wolm%5F00.doc

The **Abel Wolman Fellowship** is designed to support promising students in the U.S., Canada, and Mexico pursuing advanced training and research in the field of water supply and treatment. The fellowship provides up to two years of support. The initial award is for one year and provides a $15,000 stipend distributed over 12 months, plus $1,000 for research supplies and equipment, and an education allowance of up to $4,000 to cover the cost of tuition and other fees. To be eligible you must be anticipating completing the requirements for a Ph.D. within two years of the award and have citizenship or permanent residence in Canada, Mexico, or the United States. Contact the scholarship committee for further information.

Asian Pacific American Women's Leadership Institute

1921 Ivy Street
Denver, CO 80220
303-399-8899
http://www.apawli.org

APAWLI's periodic insitutes are held throughout the year. Each year, up to 20 Asian and Pacific American women leaders are selected to participate in the **APAWLI Fellowship Program.** Three one-week sessions are held in three different U.S. cities, with guest speakers, activities, readings, and other learning tools. The cost of the leadership training is $20,000 per person. Of this

Financial Aid

amount, $15,500 is paid by foundation, corporate, and individual contributions. Participants are asked to cover the remaining $4,500 as tuition, but this tuition is based on the fellow's ability to pay. As part of the program, each fellow develops a program that will impact the lives of at least 25 people in her community.

Association for Women in Science

1200 New York Avenue, NW, Suite 650
Washington, DC 20005
202-326-8940
http://www.awis.org

AWIS fosters the recruitment, retention, and promotion of women in science. Five to ten graduate fellowships are offered annually. The **Ruth Satter Memorial Award for Women in Science** is open to women students who interrupted their education for three or more years to raise a family.

The **Amy Lutz Rechel Award** is for an outstanding graduate student in the field of plant biology.

The **Luise Meyer-Schutzmeister Award** is for a graduate student in physics.

The **Diane H. Russell Award** is for a graduate student in the field of biochemistry or pharmacology. Female students enrolled in a life, physical, behavioral, social science, or engineering program leading to a Ph.D. may apply. There are no citizenship restrictions. An application is available on the Web site or by requesting one in writing.

Association for Women Psychiatrists

PO Box 28218
Dallas, TX 75228
972-686-6522
http://www.womenpsych.org

The **AWP/Wyeth-Ayerst Fellowship** honors outstanding women psychiatry residents. In a recent year, two recipients each received $2,500 in recognition of their accomplishments and to assist with attending the American

Psychological Association and the AWP annual meetings.

AT&T Labs

AT&T Fellowship Administrator
Room C103
180 Park Avenue
Florham Park, NJ 07932-0971
http://www.research.att.com/academic/alfp.html

AT&T Fellowships are available to outstanding women and minority students who are pursuing Ph.D. studies in computer and communications-related fields. Fellowships provide all educational expenses during the school year, a stipend for living expenses, education expenses for summer study or research, and a mentor who is a staff member at AT&T Labs. Fellowships are renewable for up to six years. Each recipient is placed in a summer internship the first summer. Visit the Web site or write.

Bell Labs—Lucent Technologies

Graduate Research Program for Women
Scholarship Management Services, CSFA
1505 Riverview Road
PO Box 297
St. Peter, MN 56082
http://www.bell-labs.com/fellowships/GR

The GRPW is designed to identify and develop research ability in women and increase representation of women in science and engineering. Women pursuing full-time doctoral studies in chemical engineering, chemistry, communications science, computer science, electrical engineering, information science, materials science, mathematics, mechanical engineering, operations research, physics, or statistics are eligible for fellowships and grants. The fellowships provides an annual stipend of $17,000, books, fees, and travel expenses and are renewable annually up to four years. Fellows will be exposed to a variety of research environments by participating in ongoing research activities at Bell Laboratories. Visit the Web site or write for information.

Business and Professional Women's Clubs of New York State

Grace Legendre Fellowship
7509 Route 5
Clinton, NY 13323

Women from New York State are eligible for the **Grace Legendre Fellowship** of $1,000 to help finance graduate study. Applicants must show a good academic record and financial need and be a New York State resident enrolled at an accredited New York State college or university. Send a SASE with a written request for application materials.

Canadian Federation of University Women

251 Bank Street, Suite 600
K2P 1X3
Ottawa, Ontario
613-234-2732
http://www.cfuw.ca

The Canadian Federation of University Women offers several fellowships and awards to Canadian women who hold at least a bachelor's degree and have been accepted into a recognized program. **The Margaret McWilliams Pre-doctoral Fellowship** of $10,000 is for women who have completed at least one full calendar year as a full-time student in doctoral level studies. She may be studying abroad.

The **CFUW Memorial/Professional Fellowship** of $5,000 is for a woman enrolled in a master's program in Canada or abroad. Several other fellowships are available. Visit the Web site or call for information.

Center for Work and Service, Wellesley College

M. A. Cartland Schackford Medical Fellowship
Committee on Graduate Fellowships and Scholarship
106 Central Street
Wellesley, MA 02181-8203
781-283-3525
http://www.wellesley.edu/CWS/step/fello

Wellesley College offers limited financial aid for women graduates of any American institution for study at an American institution. The **M. A. Cartland Shackford Medical Fellowship** is awarded for the study of medicine with a view to general practice, not psychiatry. The fellowship offers a minimum $7,000 stipend.

Chicana/Latina Research Center

122 Social Sciences and Humanities
1 Shields Avenue
University of California
Davis, CA 95616
530-752-8882
http://www.apsanet.org/POS/grants/latin

The Chicana/Latina Research Center seeks to develop and promote scholarship on Hispanic women. The fellowship program is presented to extend to other campuses opportunities available at the center. The **Dissertation Fellowship** pays a $5,400 per quarter stipend and $200 for research. The **Post-Doctoral Fellowship** pays $400 for research and the stipend is negotiable. Fellows work in-residence on Davis' campus and deliver one public lecture per quarter. Awardees will also co-edit *VOCES: A Journal of Chicana/Latina Studies.*

Henry Luce Foundation

Clare Booth Luce Program
Program Director
111 West 50th Street, 4601
New York, NY 10020
212-489-7700
http://www.hluce.org

The Clare Booth Luce Program of the Henry Luce Foundation offers awards to help women teach in fields where they have been traditionally underrepresented, including physics, chemistry, biology, meteorology, engineering, computer science and mathematics. Grants are made only through four-year degree-granting institutions, not directly to individuals. Thirteen institutions were designated permanent participants (see Web site for list) and other colleges are invited to participate on a temporary basis.

Awards are offered in three categories: Scholarships for Undergraduates—generally awarded for two academic years solely on the basis of merit; Graduate Fellowships—awarded

Financial Aid

for an initial two-year period based on academic excellence and professional potential; and Professorships for Junior Faculty—five-year tenure-track appointments at the assistant or associate professor level (appointments must be made outside an institution's existing faculty). Visit the Web site for more information.

International Women's Forum
1621 Connecticut Avenue, NW, Suite 300
Washington, DC 20009
202-775-8917
http://www.iwforum.org

The IWF Leadership Foundation supports the **Leadership Foundation Fellows Program,** designed to help "up and coming" women from a variety of fields reach the levels of achievement that IWF's members have been able to accomplish. The foundation selects twelve to fifteen women annually, who are matched with members of the IWF who are willing to act as mentors. As part of the year-long program, fellows receive six days with their mentors; ongoing leadership training; conference opportunities, a customized week-long program at the Kennedy School of Government and a four-day program at Cambridge University's Judge Institute of Management Studies. A portion of the cost of the program is paid by the foundation; participants will be required to pay approximately $5,000 toward their expenses.

Kappa Omicron Nu Honor Society
Awards Committee
4990 Northwind Drive, Suite 140
East Lansing, MI 48823-5031
517-351-8335

Kappa Omicron Nu awards fellowships on a competitive basis to its members. (Nonmembers may apply for membership at the time they apply for a fellowship). The **Hettie M. Anthony Fellowship** for doctoral students and the **Eileen C. Maddex Fellowship** for master's level students are awarded annually in the amount of $2,000. Visit the society's Web site or write for information on membership or obtaining an application. (Open to men also, but awards majority of scholarships to women).

Mary Ingraham Bunting Institute
Fellowship Office
34 Concord Avenue
Cambridge, MA 02138
617-495-8212
http://www.radcliffe.edu/bunting/apply

This multidisciplinary residential research center offers funded and unfunded fellowships for women scholars, scientists, artists, and writers. The **Affiliation Appointment** is for women scholars in any field, women creative writers, and visual or performing artists. These appointments are without stipend; women holding or seeking funding from other sources are invited to apply. The institute provides studio space, auditing privileges, and access to libraries and other resources of Radcliffe and Harvard University. **Bunting Fellowships** offer the same benefits as above, but are funded in the amount of $36,500. Eight to ten are awarded annually. Visit the Web site or write for details.

Funded by the Berkshire Conference of Women Historians, the **Berkshire Summer Fellowship at Radcliffe** provides one award of $3,000 for a summer of research. The fellowship is open to women historians at the postdoctoral level working in any field of history. Preference will be given to junior scholars and to those who do not normally have access to Boston-area resources. Visit the Web site or call to request information.

Women scientists who are U.S. citizens or permanent residents and have held a doctorate (M.D. or Ph.D. for at least two years are eligible for the **Biomedical Research Fellowship,** funded by the Burroughs Wellcome Fund. Applications are accepted from all fields of biomedical research. The stipend is $41,600 plus $3,000 in research expenses for a year appointment. Two awards are made annually. Fellows may compete for a second year of funding. Visit the Web site or call to request information.

One $32,000 **Peace Fellowship** will be awarded annually to a woman who has demonstrated practical effectiveness in projects related to peace and justice, international relations, human rights, peace negotiation, and conflict resolution in national and international contexts, and whose project has potential for significance in such areas. Visit the Web site or call to request information.

National Council for Research on Women
Women and Public Policy Fellowship
Fellowship Coordinator
Center for Women in Government, University at Albany
Draper Hall, 135 Western Avenue
Albany, NY 12222
518-442-3383
http://www.ncrw.org

The **Women and Public Policy Fellowship** seeks to encourage greater participation of women in the public policy process and encourage the formulation of state policy that responds to the need of women, children, and families. The fellowship is open to graduate students from all academic disciplines who are enrolled in a New York state college, have completed 12 hours of graduate work, and have demonstrated an interest in improving the status of women through their studies, research, paid employment, or voluntary activities. Fellows are assigned as staff to a legislator, nonprofit organization, or state agency for 30 hours each week. All placements are in Albany, NY. A stipend of $9,000 is awarded for the seven-month period of January-July. Call or write for information.

National Physical Sciences Consortium
Graduate Fellowships for Women and Minorities in the Physical Sciences
Student Recruitment Office, New Mexico State University
Box 30001
Las Cruces, NM 88003
800-952-4118
http://www.npsc.org

The **NPSC Graduate Fellowship for Minorities and Women in the Physical Sciences** pays tuition, fees, and a stipend for up to six years of study toward the Ph.D. in astronomy, chemistry, computer science, geology, materials science, math, and physics. The program involves employment at a sponsoring research institution. Guidelines state that minorities and women are eligible, but in a recent year, 19 of 20 fellows were women. Call or write for further information.

National Science Foundation
4201 Wilson Boulevard
Arlington, VA 22230
703-306-1234
http://www.fastlane.nsf.gov

The National Science Foundation is a large government organization that encourages and funds research in all fields. NSF funding consists of several thousand dollars for a major research project over several months or years. It offers three programs specifically for women researchers, and provides women with funding opportunities that are not ordinarily available through regular research and education grant programs. **POWRE Funds** are designed to provide a one-time input of funds at a critical stage in a woman's career. Eligible research areas include biochemistry, biology, cell biology, chemistry, developmental biology, microbiology, and molecular biology. Grants are for up to $75,000 over 12 to 18 months and are non-renewable. In a recent year, $13.7 million in POWRE grants were awarded to 206 applicants. Grants are for junior faculty and senior faculty/scientists.

Faculty Awards for Women are offered to expand women faculty members' access to research and tenure opportunities. A recent research offering was Tracing Sources and Sinks of Particles in the Ocean. General Faculty Awards for Women in math, science, and engineering are also offered.

Visiting Professorships for Women provide funding for women to conduct research in specific areas at various universities. Recent topics were Early Developments in Children's Understanding of the Mental State of Pretense. NSF's Fast Lane Web site gives applicants the ability to conduct NSF award searches, view notifications and requests, and submit proposals for reviews.

Financial Aid

National Urban Fellows, Inc.
55 West 44th Street, Suite 600
New York, NY 10036
212-921-9400
http://www.nuf.org

NUF offers the **National Urban/Rural Fellows** 14-month fellowship to mid-career minority and women executives in upper levels of management, with a commitment to public sector management of urban and rural environments. The $17,000 fellowship also covers travel, tuition, and other related expenses.

New Jersey Federation of Women's Clubs
55 Labor Center Way
New Brunswick, NJ 08901-1529
732-249-5474

Female graduate students (preferably from New Jersey) are eligible to apply for the **Margaret Yardley Fellowship** if they are enrolled in a master's or doctoral program. The $1,000 fellowship is tenable at any American college or university.

Newberry Library
60 West Walton Street
Chicago, IL 60610
312-943-9090
http://www.newberry.org

The **Monticello College Foundation** offers a six-month fellowship for research, writing, and participation in the intellectual life at the Newberry Library for women scholars. Applicants must have a Ph.D. and be a U.S. citizen or permanent resident. The fellowship is designed for a woman at an early stage of her academic career whose work gives clear promise of scholarly productivity. The applicant's topic should be related to the Newberry's collections; preference will be given to proposals concerned with the study of women. The fellowship carries a $12,500 stipend.

Phi Beta KappaSociety
Mary Isabel Sibley Fellowship Committee
1811 Q Street, NW
Washington, DC 20009
202-265-3808
http://www.pbk.org

The **Mary Isabel Sibley Fellowship** is awarded alternately in the fields of Greek and French. The award may be used for the study of Greek language, literature, history, or archaeology, or for the study of French language or literature. The fellowship is awarded annually and has a stipend of $20,000. The stipend will be paid in two installments. Candidates must be unmarried women between 25 and 35 who hold a doctorate or have fulfilled all the requirements for the doctorate except the dissertation. They must devote full-time work to the research during the fellowship year.

Radcliffe College
Henry A. Murray Research Center
10 Garden Street
Cambridge, MA 02138
http://www.radcliffe.edu/murray/index.htm

The **Henry A. Murray Research Center** at Radcliffe is a national repository of social and behavioral sciences data for the study of lives over time, with a special focus on the lives of American women. Grant funds for postdoctoral research using the center's resources are available.

The **Jeanne Humphrey Block Dissertation Award Program** offers a grant of $2,500 to a woman doctoral student. Proposals should focus on sex and gender differences or some developmental issues of particular concern to girls or women. Other grants are not expressly for women, but many recipients are women conducting research in women's studies.

The **Visiting Scholars Program** offers office space and access to the facilities of Radcliffe and Harvard University each year to six to eight scholars who wish to investigate some aspect of women and social change or the study of lives over time. The program does not include a stipend. Strong preference is given to scholars using the Murray Center's data resources.

The **Observational Studies Dissertation Award Program** offers grants up to $2,500 to doctoral students using data from the Manpower Demonstration Research Corporations Observational Studies, comprising two different welfare intervention programs. The data set includes computer accessible and videotaped data of mothers and their children. Visit the Web site for application information.

The **Marion Cabot Putnam Fellowship** is open to professional women in the field of infant and child development, conducting research within the framework of, or contributing to, psycho-analysis. One fellowship will be awarded at a stipend of $36,500 for the 11-month fellowship.

Ragdale Foundation
Frances Shaw Fellowship
1260 North Green Bay Road
Lake Forest, IL 60045-1106
847-234-1063

Women who began writing seriously after the age of 55 are eligible to apply for the **Frances Shaw Fellowship.** The fellowship pays travel expenses and room and board at Ragdale for two months.

Sigma Delta Epsilon/Graduate Women in Science
PO Box 240726
Apple Valley, MN 55124
http://www.gac.edu/People/orgs/gwis

SDE/GWIS offers fellowships to women study-ing science, including the social sciences at the graduate or postdoctoral level. **SDE Fellowships** are available to members and non-members alike. In a recent year, three awards ranging from $2,000 to $3,000 were given. Contact the national headquarters by mail or visit the Web site for an online application form and guide-lines and to get the addresses of current selec-tion committee chairs. There is a $20 applica-tion fee for nonmember applicants.

Society for Historians of American Foreign Relations
c/o Department of History
Wright State University
Dayton, OH 45435
937-873-3110
http://www.ohiou.edu/shafr/shafr.html

Two **Myrna Bernath Research Fellowships** are available annually to research the study of for-eign relations among women scholars. The grants are intended for women at U.S. universi-ties as well as women from abroad who wish to do research in the United States. Preference is given to graduate students and newly finished Ph.D.s. Work on purely domestic topics will not be considered. Applications should include a letter of intent and three copies of a detailed research proposal. Contact the SHAFR business office for contact information for the current fellowship chair.

Society of Women Geographers
415 East Capitol Street, SE
Washington, DC 20003
202-546-9228

The Society of Women Geographers offers fel-lowships to aid young women studying for advanced degrees in geography or its allied sci-ences. Society fellowships are awarded through collaborative arrangements with such institu-tions as Columbia University, the University of Chicago, Rutgers, and the University of California in both Berkeley and Los Angeles.

University of Florida
Office of International Studies and Programs
WorldWide Fellows Program
123 Tigert Hall, PO Box 113225
Gainesville, FL 32611-3225
352-392-7074
http://www.datexinc.com/worldwid/widdes

The **Worldwide Women-in-Development Fellows Program** is a one-year international development fellowship for mid-career profes-sionals who can apply their technical skills to U.S. foreign assistance and to incorporate gen-der and development issues in their applied work. Applicants must be U.S. citizens and have five years of experience in their area of technical expertise. Fellows receive a $2,500 monthly stipend, travel expenses, housing, and food allowance during training, and partial medical insurance. Fellows undergo a training program at the University of Florida and in Washington, DC. They report to a United States Agency for International Development mission abroad, where they will use their technical expertise to improve conditions in the country. In the final component "Bringing Home Lessons Learned," fellows provide an action plan to explain how they will integrate the experience and knowledge gained here in the United States. Visit the Web site or call for program information.

Womanist Studies Consortium

Womanist Theory and Research Institute for African-American Studies
164 Psychology Building
University of Georgia
Athens, GA 30602-3012
706-542-5197
http://www.uga.edu/~womanist/fellowship.html

The Womanist Studies Consortium seeks to support "womanists" (black feminists or feminists of color). WSC fellows will be expected to devise, develop, and disseminate scholarship that applies womanist perspectives in innovative ways in their respective disciplines. WSC provides four types of fellowships. The **Flexible Fellowship** allows fellows to engage in up to ten months of residency with a stipend of $3,300 per month for one scholar per year. Applicants are encouraged to submit projects with a community outreach component.

Single Parent Fellowships provide one quarter of residency for womanist scholars whose child care responsibilities make longer appointments prohibitive. An overall stipend of $10,000 is provided. Community outreach projects are encouraged.

Summer Seminar Fellowships provide a stipend of $3,300 for participation in the one-month Womanist Studies Seminar for six scholars per year.

Graduate Summer Internships provide a stipend of $1,000 to allow one out-of-state graduate student working in any field to reside for one month at the University of Georgia at Athens. The student participates in the summer seminar and assists with editorial and technological projects. Write or call for information.

Women in Government Relations

1029 Vermont Avenue, NW, Suite 510
Washington, DC 20005-3527
202-347-5432
http://www.wgr.org

WGR offers the **Future Leader Fellowship** of $4,000 annually to women studying in an area that will lead to a career in public policy, such as political science or law. Applicants must be residents of the DC area who have been active in the community, have financial need, and had their education or career interrupted by a major life event, such as childbirth or divorce. Undergraduate, graduate, and doctoral studies qualify. Fellowships are administered by the Union Institute Center for Women in Washington, DC. Interested applicants should call the Union Institute at 202-496-1630.

Women's International Network of Utility Professionals

PO Box 335
Whites Creek, TN 37189
615-876-5444
http://www.winup.org

WINUP, formerly the Electrical Women's Round Table, offers two fellowships to graduate women in any area of electrical energy. The **Julia Kiene Fellowship** is a $2,000 annual grant. The **Lyle Mamer Fellowship** is a $1,000 grant. Visit the Web site or write for an application.

Women's Medical Association of New York City

Mary Putnam Jacobi Fellowship
386 Park Avenue South, Room 1502
New York, NY 10016
212-545-0022

Women physicians of any country are eligible for the **Mary Putnam Jacobi Fellowship** of $2,000. Fellows are encouraged to carry out projects in institutions or countries other than their own.

Women's National Democratic Club Educational Foundation

http://www.wndcfoundation.org

The WNDC Foundation administers the **Marian O. Norby Legal Education Fellowships**. The fellowships provide $5,000 per year, renewable for three years, to women who have been employed at the White House and are admitted to an accredited law school.

Women's National Farm and Garden Association

c/o Mrs. Ronald Hudson
251 West Saint Clair Street
Romeo, MI 48065
517-793-1714

The Women's National Farm and Garden Association offers the $1,000 **Sarah Bradley Tyson Memorial Fellowship** for advanced study in agriculture, horticulture, and allied subjects. There is no application form. A letter of application containing an account of the applicant's educational training, plan of study, certification of degrees held, and testimonials as to character, ability, personality, and scholarship should be sent to the chairman of the committee. A health certificate and recent photograph are also requested.

Women's Research and Education Institute

1750 New York Avenue, NW, Suite 350
Washington, DC 20006
http://www.wrei.org

The WREI program is designed to encourage more effective participation by women in policymaking. WREI awards annual fellowships to graduate students with a proven commitment to equity for women. Fellows work for one academic year as congressional legislative aides in Washington. Major criteria are academic performance, work with community groups, and interest in analyzing the effect of gender differences on laws and lawmakers. Fellows receive stipends for tuition and living expenses. Applications are available online or by sending a SASE to the above address.

Women's Studio Workshop

Clay Fellowship
PO Box 489
New York, NY 12472
914-658-9133
http://www.wsworkshop.org

The Women's Studio Workshop, an alternative space for artists to create new work and come together to share skills, assists women artists in various mediums. The **Clay Fellowships** offer a block of uninterrupted work time in WSW's low-tech clay studio. Two- to six-week sessions are available each year from September to June. The award includes on-site housing and studio access. Cost to recipients is $200 a week plus materials and firing, approximately one-fifth the actual cost of the residency. Grant applications are available online at WSW's Web site.

Zeta Phi Beta Sorority

1734 New Hampshire Avenue, NW
Washington, DC 20009
202-387-3103
http://www.zpb1920.org

The sorority awards scholarships and fellowships to women who are not members, as well as several to ZPB members. The **Deborah Partridge Wolfe International Graduate Fellowship** is offered to Americans studying in a foreign country and to foreign students studying in the United States.

Zonta International Foundation

557 West Randolph Street
Chicago, IL 60661-2206
312-930-5848
http://www.zonta.org

Amelia Earhart Fellowship Awards are available to women pursuing graduate study in aerospace-related sciences and engineering. In a recent year, thirty-five $6,000 fellowships were awarded. Applicants need not be U.S. citizens.

Grants

Grants are similar to fellowships, although they may be given at any level, and are generally given for work on a specific project, such as research or for travel expenses to a professional conference.

Alpha Delta Kappa

1615 West 92nd Street
Kansas City, MO 64114
800-247-2311
http://www.alphadeltakappa.org

ADK awards three grants apiece in the Fine Arts-Painting and Fine Arts-Music-Strings areas. Grants are for $1,000, $3,000, and $5,000 to female graduate students or professionals in these fields. Recipients need not be members of ADK. Competitions are held every even-numbered year. See the Web site for application information or request information at the above address.

Altrusa InternationalFoundation

322 South Michigan Avenue, Suite 1123
Chicago, IL 60604-4305
312-427-4410
http://www.altrusa.org

Altrusa International Foundation, a philanthropic corporation, supplements its direct contributions to society through a program of cash grants to individuals and Altrusa clubs that support Altrusa's interests, including the well-being of women and families. Through its **Grants-in-Aid** and **Founders Fund Vocational Aid** programs, the organization has helped over 10,000 women begin professional and business careers. Grants provide vocational assistance, including job training and equipment purchases, for start-up businesses. Grants range from $250 to $1,000 based on need and funds available. Visit the Web site or call for specific grant information and current funding interests.

American Association for the Advancement of Science

1200 New York Avenue, 7th Floor
Washington, DC 20005
202-326-7027
http://www.aaas.org

The American Association for the Advancement of Science occasionally offers one-time **grants** for women only. A recent program sought to raise the profile of women scientists in Russia and encourage U.S.-Russian cooperation and information exchange among women scientists. Travel grants allowed U.S. women scientists to travel to Russia to participate in scientific meetings. Visit AAAS's Web site for information on current programs for women.

American Association of Family and Consumer Sciences

Fellowships and Grants Program
1555 King Street
Alexandria, VA 22314
703-706-4600
http://www.aafcs.org

Ruth O'Brien Project Grants are granted in varying amounts to individuals concerned with research and development in home economics. These grants are not expressly for women, but most past recipients have been women.

American Association of University Women

1111 16th Street, NW
Washington, DC 20036
800-326-AAUW
http://www.aauw.org

Two types of Scholar-in-Residence Awards are offered. **Research Scholar-in-Residence** awards are based at the headquarters in Washington, DC. Scholars will address the higher education experience or women, including topics in technology/distance learning and the economic barriers limiting access to higher education. **University Scholar-in-Residence,** located at a college or university, will undertake and disseminate research on gender equity for women and girls. Visit the Web site or call national headquarters.

American Chemical Society

Women Chemists Committee Travel Award
1155 16th Street, NW
Washington, DC 20036
202-872-4600
http://www.acs.org

The **ACS Women Chemists Committee Travel Award,** with funding from Eli Lilly & Co. and the Hoechst Celanese Corp., provides funding for undergraduate, graduate, and postdoctoral women chemists to travel to scientific meetings to present the results of their research. Grants may be applied only to registration, travel, and accommodations to meetings in the United States.

American Film Institute

Directing Workshop for Women
2021 North Western Avenue
Los Angeles, CA 90027
213-856-7628

AFI sponsors a **Directing Workshop for Women.** The workship is open to professional women in television, film, or video who have not directed films or television. Participants are awarded $5,000 per project and are provided with production equipment for the 8-month workshop. Applications are available online or call or write for information.

Association for Women in Mathematics

Mentoring/Travel Grant Committee
4114 Computer & Space Sciences Building
University of Maryland
College Park, MD 20742-2461
301-405-7892
http://www.awm-math.org

AWM, in cooperation with the National Science Foundation, offers travel grants and mentoring grants to assist women in math and science fields. The **NSF-AWM Travel Grants** enable women to attend research conferences in their fields. A maximum of $1,000 for domestic travel and $2,000 for foreign travel will be available. **AWM Mentoring Grants** fund travel, subsistence, and expenses for an untenured woman mathematician to travel to an institute to do research with a specified individual for one month. Grants are $4,000. Applicants for either grant must be women holding a doctorate with a work address in the United States.

Association of Women Surgeons Foundation

Ethicon Endo-Surgery Grant
414 Plaza Drive, Suite 209
Westmont, IL 60559
630-655-0392
http://www.womensurgeons.org

AWSF and Ethicon Endo-Surgery co-sponsor an annual grant of $25,000 for endoscopic-laparoscopic research related to clinical and basic science research. Grants are awarded in the fall for research the following year. Contact AWSF.

AT&T Labs

AT&T Grants Administrator
Room C103
180 Park Avenue
Florham Park, NJ 07932-0971
http://www.research.att.com/academic/alfp.html

AT&T Labs Grants are available to outstanding women and minority students pursuing a Ph.D. in computer and communications-related fields. Grants provide an annual stipend of $2,000; a mentoring arrangement with a staff member of AT&T Labs, conference travel support, and subsequent summer employment. Recipients are placed in a summer research internship the first summer. Grants are renewable for up to six years of recipients making progress toward their Ph.D. Visit the Web site or write.

Bell Labs—Lucent Technologies

Graduate Research Program for Women
Scholarship Management Services, CSFA
1505 Riverview Road, PO Box 297
St. Peter, MN 56082
http://www.bell-labs.com/fellowships/GR

The GRPW is designed to identify and develop research ability in women and increase representation of women in science and engineering. Women pursuing full-time doctoral studies in chemical engineering, chemistry, computer science, electrical engineering, information science, materials science, mathematics, mechanical engineering, operations research, physics, or statistics are eligible for fellowships and grants. The grants provide an annual award of $2,000, which is to be used to support aspects of the recipient's professional development not normally covered by other awards (child care expenses, computer equipment). Grants are renewable annually up to four years. Recipients will be exposed to a variety of research environments by participating in ongoing research activities at Bell Laboratories. Visit the Web site or write for information.

Computing Research Association

1100 17th Street, NW, Suite 507
Washington, DC 20036-4632
202-234-2111
http://cra.org/Activities/craw/

The **CRA Distributed Mentor Project,** funded by the National Science Foundation, seeks to increase the number of women entering graduate school in computer science. The project brings together computer science undergraduates and professors for a summer of research at the mentor's research institution. Students will be involved in research, learn how a research university operates, and meet and interact with graduate students and successful researchers. Funding for the student consists of $550 per week for research, plus travel assistance. Mentors and their universities receive no funding. Check the Web site or call for current information.

The **Committee on the Status of Women in Computing Research**, an effort of the Computing Research Association, provides opportunities for undergraduate and new graduate women to attend a research conference. **Conference Experiences for Women** provides travel and conference expenses up to $1,000 for female students accompanied by a faculty member. Support will not be provided for students who are giving papers. Visit the Web site or call for current-year information.

Educational Foundation for Women in Accounting

PO Box 1925
Southeastern, PA 19399-1925
610-407-9229
http://www.efwa.org

EFWA provides **research grants** for women faculty members to contribute to the field of accounting and assist faculty in their careers. EFWA also funds issues papers by faculty, individuals, and businesses on technical accounting issues or issues furthering women in the profession.

George Washington University Summer Program for Women in Mathematics

Mathematics Department
2201 G Street, NW
Washington, DC 20052
202-994-4857
http://www.gwu.edu/~math/spwm.html

The **Summer Program for Women in Mathematics** is a five-week intensive program for mathematically talented undergraduate women who are completing their junior year and contemplating graduate study in the mathematical sciences. Applicants need not be a George Washington University student. Goals of the program are to build enthusiasm, develop research skills, cultivate mathematical self-confidence, and promote success in graduate school. Sixteen women are selected annually. Each receives a travel allowance, campus room and board, and a stipend of $1,250. No course credits or grades will be given. Applications are available online or by calling or writing.

Infusium 23

Infusium 23 Science Awards
40 West 57th Street, 23rd Floor
New York, NY 10019

Infusium 23, a haircare brand, funds 23 **grants** of $1,000 each to provide encouragement to female high school students to pursue careers in science. The grants may be used for college, summer classes, extracurricular programs, or other educational pursuits. The award is open to all female high school students. Applicants should provide an essay or statement about the career she wants to pursue, extracurricular activities demonstrating career commitment, and a person who has influenced her career choice. Submit the essay along with the applicant's name, address, age, and school grade as of April 15.

Journalism and Women Symposium
http://www.jaws.org

The **Joan Cook Scholarship Fund** provides grants to young women, particularly women of color, in journalism, to travel to the JAWS annual camp. The annual camp is a gathering of professionals who explore issues like "ethics and equity, coverage and careers, and affirmative action and anger."

Kentucky Foundation for Women
Grants Program
332 West Broadway
1215-A Heyburn Building
Louisville, KY 40202
http://www.kfw.org

Women visual artists, writers, musicians, performers, videographers, and filmmakers who live or work in Kentucky are eligible to apply for $1,000 encouragement grants and $3,000 to $5,000 regular grants. Special grants of up to $15,000 are occasionally awarded. Artists whose work embodies a feminist consciousness are desired. Call or send SASE to request current application guidelines and application.

Leeway Foundation
123 South Broad Street, Suite 2040
Philadelphia, PA 19019
215-545-4078
http://www.libertynet.org/leeway.html

The Leeway Foundation grants substantial awards to women artists in the Philadelphia area. Applicants must be 25 or older; a resident of the Philadelphia area for at least two years; have exhibited or been published; and not be enrolled in a degree program in the field under consideration. The annual **Bessie Berman Grant** awards $50,000 to a woman artist 50 or older for

her artistic accomplishments. Up to four **Leeway Grants for Excellence** for $30,000 and up to four **Leeway Grants for Achievement** for $20,000 are awarded annually. Up to three **Edna Andrade Emerging Artist Grants** are made annually to women artists who demonstrate exceptional promise early in their careers. Applicants are encouraged to attend one of the foundation's Application Workshops. Call to request information or visit the Web site.

Money for Women Fund
P.O. Box 40-1043
Brooklyn, NY 11240-1043

Women who are not enrolled in school are eligible to apply for grants up to $5,000. Awards are designed to support feminists active in the arts who are furthering such issues as peace, social justice, and the status of women. Send a stamped, self-addressed envelope for application information.

National Museum of Women in the Arts
Library and Research Center
1250 New York Avenue, NW
Washington, DC 20005-3920
202-783-7996
http://www.nmwa.org

The **Library Fellow Grant for Book Artists** offers funding for a book's creation to female artists. The grant is used to produce an artist's book in a limited edition of 125 copies. The artist keeps 25 copies as a form of remuneration; the program keeps 50 and the remainder are sold. Send a self-addressed, stamped envelope for further information to the Library and Research Center.

Ninety-Nines
Amelia Earhart Research Scholar Grant
Box 965
7100 Terminal Drive
Oklahoma City, OK 73159-0965
800-994-1929
http://www.ninety-nines.org

Ninety-Nines is an international organization of licensed women pilots. Several scholarships and grants are offered for members and nonmembers. The **Amelia Earhart Research Scholar Grant** is awarded periodically for a highly specialized professional scholar to work in her field of expertise to expand knowledge about women in aviation and space. Contact the organization with your proposal.

P.E.O. Sisterhood
Program for Continuing Education
3700 Grand Avenue
Des Moines, IA 50312-3820
515-255-3153
http://www.peointernational.org

The P.E.O. Sisterhood, an international philanthropic organization with an interest in furthering educational opportunities for women, offers **grants** to women in the United States and Canada for purposeful educational goals of self or service. Specific guidelines are not provided. Call or write to see if your needs match funding availability.

Sociologists for Women in Society
SWS Feminist Lectureship Committee
Sociology Department
300 Bricker Hall
190 North Oval Mall
Ohio State University
Columbus, OH 43210
http://socsci.colorado.edu/sws/sws.html

SWS awards the **SWS Feminist Lecturer** a one-time honorarium of $1,000 for lectures at two sites. Hosts are expected to cover all other expenses. A written version of the lecture will appear in the SWS journal *Gender and Society.*

Thanks Be To Grandmother Winifred Foundation
P.O. Box 1449
Wainscott, NY 11975-1449

Grants of $500 to $5,000 are made to women 54 years old and older to fund projects that empower and enrich the lives of other adult (over 21) women. Funding may be requested for a specific project, to produce a report or similar project, or to improve or enhance a literary, artistic, musical, scientific, educational, or other skill or talent. Candidates must be U.S. citizens.

Write for application instructions. Include a SASE.

Women in Neuroscience
WIN President Andrea Zardetto-Smith
Creighton University Department of Physical Therapy
2500 California Plaza
Omaha, NE 68178
402-280-5946
http://www.womenCONNECT.com/WIN/index.html

WIN Travel Grants sponsor graduate students and postdoctoral fellows to attend the annual meeting of the Society for Neuroscience. Grants are given based on the scientific quality of the abstract to be presented and on financial need. Recent awards were $750 each. Awards are funded by a grant from the Eli Lilly Company and proceeds of WIN fundraising. Membership in WIN is encouraged but not required. Write to the WIN president for an application.

Women's Initiative for Self-Employment
450 Mission Street, Suite 402
San Francisco, CA 94105
415-247-9473

WI makes modest grants to help low-income women start up businesses upon completion of a 14-week training program. WI also offers business support services to women, including one-on-one consultations, peer networking and support groups, and special seminars.

Women's National Book Association
Grant Administrator
American Library Association
50 East Huron
Chicago, IL 60611

The Women's National Book Association **Ann H. Eastman Grant,** administered by the American Library Association, is available for librarians interested in learning about publishing. It offers up to $150 for women to take a course or participate in an institute on publishing. It is open to a librarian holding a master of library sciences and two years' experience.

Women's Sports Foundation

Research Grants
Eisenhower Park
East Meadow, NY 11554
800-227-3988
http://www.womenssportsfoundation.org

The Women's Sports Foundation administers research grants funded by private companies. The **Quaker Rice Cakes Exercise and Nutrition Research Grant** provides financial assistance for research on exercise and nutrition in female sports and fitness.

The **Evian Rehydration in Women's Sports Grant** provides financial assistance for research on rehydration and the sports performance of female athletes.

The **Lilo Leeds Women's Sports and Fitness Participation Endowment Research Grant** provides financial assistance for research that creates a greater understanding of the factors that influence the participation of girls and women in sports and fitness activities.

The **Women's Sports Foundation Girls and Women in Sports Research Grant** provides financial assistance for research pertaining to girls and women in sports. Apply through the foundation. Information is available on the Web site, or by calling.

Women's Studio Workshop

Artists' Book Grants
P.O. Box 489
Rosendale, NY 12472
914-658-9133
http://www.wsworkshop.org

The Women's Studio Workshop, an alternative space for artists to create new work and come together to share skills, offers assistance to women book artists. The **Artists' Book Residency Grants** enable artists to produce a limited edition bookwork at WSW. Selected artists work in the WSW studios for four to six weeks and are involved in all aspects of the design and production of their bookwork. On-site housing is provided. The grant includes a stipend of $1,800 for six week, materials up to $450, and access to all studios.

The **Artists' Book Production Grants** assist artists working in their own studios with production costs for the publication of smaller-scale projects. Assistance up to $750 is provided. Grant applications are available at WSW's Web site or call to request information.

Woodrow Wilson National Fellowship Foundation

Woodrow Wilson Dissertation Grants in Women's Studies
CN 5281
Princeton, NJ 08543-5281
609-452-7007
http://www.woodrow.org

The **Woodrow Wilson Dissertation Grants in Women's Studies** encourages original research about women that crosses disciplinary, regional, or cultural boundaries. Recent winning topics include: "Women, Law and the Victorian Novel," "Girls, Boys, and Popular Literature," and "African-American Women in Electoral Politics." Students in doctoral-level programs who have completed all predissertation requirements in any field at graduate schools in the United States may apply. Grants are $1,500 to be used for expenses connected with the dissertation, including travel, books, microfilming, taping, and computer services. An average of 15 grants are awarded annually. Applications are available on the foundation's Web site or by written request.

Loans

Loans for women-only businesses are available from lenders around the country. Your local Small Business Administration office can get you connected with specialized lenders.

Financial Aid

Business and Professional Women's Foundation

2012 Massachusetts Avenue, NW
Washington, DC 20036
202-293-1200
http://www.bpwusa.org

Loans are available to women seeking education in an engineering field or business. Applicants must demonstrate financial need, have realistic career goals, have academic or work experience showing career motivation and ability, and have written notice of acceptance or enrollment at an accredited school. Interest of 7 percent begins immediately after graduation and loans are repaid in 20 quarterly installments beginning 12 months after graduation. Request a brochure and application by sending a #10 double-stamped envelope to the above address.

Sears Roebuck Loans for Women in Graduate Business Studies are available for full or part-time female students who have been accepted for master's study in a business administration program. Applicants must be U.S. citizens and demonstrate financial need.

California Community Foundation
606 South Olive Street, Suite 2400
Los Angeles, CA 90014
213-413-4130

Loans of up to $15,000 are offered to women business owners in the Los Angeles area to help them develop their enterprises. Must be willing to work with a sponsoring agency such as the Coalition for Women's Economic Development.

National Association of Women Business Owners/Wells Fargo

Wells Fargo National Business Banking Center
800-35WELLS
http://wellsfargo.com/cra/nawbo

Wells Fargo first partnered with NAWBO in 1995 to create a $1 billion, three-year loan fund just for women-owned businesses. The response was so overwhelming that the entire $1 billion was disbursed in one year. Wells Fargo has since renewed its support by agreeing to lend $10 billion over the next ten years. For information

about obtaining a loan, call the banking center and mention the NAWBO partnership. NAWBO membership is not necessary. NAWBO headquarters can be reached at 301-608-2950.

P.E.O. Sisterhood

Educational Loan Fund
3700 Grand Avenue
Des Moines, IA 50312-2899
515-255-3153
http://www.peointernational.org

The P.E.O. Educational Loan Fund is a revolving loan fund established in 1907 to lend money to worthy women students to assist them in securing a higher education. No specific guidelines are provided; call or write to request information for your circumstances.

Small Business Administration

Office of Women's Business Ownership
800-827-5722
http://www.gov.womeninbusiness

The SBA Office of Women's Business Ownership can provide information on SBA lending programs and venture capital sources geared toward women and minorities. The 7(a) **Loan Program** makes loans to small businesses unable to secure financing on reasonable terms through normal lending channels. It operates through private lenders with loans guaranteed by the SBA up to $1 million.

The **Women's Prequalification Loan Program** uses nonprofit organizations as intermediaries to assist prospective women borrowers in developing a viable loan application package. Many of the Women's Business Centers listed in the Organizations section of this book can assist with prequalification loans.

The **LowDoc Program** streamlines the loan process to a one-page application and 36-hour response for loans up to $150,000.

The **MicroLoan Program** increases the availability of very small loans up to $25,000 for small businesses. Women seeking venture capital can inquire about SBA Small Business Investment

Companies, which are private investment firms licensed by the SBA to provide equity capital, long-term loans, and management assistance.

The **Surety Bond Guarantee Program** provides small and minority contractors with government contracting opportunities for which they would not otherwise bid. SBA also makes referrals to ACE-Net, the Access to Capital Electronic Network. ACE-Net addresses the capital gap in the $250,000 to $5 million range and works with a national network of nonprofit partners who mentor and assist business development.

Springboard 2000
Women's Venture Capital Forum
http://www.springboard200.org

Springboard 2000 is the first-ever venture capital forum to showcase women entrepreneurs. The forum is a joint project of the National Women's Business Council and the Forum for Women Entrepreneurs. The forum will bring together over 350 investors and key service providers with women seeking seed or later-round investments of $1 million to $15 million. Contact the Web site, or call the National Women's Business Council at 202/205-3850 or the Forum for Women Entrepreneurs at 650-357-0222.

Women Incorporated
333 South Grand Avenue, Suite 2450
Los Angeles, CA 90071
http://www.womeninc.org

Women Incorporated's National Financial Network offers members access to a multibillion-dollar loan pool. The financing is complemented by a national technical assistance network. If the loan is not approved, a member service representative steps in to help find a training class or a local microlender.

Women's Enterprise Society of British Columbia
14-2070 Harvey Avenue
Kelowna, BC V1Y 8P8
250-868-3454
http://www.wes.bc.ca

The WESBC encourages the establishment and growth of women-owned and controlled businesses in British Columbia. The WESBC offers loan programs to women entrepreneurs. The most important criteria for obtaining financing is a viable business plan. Visit the Web site for further information.

Women's World Banking
8 West 40th Street
New York, NY 10018
212-768-8513
http://www.soc.titech.ac.jp/icm/wind/wwb.html

WWB supports the involvement of women in enterprise creation all over the world. Loans of up to $1 million are made to help businesses started by women anywhere in the world. They must have support from a local affiliate.

Scholarships

Scholarships are offered at all levels, from high school through postdoctoral to working women.

Alpha Delta Kappa International Honorary Society for Women Educators
1615 West 92nd Street
Kansas City, MO 64114
http://www.alphadeltakappa.org

Alpha Delta Kappa offers the **International Teacher Education Scholarship** to women who are not U.S. citizens. To be eligible, you must be a single woman with no dependents and maintain that status throughout the scholarship period; under age 30 at time of application; and living outside the United States and not currently attending school in the United States. This grant-in-aid is $10,000. The program is directed to women whose major field is related to education. Application requests are available on ADK's Web site or by writing.

Alpha Epsilon Iota Scholarship Fund

c/o Society Bank Trust Department
100 South Main Street
Ann Arbor, MI 48104

Two awards are made annually to women who are U.S. citizens and enrolled or accepted in an accredited U.S. medical school. Priority is given to candidates in their first year of medical school. Scholarships are based on financial need and merit and are $3,000-$3,500. Scholarships are renewable, and are thus not offered some years because of renewals. Write for information.

America's Junior Miss

P.O. Box 2786
Mobile, AL 36652-2786
http://www.ajm.org

High school juniors and seniors are eligible for scholarships based on scholastic achievement, talent in the creative and performing arts, fitness, and poise. Awards totaling more than $5 million are granted annually. To apply, contact your state chairman during the summer between your sophomore or junior year. The Web site has contact information for state chairmen.

American Business Women's Association

National Headquarters
9100 Ward Parkway
P.O. Box 8728
Kansas City, MO 64114
800-228-0007
http://www.abwa.org

ABWA has chapters in most U.S. states, some of which award local scholarships. To find a chapter in your area, visit the Web site and look under the Councils link. Nationally, the **Stephen Bufton Memorial Fund** administers a limited number of scholarships in fields of study that vary from year to year. Call national headquarters after November 1 to learn which fields will be emphasized in the coming year.

American College of Medical Practice Executives

104 Inverness Terrace East
Englewood, CO 80112-5313
303-799-1111, ext. 573

The **Constance L. Lloyd Scholarship** of $1,500 is available for women enrolled at the undergraduate or graduate level in Georgia pursuing an administrative or clinically related degree in the health care field.

American Congress on Surveying and Mapping

5410 Grosvenor Lane, Suite 100
Bethesda, MD 20814
301-493-0200

Several scholarships are available to undergraduate and graduate students in the fields of cartography and surveying. The **Porter McDonnell Memorial Award** of $1,000 is granted to women students to assist in completion of a bachelor's degree.

American Foundation for the Blind

11 Penn Plaza South, Suite 300
New York, NY 10001
212-502-7774
http://www.irg.org/afb/index.html

The foundation offers several awards to undergraduate women who are legally blind, including the **Gillette Scholarship** in creative writing and music and the **Gladys Anderson Scholarship** for undergraduate study in classical music.

American Legion Auxiliaries

777 North Meridian Street, Third Floor
Indianapolis, IN 46204
317-635-6291
http://www.legion-aux.org

Local American Legion auxiliaries are excellent sources of scholarships for young women. High school students should contact their school's guidance office or local American Legion Auxiliary for information on essay contests and other scholarships available at the local and state levels. Nationally, the American Legion

Auxiliary sponsors **Girls Nation,** a hands-on federal government training program in Washington, DC, to teach high school girls about government and democracy.

American Mensa Education and Research Foundation

National Scholarship Chairperson
3437 West Seventh Street, Suite 105
Fort Worth, TX 76102
210-340-1966

The **Rita Levine Memorial Scholarship** is open to a woman returning to school after an absence of seven or more years who is enrolled in a degree program in an accredited United States college or university. Applications are available after October 1.

American Mothers, Inc.

301 Park Avenue
Waldorf-Astoria
New York, NY 10022
212-755-2539

Gertrude Fogelson Cultural and Creative Arts Scholarships are offered annually in the areas of art, literature, and vocals. The awards seek to encourage and honor mothers in their artistic and creative pursuits. Awards range from $100 to $1,000. Call for application information.

American Nuclear Society

555 North Kensington Avenue
LaGrange Park, IL 60526-5592
708-352-0499
http://www.ans.org

The society offers the **Delayed Education Scholarship for Women** to encourage mature women whose undergraduate studies in nuclear science, nuclear engineering, or a nuclear-related field have been delayed or interrupted for at least one year.

American Society of Landscape Architects

Landscape Architecture Foundation
636 I Street, NW
Washington, DC 20001-3736
202-216-2356
http://www.asla.org

The foundation administers a number of scholarships to men and women preparing for careers in landscape architecture. Details are available on the association's Web site. The **Harriett Barnhart Wimmer Scholarship** is a $1,000 scholarship for a woman entering her final year of undergraduate landscape studies who has demonstrated excellence in design ability and sensitivity to the environment. There is no application form. Check the Web site or write the above address for details on what to include in your application.

American Society of Women Accountants

ASWA Headquarters
60 Revere Drive, Suite 500
Northbrook, IL 60062
800-326-2163
http://www.aswa.org

The American Society of Women Accountants awards scholarships annually to women in accounting fields. In a recent year, $16,000 was awarded in one scholarship of $4,500, one scholarship of $3,500, and four scholarships of $2,000 each. Applicants can be part-time or full-time students pursuing a bachelor's or master's degree in accouting. They should have completed a minimum 60 semester hours at an accredited college. Membership in ASWA is not required. Applications are made through a local chapter. Visit the Web site or call for chapter information.

American Statistical Association

Gertrude Cox Scholarship Program
1429 Duke Street
Alexandria, VA 22314
703-684-1221
http://www.amstat.org

The American Statistical Association's Committee on Women in Statistics and the

Financial Aid

Caucus for Women in Statistics established the **Gertrude Cox Scholarship** to encourage more women to enter statistically oriented professions. Scholarships are given in a variety of fields, provided the candidate is admitted to full-time study in a graduate statistical program. Women in or entering the early stages of graduate training (M.S. or Ph.D.) are especially encouraged to apply. The award consists of a certificate and a $1,000 cash prize. Applications are available on ASA's Web site or by mail.

Arizona Association of Family and Consumer Sciences

Webber Educational Grants Committee
4861 North Via Serenidad
Tucson, AZ 85718-5715

The **Benjamin J. and Josephine M. Webber Scholarship Fund** awards seven scholarships to Mexican American bilingual females from Arizona for study in home economics or nutrition.

Association for Women Geoscientists Foundation

c/o G & H Production
518 17th Street, Suite 930
Denver, CO 80202
http://www.awg.org

The foundation offers financial assistance to women in the geosciences who need funding to complete their thesis. The $750 **Chrysalis Scholarship** may be applied to expenses related to typing, drafting, child care, or anything necessary to allow a degree candidate to finish her thesis during the current academic year.

Association for Women in Architecture—Los Angeles

2550 Beverly Boulevard
Los Angeles, CA 90057
213-389-6490
http://www.awa-la.org

AWA-LA awards scholarships annually to women studying architecture, landscape architecture, urban and land planning, interior design, environmental design, or structural, civil, mechanical, or electrical engineering as related to architecture. Students must have completed at least one year in a degree program and be residents of or attending school in California. Application forms are available on the Web site.

Association for Women in Communications—DC Chapter

Box 5465
Washington, DC 20016
202-973-2136
http://www.awc-dc.org

The AWC-DC professional chapter awards a scholarship to a junior or senior female student attending a Washington, DC-area college studying communications, advertising, journalism, public relations, marketing, or graphic arts. The award is $1,000. Applicants should have a 3.0 GPA or higher and have work experience in a communications field.

Association for Women in Science

1200 New York Avenue, NW, Suite 650
Washington, DC 20005
202-326-8940
http://www.awis.org

AWIS fosters the recruitment, retention, and promotion of women in science. The **Dr. Vicki L. Schechtman Scholarship** awards $1,000 to undergraduate women interested in pursuing a career in scientific studies. Preference is given to applicants who wish to pursue research. Must hold a minimum 3.0 GPA. The application is available on the Web site or by requesting one in writing.

Association for Women in Sports Media

PO Box 17536
Fort Worth, TX 76102
612-228-5509
http://users.southeast.net/~awsm

AWSM, an organization that supports women employed in sports writing, editing, broadcast and production, public relations, and sports information offers five annual scholarships.

First place winners in the categories of writing, copy editing, public relations, television, and radio will each receive $1,000. The scholarship is open to any female college or graduate student. Call or write for an application.

Association of Black Women in Higher Education

Delores Smalls
Nassau Community College
One Education Drive
Garden City, NY 11530-6793
516-572-7160

The association awards scholarships to African American women in higher education. Write for complete details.

Association of Black Women Physicians

ABWP Scholarship Committee
Rebecca Lee, MD
4712 Admiralty Way, 175
Marina del Ray, CA 90292

The Association of Black Women Physicians awards $500 to $1,500 scholarships annually to African American female medical students in southern California. Contact the scholarship coordinator, or the University of California—Los Angeles School of Medicine Financial Aid Office at 310-825-4181.

Association of Junior Leagues International

660 First Avenue
New York, NY 10016-3241
212-683-1515
http://www.ajli.org

The Association of Junior Leagues represents local Junior Leagues across the nation. Junior Leagues are largely service organizations, but some offer assistance in adult education, job training, and scholarship assistance to women in need. The Web site lists contact information and links to chapters on the Web.

Association of Universities and Colleges of Canada

C. D. Howe Memorial Awards Program
600-350 Albert Street
Ottawa, Ontario K1R 1B1
613-563-1236
http://www.aauc.ca

The **C. D. Howe Memorial Foundation** offers two scholarships of $6,000, one to a female and one to a male student enrolled in an engineering program at a Canadian university. Awards are renewable twice for a total of three years. This is a merit scholarship awarded to Canadian citizens and is by nomination only. Contact your AAUC or your university's engineering department for nomination information.

Augustus and Kathleen Barrows Memorial Fund

271 South Union Street
Burlington, VT 05401
802-863-4531

Women from Vermont under the age of 25 may apply for one of 27 scholarships of $200 to $400. The Trust Fund is also open to female high school seniors or undergraduate students who are residents of Vermont.

Barbara Alice Mower Memorial Scholarship

c/o Nancy Mower
1536 Kamole Street
Honolulu, HI 96821-1424
808-373-2901

Barbara Alice Mower Memorial Scholarships are available to female residents of Hawaii who are at least juniors in college and can demonstrate strong interest in women's studies and strong commitment to helping women. The stipend ranges from $1,000 to $3,000.

Beta Pi Sigma

PO Box 9112
Inglewood, CA 90305
http://members.aol.com/bpssi/index.html

Beta Pi Sigma is a business and professional sorority. Each of twenty chapters is required to present a scholarship annually. Local awards are presented to graduating high school seniors, with application requirements determined by the local chapter. National scholarships include the **Lucille Ailstock Scholarship** and the **Reynolds-Wallace Founders Award,** both presented to a high school senior with financial need. The **Helen Gaines-Cleatter Saul Memorial Supporting Award** is given to a sophomore enrolled in college full-time and is based on scholastic achievement and financial need.

Black Women Lawyers Association of Greater Chicago

321 South Plymouth Court, Sixth Floor
Chicago, IL 60604
312-554-2088

The BWLA is a professional organization of over 500 African American women lawyers in the Chicago area. BWLA has awarded over $30,000 in scholarships to outstanding Illinois law students. Its high school scholarship program is limited to its mentoring program at Hyde Park Career Academy. Call for information.

Brookhaven Women in Science

Renate W. Chasman Scholarship
PO Box 5000
Upton, NY 11973
516-344-8000

Women who are reentering the educational system are eligible for the $2,000 **Renate W. Chasman Scholarship** to pursue undergraduate or graduate study in engineering, math, or science. The applicant must be a resident of Nassau or Suffolk counties, or Brooklyn or Queens, New York City. Candidates must request an application by mail.

Business and Professional Women's Foundation

ATTN: SCHOLARSHIPS AND LOANS
2012 Massachusetts Avenue, NW
Washington, DC 20036
202-296-9118
http://www.bpwusa.org

The BPW Foundation is a major funder for working women, with hundreds of scholarships offered through local chapters nationwide as well as national scholarships and assistance. Scholarships are awarded to female students 25 and over with critical financial need seeking the education necessary for entry, re-entry, or advancement in the work force. The **Career Advancement Scholarship Program** assists women studying one of several fields, including education. Scholarships ranging from $500 to $1,000 each are awarded for full-time or part-time programs of study. Candidates should request a brochure and application by sending a #10 double-stamped envelope to BPW Foundation headquarters as listed above.

The **Avon Career Empowerment Scholarship,** administered by BPW, offers financial assistance for women on welfare in the Los Angeles area. Forty $500 to $1,500 scholarships have been created by BPW and Avon to support women going from welfare to work. Women living or going to school in the Los Angeles metro area who are looking to end their dependence on welfare are eligible. Applicants must be 25 years or older, U.S. citizens, and currently on welfare or removed from welfare in the last 24 months. Applicants must have plans to enter the workforce after they receive their degree or certificate and be acquiring marketable skills that will increase their economic security. Application materials are available in January only. Contact the BPW Foundation.

The **New York Life Foundation Scholarship,** administered by the BPW Foundation, assists women seeking the education necessary for entry or re-entry into the work force or advancement within the field of health care. A total of $50,000 in scholarships ranging from $500 to $1,000 are awarded annually. Students studying full or part-time at the undergraduate level are eligible. Study at the graduate or doctoral level is not eligible. Send a business-size SASE to the foundation for a brochure and application.

The **Wyeth-Ayerst Scholarship**, administered by the BPW Foundation, seeks to increase the number of women in underrepresented health and health business occupations, especially emerging health fields. Women studying biomedical engineering, biomedical research, medical technology, pharmaceutical marketing, public health, or other emerging fields are eligible for one of 25 $2,000 scholarships. Applicants must be studying full-time at the graduate level. Send a business-sized SASE to the BPW Foundation for a brochure and application.

California Masonic Foundation

Scholarship Committee
1111 California Street
San Francisco, CA 94108-2205
415-776-7000
http://www.freemason.org

The **Amaranth Awards** are offered to high school senior female residents of California who are United States citizens, and who are enrolled or planning to enroll in a 2-4 year postsecondary institution. The stipend is $2,000 to $2,500. Applicants must have a 3.0 GPA or higher and demonstrate financial need.

Canadian Association for Women and Sport

1600 James Naismith Drive
K1B 5N4
Gloucester, Ontario CA
613-748-5793
http://www.caaws.ca

The **Stacey Levitt Women and Sport Scholarship** is open to a young woman, girls' team, or a sport organization that demonstrates a keen interest in sports and a healthy lifestyle, takes the initiative to make positive things happen, is highly motivated and enthusiastic, and strives to be the best and doesn't give up. The $2,500 scholarship is shared by five recipients.

Canadian Congress for Learning Opportunities for Women

Mairi St. John McDonald Scholarship
CCLOW, 27 Follis Avenue
M6G 1S5
Toronto, Ontario CA
416-532-9108
http://www.nald.ca/cclow.htm

The **Mairi St. John MacDonald Scholarship** provides money to help women improve their edu-

cation. Twelve scholarships are awarded annually in various fields.

Canadian Home Economics Association

307-151 Slater Street
K1P 5H3
Ottawa, ONT Canada
613-238-8817
http://www.chea.ca

Canadians who want to study home economics are eligible for a number of scholarships administered by the association. Most are restricted to members. This association is open to men also, but a majority of members are women and many women benefit from the scholarships offered. Write for details.

Center for Work and Service— Wellesley College

Committee on Graduate Fellowships and Scholarships
106 Central Street
Wellesley, MA 02481-8203
781-283-3525
http://www.wellesley.edu/CWS/step2/fell

The **Mary McEwen Schimke Scholarship** is a supplemental award to provide relief from household and child care expenses while pursuing graduate study. Unlike most other Wellesley-affiliated awards, this award is open to women graduates of any American institution for study at any American institution. The candidate must be over 30 years of age and currently engaged in graduate study in literature and/or history, with preference given to American Studies. Awards are up to $1,000. Applications may be found online or by sending a SASE.

Chicana Foundation of Northern California

P.O. Box 27803
Oakland, CA 94602
510-869-3588

The foundation offers scholarships to Hispanic women who have completed 15 semester units with a minimum GPA of 2.5. The applicant must attend school or live in Marin, San Francisco, San Mateo, Alameda, Santa Clara, or Contra Costa counties. Call for information.

Daughters of the American Revolution
1776 D Street, NW
Washington, DC 20006-5303
202-628-1776
http://www.dar.org

The Daughters of the American Revolution is largely a service organization, advancing patriotism and citizenship. There are over 2,975 chapters in the United States. Most chapters offer some type of scholarship and some state DAR organizations sponsor statewide scholarship competitions. Do not call the national office looking for your local chapter. Instead, visit the Web site, which has links to state DAR sites, which in turn list links for local organizations.

Caroline Holt Nursing Scholarships are national scholarships open to undergraduate students enrolled in a nursing program in the United States. Selection criteria include academic standing, financial need, and letters of recommendation. Applicants need not be affiliated with DAR. Enclose a self-addressed, stamped envelope with your inquiry.

Delta Kappa Gamma Society International
PO Box 1589
Austin, TX 78767

The society has over 3,000 chapters in 75 states, with almost every chapter offering these grants to nonmembers in their state or local area. Applicants must be enrolled in college and interested in preparing for a career in education. Award amounts vary from $100 to $1,000 or more a year. Write for details or to find a chapter in your area.

Dialogue on Diversity
1730 K Street, Suite 304
Washington, DC 20006
703-631-0630
http://www.dialogueondiversity.org

Dialogue on Diversity provides opportunities and resources to build the personal and professional strengths of women of ethnically and culturally diverse backgrounds. Dialogue on Diversity sponsors a national scholarship program to serve the educational ambitions of women of ethnically and culturally diverse backgrounds. Scholarships will be offered to student and working professionals in undergraduate and graduate degree programs.

Educational Foundation for Women in Accounting
Administrative Office
P.O. Box 1925
Southeastern, PA 19399-1925
610-407-9229
http://www.efwa.org

The Educational Foundation for Women in Accounting is a joint effort of the American Society of Women Accountants and the American Woman's Society of Certified Public Accountants. The foundation's **Laurels Fund** provides scholarships for advanced degrees in accounting. At least $10,000 is available annually to fund scholarships ranging from $1,250 to $5,000. The **Women in Transition Scholarship** (formerly the Displaced Homemaker Scholarship) is awarded to a "woman in transition" so she may attain a degree in accounting. The annual scholarship of $4,000 is renewable. The foundation also funds undergraduate scholarships administered by the American Society of Women Accountants; $15,000 was available for scholarships in a recent year.

Eleanor Women's Foundation
1550 North Dearborn Parkway
Chicago, IL 60610-1402
312-664-8245

The Eleanor Women's Foundation assists with housing and education for working women and female students over 18 attending a college or vocational program in the Chicago area. Residence with two meals daily is provided six days a week. Call for a tour or an application.

Elizabeth Loudenslager Clark Scholarship for Young Women

First Union National Bank
Charitable Funds Division
600 Cuthber Boulevard
Haddon Township, NJ 08100
856-833-1249

Female residents of Camden, Cape May, Cumberland, Gloucester, and Salem counties who have been admitted to an accredited institution in the United States are eligible to apply for the **Elizabeth Loudenslager Clark Scholarship for Young Women.** The stipend is $4,000. Applications are available through local high school guidance offices.

Epsilon Sigma Alpha Foundation

PO Box 270517
Fort Collins, CO 80527
970-223-2824

The **E. M. Bullock Endowment Award** is available to help a California woman resume her education; candidates need not be ESA members to apply. Two $500 scholarships are offered annually.

ESPN, Inc.

Scholastic Sports America Scholarship
ESPN Plaza
PO Box 986
Bristol, CT 06011

ESPN awards eight scholarships annually, four each to male and female seniors graduating from high school. The scholarships are based on academics and community/school service, and not athletics (although athletics may be considered toward school service). Any field of study is eligible. U.S. citizenship is required. Write for information.

Executive Women International

515 South 700 East, Suite 2F
Salt Lake City, UT 84102
801-355-2800

The **Executive Women International Scholarship Program** awards scholarships for academic excellence to high school juniors who plan to pursue a professional or business degree. Students who live within a chapter's boundaries may compete at the local level and advance to regional and national competition. There are 85 chapters in the United States, Canada, and Europe. Also available is **Adult Students in Scholastic Transition** assistance for women who demonstrate need and a desire to improve their life status through education.

Family, Career, and Community Leaders of America

National Headquarters
1910 Association Drive
Reston, VA 20191-1584
703-476-4900
http://www.fhahero.org

Formerly the Future Homemakers of America, the FCCLA is open to men and women, but family and consumer sciences fields are still predominantly women and many women benefit from the financial assistance offered. Student members of FCCLA are eligible for scholarships through local chapters to help finance study in family and consumer sciences. The Texas chapter offers a Web site with contact information for chapters across the United States.

Financial Women's Association of San Francisco

PO Box 26413
San Francisco, CA 94126
415-333-9045
http://www.fwasf.org

FWASF offers scholarships to women in the Bay Area of California in the fields of finance or accounting. Scholars are honored at a FWASF luncheon and receive a one-year associate membership. Undergraduate scholarships are awarded to juniors and seniors; graduate scholarships are awarded to students in a graduate business program. A minimum GPA of 3.0 and financial need is required. Visit the Web site or call.

Financial Aid

Fourth Tuesday

Pat Hoban Memorial Scholarship
1387 Oxford Road, NE, Suite 801
Atlanta, GA 30307
770-662-4353
http://www.lambda.net/~4thtues/Schol.html

Fourth Tuesday is a social networking organiation for lesbians. The **Pat Hoban Memorial Scholarship** is offered to Atlanta-area lesbians attending an institution of higher education.

General Federation of Women's Clubs

1734 N Street, NW
Washington, DC 20036-2990
202-347-3168
http://www.gfwc.org

GFWC is an international organization of volunteer women's clubs. It offers a variety of scholarships and grants to women seeking to further their education and to needy women. Scholarships and grants are awarded at the local level and the state level, which is called a federation. Visit the national Web site for federation information.

Girl Scouts of America

420 Fifth Avenue
New York, NY 10018-2798
212-852-6548
http://www.girlscouts.org

A considerable number of scholarships are offered to Girl Scouts members at colleges nationwide. Contact your college about any financial aid set aside for Girl Scouts. The Girl Scouts Web site includes a list of more than 50 schools that offer scholarships and grants to Girl Scouts. Nationally, the Girl Scouts **Gold Award** is given to young women who achieve the highest ranking in Girl Scouting. Gold Award recipients are also eligible for special scholarships, including one funded by the Elks National Foundation (call 773-755-4732), which awards $6,000 to a Gold Award winner from each of the eight Girl Scout Service Areas. To apply, contact your Girl Scout Council.

Governor's Opportunity Scholarships

State Capitol, First Floor
Sacramento, CA 95814
http://www.cgcw.ca.gov/

California women are eligible for one of five scholarships to be awarded at the annual California Governor's Conference on Women. **Opportunity Scholarships** of $5,000 apiece will be awarded in each of the following career categories: business, education, health care, law enforcement/public service, and mathematics/science. Awards must be applied toward a program at an accredited California institution. The scholarship application can be found on the governor's Web site or write for an application.

Hispanic Women in Leadership

c/o Scholarship Review Committee
PO Box 701125
Houston, TX 77270-1125
713-450-4582

Hispanic Women in Leadership offers ten scholarships ranging from $500 to $1,000 to Houston area Hispanic women pursuing an education in any career field.

Hispanic Women's Corporation

PO Box 20725
Phoenix, AZ 85036-0725
602-954-7995

The Hispanic Women's Corporation seeks to help Hispanic women achieve educational and career success. The **Hispanic Scholars Program** provides financial support, advice, encouragement, peer contact, and role models. Monetary awards are based on need and range from $300 to $1,000.

Hispanic Women's Council

5803 East Beverly Boulevard
Los Angeles, CA 90022
213-743-2456

The scholarship program of the Hispanic Women's Council provides scholarships on a yearly basis to Hispanic women who demonstrate a need for financial assistance to continue their education. The applicant must be 25 or older and a resident of Los Angeles.

Hispanic Women's Network of Texas
Dallas Chapter
PO Box 516411
Dallas, TX 75251-6411

Scholarships are awarded to participants of HWNT's Education Seminar Series. The series motivates students to continue their education after high school and develop leadership skills. Students in the Dallas area are eligible.

Hitchcock Scholarship Fund
Boston Safe Deposit Company
Trust Department
1 Boston Place
Boston, MA 02108
617-722-7340

The **Susan Glover Hitchcock Scholarship** of $500 to $1,000 is awarded for undergraduate study at a Massachusetts college or university. Female residents who are graduates of Massachusetts high schools are eligible to apply. Recommendation of the music department and financial aid office of the college is required. Write for complete information.

Intel Foundation
Intel Foundation Women in Science and Engineering Scholarships
http://www.intel.lu/intel/community/scholars.htm

The Intel Foundation funds scholarships for undergraduate women enrolled at one of 11 universities. Specified degree programs include electrical engineering, computer engineering, chemical engineering, operations research, applied mathematics, and various computer and science specialties. Scholarships are renewable through the fifth undergraduate year. Scholars are assigned an Intel Mentor for academic and career guidance.

Participating universities include California Institute of Technology, Carnegie Mellon University, Cornell University, Georgia Institute of Technology, Purdue University, Stanford University, University of California at Berkeley, University of Illinois, University of Michigan, University of Texas at Austin, and University of Washington. No mail or phone contact provided; see Web site for information.

International Society of Women Airline Pilots
2250 Tropicana Avenue, Suite 19-395
Las Vegas, NV 89119
http://www.iswap.org

This national organization for women airline pilots offers scholarships for women studying aviation or pilots in training. The **International Career Scholarship** is offered to a woman pilot and is to be used solely for advanced pilot ratings, such as ATP and/or flight engineer rating. The **Fiorenza de Bernardi Merit Scholarship** is for applicants who do not meet the requirements for the International Career Scholarship. It aids pilots endeavoring to fill basic requirements, such as CFI, CFII, or MEI. The **Holly Mullins Memorial Scholarship** is reserved for applicants who are single mothers. Up to five different **Airline Scholarships** are also offered with funds from individual airlines. The number and type of scholarship vary by year. Visit the Web site to download the application or request one by mail.

International Women's Automotive Association—Chicago Chapter
c/o Cindy Henderson, Motive Parts Co.
8226 South 86th Court
Justice, IL 60458

Annual scholarships are available to women enrolled in an accredited university or community college seeking a career in the automotive industry. Write for eligibility requirements.

Iota Sigma Pi
http://chem-faculty.ucsd.edu/sawrey/ISP/awards.html

Iota Sigma Pi, a national honorary society for women chemists, recognizes the achievements of women in chemistry. Membership in Iota Sigma Pi is not necessary. The **Gladys Anderson**

Financial Aid

Emerson Scholarship is awarded to a junior member or to a qualified woman who will be made a member upon applying. The winner must be nominated by an Iota Sigma Pi member. The scholarship is for $1,000.

Jeanette Rankin Foundation

P.O. Box 6653
Athens, GA 30604-6653
http://www.wmst.unt.edu/jrf

The Jeannette Rankin Foundation awards scholarships to women 35 years old or older who are seeking to better themselves, their families, and their communities through undergraduate or vocational education. The applicant must be enrolled in a certified program of technical vocational training or in an undergraduate program. The stipend is $1,000; seven to ten nonrenewable awards are available. Prospective applicants will benefit from reading the biographies of previous winners on the Web site, to understand the level of need required. One thousand applications are received annually and only twenty awards are made. The successful applicant is a very promising student with severe financial need.

John Edgar Thomson Foundation

201 South 18th Street, Suite 318
Philadelphia, PA 19103
215-545-6083

The John Edgar Thomson Foundation offers financial aid and scholarships to girls and women from age 0 to 22 with a parent who is a deceased railroad worker. The cause of death need not be work-related. Eligibility is dependent on the daughter and surviving spouse remaining unmarried.

Junior League of Northern Virginia

Scholarship Committee
7921 Jones Branch Drive, Suite 320
McLean, VA 22102
703-893-0258

The JLNV provides scholarships of $500 to $2,000 to women over the age of 23 who are enrolled in a college or vocational training program in the northern Virginia or Washington metro area. Applicants must demonstrate financial need.

Karla Scherer Foundation

737 North Michigan Avenue, Suite 2330
Chicago, IL 60611
313-259-4520
http://comnet.org/kschererf.index.html

The Karla Scherer Foundation was founded by Karla Scherer, who was "appalled at how badly she was treated" when she led a bitter proxy battle to sell the company her father founded in the 1930s. She resolved to enable more women to attain positions of power in business. Scholarships are available to female students majoring in Finance or Economics with plans for a corporate business career in the private sector. Requests for applications are accepted from high school seniors through Ph.D. candidates. All written inquiries should be accompanied by a SASE. Approximately 25 awards of varying amounts are granted each year.

Latin American Professional Women's Foundation

PO Box 31532
Los Angeles, CA 90031
213-227-9060

The foundation operates a scholarship program and uses role models to provide guidance to young Hispanic women.

Lettie Pate Whitehead Foundation

50 Hurt Plaza, Suite 1200
Atlanta, GA 30303
404-522-6755

The foundation funds scholarships for women at colleges in Alabama, Florida, Georgia, Louisiana, Mississippi, North Carolina, South Carolina, Tennessee, and Virginia. Funds are provided to more than 200 institutions annually. Assistance is provided to undergraduates studying in health fields, especially nursing and allied health fields. Contact your school's financial aid office to see if it is funded.

Mana, A Latina Organization

Scholarships
1725 K Street, NW, Suite 501
Washington, DC 20006
202-833-0060
http://www.hermana.org

The **National MANA Scholarship Endowment** provides financial assistance to talented Hispanic women with records of academic excellence and community service. In addition to several general scholarships, the **Raquel Marquez Frankel Scholarship** is offered to a Hispanic woman studying political science. The **Rita Dimartino Scholarship** assists women studying communications. Write for eligiblity and award details.

Microsoft Corporation

Women's Scholarships
One Microsoft Way
Redmond, WA 98052-6399
http://www.microsoft.com/College/
Scholarship.htm

Microsoft funds scholarships to encourage women to pursue careers in computer science and other related technical fields. Two programs are offered specifically to women. The **Microsoft Women's Technical Scholarship** offers a full-tuition scholarship to one outstanding undergraduate at selected colleges. All recipients of this scholarship will be required to complete a salaried summer internship of 12 weeks at Microsoft Corporation in Redmond, Wash. The **Microsoft National Women's Technical Scholarship** provides five $1,000 awards. Women who are enrolled full-time in undergraduate computer science, computer engineering, or related technical programs, such as math or physics, are eligible for either scholarship. The applicant must have a 3.0 GPA or higher.

Miss America Pageant

2 Ocean Way, Suite 1000
Atlantic City, NJ 08401
609-345-7571
http://missamerica.com

Contestants in the various state and national Miss America competitions receive up to $10 million annually in scholarships at local, state, and national levels. Applicants must be single (never married) females between 17 and 26 who are high school graduates and United States citizens. Contact information for several state and local Miss America programs is on the Web site.

Miss Teen U.S.A.

http://www.missteenusa.com

Applicants for the Miss Teen Scholarship must be at least 15 and under 19 years of age. For complete eligiblity requirements, contact your state director. Contact information for all state directors can be found on the Web site.

Musicians Club of Women

Chicago, IL
http://members.aol.com/_ht?a/mcwomen/
awards.htm

The Musicians Club of Women seeks to discern and encourage talented young women musicians. An annual competition results in several scholarships and awards. Applicants must be between 23 and 30 years of age; living and studying within a 100-mile radius of the Chicago Loop; and a U.S. citizen. Awards are made in instrumental and voice in the following amounts: **Lynne Harvey Scholarship,** $5,000; **Edith Newfield Scholarship,** $3,000; and in alternate years, **Annemarie Gerts Scholarship** of $1,500 and **Louise Hammond Scholarship** of $1,000. Each winner receives a three-year membership in the club and a recital.

National Association of Black Female Executives in Music and Entertainment

http://www.womenet.org

NABFEME awards scholarships to African-American females pursuing a career in broadcasting, recorded music, journalism, and related fields.

National Association of Professional Mortgage Women

PO Box 2016
Edmonds, WA 98020-9516
800-827-3034
http://www.napmw.org

The APMW Foundation provides financial assistance for women in mortgage lending and related fields. Send a SASE or call to request scholarship guidelines.

National Association of Women in Construction

327 South Adams
Fort Worth, TX 76104-1081
817-877-5551
http://www.nawic.org

NAWIC advances the causes of all women in construction whose careers range from business ownership to the skilled trades. The **NAWIC Founders Scholarship** offers awards ranging from $500 to $2,000. The applicant must be enrolled in a construction-related degree program (high school seniors are not eligible), must desire a construction-related field; and must be enrolled full-time with a GPA of 3.0 or higher. Apply online at http://www.fastweb.com or contact NAWIC for an application.

National Chamber of Commerce for Women

10 Waterside Plaza, Suite 6H
New York, NY 10010
212-685-3454

The NCCW awards scholarships and research grants to women engaged in behavioral studies. Scholarships are based on need and applicants must submit a proposal for research that examines organizational behavior or business ethics.

National Council for Geographic Education

Indiana University of Pennsylvania
16A Leonard Hall
Indiana, PA 15705-0001
724-357-6390
http://www.ncge.org

The council offers scholarships to women pursuing undergraduate or graduate degrees in geography. Recipients must be intending a career in teaching and have a 3.0 GPA in their undergraduate program.

National Council of Jewish Women— Greater Boston Section

831 Beacon Street
Newton Centre, MA 02159
617-783-9660

Jewish women who are residents of Boston or the vicinity and attend a Massachusetts college as an undergraduate are eligible for the **Amelia Greenbaum/Rabbi Marshall Lifson Scholarship Program.** Applicants must demonstrate financial need. Priority is given to those returning to school after five or more years of absence. Maximum award is $400. Write for complete information.

National Council of Jewish Women— Los Angeles

213-651-2930
http://www.ncjwla.org

NCJW-LA offers various financial assistance and scholarships to women and others in the Los Angeles area, such as the **Jon Douglas Child Care Subsidy Fund,** for mothers seeking financial self-reliance through education; and the **June Miller Nursing Education Scholarship Fund,** for women seeking a career in nursing.

National Federation of Press Women

PO Box 5556
Arlington, VA 22205
800-780-2715
http://www.nfpw.org

Professional Development Scholarships are awarded to female junior, senior, and graduate students. The **Helen Miller Malloch Scholarship** of $1,000 is provided to women college students who wish to complete communications studies for a degree.

National Federation of Republican Women

Attn: Scholarships
124 North Alfred Street
Alexandria, VA 22314
http://www.nfrw.org

The **National Pathfinder Scholarship** was established in recognition of Nancy Reagan's efforts in the prevention of drug and alcohol abuse. Two $2,000 scholarships are awarded annually to women studying in a related field, such as chemistry, sociology, psychology, or pharmacology, with intended careers in chemical, biological, or medical research, or counseling of addicts and their families. The **Betty Rendel Scholarship** honors a past NFRW president and is awarded to an undergraduate woman majoring in political science, government, or economics. A single $1,000 scholarship is awarded. Applications are available on the NFRW's Web site, or mail your request.

National Federation of the Blind

805 Fifth Avenue
Grinnell, IA 50112
515-236-3366

The **Anne Pekar Memorial Scholarship** is open to legally blind women between the ages of 17 and 25 who are planning to attend college full-time. Award is based on academic excellence, service to the community, and financial need. The **Hermione Grant Calhoun Scholarship** is open to legally blind female undergraduate or graduate students. The award is based on academic excellence, service to the community, and financial need. Write for complete information.

National Italian American Foundation

Scholarship Committee
1860 19th Street, NW
Washington, DC 20009-5599
202-530-5315

Frances Rello Scholarships of $1,000 are open to Italian American women who are studying Italian in college and plan to teach it. The **Agnes E. Vaghi-Cornaro Scholarship** is open to Italian-American women (any major) who are currently enrolled or entering any accredited college or university in the United States. The stipend is up to $2,000. Application information should include a three-page, double-spaced essay on a famous Italian-American woman or a current issue of concern for Italian-American women.

National League of American Pen Women

1300 17th Street, NW
Washington, DC 20036
202-785-1997

Women 35 years old or older may apply for scholarships to support professional development. Women writers, artists, photographers, and composers may apply for the biennial awards of $1,000. Send a SASE for information.

National Research Council of Canada

Human Resources Branch
Montreal Road
Building M58, Room E116
Ottawa, Ontario K1A 0R6
http://www.nrc.ca

Three **NRC Scholarships for Women in Engineering and Science** are awarded by the National Research Council. Scholarships are valued at $10,000 for second-year studies; $12,000 for third-year studies; and $15,000 for fourth-year studies at a Canadian university. The applicant should be a female student enrolled at the undergraduate level in a science or engineering degree program. In addition to financial assistance, recipients will undertake career-related work at the NRC or with one of its partner organizations.

National Society of Professional Engineers

1420 King Street
Alexandria, VA 22314-2794
703-684-2800
http://www.nspe.org

Each year, NSPE awards national scholarships to high school seniors who plan to study engineering in college. Two scholarships are set aside for young women. The **Auxiliary Scholarship** is a $1,000 scholarship renewable once for a total of two years. The **Virginia D.**

Financial Aid

Henry Memorial is awarded in the amount of $1,000 for the freshman year. Both scholarships are for female students studying engineering at an accredited institution and are based solely on achievement.

National Teenager Scholarship Foundation

P.O. Box 610187
Dallas, TX 75261-0187
817-577-2220
http://www.nationalteen.com

All girls who are 12 through 19 years of age are eligible to apply for the **Miss National Teenager Scholarship Program.** Local and state pageants commence in February, and each state winner is selected on the basis of scholastic achievement, leadership, communication skills, and appearance. More than $5 million in cash, tuition scholarships, and awards are presented in the state and regional pageants. Deadline dates vary.

National Women's Studies Association

University of Maryland
7100 Baltimore Avenue, Suite 500
College Park, MD 20740
301-403-0525
http://www.nwsa.org

Financial assistance is available to women whose scholarship will help expand the boundaries and possibilities of women's studies programs. The $500 **NWSA Graduate Scholarship in Lesbian Studies** will be awarded to a student who will be doing research for or writing a master's thesis or Ph.D. dissertation in lesbian studies. The $500 **Scholarship in Jewish Women's Studies** will be given to a graduate student whose area of research is Jewish women's studies.

NCAA Women's Enhancement Program

Scholarship Coordinator
6201 College Boulevard
Overland Park, KS 66211-2422
913-339-1906
http://www.ncaa.org

The NCAA Women's Enhancement Program was established to increase the pool of qualified women candidates in coaching, athletics administration, officiating, and support services. Ten postgraduate scholarships are available annually for female college graduates who have been accepted into a sports administration or related program. Scholarships are $6,000 each. For application information, write or call.

Network of Executive Women in Hospitality

800-593-NEWH
http://www.newh.org

NEWH is a professional organization for women in all facets of the hospitality industry. It offers scholarships and student competitions to encourage students to pursue careers in hospitality, and provides financial support and recognition for young women entering the hospitality industry.

Nevada Women's Fund

P.O. Box 50428
Reno, NV 89513
775-786-2335

The **Constance H. Bishop Scholarship** is open to women in Nevada who are studying on the undergraduate level. The stipend is $1,500.

E. J. Cord Foundation Scholarship/Fellowships are open to women in Nevada who are studying on the undergraduate or graduate level. Applications are encouraged from workforce re-entry women and women who are single parents. The stipends range from $500 to $3,000.

The **Mary Davis Spirit of Enterprise Scholarship** is open to women studying on the undergraduate level in Nevada. The stipend is $1,000.

Feltner Family Scholarships are open to women studying on the undergraduate level in Nevada. The stipend is $1,500.

The **Friends of the Fund Scholarship** is open to women studying on the undergraduate level in Nevada. The stipend is $3,000.

The **Martha H. Jones Scholarship** is open to women from Nevada who are preparing for a medical career and who are working on a medical degree. The stipend is $1,500. Recipients may attend school outside the state.

Charlotte L. Mackenzie Scholarships are open to women in Nevada who are studying on the undergraduate level. The stipend is $5,000.

New Mexico Educational Assistance Foundation
3900 Osuna, NE
Albuquerque, NM 87125-7020
505-345-3371

To increase the number of ethnic minorities and women teaching engineering, physical or life sciences, and mathematics, residents of New Mexico pursuing a doctoral degree in an out-of-state institution are eligible for financial assistance. Graduate fellowships of up to $7,000 are available to minority or female residents of New Mexico pursuing degrees in computer science, mathematics, and engineering.

Northern Nevada Women Lawyers Association
co/ Debra Robinson
499 West Plumb Lane, Suite 4
Reno, NV 89509
775-334-1400
http://www.nnwla.org

The Northern Nevada Women Lawyers Association offers the **NNWLA Annual Scholarship Award** in the amount of $1,000 to a senior undergraduate or graduate student female attending an ABA-accredited Nevada law school. Visit the Web site for current scholarship information.

Odwalla, Inc.
Femme Vitale Scholarship Award
120 Stone Pine Road
Half Moon Bay, CA 94109
800-ODWALLA
http://www.odwalla.com

Women who are preparing for a career in health or nutrition are eligible for one of four **Femme Vitale Scholarship Awards.** Awards range from $1,000 to $4,000. Applicants must live in a state where Odwalla Juice is sold, including AZ, CA, CO, IL, LA, MD, MI, MN, NV, NJ, NM, OR, PA, TX, UT, WI, VA, WA, and the District of Columbia. Financial need is also considered. For details, send a stamped, self-addressed envelope with your request.

Ohio Newspaper Women's Association
840 Shroyer Road 1
Dayton, OH 45419

The Ohio Newspaper Women's Association offers four scholarships to Ohio women entering their junior or senior year at an accredited Ohio school of journalism. Recipients must promise to work on an Ohio newspaper one year after graduation.

Oregon State Scholarship Commission
Office of Scholarships and Awards
1500 Valley River Drive, Suite 100
Eugene, OR 97401
800-452-8807
http://www.ossc.state.or.us

The **Dorothy Campbell Memorial Scholarship** is offered to female Oregon high school graduates with a 2.75 GPA or better. An essay about the applicant's strong continuing interest in golf is required, but the scholarship is awarded for general studies.

Organization of Chinese Americans
Avon College Scholarship
1001 Connecticut Avenue, NW, Suite 707
Washington, DC 20036
202-223-5500
http://www.ocanatl.org

Financial Aid

The Organization of Chinese Americans has been provided funding from the **Avon Foundation** to fund college scholarships for Asian-Pacific-American women who will be entering their first year of college. In a recent year, eighteen $1,000 scholarships were awarded. The applicant should be an Asian-Pacific-American woman with financial need and a 3.0 or higher GPA, and a U.S. citizen. An application is available on the Web site or by sending a SASE.

P.E.O. Sisterhood
3700 Grand Avenue
Des Moines, IA 50312-2899
515-255-3153
http://www.peointernational.org

Female residents of California seeking a degree in medicine, and who have completed the first year of graduate work may apply for the **Ruth G. White Scholarship.** Awards are based on character, integrity, academic excellence, and financial need. Write to the committee chairwoman, stating your year in school and requesting an application.

P.E.O. Peace Scholarships are offered to female master's or doctoral students in business, education, health, science, math, and engineering. Applicants must be citizens of countries other than the United States or Canada and must have a sponsor who is a U.S. or Canadian citizen, who will act as their nonacademic adviser. The maximum amount awarded is $5,000. Funds may be used for research costs, living expenses, and/or tuition and fees in the United States or Canada. Recipients must agree to return to their home country to pursue their careers.

Professional Black Women's Enterprise
Lena Gibbs Greenwood Scholarship Award
2425 West Loop South, Suite 200
Houston, TX 77027
http://www.pbwe.org

PBWE awards four $1,500 scholarships annually to assist young black women in attaining a college degree. Two of the four scholarships will be awarded to two graduating seniors, one scholarship to a second-year college student, and one to a participant of the Fresh Start Sisterhood program (a PBWE welfare-to-work program). Applicants must be full-time students with a GPA of 3.0 or above. All fields of study are eligible. Visit the Web site for details or write to request application information.

Project for Homemakers in Arizona Seeking Employment (Phase)
1230 North Park Avenue
Tucson, AZ 85721
520-621-3902

PHASE offers scholarships of up to $1,000 to women who have completed basic vocational training and who need some additional education before entering the job market. Special targets of this program are women who are single parents. PHASE promotes the hiring and retention of women in non-traditional employment.

Rachel Royston Permanent Scholarship Foundation
Alpha Sigma State, Washington
PO Box 111595
Tacoma, WA 98411-1595

Scholarships are available to women educators who are residents of Washington State pursuing a master's or doctoral degree. Award amounts range from $500 to $2,000.

Romanian Orthodox Episcopate of America
A.R.F.O.R.A. Scholarship
PO Box 309
Grass Lake, MI 49240-0809
http://www.roea.org

Women who are members of a parish under the jurisdiction of the Romanian Orthodox Episcopate of America are eligible for the **A.R.F.O.R.A. Undergraduate Scholarship for Women.** Candidates must have completed their first year of college, and must include a letter projecting their plans and church and community involvement with their application.

Scripps College

Office of Financial Aid
1030 Columbia Avenue
Claremont, CA 91711
714-721-2233

James Scripps Scholarships of $7,000 to $10,000 and **Dean's Awards** of $4,000 are offered at this small liberal arts college for women. Write for details.

Sigma Alpha Iota Philanthropies

34 Wall Street, Suite 515
Asheville, NC 28801-2710
828-251-0606
http://www.sai-national.org

The national organization offers awards in the field of music to non-SAI members as well as the many awards available to members. Awards available to non-members include a series of $500 scholarships for summer study at institutions such as the Aspen Music Festival, Chautauqua Summer Insitition, and Sewanee Music Center. Awards are for vocal, piano, and instrumental.

Society of Daughters of Holland Dames

c/o Mrs. Barbara Harness
17 Stevens Street
Bernardsville, NJ 07924
212-870-2347

Awards are open to women of Dutch descent to help them finish their junior or senior year of college.

Society of Daughters of the United States Army

Scholarship Committee
4242 East-West Highway, Suite 910
Chevy Chase, MD 20815

The society offers scholarships to the daughters, adopted daughters, stepdaughters, and granddaughters of United States Army Commissioned and Warrant Officers who are currently on active duty, retired after twenty years of active duty or for medical reasons, or deceased. The amount of the award is a maximum of $750.

The **Margaret M. Prickett Scholarship Fund** offers a scholarship to a daughter, stepdaughter, adopted daughter, or granddaughter of a United States Army Commissioned or Warrant Officer who is on active duty, retired after at least twenty years of active duty or for medical reasons, or deceased. The amount of the award is $1,000.

The **Eugenia Bradford Roberts Memorial Fund** offers scholarships to a daughter, stepdaughter, adopted daughter, or granddaughter of a United States Army Commissioned or Warrant Officer who is on active duty, retired after at least twenty years of active duty or for medical reasons, or deceased. The amount of the award is $1,000.

The **Colonel Hayden W. Wagner Memorial Fund** offers scholarships to a daughter, stepdaughter, adopted daughter, or granddaughter of a United States Army Commissioned or Warrant Officer who is on active duty, retired after at least twenty years of active duty or for medical reasons, or deceased. The amount of the award is $1,000.

Society of Women Engineers

120 Wall Street, 11th Floor
New York, NY 10005-3902
212-509-9577
http://www.swe.org

SWE administers approximately 90 scholarships annually, ranging from $200 to over $5,000. All SWE scholarships are open only to women majoring in engineering or computer science in a college or university with an accredited program. Applicants for sophomore, junior, senior, and graduate scholarships must have a grade point average of 3.5 or above. Various scholarships have additional specific requirements as listed below. Applications can be obtained through the engineering departments of eligible schools or from SWE headquarters, accompanied by a SASE. A general application form is available on SWE's Web site.

Freshman scholarships are as follows: **Chrysler Corporation Scholarship,** two $1,500 awards to students majoring in engineering or computer science; **Admiral Grace Murray Hopper Scholarships,** five $1,000 awards for women studying computer engineering or computer science in any form of a four-year program; **Northrop Grumman Scholarships,** one $1,500 and two $1,000 scholarships to students majoring in engineering or computer science.

Sophomore, Junior and Senior Scholarships: **Central Intelligence Agency Scholarship,** one $1,000 award to an entering sophomore student majoring in electrical engineering or computer science; **Chrysler Scholarship,** one $1,750 scholarship to an entering sophomore, junior, or senior woman who is a member of an under-represented group in engineering or computer science; **Lillian Moller Gilbreth Scholarship,** one $5,000 scholarship to an engineering or computer science student of outstanding potential and achievement entering her junior or senior year; **GTE Foundation Scholarships,** nine $1,000 awards for sophomore or junior women majoring in electrical engineering or computer science; **Dorothy Lemke Howarth Scholarships,** five $2,000 awards for engineering or computer science students entering their sophomore year. U.S. citizens only: **MASWE Scholarships,** two $2,000 and one $1,000 scholarship by the Men's Auxiliary of SWE to engineering or computer science students entering sophomore, juniors, or seniors; **Microsoft Scholarships,** ten $1,000 awards to sophomore, junior, or senior students in computer science or computer engineering; **Ivy Parker Scholarship,** one $2,000 scholarship to an engineering or computer science junior or senior with financial need; **Rockwell International Scholarships,** two $3,000 scholarships to minority women entering junior year in engineering or computer science; **David Sarnoff Research Center Scholarship,** one $1,500 award to a woman engineering or computer science student who is a U.S. citizen entering her junior year; **Stone and Webster Scholarships,** one $1,500 award and three $1,000 awards to sophomore, junior, or senior engineering or computer science students.

Graduate Scholarships: **Microsoft Scholarships,** ten $1,000 scholarships to entering master's students in computer science or computer engineering.

Re-entry Scholarships (for women who have been out of the engineering job market as well as out of school for two years or more): **Olive**

Lynn Salembier Scholarship, one $2,000 award for a student entering undergraduate or graduate level as a full- or part-time student; **B. K. Krenzer Memorial Scholarship,** one $1,000 award to degreed engineers desiring to return to the workforce after temporary retirement; for undergraduate or graduate, full- or part-time; **Chrysler Re-entry Scholarship,** one $2,000 scholarship to an engineering or computer science student.

Sociologists for Women in Society

Barbara Rosenblum Scholarship Committee
Department of Sociology
San Francisco State University
San Francisco, CA 94132
http://socsci.colorado.edu/sws/sws.html

The **Barbara Rosenblum Scholarship** encourages doctoral research in sociology, anthropology, psychology, and related fields on women's experience of breast cancer and other reproductive cancers and the prevention of these cancers. The applicant must be a woman with a feminist orientation with approval of prospectus for doctoral research that will be useful not only academically but also practically. The award is $1,500 to support any aspect of research or publication and presentation of results.

Sons of Norway Foundation

Nancy Lorraine Jensen Memorial Scholarship Fund
1455 West Lake Street
Minneapolis, MN 55408
http://www.sonf.com

Women between the ages of 17 and 35 who are members or are the daughters or granddaughters of members of the Sons of Norway, or current employees or daughters or granddaughters of employees of the NASA Goddard Space Center are eligible for a scholarship. The applicant must be studying chemistry, physics, or chemical, electrical, or mechanical engineering at the undergraduate level.

Theodora Bosanquet Bursary Fund

26 Moorfield
Canterbury, Kent CT2 7AN, England

Female undergraduate or graduate students from any country are eligible for research scholarships to travel to London for a month to pursue research in English literature or history. Scholarships provide room and board; write for further information.

Transportation Clubs International

7116 Stinson Avenue, NW, Suite B315
Gigs Harbor, WA 98335
253-858-8627
http://www.trans-clubs.org

TCI awards several scholarships to students enrolled in an accredited institution of higher learning in a vocational or degree program in the fields of transportation logistics or traffic management. The **Hooper Memorial Scholarship** is a $1,500 award offered annually, in memory of the founder of the first Women's Transportation Club in the U.S.

Uncommon Legacy Foundation

150 West 26th Street, Suite 602
New York, NY 10001
212-366-6507
http://www.uncommonlegacy.org

Uncommon Legacy is a foundation that seeks to enhance the strength and vitality of the lesbian community. It awards $1,000 scholarships to outstanding lesbian undergraduate and graduate full-time students. The applicant must have a GPA of 3.0 or better, demonstrate a commitment or contribution to the lesbian community, and demonstrate financial need. A scholarship application is available on the Web site, or by calling.

Union College

ACSEE Scholarship Director
EE/CS Department
Schenectady, NY 12308
518-388-6326
http://doc.union.edu/acsee.html

The **Advancement in Computer Science and Electrical Engineering Scholarship** seeks to increase the pool of women and minorities in electrical engineering and computer science careers. Scholarships of $4,000 per year are awarded annually to high school senior women or minorities who have a 3.0 GPA or better and have demonstrated high achievement in math and science courses. Financial need must be demonstrated. U.S. citizenship is not required. For an application, send a full postal address to the above address.

United Methodist Church

Office of Scholarships
P.O. Box 871
Nashville, TN 37202
615-340-7344

The **Esther Edwards Graduate Scholarship** of $5,000 is awarded to female administrative or faculty members pursuing an advanced degree that will provide the basis for a leadership role at a United Methodist-related college or university. Applicants must be active members of the United Methodist Church for at least one year.

United States Tax Court

Edith Seville Coale, M.D., Scholarships
Scholarship Committee
400 2nd Street, NW, Room 332
Washington, DC 20217

The **Edith Seville Coale, M.D., Scholarship** is offered to women medical students attending schools in the Washington, DC, area. Awards range from $500 to $2,000. Write for application information.

Van Wert County Foundation

138 East Main Street
Van Wert, OH 45891
419-238-1743
http://www.vanwert.com/foundation/

Women from Van Wert and Paulding counties are eligible for **Eirich Scholarships** of $200 to $1,000. They must have a 3.0 GPA. Priority is given to those planning to enroll for undergraduate study in agriculture or home economics at either the University of Michigan or Ohio Wesleyan University.

Virginia Association of Female Executives

P.O. Box 3308
Reston, VA 20195-1308
703-476-0089
http://orgs.womenconnect.com/vafe/

The VAFE offers scholarships of up to $1,000 to help women from northern Virginia who show financial need and who plan a college program leading to a career in executive management.

Washington Fashion Group

Scholarship Committee
P.O. Box 50139
Washington, DC 20004

Scholarships of up to $3,000 are open to women from the Greater Washington area to help finance study leading to a career in fashion. Applications are due in April.

Wellesley College

Committee on Graduate Fellowships and Scholarships
Center for Work and Service
106 Central Street
Wellesley, MA 02481-8203
781-283-3525

The **Mary McEwen Schimke Scholarship** is a supplemental award to provide relief from household and child care expenses while pursuing graduate study. Unlike most other Wellesley-affiliated awards, this award is open to women graduates of any American institution for study at any American institution. The candidate must be over 30 years of age and currently engaged in graduate study in literature and/or history, with preference given to American Studies. Awards are up to $1,000. Applications can be found online.

Whirly Girls

Executive Director
PO Box 7446
Menlo Park, CA 94026-7446
http://www.whirlygirls.org

The **Whirly Girls Scholarship Fund** provides assistance to women helicopter pilots and pilots in training. The $4,500 **Whirly Girls Helicopter Flight Training Scholarship** assists a rated woman pilot in earning her add-on training. Several other scholarships are awarded to Whirly Girls members.

Women Band Directors International, Inc.

2501 Madison Street
Waukesha, WI 54188
262-549-3227

Women enrolled in a college program and working toward a degree in music education with the intent of becoming a band director are eligible for one of five scholarships. Write for an application.

Women Basketball Coaches Association

WBCA
4646 Lawrenceville Highway
Lilburn, GA 30047-3620
770-279-8027
http://www.wbca.org

The **Charles T. Stoner Law Scholarship** is a $500 scholarship offered to a woman collegiate basketball player who intends to pursue a career in law. Female basketball players in all five intercollegiate divisions are eligible. The **WBCA Scholarship Award** is presented annually to two women's basketball players who have demonstrated outstanding commitment to the sport and academic excellence. Female basketball players in all five intercollegiate divisions are eligible for the $1,000 award.

Women Executives in Public Relations

P.O. Box 609
Westport, CT 06881
203-226-4947
http://www.wepr.org

The **WEPR Foundation Scholarship Assistance Program** offers scholarships to deserving senior students majoring in public relations. Many past winners have been members of the Public Relations Students Society of America (PRSSA), but membership is not a requirement.

Women in Aviation International

3647 S.R. 503 S
West Alexandria, OH 45381
937-839-4647
http://www.wiai.org

Women in Aviation awarded $380,000 in scholarships to 38 women in a recent year. Selection factors include achievements, attitude toward self and others, commitment to success, dedication to career, financial need, motivation, reliability, responsibility, and teamwork. Scholarships are awarded in flight training (private pilot, flight instructor, type ratings), maintenance, and aviation management. The scholarships are funded by commercial airlines, organizations, and individuals. Some recipients are also offered interview dates with a major airline.

Women in Defense

Horizons Foundation
2111 Wilson Boulevard, Suite 400
Arlington, VA 22201-3061
703-247-2552
http://www.adpa.org/wid/default.hm

The **Horizons Scholarship Program** provides scholarships of at least $500 to assist individuals either employed or planning careers in the defense or national security areas. The applicant must be currently enrolled, either full- or part-time; have financial need; demonstrate an interest in national security; have a minimum GPA of 3.25; and be a U.S. citizen. Both undergraduate and graduate students are eligible; undergraduates must be at least juniors. Law, international relations, political science, physics, operations research, mathematics, engineering, computer science, operations research, business, and economics are among the fields preferred. Others will be considered if the candidate can demonstrate relevance to a career in the areas of national security or defense.

Women in Management

30 North Michigan Avenue
Chicago, IL 60602
http://www.opri.com/WIM/

The Chicago chapter of Women in Management offers a **Returning Scholar Scholarship** to a woman over 25 returning to higher education. A scholarship is also offered to a woman high school graduate entering college for the first time. In a recent year, both awards were $1,000. Applicants should be from the Chicago area.

Women in Mining

1801 Broadway, Suite 760
Denver, CO 80202
303-298-1535
http://www.womeninmining.org

The WIM Foundation provides technical education and scientific programs, conducts field trips and seminars, and bestows annual scholarships to upper-level undergraduates enrolled in a mineral engineering degree program. Write for further information.

Women in Wireless Communications

c/o Allen Telecom, Inc.
30500 Bruce Industrial Parkway
Solon, OH 44139
http://www.wiwc.org

Women in Wireless Communications provides a minimum $500 scholarship to assist a women in the wireless communications industry. The applicant must be enrolled in a college or technical program working toward a degree in a wireless industry related field and have a 3.0 GPA.

Women International Publishing

PMB 327
91-590 Farrington Highway, Suite 210
Kapolei, HI 96707-2002
http://www.womentakecontrol.com

Women International Publishing is an independent publishing company that publishes and promotes books and information that improve women's economic and personal well-being. It offers the **Women Opportunity Scholarship,** designed to promote higher education for young women who excel academically and positively impact their community. Applicants must be U.S. citizens and high school seniors who will enter college or vocational school full-time. The number of scholarships awarded is dependent on the company's book sales.

Women Marines Association

9608 North May Avenue, Box 265
Oklahoma City, OK 73120-2798
http://www.womenmarines.org

Women Marines Association Scholarships are available to women who have at least a 3.0 GPA during the last three years of high school. Applicants must be sponsored by a member of the Women Marines Association who has been a member for at least two years. The amount of the scholarship is $500. The organization will not give out members' names by request. The applicant must be acquainted with the member herself.

Women of the Evangelical Lutheran Church of America

8765 West Higgins Road
Chicago, IL 60631-4189
800-638-3522
http://www.elca.org/wo/

Women of the ELCA offers several scholarships to women who are members of a congregation of the Evangelical Lutheran Church of America. The **Kahler-Vickers/Raup-Emma Wettstein Scholarship** assists ELCA women studying for service in health professions associated with ECLA projects abroad. The applicant must be a U.S. citizen, church member, at least 21 years old, and have experienced an interruption in education of two or more years since the completion of high school. Request an application through a link on the Web site or by mail.

The **Herbert and Corrine Chilstrom Scholarship** provides assistance to Lutheran women who are second-career students preparing for the ordained ministry at Evangelical Lutheran Church of America Seminaries. The applicant must be a U.S. citizen, have experienced an interruption in education of at least five years since college graduation, be a student in the master of divinity program at an ELCA seminary, and be a member of the ELCA. Request an application through a link on the Web site or by mail.

Minority women who wish to continue their education after an interruption may apply for the **Amelia Kemp Scholarship** for up to $2,000. The applicant must be a U.S. citizen, enrolled in undergraduate, graduate, or professional study, at least 21 years old, and a member of the Evangelical Lutheran Church of America. Women studying church-certified professions are not eligible. Request an application through a link on the Web site or by mail.

Women Peace Officers Association of California

39525 Los Alamos Road, Suite A
Murrieta, CA 92563

The **WPOA of California Scholarship** is open to members and non-members. The applicant must be an active peace officer in California. For an application, write the scholarship commitee.

Women's Jewelry Association

333 B. Route 46 West
Suite B201
Fairfield, NJ 07004
973-575-7190
http://www.womensjewelry.org

The **WJA Scholarship Program** provides annual awards for women based on juried applications. The program is funded by individuals and corporations in the jewelry industry.

Women's Overseas Service League

PO Box 39058
Friendship Station
Washington, DC 20009
714-380-7484

Women's Overseas Service League provides scholarship assistance to women who are committed to advancement in military or other public service careers and have completed 12 semester hours with a 2.5 GPA in a degree-granting program.

Women's Sports Foundation

Eisenhower Park
East Meadow, NY 11554
800-227-3988
http://www.womenssportsfoundation.org

The Women's Sports Foundation, a national organization that supports women and girls in sports, offers several scholarships. The **Dorothy Harris College Scholarship** assists women graduate students in physical education, sport management, sport psychology, or sport sociology.

The **Mervyn's/Women's Sports Foundation College Scholarship** provides female high school student-athletes with a means to continue their athletic participation as well as their college education. One hundred $1,000 scholarships are awarded annually.

The **Gart Sports Sportmart/Women's Sports Foundation Scholarship** provides female high school student-athletes with a means to continue athletic participation as well as a college education. Eight $5,000 scholarships are awarded annually.

The **Linda Riddle/SGMA College Scholarship** provides young women athletes of limited financial means the opportunity to continue to pursue their sport as well as attend college. Details are available on the Web site or by calling.

Women's Transportation Seminar

One Walnut Street
Boston, MA 02108-3616
617-367-3273
http://www.wtsnational.org

This national organization for women working in the field of transportation offers scholarships to encourage women to pursue careers in transportation. The **Helene Overly Scholarship** of $3,000 is awarded to a graduate student. The **WTS Chapters' Undergraduate Scholarship** is awarded to undergraduate students. Both scholarships are competitive and based on the applicants' transportation goals, academic record, and transportation-related activities or job skills. Applicants must have a 3.0 GPA and be enrolled in a transportation-related field such as engineering, planning, finance, or logistics. Visit the Web site for application and local chapter information.

Women's Western Golf Association Foundation

PO Box 85
Golf, IL 60029
800-753-WWGA
http://www.mcs.net/~wwga/

The WWGA seeks to advance women in scholastic achievement and intercollegiate golf. The Women's Western Golf Foundation offers scholarships for female high school seniors who plan to attend college and are involved in the sport of golf. A GPA of 3.5 or higher is required; level of skill in golf is not a criterion. Contact the WWGA in writing for an application.

Young American Bowling Alliance

Alberta E. Crowe Star of Tomorrow Scholarship
5301 South 76th Street
Greendale, WI 53129

The **Alberta E. Crowe Star of Tomorrow $4,000 scholarship** is open to women who are amateur bowlers and members in good standing of YABA or the Women's International Bowling Congress. The applicant must be 22 or younger and a senior in high school or attending college.

Financial Aid

Zeta Phi Beta Sorority

1734 New Hampshire Avenue, NW
Washington, DC 20009
202-387-3103
http://www.zpb1920.org

The sorority awards scholarships and fellowships to women who are not members, as well as several to ZPB members. The **Lullelia W. Harrison Scholarship in Counseling** is offered to a graduate or undergraduate woman pursuing a degree in counseling and/or guidance services.

The **Isabel M. Herson Scholarship in Education** is offered to any graduate or undergraduate woman pursuing a degree in education, either elementary, secondary, or post-secondary. Write to obtain a copy of guidelines and applications.

Zonta International Foundation

557 West Randolph Street
Chicago, IL 60661-2206
312-930-5848
http://www.zonta.org

The **Jane M. Klausman Women in Business Scholarship** program was established to encourage undergraduate women to enter careers and seek leadership positions in business-related fields. Any woman who is enrolled in the second or third year of a business-related undergraduate degree program during the current school year is eligible to enter the competition. The program operates at the club, district, and international levels. Applications of club winners are forwarded to the district level. District winners are selected and receive $400 and advance to the international level. International winners receive a $4,000 scholarship. Application information is available on the Web site, or by contacting your local club.

Section B
Organizations

A wide range of organizations make up Section B. All work on behalf of women, but their structure, goals, services, and activities vary greatly. In addition to being women-oriented, organizations selected for listing in this directory also were required to have a career or educational focus.

Commissions

Commissions are created by government to improve the status of women and to work toward equality and justice for all women. The National Association of Commissions for Women is an umbrella organization for government-sanctioned regional, state, county, and local commissions across the United States. These commissions have been created by law and are service delivery organizations with a grassroots network of volunteers. Commissions act as information and referral resources for women in employment and education, as well as domestic violence, health, and child care. The National Association of Commissions for Women (NACW) can be reached at 8630 Fenton Street, Silver Spring, MD 20910-3808. Telephone: 301-585-8101. Internet: http://www.nacw.org.

Alabama

Alabama Women's Commission
200 South Franklin Drive
Troy, AL 36081-4508
205-566-8744

Alaska

Anchorage Women's Commission
Municipality of Anchorage
PO Box 196650
Anchorage, AK 99519-6650
907-343-6310

Juneau Women's Council
155 South Seward
Juneau, AK 99801
907-586-5257

Arizona

Phoenix Women's Commission
Equal Opportunity Department-Human Resources
251 West Washington, Seventh Floor
Phoenix, AZ 85003-6211
602-261-8242

Organizations

Pima County/Tucson Women's Commission
240 North Court Avenue
Tucson, AZ 85701
520-624-8318

California

Alameda County Commission on the Status of Women
22225 Foothill Boulevard, Suite 4
Hayward, CA 94541-2713
510-670-5743

Berkeley Commission on the Status of Women
2180 Milvia Street, Fourth Floor
Berkeley, CA 94704
510-644-6080

California Commission on the Status of Women
1303 J Street, Suite 400
Sacramento, CA 95814-2900
916-445-3173

City of San Diego Commission on the Status of Women
202 C Street, Eleventh Floor
San Diego, CA 92101
619-236-7072

Compton Commission for Women
205 South Willowbrook Avenue
Compton, CA 90220
310-605-5590

Concord Status of Women Committee
City of Concord
1950 Parkside Drive
Concord, CA 94520
510-671-3374

Contra Costa County Women's Advisory Committee
20 Allen Street
Martinez, CA 94553
510-370-5056

El Dorado County Commission on the Status of Women
901 H Street, Suite 310
Sacramento, CA 95814
916-444-7486

Fresno City/County Commission on the Status of Women
Human Resources Department
2600 Fresno Street
Fresno, CA 93721-3650
209-431-9107

Humboldt County Commission on the Status of Women
County Courthouse
825 Fifth Street
Eureka, CA 95501
707-445-6395

Los Angeles City Commission on the Status of Women
City Hall East, Room 700
200 North Main Street
Los Angeles, CA 90012
213-485-6533

Los Angeles County Commission for Women
500 West Temple Street, Room 383
Los Angeles, CA 90012
213-974-1455

Lynwood City Women's Commission
11330 Bullis Road
Lynwood, CA 90262
310-603-0220

Marin County Commission on the Status of Women
3501 Civic Center Drive, Room 403
San Rafael, CA 94903
415-499-6195

Mendocino County Commission on the Status of Women
150 North McPherson Street
Fort Bragg, CA 95437
707-961-0326

Napa County Commission on the Status of Women
1820 Jefferson Street
Napa, CA 94558
707-253-6272

Pasadena City Commission on the Status of Women
Security Pacific Building
234 East Colorado Boulevard, Suite 205
Pasadena, CA 91101
626-744-6940

Riverside County Commission for Women
4080 Lemon Street, First Floor
Riverside, CA 92501-3851
909-275-5493

San Bernadino County Commission on the Status of Women
157 West Fifth Street
San Bernadino, CA 92415-0400
909-387-5543

San Diego County Commission on the Status of Women
591 Camino de la Reina, Suite 620
San Diego, CA 92108
619-296-7341

San Francisco Commission on the Status of Women
25 Van Ness Avenue, Room 130
San Francisco, CA 94102
415-252-2570

Santa Monica Commission on the Status of Women
1685 Main Street, Room 212
Santa Monica, CA 90401
310-458-8701

Sonoma County Commission on the Status of Women
2300 County Center Drive, Suite B-167
Santa Rosa, CA 95403
707-527-2693

Stanislaus County Commission for Women
P.O. Box 4254
Modesto, CA 95352
209-524-3987

Ventura County Commission for Women
505 Poli Street
Code: 4400
Ventura, CA 93001
805-652-7611

Colorado

Denver Women's Commission
303 West Colfax Avenue, Suite 1600
Denver, CO 80204
303-640-3955

Fort Collins City Commission on the Status of Women
Human Resources
P.O. Box 580
Fort Collins, CO 80522
970-221-6535

Connecticut

Bridgeport Permanent Commission on the Status of Women
Office of the Mayor
45 Lyon Terrace
Bridgeport, CT 06604
203-576-7201

Connecticut Permanent Commission on the Status of Women
18-20 Trinity Street
Hartford, CT 06106-1628
860-240-8300
http://www.cga.state.ct.us/PCSW/

Danbury Commission on the Status of Women
City Hall
155 Deer Hill Avenue
Danbury, CT 06810
203-797-4511

Organizations

Norwalk Commission on the Status of Women

62 William Street
Norwalk, CT 06851
203-226-1206

Permanent Commission on the Status of Hartford Women

550 Main Street, Room 5
Hartford, CT 06103-2913
860-543-8595

Delaware

Delaware Commission for Women

4425 North Market Street, Fourth Floor
Wilmington, DE 19802
302-761-8005

District of Columbia

DC Commission for Women

1366 Barnaby Terrace, SE
Washington, DC 20032
202-833-6917

Florida

Brevard County Commission on the Status of Women

2725 Judge Fran Jamieson Way B
Melbourne, FL 32940
407-633-2007

Broward County Commission on the Status of Women

Human Services Department
Governmental Center
115 South Andrews Avenue, Room 433
Fort Lauderdale, FL 33301
954-357-6399

City of South Miami Commission for Women

1501 Venera, #213
Coral Gables, FL 33146
305-666-5319

Commission on the Status of Women Advisory Committee—Manatee County

Bradenton Academy
6210 17th Avenue West
Bradenton, FL 34209
813-748-0137

Duval County Mayor's Commission on the Status of Women

117 West Duval Street, Suite M100
Jacksonville, FL 32202
904-630-1650

Florida Commission on the Status of Women

Office of the Attorney General
The Capitol
Tallahassee, FL 32399-1050
850-414-3300

Miami Beach Commission on the Status of Women

4410 Alton Road
Miami Beach, FL 33140
305-672-4287

Miami City Commission on the Status of Women

2600 South Bayshore Drive, Second Floor
Miami, FL 33133
305-579-3473

Miami-Dade County Commission for Women

111 Northwest First Street, Suite 660
Miami, FL 33128-1989
305-375-4967

Monroe County Commission on the Status of Women

217 Coral Road
Islamorada, FL 33036
305-451-6037

North Miami Beach Commission on the Status of Women
City Hall
17011 Northeast 19th Avenue
North Miami Beach, FL 33162
305-948-2986

Orange County Commission on the Status of Women
948 Versailles Circle
Maitland, FL 32751

Palm Beach County Commission on the Status of Women
420 Columbia Drive
West Palm Beach, FL 33401
407-684-6686

Sarasota Advisory Commission on the Status of Women
1938 Laurel Street
Sarasota, FL 34236
941-316-1077

Volusia County Commission on the Status of Women
County Manager's Office
123 West Indiana Avenue
Deland, FL 32720-4612
904-736-5920

Georgia

Georgia State Commission on Women
148 International Boulevard, NE, Suite 600
Atlanta, GA 30303-1751
404-657-9260

Hawaii

Hawaii County Committee on the Status of Women
Mayor's Office
25 Aupuni Street
Hilo, HI 96720
808-961-8211

Hawaii State Commission on the Status of Women
235 South Beretania Street, Room 407
Honolulu, HI 96813
808-586-5757

Honolulu County Committee on the Status of Women
Department of Human Resources
715 South King Street
Honolulu, HI 96813
808-523-4073

Maui County Committee on the Status of Women
Office of the Mayor
200 South High Street
Wailuku, HI 96793
808-243-7855

Idaho

Idaho Women's Commission
P.O. Box 83720
Boise, ID 83720-0036
208-334-4673

Illinois

Chicago Advisory Council on Women
510 North Peshtigo Court, Room 6B
Chicago, IL 60611
312-744-4113

Cook County Commission on Women's Issues
69 West Washington, Suite 2900
Chicago, IL 60602-3307
312-603-1100

Governor's Commission on the Status of Women
James R. Thompson Center
100 West Randolph Street, Suite 16-100
Chicago, IL 60601
312-814-5743

Organizations

Indiana

Bloomington City Commission on the Status of Women
Human Resources Department
P.O. Box 100
Bloomington, IN 47402-0100
812-331-6430

Crawfordsville Commission on the Status of Women
300 East Pike Street
Crawfordsville, IN 47933
317-364-5160

East Chicago Women's Commission
3901 Indianapolis Boulevard
East Chicago, IN 46312-2555
219-391-8467

Gary Commission on the Status of Women
475 Broadway, Suite 508
Gary, IN 46402
219-883-4155

Indiana Commission for Women
Indiana Civil Rights Commission
100 North Senate Avenue, Room N103
Indianapolis, IN 46204-2211
317-233-6303
http://www.state.in.us/icw

Mishawaka City Commission on the Status of Women
City Hall 600 East Third Street
Mishawaka, IN 46544
219-258-1601

South Bend Committee on the Status of Women
Human Rights Commission
227 West Jefferson Boulevard
1440 County Building
South Bend, IN 46601
219-284-9355

Iowa

Iowa Commission on the Status of Women
Lucas State Office Building
Des Moines, IA 50319
515-281-4461

Kansas

Topeka Mayor's Commission on the Status of Women
City Hall
215 East Seventh Street
Topeka, KS 66603
913-266-3299

Kentucky

Jefferson County Office for Women
Jefferson County Courthouse
527 West Jefferson Street
Louisville, KY 40202-2819
502-574-5360

Kentucky Commission on Women
614A Shelby Street
Frankfort, KY 40601
502-564-6643

Louisiana

Bossier City Mayor's Commission for Women
1984 Airline Drive
Bossier City, LA 71112
318-742-6000

Lafayette Commission on the Needs of Women
P.O. Box 52082
Lafayette, LA 70505-2082
318-261-8447

Lake Charles Mayor's Commission for Women
PO Box 6712
Lake Charles, LA 70606-6712

Louisiana Office of Women's Services
1885 Woodale Boulevard
P.O. Box 94095
Baton Rouge, LA 70804-9095
504-922-0960

Monroe Mayor's Commission on the Needs of Women
P.O. Box 123
Monroe, LA 71210
318-329-2310

New Orleans Women's Office
City Hall, Room 2W02
New Orleans, LA 70122
504-586-3165

Ruston Mayor's Commission for Women
PO Box 576
Ruston, LA 71273-3165

Shreveport Women's Commission
3045 Sandra Drive
Shreveport, LA 71119

Terrebone Women's Commission Inc.
116 Lewald Drive
Houma, LA 70360

Maryland

Anne Arundel County Commission for Women
P.O. Box 3492
Crofton, MD 21114

Baltimore City Commission for Women
10 South Street, Suite 600
Baltimore, MD 21202
410-396-4274

Baltimore County Commission for Women
Courthouse, Suite 124
400 Washington Avenue
Towson, MD 21204-4610
410-887-3448

Calvert County Commission for Women
Courthouse
175 Main Street
Prince Frederick, MD 20678-3337
410-535-1600

Cecil County Women's Council
21 Beach Street
North East, MD 21921
410-287-5173

Frederick County Commission for Women
Winchester Hall
12 East Church Street
Frederick, MD 21701-5243
301-694-1066

Garrett County Commission for Women
P.O. Box 623
Oakland, MD 21550
301-334-4810

Harford County Commission for Women
220 South Main Street
Bel Air, MD 21014-3829
410-879-2000, ext. 373

Howard County Commission for Women
6751 Columbia Gateway Drive
Columbia, MD 21046-2150
410-313-6400

Maryland Commission for Women
311 West Saratoga Street, Room 232
Baltimore, MD 21201
410-767-7137

Organizations

Montgomery County Commission for Women

255 North Washington Street, Fourth Floor
Rockville, MD 20850
301-279-8301

The Prince George's County Commission for Women

5012 Rhode Island Avenue
Hyattsville, MD 20787
301-699-2672

St. Mary's County Commission for Women

Governmental Center
P.O. Box 653
Leonardtown, MD 20650
301-475-4632

Washington County Commission for Women

100 West Washington Street
Hagerstown, MD 21740
301-791-3090

Wicomico County Commission for Women

P.O. Box 1309
Salisbury, MD 21802
410-546-8033

Massachusetts

Berkshire County Commission on the Status of Women

Berkshire Community College
Pittsfield, MA 01201
413-499-4660

Boston Women's Commission

City Hall, Room 716
1City Hall Plaza
Boston, MA 02201
617-635-4427

Cambridge Commission on the Status of Women

51 Inman Street
Cambridge, MA 02139-1730
617-349-4697
www.ci.cambridge.ma.us/~women#http://www

Massachusetts Governor's Advisory Committee on Women's Issues

State House Room 360
Boston, MA 02133
617-727-3600

Massachusetts Permanent Commission on the Status of Women

State House, Room 332
Boston, MA 02133

Quincy Mayor's Commission on the Status of Women

1305 Hancock Street
Quincy, MA 02170
617-773-1380

Somerville Commission for Women

Mayor's Office of Human Services
167 Holland Street, Room 208
Somerville, MA 02144-2401
617-625-6600, ext. 2400
http://www.somervillewomen.com

Worcester City Manager's Committee on the Status of Women

Office of City Manager
City Hall-455 Main Street
Worcester, MA 01608
508-799-1175

Michigan

Ingham County Women's Commission

5303 South Cedar Street
Lansing, MI 48911-3800
517-887-4558

Michigan Women's Commission
741 North Cedar Street, Suite 102
Lansing, MI 48913
517-334-8622

Minnesota

**Minnesota Commission on the
Economic Status of Women**
85 State Office Building
St. Paul, MN 55155
612-296-8590

Missouri

**Missouri Council on Women's
Economic Development and Training**
P.O. Box 1684
Jefferson City, MO 65102
314-751-0810

Montana

**Montana Women in Employment
Advisory Council**
Mitchel Building, Room 130
Helena, MT 59624
406-444-3111

Nebraska

**Columbus Mayor's Commission on
the Status of Women**
107 Cottonwood Drive
Columbus, NE 68601

**Lincoln/Lancaster Commission on the
Status of Women**
2202 South Eleventh Street, #110
Lincoln, NE 68502
402-441-7716

**Nebraska Commission on the Status
of Women**
301 Centennial Mall South
P.O. Box 94985
Lincoln, NE 68509-4985
402-729-2308

Nevada

Nevada Commission for Women
198 Carson Street, Capitol Complex
Carson City, NV 89710
702-687-4170

**Reno City Commission on the Status
of Women**
P.O. Box 1900
Reno, NV 89509

New Hampshire

**New Hampshire Commission on the
Status of Women**
State House Annex, Room 334
Concord, NH 03301
603-271-2660

New Jersey

**Atlantic County Advisory
Commission on Women**
354 Chestnut Neck Road
Port Republic, NJ 08241

**Bergen County Commission on
Women**
115-W Court Plaza South
21 Main Street
Hackensack, NJ 07601
201-646-3700

**Burlington County Commission on
Women**
49 Rancocas Road
Mount Holly, NJ 08060
609-265-5538

Organizations

Camden City Advisory Commission on the Status of Women

Cape May Court House
4 Moore Road
Cape May, NJ 08210
609-463-6695

Camden County Commission on Women

520 Market Street, Second Floor
Camden, NJ 08102-1375
609-225-5454

Cape May County Advisory Commission on the Status of Women

Cape May Court House
4 Moore Road
Cape May, NJ 08210
609-463-6695

East Orange City Committee on the Status of Women

City Council Office
44 City Hall Plaza
East Orange, NJ 07019
201-266-5120

Essex County Advisory Board on the Status of Women

Hall of Records
465 Dr. Martin Luther King, Jr. Boulevard
Newark, NJ 07102
201-621-4432

Gloucester County Commission on Women

7 North Jackson Avenue
Wenonah, NJ 08090
609-468-7733

Mercer County Advisory Commission on the Status of Women

McDade Administration Building
640 South Broad Street, Box 8068
Trenton, NJ 08650-8068
609-989-6033

Monmouth County Commission on the Status of Women

Human Services Building, Box 3000
Kozloski Road
Freehold, NJ 07728
908-577-6681

New Jersey Advisory Commission on the Status of Women

Department of Community Affairs
101 South Broad Street, CN 801
Trenton, NJ 08625-0801
609-292-8840

Newark City Mayor's Commission on the Status of Women

Office of the Mayor-Newark
920 Broad Street, Room 200
Newark, NJ 07102
201-733-6400

Ocean County Commission on Women

Ocean County Administration Building
1027 Hooper Avenue, Third Floor, Building 2
Toms River, NJ 08754-2191
908-929-2136

Salem County Commission on Women

Courthouse
92 Market Street
Salem, NJ 08079

Somerset County Commission on the Status of Women

County Administration Building
P.O. Box 3000
North Bridge/High Streets
Somerville, NJ 08876-1262
908-231-7036

Union County Advisory Commission on the Status of Women

Freeholders' Office
County Administration Building
Elizabethtown Plaza
Elizabeth, NJ 07207

Warren County Commission for Women
Freeholders' Office
Wayne Dumont Jr. Administration Building
165 County Road-519 South
Belvidere, NJ 07823-1949
908-475-6500

New Mexico

New Mexico Commission on the Status of Women
2401 Twelfth Street, NW
Albuquerque, NM 87104-2302
800-432-9168

New York

Erie County Commission on the Status of Women
95 Franklin Street, Room 1655
Buffalo, NY 14202-3904
716-858-8307

Nassau County Office of Women's Services
250 Fulton Road, Mezz.
Hempstead, NY 11550

New York City Commission on the Status of Women
100 Gold Street, Second Floor
New York, NY 10038
212-788-2738
http://www.ci.nyc.ny.us/women

New York State Division for Women
State of New York Executive Chambers
633 Third Avenue, 38th Floor
New York, NY 10017-6706
212-681-4547
http://www.Women.state.ny.us

Rockland County Commission on Women's Issues
11 New Hempstead Road
New City, NY 10956
914-638-5100

Suffolk County Women's Services
396 Oser Avenue
Hauppauge, NY 11788
516-853-3762

Syracuse Commission for Women
City Hall Commons
201 East Washington Street, Room 200
Syracuse, NY 13202-1427
315-448-8620

Town of Islip Women's Services
Division of Human Development
401 Main Street
Islip, NY 11751
516-224-5397

Westchester County Office for Women
150 Grand Street, Sixth Floor
White Plains, NY 10601
914-285-5972

North Carolina

Buncombe County Women's Involvement Council
60 Court Plaza 29
Asheville, NC 28801
828-255-7641

Burke County Council for Women
203 Shamrock Drive
Morganton, NC 28655
828-439-2326

Caldwell County Council on the Status of Women
109 Valencia Place, NE
Lenoir, NC 28645
828-758-9364

Carteret County Council for Women
P.O. Box 1821
Morehead City, NC 28557
252-247-0177

Organizations

Catawba Council for Women
Women's Resource Center
328 North Center Street
Hickory, NC 28601
704-328-6738

Cherokee County Council for Women
118A Peachtree Street
Murphy, NC 28906

Cleveland County Council on the Status of Women
Cleveland County DSS
130 South Post Street
Shelby, NC 28150
704-484-0959

Craven County Council on Women, Inc.
P.O. Box 1285
New Bern, NC 28563
252-638-3381

Durham County Women's Commission
15 Bonsell Place
Durham, NC 27707

Gaston County Council on the Status of Women
4109 Stoneleigh Place
Gastonia, NC 28056
704-865-7463

Greensboro Commission on the Status of Women
3 Bent Oak Court
Greensboro, NC 27455
336-373-2390

Harnett County Council for Women
PO Box 55f3
Lillington, NC 27546

Henderson County Council for Women
10455 Armstrong Street
Route 3, Box 375
Hendersonville, NC 28742
828-891-3317

Johnston County Council on the Status of Women
400 Dogwood Street
Smithfield, NC 27577
910-934-0791

Lee County Council for Women
225 South Steele Street
Sanford, NC 27330

Martin County Council for Women
1966 Lum Brown Road
Williamston, NC 27835-3503
919-792-1679

Mecklenburg County Women's Commission
700 North Tryon Street
Charlotte, NC 28202
704-336-3210

Moore County Council for Women
205 Poplar Street
Carthage, NC 28327

New Hanover County Council for Women
PO Box 15056
Wilmington, NC 28408
919-763-3524

North Carolina Council for Women
Southwestern Regional Office
June M. Kimmel
500 West Trade Street, Suite 360
Charlotte, NC 28202-1153
704-342-6367

North Carolina Council for Women
526 North Wilmington Street
Raleigh, NC 27604-1199
919-733-2455

Onslow County Council for Women
117 Cherrywood Court
Jacksonville, NC 28546
910-355-9479

Orange County Commission for Women
110 South Churton Street
Hillsborough, NC 27278
919-732-8181

Pitt County Council on the Status of Women
P.O. Box 3503
Greenville, NC 27835-3503
252-756-9750

Sampson County Council for Women
PO Box 296
Garland, NC 28441
910-592-8081

Wake County Commission for Women
3012 Legging Lane
Raleigh, NC 27615

Watauga County Council on the Status of Women
243 Red Oak Trail
Boone, NC 28607
828-963-4630

Winston-Salem/Forsyth County Council on the Status of Women
660 West 5th Street
Winston-Salem, NC 27106
336-727-8409

North Dakota

North Dakota Governor's Commission on the Status of Women
Department of Economic Development and Finance
1833 East Bismarck Expressway
Bismarck, ND 58504-6708
701-328-5310

Ohio

Ohio Women's Policy and Research Commission
77 South High Street, 24th Floor
Columbus, OH 43266
614-466-5580

Oklahoma

Lawton Mayor's Commission on the Status of Women
102 Southwest Fifth Street
Lawton, OK 73501
405-581-3260

Oklahoma Commission on the Status of Women
101 State Capitol Building
2300 North Lincoln Boulevard
Oklahoma City, OK 73105-4897
918-492-4492

Tulsa Mayor's Commission on the Status of Women
Department of Human Rights
200 Civic Center
Tulsa, OK 74103
918-582-0558

Oregon

Eugene City Women's Commission
777 Pearl Street
Eugene, OR 97401

Jackson County Women's Commission
Jackson County Courthouse
Medford, OR 97501

Oregon Governor's Commission for Women
PO Box 751-CW
Portland, OR 97207
503-725-5889

Organizations

Pennsylvania

Berks County Commission for Women

Berks County Services Center
633 Court Street
Reading, PA 19601
610-478-6124

Bucks County Commissioner's Advisory Council for Women

Administration Building
Broad and Court Street
Doylestown, PA 18901
215-348-6676

Delaware County Women's Commission

20 South 69th Street, Fourth Floor
Upper Darby, PA 19082
610-713-2308

Greater Pittsburgh Commission for Women

425 Sixth Avenue
Pittsburgh, PA 15219-1819
412-281-5533

Lackawanna County Commission for Women

200 Adams Avenue
Scranton, PA 18503-1607
507-963-6750

Luzerne County Commission for Women

Luzerne County Courthouse
North River Street
Wilkes-Barre, PA 18711
717-825-1727

Mercer County Commission for Women

103 Courthouse
Mercer, PA 16137

Montgomery County Commission on Women and Families

Courthouse
PO Box 311
Norristown, PA 19404-0311
610-292-5000

Pennsylvania Commission for Women

205 Finance Building
Harrisburg, PA 17120
717-787-8128

Philadelphia Mayor's Commission for Women

City Hall, Room 214
Philadelphia, PA 19107
215-686-2171

Puerto Rico

Office of Integral Development of Women

Municipality of San Juan
1127 Munoz Riverda Avenue
San Juan, PR 00925
787-758-5400

Puerto Rico Commission for Women's Affairs

Office of the Governor
Commonwealth of Puerto Rico
P.O. Box 11382
Fernandez Juncos Station
Santurce, PR 00910
787-721-0606

Rhode Island

Rhode Island Commission for Women

260 West Exchange Street, Suite 4
Providence, RI 02093
401-277-6105

South Carolina

Charleston Commission for Women
City Hall
80 Broad Street
Charleston, SC 29401
803-577-6970

South Carolina Governor's Office Commission on Women
Edgar A. Brown Building
1205 Pendleton Street
Columbia, SC 29201
803-734-1665

Texas

Austin Commission for Women
Austin Human Resources Department
P.O. Box 1088
Austin, TX 78767-1088
512-499-3215

Corpus Christi Commission for Women
320 Laurel
Corpus Christi, TX 78404
512-888-0410, ext. 2567

Fort Worth Commission on the Status of Women
City Manager's Office
1000 Throckmorton
Fort Worth, TX 76102
817-871-8552

Longview Commission on the Status of Women
Public Information Office
P.O. Box 1952
Longview, TX 75606
903-237-1096

Lubbock Mayor's Committee for Women
P.O. Box 2000
Lubbock, TX 79457
806-657-6411, ext. 2282

San Angelo Mayor's Commission on the Status of Women
2605 Southland Boulevard, Number 4
San Angelo, TX 76904
915-657-4499

San Antonio Commission on the Status of Women
P.O. Box 839966
San Antonio, TX 78283-3966
210-207-7067

San Marcos Commission for Women
111 West Holland
San Marcos, TX 78666
512-353-1111

Texas Governor's Commission for Women
P.O. Box 12428
Austin, TX 78711-2428
512-475-2615

Wichita Falls Mayor's Commission on the Status of Women
P.O. Box 1431
Wichita Falls, TX 76307
817-761-7601

Utah

Utah Governor's Commission for Women and Families
1160 State Office Building
Salt Lake City, UT 84114
801-538-1736

Vermont

Burlington Council on Women
City Hall
Burlington, VT 05401
802-658-9300

Organizations

Vermont Governor's Commission on Women

126 State Street, Drawer 33
Montpelier, VT 05633-6801
802-828-2851

Virgin Islands

Virgin Islands Commission on the Status of Women

PO Box 6334
St. Thomas, USVI 00804
340-693-1265

Virginia

Alexandria Council on the Status of Women

110 North Royal Street, Suite 201
Alexandria, VA 22314
703-838-5030

Arlington County Commission on the Status of Women

2100 Clarendon Boulevard, Suite 314
Arlington, VA 22201
703-358-3257

Fairfax City Commission for Women

10455 Armstrong Street
Fairfax, VA 22030
703-385-7894

Fairfax County Commission for Women

12000 Government Center Parkway, Suite 318
Fairfax, VA 22035-0001
703-324-5720

Falls Church City Commission for Women

300 Park Avenue
Falls Church, VA 22046
703-241-5005

Loudon County Commission for Women

17585 Wadell Court
Hamilton, VA 20158
540-338-3609

Prince William County Commission for Women

4370 Ridgewood Center Drive, Suite D
Woodbridge, VA 22192
703-792-6611

Richmond Mayor's Commission on the Concerns of Women

City Hall, Suite 201
900 East Broad Street
Richmond, VA 23219
804-698-3672

Virginia Council on the Status of Women

7805 Kahlua Drive
Richmond, VA 23227
804-786-7765

Washington

Seattle Women's Commission

Seattle Office for Civil Rights
700 Third Avenue, Suite 250
Seattle, WA 98104
206-684-0549

West Virginia

West Virginia Women's Commission

Capitol Complex
Building 6, Room 637
Charleston, WV 25305
304-558-0070

Wisconsin

Kenosha Commission on Women's Issues
6720 49th Avenue
Kenosha, WI 53142
404-658-8166

Wausau Mayor's Commission on the Status of Women
City Hall
407 Grant Street
Wausau, WI 54401
715-843-1200

Wisconsin Women's Council
16 North Carroll Street, Suite 720
Madison, WI 53702-2728
608-266-2219

Wyoming

Wyoming Commission for Women
Herschler Building
122 West 25th Street
Cheyenne, WY 82002
307-777-7349

Professional Organizations

In this directory, professional organizations cover a range of groups working on behalf of women. Most included here are trade and professional associations that recruit members, hold meetings, and offer training. Also listed are organizations that advocate on behalf of women without offering specific membership activities, but instead keep women apprised of developments in the field and women's rights in general.

Many organizations listed here also accept men, but maintain a primary focus of advancing and recognizing women in the field.

Advocates for Women in Science, Engineering, and Math
PO Box 91000
Portland, Oregon 92791-1000
503-690-1261
http://www.awsem.org

AWSEM is an advocacy project that encourages girls and young women to pursue careers in science-related fields. It brings together parents, educators, and women professionals. AWSEM works with Women in Technology International to facilitate regional advocacy efforts for girls nationwide. AWSEM provides guidelines for educators and organizations seeking to establish a local resource to introduce girls to technology careers.

AFL-CIO
Working Women's Department
815 16th Street, NW
Washington, DC 20006
202-637-5000
http://www.aflcio.org/women/index.htm

The **Working Women's Department** of the AFL-CIO works with women's civil rights, community, and religious organizations. Documentation available on the Web site includes results of the Ask a Working Woman Survey, Facts About Working Women, and How Much Will the Pay Gap Cost You?

African American Women's Clergy Association
214 Paul Street, NW
Washington, DC 20001
202-518-8488

The African American Women's Clergy Association is a membership organization for ordained and lay clergy women. The group operates a shelter in the Washington, DC, area, and shares information about African American women and religion through a newsletter.

Organizations

African-American Women Business Owners Association

3363 Alden Place, NE
Washington, DC 20019
202-399-3645
http://www.angelfire.com/biz2/aawboa.html

The association is open to any type of business. Benefits include financial support and information, emotional support, free subscription to *Black Enterprise* magazine, and networking with other businesses and possible customers/clients. Regular meetings are held twice a month in Washington, DC. Services include discount Web design, notary service, desktop publishing, and broadcast faxing.

African-American Women's Association

c/o June P. Bland, Ph.D.
PO Box 55122
Washington, DC 20011
202-723-4986

The African-American Women's Association seeks to establish closer relationships and understanding among women of Africa and America through cultural, educational, and social activities. The organization provides scholarships to African and American women and contributes to worthwhile developmental and educational projects in the United States and Africa that support women and children. The organization meets monthly in the District of Columbia area and publishes a quarterly newsletter. Send a SASE for scholarship or membership information.

Alberta Women's Science Network

PO Box 6912
Station D
Calgary, Alberta AB T2P 2G1
888-880-1788
http://www.awsn.com

The Alberta Women's Science Network is a coalition of several groups supporting women in science and engineering. Women in Scholarship, Engineering, Science, and Technolog, sponsors a mentoring and a summer research program for girls. Chapters of the Association of Women in Engineering and Science in Calgary and Edmonton are associate organizations.

All Navy Women's National Alliance

http://www.anwa.com

ANWA is devoted to the more than 400,000 active duty, reserve, retired, and women veterans of the Navy, Coast Guard, and Marines, as well as women who served with U.S. Forces in other branches of the Department of Defense, including women who serve in NATO forces around the world. It coordinates educational programs and seminars, and celebrates and recognizes significant accomplishments, milestones, and acts of heroism. It assists recruiters in their efforts and provides liaison to the civilian community.

Alliance of Black Women Attorneys

PO Box 13460
Baltimore, MD 21203-4460
410-377-1019

The Alliance of Black Women Attorneys provides a network for and seeks to improve the professional environment of black women attorneys.

Alpha Delta Kappa

1615 West 92nd Street
Kansas City, KS 64114
816-363-5525
http://www.alphadeltakappa.org

Alpha Delta Kappa is an international honorary sorority for women educators. Membership eligibility requirements are a bachelor's degree, teacher certification, and three years of professional experience. ADK offers workshops, training sessions, conferences, and conventions and publishes the *Alpha Delta Kappan* for its members.

Alumnae Resources

120 Montgomery Street, Suite 600
San Francisco, CA 94104
415-274-4700
http://www.ar.org

Alumnae Resources is a national organization offering assistance to college-educated women in career transition and management. Alumnae Resources offers hundreds of workshops, counseling, and research facilities. It serves over 100 companies and 8,500 individual members.

American Academy of Medical-Surgical Nurses

East Holly Avenue, Box 56
Pitman, NJ 08071-0056
856-256-2323
http://amsn.nurse.com

Membership benefits of the American Academy of Medical-Surgical Nurses include an annual convention, educational opportunities, and a subscription to AMSN's journal and newsletter.

American Academy of Religion

Committee on the Status of Women in the Profession
c/o Saint Paul School of Theology
5213 Truman Road
Kansas City, MO 64127
816-483-9604
http://www.aar-site.org

The **Committee on the Status of Women in the Profession** studies the problems of women in religious studies, proposes remedies and initiatives, and develops ways to involve men and women in addressing these issues.

American Agri-Women

http://www.americanagriwomen.com

American Agri-Women is a national coalition of farm, ranch, and agri-business women's organizations. AAW members work on national issues of mutual interest and hold a national convention annually. On the local level, AAW members work in areas of legislation, regulations, consumer relations promotion, and education. Members are eligible for financial aid through the **Helen Whitmore Memorial Fund.**

American Agricultural Economics Association Foundation

Committee on Women in Agricultural Economics
415 South Duff
Ames, IA 50010
515-233-3202
http://www.aaea.org

The **Committee on Women in Agricultural Economics** administers a fellowship fund and coordinates AAEA activities geared for women.

American Anthropological Association

Association for Feminist Anthropology
4350 North Fairfax Drive, Suite 640
Arlington, VA 22203-1620
703-528-1902
http://www.aaanet.org

The **Association for Feminist Anthropology** is a section of the AAA that publishes a newsletter, lists job openings, and issues announcements for calls for papers, fellowships, and travel grants for AFA members.

American Association for Cancer Research

Women in Cancer Research
Public Ledger Building, Suite 816
150 South Independence Mall West
Philadelphia, PA 19106-3483
215-440-9300
http://www.aacr.org

Women in Cancer Research is a new affiliate organization of the American Association of Cancer Research, a scientific society of over 15,000 laboratory and clinical researchers. AACR publishes four journals, hosts an annual meeting, and organizes scientific conferences.

American Association for Higher Education

Women's Caucus
One Dupont Circle, NW, Suite 360
Washington, DC 20036-1110
202-293-6440
http://www.aahe.org

141

Organizations

The **Women's Caucus** of the AAHE seeks to enrich and enhance the role of women in the academy. Through special sessions at the AAHE National Conference, and other meetings and opportunities, the caucus provides opportunities for sharing, learning, and growth. AAHE members are eligible to join.

American Association for Neuroscience Nurses

4700 West Lake Avenue
Glenview, IL 60025-1485
847-375-4733
http://www.aann.org

AANN seeks to provide the essential nursing education and networking opportunities required for neuroscience nursing professionals. Membership benefits include the *Journal of Neuroscience Nursing* and a newsletter, educational programs, an annual meeting, discounts on Certified Neuroscience Register Nurse examinations at the annual meeting, and discounts on educational products.

American Association for Women Podiatrists

5900 Princess Garden Parkway, Suite 420
Lanham, MD 20706
301-577-4464
http://www.aawp.org

The American Association of Women Podiatrists promotes the interests common to women podiatrists and the public and make more visible the talent, training, and work of women podiatrists.

American Association for Women Radiologists

1891 Preston White Drive
Reston, VA 22091
703-648-8939

AAWR seeks to address socioeconomic issues of interest to women in radiology, serve as a resource organization for women in the practice, support women in radiology residency, and encourage participation of women at all levels in national radiological societies. It holds an annual meeting and a refresher course in conjunction with the Radiological Society of North America meeting. It holds a business meeting and president's program at the American Roentgen Ray Society meeting. A quarterly newsletter and membership directory are available to members.

American Association of Colleges of Nursing

1 Dupont Circle, NW, Suite 530
Washington, DC 20036
202-463-6930
http://www.aacnche.edu

AACN serves as a national voice for America's baccalaureate and higher-degree nursing programs. Students can access a list of AACN member schools and contact information on AACN's Web site.

American Association of Critical Care Nurses

101 Columbia
Aliso Viejo, CA 92656
949-362-2000
http://www.aacn.org

AACN has chapters in every state and overseas. It offers members access to training, publications, an annual conference, scholarships, and research grants. Its Practice Resource Network provides members with clinical information through telephone, e-mail, fax, and its Web site.

American Association of Immunologists

Committee on the Status of Women
9650 Rockville Pike
Bethesda, MD 20814
301-530-7178
http://www.sciencexchange.com/aai

The AAI **Committee on the Status of Women** generates and develops programs that assure equal treatment of all immunologists on the basis of merit. It assists in planning sessions at the annual AAI meeting and assesses the needs of women immunologists.

American Association of Medical Assistants

20 North Wacker Drive, 1575
Chicago, IL 60606-2903
312-899-1500
http://www.aama-ntl.org

The AAMA serves the medical assistants who perform administrative and clinical duties in ambulatory or immediate care settings. Members in the 43 state societies include practicing medical assistants, medical assisting educators, students, and office managers. Members receive a subscription to *PMA*—a bimonthly publication that provides educational articles, current medical news, and health legislation updates. Group insurance rates, accreditation access, and an annual national convention are other benefits of membership. This organization is predominantly made up of women, but also serves men in the field.

American Association of Nurse Anesthetists

222 South Prospect Avenue
Park Ridge, IL 60068-4001
847-692-7050
http://www.aana.org

AANA promotes and supports the nurse anesthetist profession through the bimonthly *AANA Journal,* a bimonthly newsletter, patient information brochures, assistance with employment practice and clinical practice issues, and other educational and professional development opportunities.

American Association of Occupational Health Nurses

2920 Brandywine Road, Suite 100
Atlanta, GA 30341
770-455-7757
http://www.aaohn.org

AAOHN works to advance the profession of occupational and environmnental nursing. It offers continuing education and certification information, the *AAOHN Journal,* a newsletter, educational publications, and employment information to its members.

American Association of Retired Persons

Women's Initiative
601 E Street, NW
Washington, DC 20049
202-434-2400
http://www.aarp.org/programs/women/
wiwhome.html

AARP **Women's Initiative** is not a membership group. Rather, it is a resource for older women, offering advice and contact information for resources on older women's issues, such as low retirement income, lack of financial planning skills, special health concerns, and workplace inequities.

American Association of Spinal Cord Nurses

75-20 Astoria Boulevard
Jackson Heights, NY 11370
718-803-3782
http://www.aascin.org

The AASCIN promotes quality care for individuals with spinal cord impairment and advances the nursing practice through education, research, advocacy, health care policy, and collaboration with consumers and health advocacy systems. It conducts an annual conference for members, who also receive a newsletter, research notices, and recognition through an annual awards program.

American Association of University Professors

Committee on Status of Women in the Academic Profession
1012 14th Street, NW, Suite 500
Washington, DC 20005
202-737-5526

The **Committee on the Status of Women in the Academic Profession** seeks to help women in academia gain access to equal opportunities for tenure and advancement and advocates for issues such as maternity leave and equal pay.

Organizations

American Association of University Women Legal Advocacy Fund

Department LAF. INT
1111 16th Street, NW
Washington, DC 20036-4873
800-326-AAUW
http://www.aauw.org

The AAUW Legal Advocacy Fund is focused solely on sex discrimination in higher education. It provides funding and support to women seeking judicial redress for sex discrimination. The Web site lists helpful information on case support, programming ideas, and the Legal Advocacy Fund Network. An application for case support is also available on the Web site.

American Association of University Women

1111 16th Street, NW
Washington, DC 20036
800-326-AAUW
http://www.aauw.org

AAUW is a national organization that promotes education and equity for women in girls in all aspects and fields of education. Its three branches include the association, a 150,000-member organization with more than 1,500 branches; the foundation, one of the largest private funding sources for women; and the Legal Advocacy Fund, which provides funds and a support system for women seeking judicial redress for sex discrimination in higher education. It offers scholarships and fellowships in virtually every field of study and issues numerous publications on education issues for women. Branches host networking events, workshops, and seminars. Many state and regional branches offer scholarships to students in their state. The Web site has contact information for AAUW branches.

American Association of Women Dentists

645 North Michigan Avenue, Suite 800
Chicago, IL 60611
800-920-2293
http://www.womendentists.org

The American Association of Women Dentists provides a global network of mentoring and support for colleagues, both aspiring and established women dentists. It offers loans to students and professional members.

American Association of Women Emergency Physicians

3020 Legacy Drive, Suite 100-102
Plano, TX 75023
972-208-4543
http://www.aawep.org

AAWEP is a national, professional organization for women emergency physicians. It offers networking forums on issues of common interest, such as resources on litigation, wellness, and professional development. An annual conference offers educational seminars with continuing education unit opportunities. An annual membership directory and quarterly newsletter are other membership benefits. AAWEP also presents awards to women in emergency medicine.

American Association of Women in Community Colleges

1202 West Thomas Road
Phoenix, AZ 85013
203-344-3001
http://www.maricopa.edu/commmunity/aawcc/geninf1.html

The AAWCC, formerly the American Association of Women in Junior and Community Colleges, is a national organization working for the concerns of women in community, junior, and technical colleges. Membership benefits include professional development activities at the national, regional, and local levels that provide insights for career development and opportunities to give presentations; and the annual *AAWCC Journal* and four AAWCC quarterly publications. AAWCC advocates for issues important to its consitituents such as child care, equal access, affirmative action, welfare issues, and wellness.

American Astronomical Society

Committee on the Status of Women in Astronomy
2000 Florida Avenue, NW, Suite 400
Washington, DC 20009
202-328-2010
http://www.aas.org/~cswa/

The AAS **Committee on the Status of Women** makes recommendations to the AAS Council on practical measures it can take to improve the status of women in astronomy and encourage their entry into the field. It offers an annual meeting and an online women in astronomy database. It publishes a weekly electronic newsletter, *AASWomen. Status* is the committee's biannual printed publication of original and reprinted articles on topics relating to women in astronomy.

American Bar Association

Commission on Women in the Profession
750 North Lake Shore Drive
Chicago, IL 60611
312-988-5000
http://www.abanet.org/women/activities.html

The **Commission on Women in the Profession** works on issues related to gender equity for women law professionals and students through publications and public education. It meets with bar associations and law firms about developing gender-neutral evaluation procedures. It is working on a manual for law firms and corporations on facilitating women's elevation to prominent positions. It also seeks to help women to progress to leadership positions in the ABA.

American Bar Association

Women's Interest Network
International Law and Practice
750 North Lake Shore Drive
Chicago, IL 60611
312-988-5000
http://www.abanet.org

The **Women's Interest Network** of the ABA Section of International Law and Practice was founded to provide a forum in which section members could identify and discuss practice issues of special interest to women in international law. It offers periodic national meetings, networking programs, newsletters, and regional meetings, considering issues such as rainmaking in international law and cultural challenges for women practicing abroad.

American Business Women International

PO Box 1137
Palm Desert, CA 92260
760-346-ABWI
http://www.abwiworld.com

ABWI is a U.S. organization with an international bent. It makes introductions to form global business partnerships, helps businesses take their first steps into worldwide markets and expand current international markets, and creates business missions with other countries for growth into common global areas. ABWI is supported by women entrepreneurs, women in corporate America, and women in politics, government, film, agriculture, and educational and cultural sectors. Membership benefits include access to an international advisory board, an online marketplace, educational programs and seminars, regional and international conventions, and discounted products and services. A request for a membership kit is available on the Web site.

American Business Women's Association

9100 Ward Parkway
PO Box 8728
Kansas City, MO 64114
800-228-0007
http://www.abwa.org

The American Business Women's Association is a large national organization with 1,400 chapters. Members meet monthly and for networking and educational and training opportunities, receive a subscription to *Women in Business,* and discounts on business products and services.

American Chemical Society

Women Chemists Committee
1155 16th Street
Washington, DC 20036
800-227-5558
http://www.acs.org

Organizations

The **Women Chemists Committee** of the American Chemical Society provides an additional focus on issues for women chemists. The committee administers its own grants and awards, posts notices of educational and funding opportunities, and shares news in the field with the *WCC Newsletter.*

American College of Healthcare Executives

1 North Franklin, Suite 1700
Chicago, IL 60606-3491
312-424-2800
http://www.ache.org/MBERSHIP/HEG_WHEN/

The American College of Healthcare Executives maintains formal relationships with women's health care executive networks (WHENs), which conduct educational programs and sponsor social functions to provide networking opportunities.

American College of Nurse Midwives

818 Connecticut Avenue, NW, Suite 900
Washington, DC 20006
202-728-9860
http://www.acnm.org

The American College of Nurse Midwives represents certified nurse midwives, certified midwives, and student nurse midwives. Membership benefits include scholarship opportunities, a newsletter and journal, member discounts on publications and meetings, group-rate insurance, and listing in the annual membership directory.

American College of Nurse Practitioners

503 Capitol Court, NE, Suite 300
Washington, DC 20002
202-546-4825
http://www.nurse.org/acnp/

The American College of Nurse Practitioners is a national nonprofit membership organization with three types of memberships. Licensed nurse practitioners or student nurse practitioners are eligible for member-at-large status. State associations and national organizations are the other two types of membership. Benefits include local chapter meetings, a journal, and discounts on educational materials, such as the individual risk management self-study course.

American Council on Education

Office of Women in Higher Education
1 Dupont Circle, NW
Washington, DC 20036-1193
202-939-9390

The **Office of Women in Higher Education** seeks to identify qualified women leaders, develop their leadership skills, and advance them into deanships, presidencies, or equivalent positions. The Network is a state-based affiliate whose members are women leaders in higher education.

American Economics Association

Committee on Status of Women in the
Economics Profession
2014 Broadway, Suite 305
Northwestern University
Nashville, TN 37203
615-322-2595

The **Committee on Status of Women in the Economics Profession** is an arm of the American Economics Association. It publishes a thrice-yearly newsletter and arranges special sessions for women in the profession at the annual meetings of the AEA.

American Federation of State, County and Municipal Employees, AFL-CIO

Women's Rights Department
1625 L Street, NW
Washington, DC 20036
202-429-1000
http://www.afscme.org

The **Women's Rights Department** encourages women's leadership in the union and the workplace and works on issues of concern to its women members. It holds regional women's conferences. Information on issues of interest to working women, such as the Family and Medical Leave Act, child care, and pay equity, are available on the Web site.

American Historical Association

400 A Street, SE
Washington, DC 20003-3889
202-544-2422
http://www.theaha.org/affiliates/ccwh.htm

The **Coordinating Council for Women in History**, an affiliate of the AHA, encourages the recruitment of women in the profession and helps develop research and instruction in women's history.

The AHA **Committee on Women Historians** supports the interests of women in history through the AHA activities of promoting historical studies, collection of historical artifacts, dissemination of research programs, and scholarly meetings.

American Holistic Nurses' Association

PO Box 2130
Flagstaff, AZ 86003-2130
http://www.ahna.org

The American Holistic Nurses Association is an educational organization that supports the concepts of holism. There are over 4,000 members internationally who work together to support the education of nurses, allied health professionals, and the general public on health-related issues.

American Intellectual Property Law Association

Women in Intellectual Property Law Committee
2001 Jefferson Davis Highway, Suite 203
Arlington, VA 22202
703-415-0780
http://www.aipla.org

The **Women in Intellectual Property Law Committee** works to include women in leadership positions within the AIPLA and the field in general. It hosts its own annual meeting and conducts meetings in conjunction with the AIPLA. Call the AIPLA for contact information for the current president or membership coordinator.

American Library Association

Committee on the Status of Women in Librarianship
50 East Huron Street
Chicago, IL 60611
800-545-2433
http://www.ala.org/coswl/

The **Committee on the Status of Women in Librarianship** represents women's interests within the ALA. It promotes and initiates the collection, analysis, and dissemination of information on the status of women librarians.

American Mathematical Society

Committee on Women in the Mathematical Sciences
P.O. Box 6248
Providence, RI 02940-6248
800-321-4AMS
http://www.ams.org

The AMS **Committee on Women in the Mathematical Sciences** furthers mathematical research and scholarship for women. It advocates for women's interests within the organization and the field in general.

American Medical Association

Women Physicians Congress
515 North State Street
Chicago, IL 60610
http://www.ama-assn.org

The AMA **Women Physicians Congress** provides an expanded opportunity to participate directly in the AMA and to influence national health policy and advocacy on women's health and women physician professional issues. It fosters collaboration among the AMA, American Medical Women's Association, national women's health groups, and other organizations with mutual concerns.

American Medical Student Association

Women in Medicine Committee
1902 Association Drive
Reston, VA 20191
800-767-2266
http://www.amsa.org/sc/wim/html

Organizations

The **Women in Medicine Committee** advocates for the interests of women in medicine, particularly physicians-in-training and women patients. Members receive a newsletter and communicate through a listserv. Local chapters are found at medical schools nationwide and interact with the American Medical Women's Association.

American Medical Women's Association

801 North Fairfax Street, Suite 400
Alexandria, VA 22314
703-838-0500
http://www.amwa-doc.org

AMWA addresses the challenges specific to women physicians and the needs particular to women patients. Members receive publications such as the peer-reviewed *JAMWA*, and networking and personal development opportunities through national and regional meetings. Student members are eligible for several scholarships and awards, and student loans are offered to members. The bed and breakfast program assists students traveling for a residency or interview by providing a list of volunteers who will provide accommodations in the area. An online membership form is available.

American Mothers, Inc.

301 Park Avenue
Waldorf-Astoria
New York, NY 10022
212-755-2539

American Mothers, Inc., offers educational, cultural, and spiritual programs for mothers of all ages including workshops and seminars, an annual convention, mentor mother program, and arts scholarships for mothers. AMI publishes *American Mother* magazine quarterly for its members. Copies are $3 an issue for nonmembers. Call to request membership information.

American National Cattle Women

PO Box 3881
Englewood, CO 80155
303-694-0313
http://www.beef.org/organzns/ancw.htm

The American National Cattle Women a is promotion and consumer education organization regarding beef as a nutritious food, but it also serves as a networking forum for its members. ANCW's members remain current on food trends, nutrition, and food safety. They seek to address issues critical to the U.S. beef cattle industry and those it employs.

American Nephrology Nurses Association

East Holly Avenue
Box 56
Pittman, NJ 08071-0056
888-600-ANNA
http://www.annanurse.org

ANNA is a membership organization for nephrology nurses and other health care professionals with varying experience and expertise in conservative management, peritoneal dialysis, hemodialysis, renal replacement therapy, and renal transplantation. Members receive the *ANNA Journal* and access to publications such as *Nephrology Nursing: A Guide to Professional Development* and other educational materials.

American News Women's Club

1607 22nd Street
Washington, DC 20008
202-332-6770
http://www.anwc.org

ANWC provides women in the media profession with opportunities to network, participate in professional programs, and honor members' achievements in the field. Members include professionals in journalism, public relations, new media, and publishing.

American Nurses Association

600 Maryland Avenue, SW, Suite 100 West
Washington, DC 20024-2571
800-274-4ANA
http://www.nursingworld.com

The American Nurses Association is a professional organization thatworks to advance the nursing profession by fostering high standards of nursing practice, promoting the economic and general welfare of nurses in the workplace and projecting a positive and realistic view of nursing. Many educational opportunities are available, including a number of fellowships and scholarships.

American Pharmaceutical Association

Committee on Women's Affairs
2215 Constitution Avenue, NW
Washington, DC 20037-2985
202-628-4410
http://www.aphanet.org

The American Pharmaceutical Association is a national professional society for pharmacists. It publishes a journal and newsletter, and organizes an annual meeting with over 150 hours of educational sessions.The **Committee on Women's Affairs** addresses the concerns of women in the profession.

American Philosophical Association

Committee on the Status of Women
University of Delaware
Newark, DE 19716
302-831-1112
http://www.udel.edu/apa

The APA's **Committee on the Status of Women** advises women philosophers on overcoming discrimination they may encounter and makes recommendations to the APA board on ways to provide full equality to all in the philosophy field. The committee seeks to facilitate an understanding of gender issues and positions represented in feminist theories and is concerned with teaching and research. It publishes the *Newsletter on Feminism and Philosophy*.

American Physical Society

Committee on the Status of Women in Physics
1 Physics Ellipse
College Park, MD 20740-3844
301-209-3231
http://www.aps.org

The **Committee on the Status of Women in Physics** is an outreach committee of the American Physical Society. It sponsors studies, programs, and publications, including a women's colloquium, forum on education, travel grants, and speakers bureau. It hosts WIPHYS,

a listserve for women around the world to exchange advice, network, and discuss issues of interest to women in physics.

American Physical Therapy Association

Department of Women's Initiatives
703-706-8536
http://www.apta.org

The **Department of Women's Initiatives** of the APTA provides leadership, coordination, and accountability on women's issues in physical therapy.

American Planning Association

Planning and Women Division
122 South Michigan Avenue, Suite 1600
Chicago, IL 60603
312-431-9100
http://www.planning.org

Divisions of the American Planning Association, such as the **Planning and Women Division**, provide APA members with an opportunity to join others with common interests. The Planning and Women Division publishes a newsletter, organizes workshops and meetings, and assists in policy development and implementation.

American Psychiatric Nurses Association

1200 19th Street, NW, Suite 300
Washington, DC 20036-2422
202-857-1133
http://www.apha.org

APHA facilitates the professional development of psychiatric-mental health nurses through programs and services related to the creation, exchange, and engineering of new knowledge and skills.

American Psychological Association

Women's Program Office
750 First Street, NE
Washington, DC 20002
http://www.apa.org/pi/wpo/homepage.html

Organizations

The **Women's Program Office** coordinates the APA's efforts to ensure equal opportunities for women psychologists as practitioners, educators, and scientists and to eliminate gender bias in training, education, research, and diagnosis. It serves as an information and referral resource and develops reports and pamphlets on professional and consumer issues.

American Public Health Association

800 I Street, NW
Washington, DC 20001-3710
202-777-APHA
http://www.apha.org

APHA represents members of over 50 occupations in the public health field. The **Women's Caucus** works on behalf of women in the organization and the public health field in general. Contact the APHA for contact information for the current Women's Caucus chair.

American Society for Cell Biology

Women in Cell Biology Committee
9650 Rockville Pike
Bethesda, MD 20814
301-530-7153

The **Women in Cell Biology Committee** of the American Society of Cell Biology participates fully in ASCB programs and also offers a newsletter geared to women and a resource bureau of prominent women scientists. The committee awards two **Career Recognition Awards** to women at the ASCB annual meeting.

American Society for Microbiology

Committee on the Status of Women in Microbiology
1325 Massachusetts Avenue, NW
Washington, DC 20005-4171
202-942-9319
http://www.asmusa.org

The **Committee on the Status of Women in Microbiology** is a section of the American Society for Microbiology, which publishes a newsletter and professional journal, offers career assistance, and conducts workshops.

American Society for Public Administration

Section for Women in Public Administration
1120 G Street, NW, Suite 700
Washington, DC 20005
202-393-7878
http://www.aspanet.org

The **Section for Women in Public Administration** develops programs that promote the full participation and recognition of women in all levels and areas of public service. SWPA publishes a newsletter, awards grants to local ASPA chapters, and publishes monographs, such as *The Right Word: Guidelines for Avoiding Sex-Based Language.*

American Society for Training and Development

Women's Network
1640 King Street, Box 1443
Alexandria, VA 22313-2043
703-683-8100
http://www.astd.org

The American Society of Training and Development coordinates 47 special interest areas, including the **Women's Network**, for women employed in human resources.

American Society of Biochemistry and Molecular Biology

Committee on Equal Opportunities for Women
9650 Rockville Pike
Bethesda, MD 20814
301-530-7145
http://www.aai.org/asbmb/index.html

The **Committee on Equal Opportunities for Women** advocates for equal opportunity in biochemistry and molecular biology education and careers for women and minorities.

American Society of Preianesthesia Nurses

6900 Grove Road
Thorofare, NJ 08086
856-845-5557
http://www.aspan.org

The American Society of Preanesthesia Nurses is the professional specialty nursing organization representing more than 10,000 nurses in all phases of ambulatory surgery, preanesthesia, and postanesthesia care. There are 40 chartered state and regional associations.

American Society of Plastic and Reconstructive Surgical Nurses

East Holly Avenue, Box 56
Pitman, NJ 08071-0056
609-256-2340
http://www.asprn.nurse.com

Members of ASPRN are registered nurses, licensed practical nurses, and licensed vocational nurses, technicians, and medical assistants. The organization provides educational forums and training.

American Society of Women Accountants

60 Revere Drive, Suite 500
Northbrook, IL 60062
800-326-2163
http://www.aswa.org

The American Society of Women Accountants helps women in all fields of accounting achieve their personal, professional, and economic potential and contributes to the future development of the profession. The majority of its members have attained professional certifications such as CPA, CMA, CIA, and CFP. Visit the Web site or call for membership information.

American Statistical Association

Committee on Women in Statistics
1429 Duke Street
Alexandria, VA 22314-3402
703-684-1221
http://www.amstat.org

The **Committee on Women in Statistics** works to make members of the ASA more aware of the professional interests of women members of ASA and encourages women to enter the field of statistics. It jointly coordinates the **Gertrude Cox Scholarship** for women in statistics.

American Woman's Economic Development Corporation

71 Vanderbilt Avenue, Suite 320
New York, NY 10169
212-692-9100
http://orgs.womenconnect.com/awed/

AWED provides entrepreneurial training and counseling for women business owners. AWED participants represent all socioeconomic backgrounds of women including employed and formerly employed women, women entering the workplace for the first time, and women who have started and want to grow new businesses.

American Woman's Society of Certified Public Accountants

401 North Michigan Avenue
Chicago, IL 60611
800-AWSCPA1
http://www.awscpa.org

The AWSCPA seeks to promote equity within the accounting profession. It facilitates networking and mentoring and publishes a bimonthly newsletter and membership directory. AWSCPA also recognizes its members with annual awards.

American Women in Radio and Television

1650 Tysons Boulevard
McLean, VA 22102
703-506-3290
http://www.awrt.org

AWRT is a national organization of professionals working in the electronic media and closely allied fields. AWRT works to improve the quality of electronic media, serves as a medium of communications and idea exchange, and promotes the entry, development, and advancement of women in electronic media. The AWRT Foundation bestows awards to members and non-members There are more than 40 chapters nationwide. Visit the Web site for membership information.

Organizations

American Women's Hockey Coaches Association
http://rpi.edu/dept/athletics/w_hockey/awhca/

The American Women's Hockey Coaches Association is open to all women's hockey coaches in the United States. AWHCA works to promote, develop, and facilitate the growth of girls' and women's ice hockey in the United States.

Army Women's Professional Association
2550 Huntington Avenue, Suite 202
Alexandria, VA 22303-1499

The AWPA supports opportunities for women in the military and serves as an educational resource on issues that affect women in the military and national defense. It offers monthly guest speakers, professional development sessions, and networking social events, mainly in the Washington, DC, area.

Artists in Residence (A.I.R.) Gallery
40 Wooster Street, Second Floor
New York, NY 10013
212-966-0799

The gallery exhibits women's visual artwork. Send a self-addressed, stamped envelope for a prospectus. The gallery also offers an internship for women to assist in the daily operation of the gallery. Send a resume and letter of interest.

Asian American Women's Alliance
1894 18th Avenue
San Francisco, CA 94122
415-681-9229

AAWA represents a diverse group of Asian American women from various professional career fields in the Bay Area. Membership benefits include free or discount rate to all AAWA functions, access to employment opportunities, and eligiblity for academic and career scholarships.

Asian Immigrant Women Advocates
310 Eighth Street, Suite 301
Oakland, CA 94604
510-268-0192

This organization seeks to empower low-income Asian immigrant women by encouraging them to exercise their rights and develop the skills necessary to advocate for justice and dignity in their lives and workplace.

Asian Pacific American Women's Leadership Institute
1921 Ivy Street
Denver, CO 80220
303-863-8899

APAWLI seeks to address the specific challenges facing Asian and Pacific American women as leaders. It offers fellowships that partially fund participation in the APAWLI Fellowship Program. The program consists of three one-week sessions in three U.S. cities with guest speakers, activities, readings, and other learning tools. Members also receive a newsletter and access to periodic workshops.

Asian Women in Business
1 West 34th Street, Suite 200
New York, NY 10001
http://www.awib.org

AWIB was founded to assist Asian women realize their entrepreneurial potential. It sponsors conferences and workshops, provides individualized technical assistance, and serves as a support mechanism for small business owners. It offers consulting services for assistance in obtaining Minority/Women Owned Business Enterprise certification.

Association for Women Geoscientists
PO Box 280
Broomfield, CO 80038-0280
http://www.awg.org

AWG encourages the participation of women in the geosciences and the exchange of educational, technical, and professional information. AWG offers scholarships and awards to precollege and college women and answers questions about careers in geosciences from students and teachers. It publishes *Gaea,* the journal of the association, provides a speakers bureau, offers field trips to members, and provides networking opportunities through local chapters. Visit the Web site for membership information.

Association for Women in Architecture—Los Angeles

2550 Beverly Boulevard
Los Angeles, CA 90057
323-389-6490
http://www.awa-la.org

AWA-LA seeks to forward the position of women in architecture and related fields and to advance these professions. Members receive a monthly newsletter, meetings, tours of places of interest, and networking opportunities. AWA-LA also offers scholarships to young women enrolled in architecture programs in California.

Association for Women in Aviation Maintenance

PO Box 1030
Edgewater, FL 32132-1030
http://www.awam.org

AWAM supports women's professional growth and enrichment in aviation maintenance fields. Its membership consists of maintenance technicians, engineers, teachers, scientists, vendors, and pilots. AWAM publishes a quarterly newsletter and maintains a speakers network. It holds meetings annually at the Women in Aviation Conference of Women in Aviation International.

Association for Women in Communications

1244 Ritchie Highway, Suite 6
Arnold, MD 21012-1887
410-544-7442
http://www.womcom.org

AWC (formerly **Women in Communications**) is a professional organization for women in all communications disciplines. Members work in print and broadcast journalism, television and radio production, film, advertising, marketing,

graphic design, multimedia design, and photography. AWC seeks to advance women in these professions by recognizing excellence through annual awards, offering networking and educational opportunities, and promoting leadership. Awards are offered for members and non-members.

Association for Women in Computing

41 Sutter Street, Suite 1006
San Francisco, CA 94104
415-905-4663
http://www.awc-hq.org

The mission of the Association for Women in Computing is to advance women in the computing fields in business, industry, science, education, government, and the military. It sponsors national meetings, publishes both print and electronic newsletters, and supports networking both in person and via the Internet. Visit the Web site for chapter information. It gives the annual **Augusta Ada Lovelace Award** for a woman in computing.

Association for Women in Development

1511 K Street, NW, Suite 825
Washington, DC 20005
202-628-0442

AWID is an international organization that works to redefine development with women's perspectives. It promotes research, policy, and practice to engage women in building a just and sustainable development process. AWID holds biannual forums and workshops and institutes. It publishes a quarterly newsletter.

Association for Women in Mathematics

4114 Computer and Space Sciences Building
University of Maryland
College Park, MD 20742-2461
http://www.awm-math.org

AWM is a national organization that encourages women in the mathematical sciences. Membership benefits include the AWM newsletter six times a year, eligibility for AWM programs and awards, participation in AWM-Net, an e-mail forum, and career workshops and seminars.

Association for Women in Psychology

Women's Program Office—American
Psychological Association
750 First Street, NE
Washington, DC
http://www.iup.edu/counsl/awpac

The Association for Women in Psychology grew from the women's liberation movement within the American Psychological Association. Its efforts helped create the Women's Program Office of the APA. The AWP continues to play an active role outside the APA, sponsoring annual and occasional regional conferences on feminist psychology and publishing a newsletter. It makes several awards annually on topics relevant to feminist psychology.

Association for Women in Science

1200 New York Avenue, NW, Suite 650
Washington, DC 20005
202-326-8940
http://www.awis.org

AWIS is a national, professional organization for women in all scientific disciplines. It fosters the recruitment, retention, and promotion of women in science and seeks to educate the public about women in science and encourage girls' interest in science. AWIS offers scholarships, fellowships, and annual awards. Membership benefits include an annual conference, meetings at the local level, internships, mentoring, *AWIS Magazine*, job listings, a database of women in science, technology, and engineering jobs, and several other publications. Students and professionals may join.

Association for Women in Sports Media

PO Box 17536
Fort Worth, TX 76102
612-228-5509
http://users.southeast.net/~awsm

AWSM is a national organization for women employed in sports writing, editing, broadcast

and production, public relations, and sports information. AWSM holds annual conventions addressing issues such as access to athletes, Title IX, hiring and promotion practices, and sexism. Members are listed in a membership directory, receive a quarterly newsletter, and can participate in a job bank. AWSM also sponsors scholarships and internships for college students.

Association for Women in the Metal Industries

515 King Street, Suite 420
Alexandria, VA 22314-3137
703-739-8335
http://www.awmi.com

AWMI is a professional society that seeks to foster the professionalism and personal growth of women in the metal industries, address their unique challenges, and publicize their achievements. Membership benefits include networking at meetings and events on a local, regional, and national basis; seminars, workshops, and facility tours; a membership directory; and a national newsletter. Scholarships are given at the chapter level to members for career development and the enhancement of educational qualifications. Membership and chapter contact information is available on the Web site.

Association for Women Journalists

http://www.awjchicago.com

The AWJ is a group of regional organizations of women working in all mediums who gather to network, learn, and advance the status of women as professional journalists. Chapters sponsor "off-the-record" breakfast meetings with news sources and panel discussions. Chapters are in Dallas/Fort Worth, Chicago, Minneapolis/St. Paul, and St. Petersburg, Florida.

Association for Women Veterinarians

32205 Allison Drive
Union City, CA 94587
510-471-8379

The Association of Women Veterinarians promotes the role of women in veterinary medicine. Headquarters is in California, with chapters also in several cities. The Web site was under construction at the time of publication. The association publishes a quarterly bulletin and awards scholarships for second- and third-year students in veterinary school. Awards are also given annually to men or women who promote the role of women veterinarians. **Outstanding Woman Veterinarian** and **Distinguished Service Awards** are given for a person who does most to promote the role of women in veterinary medicine.

Association of African Women Scholars

c/o Obioma Nnaemeka
French and Women's Studies, Cavanaugh Hall
Indiana University, 425 University Boulevard
Indianapolis, IN 46202
317-278-2038
http://www.iupui.edu/~aaws.htm

AAWS is a worldwide organization dedicated to promoting and encouraging scholarship on African women in African studies, and forging networks with scholars, activists, students, and policy makers inside and outside Africa on issues specifically relevant or related to African women.

Association of American Colleges and Universities

Program on the Status and Education of Women
1818 R Street, NW
Washington, DC 20009-1604
202-387-3760
http://www.aacu-edu.org/initiatives/psew.html

The **Program on the Status and Education of Women** advocates for and supports women in higher education. Its current priorities are curriculum and campus climate and promoting women's leadership. It issues several publications and disseminates research on women in higher education, including its quarterly subscription newsletter, *On Campus With Women.*

Association of American Foreign Service Women

5125 MacArthur Boulevard, Suite 36
Washington, DC 20016
202-362-6514
http://www.kreative.net/fslifelines/aafsw/htm

The AAFSW is an advocate for foreign services spouses, employees, and retirees. Membership is open to all adult family members of the Foreign Affairs agencies who have served or are subject to serve at a U.S. diplomatic mission. It publishes a newsletter and serves as a forum for information on Americans living abroad.

Association of American Geographers

Geographic Perspectives on Women Specialty Group
1710 16th Street, NW
Washington, DC 20009
http://www.masu.nodak.edu/nssdiv/meartz/gpow/gpow.htm

The purpose of the **Geographic Perspectives on Women Specialty Group** is to promote geographic research and education on topics relating to women and gender. Membership is open to any member of the Assocation of American Geographers.

Association of American Law Schools

Section on Women in Legal Education
1201 Connecticut Avenue, NW, Suite 800
Washington, DC 20036-2605
202-296-8851
http://www.aals.org

The **Section on Women in Legal Education** consists of faculty members and professionals. It presents programs at AALS meetings, and publishes a newsletter and directory.

Association of American Medical Colleges

Women in Medicine Program
2450 N Street, NW
Washington, DC 20037-1126
202-828-0521
http://www.aamc.org

Organizations

The AAMC **Women in Medicine Program** offers activities and information concerning women who work in medicine. It compiles statistics on women in academic medicine in the U.S. and has established the Increasing Women's Leadership in Academic Medicine Initiative. It sponsors about 12 sessions at the AAMC annual meeting. AAMC's Professional Development Seminar for Senior Women in Medicine is offered during the summer for associate or full professors with clear potential for advancement to a major administrative position. The Professional Development Seminar for Junior Women Faculty in the fall is tailored to women early in their first faculty appointment who are aiming for a leadership position in academic medicine. It publishes the quarterly newsletter *Women in Medicine Update.*

Association of Black Women in Higher Education

PO Box 210
Princeton, NJ 08542-0210

ABWHE is a professional organization for women in higher education with five chapters in the United States. Regional and national chapter meetings and a biennial conference offer opportunities for networking and professional development. The group also recognizes the achievements of black women in higher education with awards.

Association of Canadian Women Composers

ACWC Bulletin
20 St. Joseph Street
Toronto, Ontario
M4Y 1J9 Canada
416-239-5195
http://music.acu.edu/www/iawm/acwc/index.html

The ACWC, a professional organization for women composers in Canada, promotes music written by Candian women composers and helps these composers achieve a higher profile. The association issues a newsletter three times a year and has published a directory of Canadian women composers. An annual meeting includes discussions, seminars, and concerts and networking opportunities.

Association of Chicago Bank Women

http://www.acbw.com

ACBW seeks to strengthen the personal and professional relationship among members of banks, banking associations, trust companies, and related banking and financial institutions. It provides a forum for mentoring young professionals, supports educational development of students interested in careers in the financial industry, and gives back to the community through social and financial contributions to various charities and causes. Its scholarship fund supports students enrolled in the City of Chicago Colleges by way of donation to the Professional Bank Teller and Beyond program.

Association of College and Research Libraries

Women's Studies Section
50 East Huron Street
Chicago, IL 60611
800-545-2433
http://www.ala.org/acrl/ww/wsshp.html

The **Women's Studies Section** of the ACRL was formed to discuss, promote, and support women's studies collections and service in academic and research libraries.

Association of Flight Attendants— AFL-CIO

1625 Massachusetts Avenue, NW
Washington, DC 20036
202-328-5400

The Association of Flight Attendants of the AFL-CIO is a labor union representing flight attendants. AFA's membership is 86 percent women.

Association of Nurses in AIDS Care

11250 Roger Bacon Drive, Suite 8
Reston, VA 20190-5202
800-260-6780
http://www.anacnet.org

The Association of Nurses in AIDS Care is a nonprofit professional nursing organization committed to fostering the individual and collective professional development of nurses involved in the delivery of health care to persons infected or affected by HIV. It publishes a newsletter, coordinates an annual conference, and works at the grassroots level through local chapters.

Association of Pediatric Oncology Nurses

4700 West Lake Avenue
Glenview, IL 60025
847-375-4724
http://www.apon.org

The Association of Pediatric Oncology Nurses strives to improve the care given to children who have cancer and their families. It supports members by encouraging them to contribute to professional and lay literature on nursing care for pediatric patients, providing national and regional training programs, and maintaining nursing practice standards it has developed.

Association of Perioperative Nurses

2170 South Parker Road, Suite 200
Denver, CO 80231-5711
800-755-2676
http://www.aoon.org

AOPN works to promote quality patient care by providing its members with education, standards, services, and representation. There are over 340 chapters.

Association of Professional Insurance Women

285 Hunting Ridge Road
Stamford, CT 06903
203-968-1548
http://www.apiw.org

APIW is a professional organization for women in insurance, reinsurance, and risk management. Member benefits include job placement service, college scholarships, a mentoring program, and membership directory and newsletter. To qualify for membership, women should have been employed in the insurance industry for at least three years in a professional or management capacity. Visit the Web site or call to request membership information.

Association of Professional Sales Women

Fort Lauderdale, FL
http://www.internetfl.com/apsw

APSW is a regional organization that provides educational programs and networking opportunities for women who work in sales.

Association of Rehabilitation Nurses

4700 West Lake Avenue
Glenview, IL 60025-1485
800-229-7530
http://rehabnurse.org

The Association of Rehabilitation Nurses promotes excellence in rehabilitation nursing practice and advances the specialty of rehabilitation nursing through certification standards, educational offerings, and publications.

Association of Women Industrial Designers

PO Box 468, Old Chelsea Station
New York, NY 10011
http://www.core77.com/AWID/

AWID is a professional organization addressing the issues that women in the industrial design field face. It is associated with the Pratt Institute and Parsons School of Design and offers a job board, meetings, and a resume bank. The Web site features links and information on *Goddess in the Details: Product Design by Women,* a 60-page catalogue of historical information and photos on women who have designed furniture, medical equipment, airport seating, speedboats, car batteries, and more.

Association of Women Surgeons

414 Plaza Drive, Suite 209
Westmont, IL 60559
630-655-0392
http://www.womensurgeons.org

The Association of Women Surgeons seeks to inspire, encourage, and enable women surgeons to realize their professional and personal goals. Through various networking forums, it supports the exchange of experiences, advice, and strategies among female surgeons around the world.

Organizations

It works with organizations such as the American College of Surgeons to bring down barriers to women surgeons. It co-sponsors an annual research grant for women surgeons.

Association of Women's Health, Obstetric, and Neonatal Nurses

2000 L Street, NW, Suite 740
Washington, DC 20036
800-673-8499
http://www.awhonn.org

AWHONN members practice in a variety of settings such as hospitals, home health agencies, physician's offices, universities, and public health agencies, and include staff nurses, nurse midwives, nurse practitioners, professors, nurse scientists, and administrators. It offers research-based practice projects, clinical publications, and continuing education.

At Home Mothers

406 East Buchanan Avenue
Fairfield, IA 52556
515-469-3068
http://www.athomemothers.com

At-Home Mothers is a membership organization that provides support and information for at-home mothers. Members receive *At-Home Mother* magazine. Also available are publications such as *Stay-At-Home Mom's Guide to Making Money*, and *College Degrees by Mail and Money*.

Berkshire Conference of Women Historians

c/o Barbara Winslow
124 Park Place
Brooklyn, NY 11217
http://www-berks.aas.duke.edu/index.htm

The Berkshire Conference of Women Historians was formed to establish a network among female historians and to exchange ideas on professional activities. The Berkshire Conference is a large meeting held every year for all those interested in women's history. Smaller conferences are also held periodically. The Berkshire Conference also administers a summer fellow-

ship at the Radcliffe College Bunting Institute and two graduate student awards.

Biophysical Society

Committee on Professional Opportunities for Women
9650 Rockville Pike, Room 0512
Bethesda, MD 20814
301-530-7114
http://www.biophysics.org

The **Committee on Professional Opportunities for Women** seeks to increase recognition and opportunities for women biophysicists in the Biophysical Society and the scientific professions. It sponsors a symposium and a workshop at the annual meeting, and publishes a newsletter.

Black Career Women

PO Box 19332
Cincinnati, OH 45219
513-531-1932

BCW was conceived by black women for the professional development of black women. It has implemented a series of programs that provide a forum for learning, enrichment, and encouragement for black women who may encounter racism, sexism, and economic, political, and societal forces that thwart their career successes. BCW has been recognized for its workshops and seminars. Offered annually, these one- and two-day seminars attract achieving women in multiple career arenas nationwide. Past themes have included Career Exploration and Self-Assessment; Negotiating Salary, Benefits, and Other Perks; and Preparing for Professional Advancement. BCW also develops information and research on black women workers, publicizes the achievements of black career women, and assists in the establishment of black women's networks, both locally and nationally.

Black Women in Church and Society

c/o Interdenominational Theological Center
700 Martin Luther King Drive
Atlanta, GA 30314
404-527-7740

Black Women in Church and Society is a national organization that promotes women in spirituality and religion. It offers the Womanist Scholars Program for Ph.D.s or senior scholars for a year's sabbatical of teaching, lecturing, and research in an area of religion, spirituality, or black women and family. Living expenses are paid. The Black Women in Ministry is a summer course offered in the evenings.

Black Women in Publishing

PO Box 6275, FDR Station
New York, NY 10150
212-427-8100
http://www.bwip.org

Black Women in Publishing is an employee-based trade association that seeks to increase the presence and support the efforts of African American women in the publishing industry. Members are writers, publishers, freelancers, agents, attorneys, CEOs, VPs, and business owners. Its meetings and publications facilitate learning and networking and recognize initiative and achievement.

Black Women in Sisterhood for Action

P.O. Box 1592
Washington, DC 20013
301-460-1565
http://www.feminist.com/bisas1.htm

BISA seeks to develop and promote alternative strategies for educational and career development of black women in the world of work, and provide scholarship assistance to youths, and leaderships, role models, and mentors for young people. BISA members learn and develop leadership and management skills through work on its committees.

Black Women in Sport Foundation

PO Box 2610
Philadelphia, PA 19130
http://www.blackwomeninsport.org

Black Women in Sport Foundation facilitates the development of black women in every aspect of sport through "hands-on" development and management of grassroots level outreach programs. The foundation has developed mentoring clinics in golf, tennis, and fencing for young women and girls in eight states. It produced the video and companion manual "Amazing Grace," emphasizing the process of developing and sustaining an interest in sport activity. It also holds annual conferences.

Black Women Lawyers Association of Greater Chicago

321 South Plymouth Court, Sixth Floor
Chicago, IL 60604
312-554-2088

The BWLA is a professional organization of over 500 African American women lawyers in the Chicago area. It seeks to identify and address issues unique to African American women lawyers, and improve the adminstration of justice by increasing participation of African-American women and other minorities throughout the legal system. It serves the community through educational programs, high school mentoring programs, scholarships, and recognition of the achievements of its members and other notable African-American women.

Black Women Organized for Educational Development

499 15th Street, Suite 310
Oakland, CA 94612
510-763-9501

BWOED assists low-income African-American women and their families by fostering economic preservation through self-sufficiency. A mentoring program for youth and support group sessions for adults are two ways BWOED works toward its goals. Workshops and training are provided, and a resource center provides information and referral services on employment opportunities.

Black Women's Agenda

202-289-7769

The Black Women's Agenda protects and advances the needs and rights of black women in society through research, dissemination of information, advocacy, education, and training.

Organizations

Business and Professional Women

2012 Massachusetts Avenue, NW
Washington, DC 20036
202-296-9118
http://www.bpwusa.org

BPW is one of the largest organizations for working women, with over 70,000 members nationwide. BPW promotes equity for women in the workplace through advocacy and education. The BPW Foundation helps low-income women and other women pursuing degrees in a variety of fields. Members receive a newsletter and access to national and regional conventions and educational seminars. Members-at-large join the national association directly and receive national publications and benefits. More than 2,000 local chapters exist that offer additional benefits. Contact the national organization to find a local chapter in your area.

Canadian Association for Women and Sport

1600 James Naismith Drive
Gloucester, Ontario
K1B 5N4 Canada
613-748-5793
http://www.caaws.ca

CAAWS is a national organization that works with Sport Canada and with Canada's sport and active living communities to achieve gender equity in sports. It publishes materials in this area and offers awards and scholarships.

Canadian Congress for Learning Opportunities for Women

27 Follis Avenue
Toronto, Ontario
M6G 1S5 Canada
416-532-9108
http://www.nald.ca/cclow.htm

CCLOW is a national, feminist organization that seeks to address education and training issues for girls and women. It strives to achieve women's social, political, and economic equality through expanded learning opportunities. A national convention is held annually and scholarships are available to needy women.

Canadian Federation of Business and Professional Women's Clubs

950 Auger Street
Sudbury, Ontario
P3E 4A9 Canada
http://www.bpwcanada.com

The Canadian Federation of BPW Clubs provides opportunities for interaction between members and clubs. It encourages women to pursue business, the professions, and industry and works toward the improvement of economic, employment, and social conditions for women. It holds national and regional events, issues a newsletter, and offers scholarships at the provincial and local level. Contact national headquarters for information on local clubs.

Canadian Federation of University Women

251 Bank Street, Suite 600
Ottawa, Ontario
K2P 1X3 Canada
613-234-2732
http://www.cfuw.ca

CFUW is a national organization with clubs at the local level. It provides opportunities to network with members at the local, regional, provincial, national, and international levels. Local clubs hold meetings on educational, cultural, and social issues with emphasis on the status of women; offer scholarships and awards; and research and present solutions to women's educational issues.

Canadian Women's Business Network

3995 MacIsaac Drive
Nanaimo, British Columbia
V9T 3VS Canada
250-518-0567
http://www.cdnbizwomen.com

The Canadian Women's Business Network offers networking and resources for businesswomen in Canada. The Web site features a members' showcase, the CWBN Marketplace of member and relevant businesses, and other business resources. It also publishes a newsletter.

Catalyst

120 Wall Street
New York, NY 10005
212-514-7600
http://www.catalystwomen.org/home.html

This organization is of interest to women business owners and managers rather than individuals. Catalyst no longer advises individuals on career development. It works with corporations and professional firms to effect change for women in the workplace. It advises companies where women are underrepresented on improving their work environment for women. It also offers a speakers bureau and assists in placing women on corporate boards.

Center for the American Woman and Politics

191 Ryders Lane
Rutgers University
New Brunswick, NJ 08901
732-932-9384
http://www.rci.rutgers.edu/~cawp/

CAWP is a university-based research, education, and public service center that seeks to promote greater understanding of women's relationship to politics and government. CAWP publishes information on women and politics, such as fact sheets on women officeholders, and compiles a directory of women public officials. Every four years, CAWP holds the National Forum for Women State Legislators, as well as other national conferences. It co-sponsors the **Good Housekeeping Award for Women in Government** and offers internships.

Center for the Child Care Workforce

733 Fifteenth Street, NW, Suite 1037
Washington, DC 20005
202-737-7700
http://www.ccw.org

The Center for the Child Care Workforce is a nonprofit, research, education, and advocacy organization seeking to improve child care quality by upgrading the compensation, working conditions, and training of child care teachers and family child care providers. It coordinates the Worthy Wage campaign, a grassroots effort to press for staffing solutions. Many articles are available on the Web site, including "Rights in the Workplace: A Guide for Child Care Teachers." Surveys, studies, reports, and trainer's guides are available for purchase. Members receive a newsletter, technical assistance, and discounts on publications and products.

Center for Women and Information Technology

University of Maryland, Baltimore County
1000 Hilltop Circle
Baltimore, MD 21250
410-455-2822
http://www.umbc.edu/cwit/index.html

The Center for Women and Information Technology seeks to address and rectify women's underrepresentation in information technology and to enhance the understanding of the relationship between gender and IT. It encourages more women and girls to study computer science and encourages research concerning the relationship between gender and IT. IT offers online resources, lecture series, workshops, internship assistance for undergraduate and graduate women, and encourages corporate involvement with women and information technology.

Center for Women In Politics and Public Policy

The Network
Program for Women in Politics and Government
University of Massachusetts-Boston, Division of Continuing Education
100 Morrissey Boulevard
Boston, MA 02725-3393
617-287-6785
http://tap.epn.org/cwppp/

The Network is the membership component of the Center for Women in Politics and Public Policy. Members participate in the Women's Research Forum, Woman of the Year Celebration, and receive a membership directory. The center offers the Graduate Program for Women in Politics and Government. It administers the **Betty Taymor Fund,** which provides scholarships to help women participate in the program.

Organizations

Center for Women Policy Studies

1211 Connecticut Avenue, NW, Suite 312
Washington, DC 20036
http://www.centerwomenpolicy.org

The Center for Women Policy Studies addresses issues that have significant implications for women at work and in their personal lives. The center conducts research, analyzes policy and legislation, convenes leaders, publishes reports, and conducts advocacy. It issues various publications and offers internships for women.

Chicago Women in Publishing

PO Box 268107
Chicago, IL 60626
312-641-6311
http://www.cwip.org

CWIP is a regional organization for women in the publishing industry. It seeks to recognize, promote, and advance women in all fields of publishing. Membership benefits include career workshops, a newsletter, membership directory, freelance directory, annual job fair, and Jobvine, a phone listing of publishing jobs.

Christian Business and Professional Women's Ministries

PO Box 6211
Laguna Niguel, CA 92607
949-443-0016
http://www.cbpwm.org

Christian Business and Professional Women's Ministries is largely a community service and spiritual organization, but also fosters personal and leadership development for Christian businesswomen through training and workshop opportunities. It also offers a mentoring program.

Church Women United

475 Riverside Drive, Room 812
New York, NY 10115
212-870-2347

Church Women United was organized before World War II to give women of faith a voice in the church and the community. This ecumenical organization for laywomen organizes World Day of Prayer, May Friendship Day, and World Community Day. It publishes a newsletter and meetings are held at the local level through chapters across the country.

Clearinghouse on Women's Issues

P.O. Box 70603
Friendship Heights, MD 20813

The Clearinghouse on Women's Issues provides a channel for dissemination of information on a variety of issues of mutual concern, such as equality in the workplace, advancement of educational opportunities for women, status of the family, and others. Membership includes a subscription to the CWI newsletter, published nine times a year. It holds monthly meetings in Washington, DC.

The Coalition for Women's Economic Development and Global Equality

Women's EDGE
1825 Connecticut Avenue, NW, Suite 800
Washington, DC 20009
202-884-8396
http://www.womensedge.org

Women's EDGE educates the public and policy makers on women's and developmental issues and works to increase the United States' investment in international aid programs. Membership benefits include a newsletter, opportunities to participate in state-level advocacy programs, email job and internship announcements, and discounts on Women's EDGE events.

Coalition of Labor Union Women

1126 16th Street, NW
Washington, DC 20036
202-466-4610
http://www.cluw.org

The Coalition of Labor Union Women seeks to implement the agenda of women laborers through education, negotiations, legislation, and media events. It publishes *CLUW News*, a newsletter for members. There are over 75 chapters. A membership application is available on the Web site.

College Music Society

Committee on the Status of Women
202 West Spruce Street
Missoula, MT 59802
406-721-9616
http://www.music.org

The **Committee on the Status of Women** is a part of the College Music Society, which gathers, considers, and disseminates ideas on the philosophy and practice of music. The committee supports the professional development of women musicians and teachers and discusses issues in teaching and women and gender.

Computing Research Association

Committee on the Status of Women in Computer Science and Computer Engineering
1100 17th Street, NW, Suite 507
Washington, DC 20036-4632
202-234-2111
http://cra.org/Activities/craw/

The Computing Research Association formed the **Committee on the Status of Women in Computer Science and Computer Engineering** to eliminate barriers to women in CS and CE research. It coordinates the Conference Experiences for Women Program (travel grants) and maintains a large amount of information on its Web site for women in science, math, engineering, and technology. It also administers the CRA Distributed Mentor Project for undergraduate women, funded by the National Science Foundation.

Cosmetic Executive Women

20 East 69th Street, Suite SC
New York, NY 10021
212-717-2415
http://www.cew.org

Cosmetic Executive Women is a professional association for executives from beauty, cosmetics, and related industries. It offers career luncheons, seminars, newsmaker forums, and panel discussions to help its members keep up-to-date on industry trends and issues.

Dermatology Nurses Association

East Holly Avenue, Box 56
Pitman, NJ 08071-0056
800-454-4362
http://dna.inurse.com

The Dermatology Nurses Association's membership includes registered nurses, licensed practical nurses, licensed vocational nurses, and individuals involved in the care of the dermatology patient. It publishes a journal and newsletter, grants specialty certification, and offers scholarships, awards, and grants to its members.

Developmental Disabilities Nurses Association

228 Grimes Street, Suite 246
Eugene, OR 97402
800-888-6733
http://www.ddna.org

The Developmental Disabilities Nurses Association is a professional organization for nurses serving individuals with developmental disabilities in a variety of settings. It offers the Certified Developmental Disabilities Nurse (CDDN) certification. Membership benefits include a newsletter and annual conference.

Dialogue on Diversity

1730 K Street, Suite 304
Washington, DC 20006
703-631-0630
http://www.dialogueondiversity.org

Dialogue on Diversity provides opportunities and resources to build the personal and professional strengths of women of ethnically and culturally diverse backgrounds. Members benefit by a newsletter, national programs and events, networking, mentoring programs, leadership development, internships, scholarships, resource connections, a membership directory, and entrepreneurship training and awards. Internships will be available for student members of the organization. Call or visit the Web site for membership information.

Organizations

Disabled Peoples International

Women's Committee
101-7 Evergreen Place
Winnipeg, Manitoba R3L 2T3
204-827-8010
http://www.dpi.org/women.html

The DPI **Women's Committee** provides a structure within DPI to work for the special interests of girls and women. It monitors the disability movement within and outside the DPI system to ensure its full participation in all areas, including the workplace.

Disabled Women's Alliance

World Institute on Disability
510 16th Street, Suite 100
Oakland, CA 94612
510-251-4355
http://www.igc.org/beijing/ngo/widnet.html

The Disabled Women's Alliance is a network of women from the U.S. and Canada with physical disabilities. Almost half of the group lives in the San Francisco Bay area, where the independent living movement has its roots. Members advocate for disabled women's rights both on the job and regarding health care and parental rights.

Disabled Women's Network—Canada

http://www.indie.ca/dawn/indext.htm

DAWN Canada is a national, cross-disability organization of women with disabilities in Canada. Its focus is research, defining the needs and concerns of women with disabilities, and designing programs to address those needs and concerns.

Educational Foundation for Women in Accounting

PO Box 1925
Southeastern, PA 19399-1925
610-407-9229
http://www.efwa.org

The Educational Foundation for Women in Accounting funds and awards several scholarships annually. EFWA also conducts a biannual demographic survey of women in accounting; funds issues papers by faculty, individuals, or

business to research technical accounting issues or issues furthering women in the accounting profession; and provides research grants for women faculty members to contribute to the field of accounting.

Educational Foundation for Women in Accounting—San Francisco

PO Box 26413
San Francisco, CA 94126
415-333-9045
http://www.efwa.org

FWASF seeks to further the advancement of women who work in the financial sector of the Bay Area of California. It provides a supportive network, mentoring opportunities, monthly luncheons, and committee experience for its members. Members include executive-level women with expertise ranging from investment management and research to accounting, banking, marketing, communications, corporate treasury, financial underwriting, and estate and personal planning. FWASF also offers scholarships in the Bay Area.

Emergency Nurses Association

847-460-4000
http://www.ena.org

ENA is a membership organization for Emergency Department nurses and other health care professionals. Membership benefits include information, education, networking, and representation.

Entitled Black Women Artists

c/o Pindell
PO Box 20566
Columbus Circle Station
New York, NY 10023
http://www.entitled-bwartists.com

Entitled Black Women Artists was formed to provide a support network for women visual artists of African descent. It is a cross-generational coalition of artists and arts professionals working in diverse media. It promotes increased exhibition opportunities for members and maintains a database of opportunities for artists.

Equal Employment Opportunity Commission

1801 L Street, NW
Washington, DC 20507
800-669-4000
http://www.eeoc.gov

Call this federal agency to report sexual discrimination or harassment.

Executive Women International

515 South 700 East, Suite 2F
Salt Lake City, UT 84102
801-355-2800

Executive Women International brings together individuals from diverse areas of business to promote member firms, enhance personal and professional development, and encourage community involvement. EWI offers an annual convention and trade show and members receive *Pulse Magazine* quarterly. Local chapters offer the opportunity to get involved and network at the local level.

Executive Women's Golf Association

300 Avenue of the Champions
Palm Beach Gardens, FL 33418
800-407-1477
http://www.ewga.com

EWGA was formed to promote and foster a spirit of acceptance, dignity, and respect for career-oriented women golfers nationwide. Local chapters organize a variety of clinic and events. Nearly half of members are in key management positions, providing an environment for networking with other businesswomen in a relaxed atmosphere. Contact information for individual chapters and a membership application is available on the Web site.

Federal Women in Science and Engineering (FedWise)

http://www.fedwise.org

FedWise is a federal interagency committee of women scientists and engineers. It is not a membership organization; rather, it encourages all scientists, engineers, and other professional women to take part in its activities. Chapters are found in individual federal agencies and regions. FedWise coordinates annual training and development programs at its annual conference. It sponsors awards for women in science and engineering, and conducts the Student Challenge, for ninth and tenth grade girls in the Washington, DC, area.

Federally Employed Women

1400 Eye Street, NW, Suite 425
Washington, DC 20005-2252
202-898-0994
http://www.few.org

FEW's membership consists of people employed by or retired from the federal government. It works in four program areas to improve the status of women employed by the federal government: legislative, training, compliance, and diversity. The national office publishes a newsletter.

Federation of American Women's Clubs Overseas

http://www.fawco.org

The Federation of American Women's Clubs Overseas is an international network for American women living and working abroad and is active in the fields of U.S. citizens' concerns, education, environmental protection, and women's and children's rights. Members and their daughters are eligible for FAWCO undergraduate and graduate scholarships. Members share travel trips and information on the overseas experience, and hold conferences.

Female Anglers Network

253 Old Ridge Road
Hollsopple, PA 15935
888-FISHFAN
http://www.femaleangler.org

The Female Anglers Network provides support, education, and camaraderie for women anglers

Organizations

nationwide. It publishes a bi-monthly magazine and hosts women-only basic fishing seminars.

Feminist Majority

1600 Wilson Boulevard, Suite 801
Arlington, VA 22209
703-522-2214
http://www.feminist.org

The Feminist Majority and the **Feminist Majority Foundation** are non-profit research and advocacy organizations dedicated to promoting equality for women. A number of publications on women's issues and statistics are available.

Feministas Unidas

(allied organization of the Modern Language Association)
Arizona State University West
Women's Studies - Mail Code 2151
PO Box 37100
Phoenix, AZ 85069-7100
http://www.west.asu.edu/femunida

Feministas Unidas is an affiliate of the Modern Language Association and sponsors a panel at the annual MLA convention and publishes a newsletter twice yearly. It is a coalition of feminist scholars in Spanish, Spanish-American, Luso-Brazilian, Afro-Latin American, and U.S. Latino/a Studies.

Fifty Plus One

817 Silver Spring Avenue
Silver Spring, MD 20910
301-587-8061
http://www.interguru.com/fiftyplusone/front.htm

Fifty Plus One offers training to women candidates and campaign workers. During intensive two-day training sessions, participants learn from women elected officials and campaign professionals how to effectively manage an electoral campaign. Participants receive a campaign tool kit and list of organizations and publications they can consult further should they decide to run for office.

Financial Women International

200 North Glebe Road, Suite 1430
Arlington, VA 22203
703-807-2007
http://www.fwi.org

FWI serves women in the financial services industry who seek to expand their personal and professional capabilities. There are more than 250 local groups across the United States. FWI offers seminars on topics such as leadership and presentation skills, an annual conference, and a newsletter to its members. It also publishes *Financial Woman Today*, a quarterly magazine.

Financial Women's Association of New York

215 Park Avenue South, Suite 1713
New York, NY 10003
212-533-2141
http://www.fwa.org

FWA offers leadership development and networking opportunities to women employed in the financial industry in and around New York City. FWA sponsors more than 100 activities every year, including forums with CEOs, mentoring programs, and professional workshops. FWA works to identify opportunities for women to serve on corporate boards and educates members about issues involved in serving on corporate boards.

Forum for Women Entrepreneurs

420 Florence Avenue, Suite 100
Palo Alto, CA 94301
650-470-0938
http://www.fwe.org

The Forum for Women Entrepreneurs is a trade association that fosters, supports, and promotes entrepreneurship for women in technology and the life sciences. It has offices in the Bay Area and Seattle. It seeks to assist women in Silicon Valley in building venture-fundable businesses by offering panels, workshops, dinners, and seminars, and connecting entrepreneurs with investors.

Foundation for African-American Women

55 West 68th Street
New York, NY 10023
212-799-0322

The foundation serves as a resource center for African-American women in the New York area. It provides information and support in many areas, including career assistance.

Foundation for Women's Resources

3500 Jefferson, Suite 210
Austin, TX 78731
512-459-1167

The Foundation for Women's Resources is an international educational organization that develops nonpartisan projects and programs to improve the status of women.

Friends of Lulu

4657 Cajon Way
1250 New York Avenue, NW
San Diego, CA 92115
http://www.friends-lulu.org

Friends of Lulu is a national organization aimed at getting more women and girls involved in comic books. Friends of Lulu publishes a directory of women in the industry, a guide for comics retailers "How to Get Girls Into Your Store", and a regular newsletter. It also offers a mentoring program, workshops, support groups, and an annual awards program. Visit the Web site or write for membership information.

Fund for Women Artists

351 Pleasant Street, Suite 108
Northampton, MA 01060
413-585-5968
http://www.womenarts.org

The Fund for Women Artists is a nonprofit arts service organization that encourages diversity and employment for women in theater, film, and video. It provides grant writing and other management services to women in the arts and funds plays, films, videos, and educational projects.

General Federation of Women's Clubs

1734 N Street, NW
Washington, DC 20036-2990
202-347-3168
http://www.gfwc.org

GFWC is an international organization of community-based volunteer women's clubs. Club membership offers women of all ages an opportunity to serve their communities and exchange ideas. Members belong to a local club, which belongs to one of 52 state federations.

Graduate Women in Business Network

c/o Darden Graduate School of Business Administration
PO Box 6550`
Charlottesville, VA 22906-6550
804-924-6981
http://www.gwib.org

The Graduate Women in Business Network seeks to promote and enhance the role of women in business. An annual national conference is sponsored and held by an accredited MBA school. GWIB members receive a quarterly newsletter, *Network Exchange,* and have access to resources including lists of speakers, panelists, company and industry contacts, alumnae and professional women, Web sites, and literature on women's issues.

Great Lakes Tradeswomen Alliance

http://www.womeninthetrades.org

Great Lakes Tradeswomen Alliance is a collaboration of six community-based organizations in the Midwest: Chicago Women in Trades, Minnesota Women in Trades, Hard Hatted Women, Employment Options Inc., Women's Resource Center, and YWCA of Milwaukee—Non-traditional Employment Training. The GLTA works to create, expand, and improve services for the recruitment of women in the skilled trades and other nontraditional occupations.

Organizations

Great Lakes Women's Leadership Network

394 Lake Avenue South, Suite 308
Duluth, MN 55802
218-726-1828
http://www.cp.duluth.mn.us/~lakes/mission.html

GLWLN was formed to mentor and support Great Lakes women and foster empowerment and social change through leadership skills training, education, and networking. Members are Canadian and American women. A directory of women with skills and issues expertise from around the Great Lakes is available and regional training is held periodically.

Hard Hatted Women

4207 Lorain
Cleveland, OH 44113
216-961-4449
http://www.stratos.net/hhw

Hard Hatted Women promotes women's economic empowerment by ensuring equal access to all jobs, especially nontraditional jobs. Activities include a preapprenticeship training program; *Riveting News,* its newsletter; a job bank; annual career fair; and the women in highways project, to increase the number of women working on road and bridge construction jobs.

Health Care Executive Assistants

c/o The American Hospital Association
1 North Franklin
Chicago, IL 60606
312-422-3870
http://www.hceaonline.org

HCEA is a professional association for executive assistants, administrative assistants, and other professionals reporting to health care management. It provides its members with opportunities for education, networking, and recognition.

Hispanas Organized for Political Equality

634 South Spring Street, Suite 290
Los Angeles, CA 90014
213-622-0606
http://www.latinas.org

HOPE seeks to further the education and participation of Hispanic and all other women in the political process. Through town hall meetings, debates, educational seminars, and practical workshops, HOPE seeks to empower Hispanic women. The HOPE-PAC generates seed money for Latinas seeking elective office. The Hope Leadership Institute is an eight-month leadership training program designed to empower Hispanic women to create critical changes in the areas of health, education, and economics.

Hispanic Women's Corporation

PO Box 20725
Phoenix, AZ 85036-0725
602-954-7995

The Hispanic Women's Corporation is a national organization that seeks to ensure Hispanic women are active participants in the workforce by promoting them in the educational and work communities, and recognizing their achievements. It sponsors an annual conference of educational and motivational presentations, panel discussions, and forums. The Hispanic Women's Leadership Institute provides leadership training to Hispanic women in the Southwest to promote them to management positions. The Hispanic Scholars Program provides scholarships to Hispanic women in need.

Hispanic Women's Network of Texas

Dallas Chapter
PO Box 516411
Dallas, TX 75251-6411

The Hispanic Women's Network of Texas is a statewide organization of individuals from diverse backgrounds who seek to promote the participation of Hispanic women in public, cultural, and civic arenas. Chapters are in Austin, Corpus Christi, Dallas, El Paso, Fort Worth, Rio Grande Valley, and San Antonio.

Independent Means

126 Powers Avenue
Santa Barbara, CA 93103
800-350-1816
http://www.anincomeoftheirown.com

Independent Means is a national organization that seeks to instill in girls under 20 the desire and the means to attain financial independence and maintain it throughout adult life. One-day programs bring women entrepreneurs together with teenage women to explore ownership and entrepreneurship as career options. It also offers the National Business Plan Competition for girls 13-19. Offices are in California, but programs are run all over the United States.

Indian Business and Professional Women

278 Bayberry Common
Fremont, CA 94539
650-506-2257
http://www.ibpw.org

IBPW seeks to enhance the business, professional, and self-enrichment skills of Indian women. It offers workshops and training, recognizes accomplishments, and publishes a newsletter and membership directory.

Indigenous Women's Network

PO Box 2967
Rapid City, SD 57709-2967
605-399-0867

This national coalition of native women is mainly a social service organization, but also encourages the self-determination of indigenous women through attainment of self-sufficiency, and assists women who are seeking education or vocational training.

Institute for Women and Work

New York School of Industrial and Labor Relations
Cornell University
16 East 34th Street, Fourth Floor
New York, NY 10016
212-340-2800

The institute develops research for policy analysis on working women's progress in New York and nationally; develops educational and training programs; provides legislators, unionists, workplace leaders, and advocates with technical assistance to advance working women's policy agenda; and develops public forums, seminars, and conferences on topics that concern women's status and progress.

Institute for Women in Technology

3333 Coyote Hill Road
Palo Alto, CA 94304
650-812-4496
http://www.iwt.org

The Institute for Women and Technology works in areas that engage women and men in industry, academia, government, and communities to imagine, design, create, and deploy technologies that have positive impacts on women around the world. The institute holds meetings and workshops and pursues research and development through development projects and virtual development centers.

Institute for Women in Trades, Technology, and Science

3010 Wisconsin Avenue, NW, Suite E10
Washington, DC 20016
202-686-7275
http://www.iwitts.com

IWITTS seeks to integrate women into the full range of trades, technology, and science careers in which they are underrepresented, such as police officer, pilot, automotive technician, electrician, and Web master, just to name a few. IWITTS conducts training workshops for teachers and industry on recruiting young girls to male-dominated courses and professions. IWITTS serves as a resource for employers and women who work in male-dominated professions.

Institute of Electrical and Electronics Engineers

Women in Engineering Committee
445 Hoes Lane
PO Box 459
Piscataway, NJ 08855-0459
800-678-IEEE
http://www.ieee.org/organizations/commi

The IEEE **Women in Engineering Committee** promotes membership in IEEE, gathers and disseminates information about the status of women in engineering, and facilitates the development of mentoring and educational programs within IEEE.

Intercollegiate Women's Lacrosse Coaches Association

http://www.iwlca.org

The IWLCA is a non-profit corporation of Division I, II, and III coaches from across the United States. IWLCA works to promote the game of lacrosse and the education of its member coaches.

The International Alliance

PO Box 1119
Sparks-Glencoe
Baltimore, MD 21152
410-472-4221
http://www.t-i-a.com

The International Alliance is an umbrella organization that links over 30 women's business organizations and networks. It seeks to assist women in reaching their potential and enable them to contribute in business, the professions, academia, government, and the not-for-profit sector.

International Alliance for Women in Music

IAWM/Department of Music
Indiana University of Pennsylvania
422 South 11th Street, Room 209
Indiana, PA 15705-1070
724-357-7918
http://150.252.8.92/www/iawm/

The International Alliance for Women in Music was formed in 1995 through the merger of the International Congress for Women in Music, American Women Composers, and International League of Women Composers. The organization publishes the *IAWM Journal.*

International Association of Administrative Professionals

10502 NW Ambassador Drive
PO Box 20404
Kansas City, MO 64195-0404
816-891-6600
http://www.iaap-hq.org

Formerly known as **Professional Secretaries International**, the International Association of Administrative Professionals includes as its members adminstrative assistants, executive secretaries, office coordinators, information specialists, and related administrative professionals. There are over 40,000 members. Membership benefits include access to research findings, *OfficePro* magazine, discounts on educational products and services, a newsletter, and travel and insurance discounts. IAAP holds an annual international convention and education forum.

International Association of Physical Education and Sport for Girls and Women

c/o University of Delaware
Carpenter Sports Building
Newark, DE 19716
302-831-2644
http://www.udel.edu/PhyEd/bkelly/iapesgw.html

IAPESGW supports its members working for women's and girls' sport and physical education and provides opportunities for professional development and international cooperation. It holds Scientific Congresses every four years.

International Association of Women Ministers

579 Main Street
Stroudsburg, PA 18360
570-421-7751

The International Association of Women Ministers is a professional organization for women who minister in the United States and around the world. It offers a newsletter, a convention, and annual meetings.

International Association of Women Police

IAWP Administrative Assistant
Rural Route 1, Box 149
Deer Isle, Maine 04627
http://www.iawp.org

The purpose of IAWP is to increase professionalism in police work; further the utilization of women in law enforcement; and provide a forum for sharing developments in police administration. Full-time law-enforcement officers as well as retired law enforcement officers, and security officers, are eligible for membership. Members receive IAWP's publication *Women Police*, reduced registration at the annual conference, and timely information on IAWP activities, projects, and programs.

International Black Women's Congress

555 Fenchurch Street, Suite 102
Norfolk, VA 23510
757-625-0500

IBWC works collectively with women of African ancestry and addresses issues of social, economic, and political empowerment.

International Centre for Women Playwrights

PO Box 86219
Portland, OR 97286
http://www.cadvision.com/sdempsey/
icwphmpg.htm

The mission of ICWP is to support women playwrights around the world by bringing international attention to their achievements, encouraging production of their plays, and translation, publication, and international distribution of their works. Its principal communications forum is the ICWP listserve, a high-volume e-mail forum for playwrights, directors, performers, poets, other genre writers, teachers, critics, students, and others.

International Federation of University Women

8 rue de l'Ancien-Port
CH-1201
Geneva, Switzerland
(41.22) 731 23 80
http://www.ifuw.org

IFUW is an organization of over 180,000 women graduates worldwide. It seeks to improve the status of women and girls, promote lifelong education, and to enable graduate women to use their expertise to effect change. It offers fellowships and grants to its members.

International Federation of Women's Travel Organizations

13901 North 73rd Street, Suite 210B
Scottsdale, AZ 85260-3125
602-596-6640
http://www.ten-io.com/ifwto/index.html

IFWTO is an umbrella organization for women's travel and tourism professional organizations. It seeks to address the concerns of women actively engaged in the sale and promotion of travel by assisting in the development of women's travel organizations where none exist, and in being involved in the planning and development of travel industry affairs.

International Lactation Consultants Association

4101 Boone Lake Trail, Suite 201
Raleigh, NC 27607
919-787-5181
http://www.ilca.org

Membership is open to all who care for mothers and infants and includes lactation consultants, nurses, physicians, dietitians, midwives, researchers, and others. ILCA publishes a peer-reviewed quarterly journal, *Journal of Human Lactation*. It also provides a member newsletter and a publications department that issues position papers, books, and breastfeeding promotional and educational materials. ILCA provides Standards of Practice and workshops for lactation consultants.

Organizations

International Nanny Association

Station House, Suite 438
900 Haddon Avenue
Collingswood, NJ 08108
609-858-0808
http://www.nanny.org

The International Nanny Association serves as a clearinghouse for information on the in-home child care industry. Membership is made up of nannies, nanny educators, and nanny referral agency owners. Group rate insurance is available to members, as well as a newsletter, annual conference, listing in the membership directory, and travel discount programs.

International Organization of Pakistani Women Engineers

http://www.iopwe.org

The IOPWE provides a forum for discussion of issues specific to women engineers of Pakistani origin. It distributes a bimonthly newsletter, offers advice on finding jobs and applying to undergraduate and graduate engineering programs, provides assistance on technical and non-technical problems, and supports and encourages young women of Pakistani origin to enter science and engineering fields.

International Society of Nurses in Genetics

http://nursing.creighton.edu/isong/

The International Society of Nurses in Genetics is a nursing specialty organization that works to foster the scientific and professional growth of nurses in human genetics. It provides a forum for education and support for nurses providing genetic health care and promotes the integration of the nursing process into the delivery of genetic health care services. It publishes a newsletter and advances nursing research in human genetics.

International Society of Women Airline Pilots

2250 Tropicana Avenue, Suite 19-395
Las Vegas, NV 89119
http://www.iswap.org

The International Society of Women Airline Pilots seeks to promote the role of women as airline pilots and encourage young women interested in aviation careers. It administers a national scholarship program. It provides a speakers bank of women pilots to schools and youth organizations. ISWAP also maintains a library of books, manuals, and videos for members and provides information on maternity/family leave, loss of license, and related medical problems, furloughs, and other pilot concerns. It maintains a database of current pregnancy policies of airlines. Visit the Web site or write for membership information.

International Statistical Institute

PO Box 950
2270 AZ Voorburg
The Netherlands
31-70-3375737
http://www.cbs.nl/isi

The ISI **Committee on Women in Statistics** promotes and strengthens the representation of women statisticians in the ISI and the field of statistics in general. It hosts periodic meetings and publicizes scholarly papers on the status of women working in statistics all over the world.

International Triathlon Union

Women's Committee
604-926-7250
http://www.triathlon.worldsport.com

The ITU **Women's Committee** encourages the growth of women's involvement in triathlon. The Web site provides information on the committee's work, including action plans and reports to the ITU Congress. It participates in the annual Women's Masters Breakfast.

International Woman's Writing Guild

P.O. Box 810, Gracie Station
New York, NY 10028-0082
212-737-7536
http://www.iwwg.com

The International Women's Writing Guild is a network for the personal and professional empowerment of women through writing. Membership benefits include contest, award, and publication opportunities; free announcement of members' newly published works; news of upcoming local meetings and workshops; a list of literary agents and independent small presses; and health insurance at group rates.

International Women's Automotive Association

c/o Northwood University
3250 West Big Beaver Road, Suite 300
Troy, MI 48084
248-646-5250

The International Women's Automotive Association is a professional organization that seeks to further the principles and education of women in the automotive industry. Chapters across the country offer scholarships.

International Women's Bowling Congress

414-423-3260
http://www.bowl.com/wibc/index.html

International Women's Brass Conference

IBWC Executive Director
1007 Carolina Street
San Francisco, CA 94107
http://uptown.turnpike.net/~iwbc/about.html

The IWBC provides for the exchange of information among women brass performers, composers, and educators. Preserving recordings and documentation of the past, present, and future of women brass musicians is a priority. At its conference, held every three to five years, IWBC holds a solo competition and awards prize money to a soloist (man or woman). Plans include the formation of an all-women brass ensemble to tour the major concert venues of the world to dispel the notion that women don't have the physical or mental strength to perform on brass instruments. Write to the executive director or visit the Web site for membership or conference information.

International Women's Fishing Association

106 Woodhall Drive
Richmond, VA 23229

International Women's Forum

1621 Connecticut Avenue, NW, Suite 300
Washington, DC 20009
202-775-8917
http://www.iwforum.org

The International Women's Forum is a professional organization for influential women athletes, film stars, writers, composers, scientists, diplomats, academics, corporate chief executives, journalists, artists, and other women world leaders. The IWF Foundation supports the Leadership Foundation Fellows Program, designed to promote women in leadership positions.

International Women's Media Foundation

1726 M Street, NW, Suite 1002
Washington, DC 20036
202-496-1992
http://www.iwmf.org

The mission of the IWMF is to strengthen the role of women in the news media worldwide and to reduce discrimination and eliminate persecution of women in the news. It sponsors seminars and training sessions, critical leadership development tools, and training in the techniques of a free press and business of the media. It sponsors the IWMF African Women's Media Center to address the concerns specific to African Americans and other women of color in the media.

Intravenous Nurses Society

800-694-0298
http://www.ins1.org

The Intravenous Nurses Society is a national membership organization that provides educational programs and professional development opportunities. Members receive a newsletter, and discounts on products and services.

Organizations

Iranian Women's Studies Foundation

PO Box 380882
Cambridge, MA 02238-0882
617-492-9001
http://www.iwsf.org

The Iranian Women's Studies Foundation provides a forum for the exchange of ideas on issues related to Iranian women. It hosts an annual conference with scholarly presentations, art exhibitions, and artistic performances by Iranian women. It publishes the *Journal of the IWSF* and forwards calls for papers.

Journalism and Women Symposium

http://www.jaws.org

The symposium brings together women journalists and journalism educators and researchers from across the country to meet in an atmosphere of mutual support and professional growth. It holds an annual JAWS Camp, where professionals gather to explore issues like "ethics and equity, coverage and careers, and affirmative action and anger."

Ladies Professional Golf Association

100 International Gulf Drive
Daytona Beach, FL 32124-1092
904-274-6200
http://www.lpga.com

The LPGA Tour Season includes 43 events and a purse worth more than $36.2 million. LPGA coordinates a youth program to introduce young people, especially young women, to the game of golf through its Girls Golf Club, Urban Youth Program, and Crayola Junior Clinics. It also sponsors golf clinics for women. The LPGA Teaching and Professional Division has more than 1,100 members who advance the game of golf through teaching, managing golf facilities, and coaching.

Leadership Conference of Women Religious

8808 Cameron Street
Silver Spring, MD 20910-4113
301-588-4955
http://www.lcwr.org

Membership in LCWR is open to Catholic sisters who are principal administrators of their religious institutes (orders) in the United States. Associate membership is open to prioresses of contemplative communities of sisters, and to major offices of related national organizations. The organization seeks to promote understanding of religious life through an annual assembly, regular publications, and educational programs.

Lex Mundi

Women and the Law Committee
2100 West Loop South, Suite 1000
Houston, TX 77027
713-626-9393
http://www.lexmundi.org

Lex Mundi is an association of large law firms. The **Women and the Law Committee** helps develop the means to attract and retain qualified women attorneys. It provides a forum for discussing women's issues and encourages and helps women become more active in Lex Mundi. Contact Lex Mundi for contact information for the current women's committee chair.

Linguistic Society of America

Committee on the Status of Women in Linguistics
1325 18th Street, NW, Suite 211
Washington, DC 20036

The **Committee on the Status of Women in Linguistics** consists of two student members and seven faculty or postgraduate members. The committee seeks to help monitor and improve the status of women in linguistics, especially with regard to discrimination, harassment, and advancement. It hosts a workshop at the LSA conference and publishes a number of items, including guidelines for nonsexist usage across all disciplines. The Women in Linguistics Mentoring Alliance provides undergraduates, graduates, faculty, and women outside academia with mentors to help them with general skills and advice.

The Links Inc.

1200 Massachusetts Avenue, NW
Washington, DC 20005-4501
202-842-0123
http://www.smartek.com/links/pages/abou

The Links is an organization of women achievers who are role models, mentors, activists, and volunteers who work toward the realization of the vision for African Americans worldwide by linking like-minded organizations and individuals for partnership. Through established and new programs, the Links works to improve education and career opportunities for African American women and children.

Los Angeles Women in Music

PO Box 1817
Burbank, CA 91507-1817
213-243-6440
http://www.lawim.org

LAWIM promotes equal opportunities for women in the music industry by organizing and supporting special events, music showcases, expert panels, and educational seminars. Members are recording artists, musicians, songwriters, producers, engineers, attorneys, publishers, managers, accountants, and personnel from radio, recording companies, and recording rights societies. Benefits include a job bank, workshops, a newsletter, and educational workshops.

Mana, A Latina Organization

1725 K Street, NW, Suite 501
Washington, DC 20006
202-833-0060
http://www.hermana.org

MANA seeks to empower Hispanic women through leadership development and community action. It offers an annual leadership development conference, mentoring program, scholarships, and "Las Primeras," a national public recognition event that features Hispanic women considered firsts in their respective fields.

Mid-Atlantic Association of Women in Law Enforcement

PO Box 27472
Richmond, VA 23261-7472
http://state.vipnet.org/maawle/home.html

MAAWLE is a professional organization of law enforcement officers promoting women in the field of law enforcement from Delaware, Maryland, Virginia, District of Columbia, New Jersey, and Pennsylvania. It offers an annual training conference, networking, annual awards ceremony, retirement planning, and inservice credits for training.

Modern Language Association

Commission on the Status of Women in the Profession
10 Astor Place
New York, NY 10003-6981
212-475-9500
http://www.mla.org

The MLA **Committee on the Status of Women in the Profession** investigates and reports on the situation of women in the profession and promotes the study and teaching of women's literature.

Multicultural Women Attorneys Network

American Bar Association
750 North Lake Shore Drive
Chicago, IL 60611
312-988-5000
http://www.abanet.org/women/mwan.html

The network is a joint project of the American Bar Association's Commission on Women in the Profession and its Commission on Opportunities for Minorities in the Profession. It addresses issues of special concern to multicultural women lawyers with programs, roundtables, and publications to identify the impact of ethnicity and gender on the professional development of lawyers. It published the report *The Burdens of Both, the Privileges of Neither.*

Organizations

National Academy of Sciences
Women in Science and EngineeringGroup
2101 Constitution Avenue, NW
Washington, DC 20418-0007
202-334-2000
http://www.nas.edu

The National Research Council and the National Academies complex created the **Women in Science and Engineering Group** as a "sister effort" to existing WISE groups in federal agencies. The NRC's WISE members search for ways to increase the participation and visibility of women in Research Council activities and in the scientific community as a whole. Programs include bi-monthly brownbag seminars, a book club, and a career day for DC-area high school students. The Web site has an extensive list of organizations encouraging women in science and engineering.

National Assocation for Family Child Care
525 Southwest Fifth Street, Suite A
Des Moines, IA 50309
515-282-8192
http://www.nafcc.org

The NAFCC seeks to improve the quality of care provided by family child care providers. It offers accreditation standards and an online resource, "Starting Your Own Family Child Care Business," with advice on legal and practical considerations for families considering establishing a child care business in their home or elsewhere. Members receive a quarterly newsletter, access to publications and resources, and an annual conference.

National Assocation of Child Care Professionals
207 West Main Street, Suite 1
Christiansburg, VA 24073
540-382-5819
http://www.naccp.org

NACCP seeks to enhance the credibility and professionalism of the people who lead the child care industry; members are child care owners, directors, and administrators. It offers a national accreditation program for child care

managers, educational publications, product discounts, and administrative training.

National Association for Female Executives
135 W. 50th St., Suite 16
New York, NY 10020-1201
800-634-6233
http://www.nafe.org

NAFE is among the nation's largest business-women's organizations, with more than 150,000 members. Membership benefits include a subscription to *Executive Female* magazine, a bimonthly publication with a circulation of 600,000; a subscription to *Working Woman* magazine; corporate and travel discount programs; free small business resource center; resume service; nationwide job-find service; career development conferences; and networking opportunities. Visit the Web site for regional information.

National Association for Girls and Women in Sport
1900 Association Drive
Reston, VA 20191-1599
703-476-3450
http://www.aahperd.org/nagws/nagws-main.html

NAGWS champions equal funding, quality, and respect for women's sports programs. Its members are teachers, coaches, administrators, officials, and students. Membership in NAGWS is through the American Alliance for Health, Physical Education, Recreation and Dance. Members can join a second AAHPERD association at no cost. NAGWS benefits include workshops and seminars at the local, state, and regional levels, a national convention, and a newsletter.

National Association for Hispanic Nurses
1501 Sixteenth Street, NW
Washington, DC 20006
202-387-2477
http://www.incacorp.com/nahn

The National Association for Hispanic Nurses works toward the recruitment and retention of Hispanic students in nursing education programs and the identification of barriers to quality education and find solutions. It also provides leadership and educational opportunities for working professionals, including scholarships and awards for members at the local and national levels, an annual conference, a quarterly newsletter, and networking opportunities.

National Association for the Education of Young Children

1509 Sixteenth Street, NW
Washington, DC 20036
http://www.naeyc.org

NAEYC is a membership and advocacy organization on behalf of children birth through eight and those who serve them in early childhood education programs. It offers professional development assistance, including teacher preparation standards, the development of state certification standards, and in-service training. It offers accreditation of child care centers through its program review system.

National Association for Women in Education

1325 18th Street, NW, Suite 210
Washington, DC 20036
202-659-9330
http://www.nawe.org

NAWE seeks to advance and support women in higher education careers. Members receive the publications *Initiatives-The Journal of NAWE,* devoted to research and scholarship on women; *About Women on Campus,* with reports on issues and legislation impacting women in higher education; and discounts on the monthly newsletter *Women in Higher Education* and on NAWE books and other publications. NAWE also sponsors national conferencs, institutes, awards, and advocacy.

National Association of Asian American Professional Women

P.O. Box 494
Washington Grove, MD 20880-0494
301-854-0535
http://www.napaw.org

NAPAW's goals are to promote the social status of Asian American professional women, improve educational and training opportunities, stimulate and implement research, and enhance leadership skills. The organization provides workshops, seminars, networking, a newsletter, and resource specialists in leadership, management, communication, human resource development, small business strategies, public relations, financial management, and publications.

National Association of Black Female Executives in Music and Entertainment

http://www.womenet.org

NABFEME promotes career advancement of African-American women in the various sectors of the music and entertainment industry through networking, advocacy, and education. The Mentor Connection links women with varied experiences to learn from each other. Members also receive a newsletter and enjoy career development and training opportunities. The organization also sponsors scholarships for African-American females.

National Association of Collegiate Women Athletic Administrators

4701 Wrightsville Avenue
Oak Park D-1
Wilmington, NC 28403
910-793-8244
http://www.nacwaa.org

NACWAA was formed after the dissolution of the Association of Intercollegiate Athletics for Women in 1979 by 12 women athletic administrators from around the nation. The organization seeks to preserve and enhance opportunities for leadership and career development of women athletic administrators and to strengthen collegiate athletic programs as they relate to

Organizations

women. Members meet once annually at the annual convention and communicate throughout the year through networking and a newsletter. Mentoring and professional development training are other membership benefits.

The NACWAA/HERS **Institute for Administrative Advancement** is an annual week-long residential program designed to offer women coaches and administrators intensive training in athletic administration. Follow-up events include seminars for institute alumni and mentoring and networking programs. The institute is held on the campus of Bryn Mawr women's college in Pennsylvania.

National Association of Colored Women's Clubs

5808 16th Street, NW
Washington, DC 20011
202-726-2044

The NACWC, founded in 1896, claims to be America's oldest black women's organization. The organization is largely a service organization, but also seeks to promote education and economic betterment for African-American women and families.

National Association of Commissions for Women

8630 Fenton Street, Suite 984
Silver Spring, MD 20910-3808
301-585-8101
http://www.nacw.org

The National Association of Commissions for Women is an umbrella organization for the 270 state and local commissions for women. These government-sanctioned commissions were created to improve the status of women and to work toward equality and justice. NACW commissions provide support and information referral to women in the form of training, networking, mentoring, displaced homemaker service, and social service.

National Association of Counties

Women's Officials Caucus
440 First Street, NW, Suite 800
Washington, DC 20001
202-393-6226
http://www.naco.org

The National Association of Counties is a discussion forum and support network for elected and employed county government officials. The Women's Officials Caucus is a support system for women county officials and meets during NACO's conferences to discuss issues unique to women county government officials.

National Association of Executive Secretaries and Administrative Assistants

900 South Washington Street, Suite G13
Falls Church, VA 22046
703-237-8616
http://www.naesaa.com

The NAESAA seeks to promote the professional stature of the adminstrative profession. Over 95 percent of members are women. Members receive a newsletter and access to home study courses and seminars.

National Association of Female Paramedics

c/o Debbie Duma
1703 Paradise Drive
Kissimmee, FL 34741
http://nafp.webjump.com

This relatively new organization offers job placement assistance, a national awards program, travel program, seminars, and an association newsletter for women paramedics.

National Association of Independent Schools

Council for Women in Independent Schools
1620 L Street, NW
Washington, DC 20036
202-973-9700

The NAIS **Council for Women in Independent Schools** supports gender equity for women in independent schools.

National Association of Insurance Women

Tulsa, OK
800-766-6249
http://www.naiw.org

NAIW serves women working in various aspects of the insurance industry with local, regional, and national conferences and seminars. NAIW committees provide an arena for members to develop leadership skills. Members may submit articles for publication in NAIW publications such as *Today's Insurance Woman, NAIW Now!,* and the NAIW Web site. Visit the Web site for further information.

National Association of Negro Business and Professional Women's Clubs, Inc.

1806 New Hampshire Avenue, NW
Washington, DC 20009-3208
202-483-4206
http://www.nanbpwc.org

NANBPWC is a diverse organization of African-American women educators, executives, nurses, secretaries, lawyers, accountants, and students. It recognizes members' achievements with an awards program, offers a national convention and publishes *Responsibility*, the national newsletter. Members volunteer for community service projects that benefit women and families.

National Association of Neonatal Nurses

701 Lee Street, Suite 450
Des Plaines, IL 60016
800-451-3795
http://nann.org

NANN furthers the work of neonatal nurses in the provision of newborn and family care. Membership benefits include research grants and scholarships, group insurance, a newsletter, and four educational meetings a year.

National Association of Professional Mortgage Women

23607 Highway 99, Suite 2C
Edmonds, WA 98026
800-327-3034
http://www.napmw.org

NAPMW includes over 4,000 members in 80 local associations. The association fosters educational opportunities, works for equal recognition for women, and encourages women to choose mortgage banking as a career. Visit the Web site for details on the national organization and assistance finding an association in your area.

National Association of Professionals in Women's Health

175 West Jackson Boulevard, Suite A-1711
Chicago, IL 60604
312-786-1468
http://www.napwh.org

NAPWH is an organization for professionals working in the field of women's health. It provides a membership directory, quarterly newsletter, an annual women's health conference, awards for excellence, peer mentoring, and an extensive information library and database.

National Association of Railway Business Women

PO Box 500164
Austin, TX 78750
800-67-NARBW
http://www.narbw.org

The NARBW seeks to stimulate interest in the railroad industry; further educational, social, and professional interests of its members; and foster cooperation within the industry. It offers scholarships to its members and their dependents.

National Association of School Nurses

PO Box 1300
Scarborough, ME 04070-1300
207-883-2117
http://www.nasn.org

Organizations

The National Association of School Nurses provides educational opportunities and leadership development for school nurses. It publishes a professional journal five times a year with articles on clinical subjects and issues in school nursing. An annual conference, regional conferences, scholarships, and home study lessons are other membership benefits.

National Association of Securities Professionals

1212 New York Avenue, NW, Suite 210
Washington, DC 20005-3987
202-371-5535
http://www.naspnet.org

NASP was founded and developed by underrepresented individuals in the securities industry. It seeks to ensure equal opportunities for women and minorities in the securities industry through annual meetings, mentor luncheons, an internship program, newsletter, jobs bulletin, and conferences on specific topics, such as pension funds, and retail development.

National Association of Women Artists

41 Union Square West 906
New York, NY 10003-3278

NAWA is an organization of women in the arts, with a primary purpose of encouraging and promoting the creative output of women artists. NAWA seeks exhibition opportunities for its members and awards scholarships through the Art Students Leagues of New York. For information, send a SASE.

National Association of Women Business Owners

1100 Wayne Avenue, Suite 830
Silver Spring, MD 20910
301-608-2950
http://www.nawbo.org

NAWBO works to "propel women entrepreneurs into economic, social, and political spheres of power worldwide." There are over 75 chapters. Membership is open to sole proprietors, partners, and corporate owners with day-to-day management responsibility. Active members who live in a chapter area automatically join both chapter and national. Those who do not live in a chapter area join as at-large members. Members qualify for business product and service discounts, and loans.

National Association of Women in Chambers of Commerce

P.O. Box 4552
Grand Junction, CO 81502-4552
303-242-0075
http://www.expressnet.com/NAWCC/

NAWCC provides education, management tools, recognition, and information for business improvement. Its members are affiliates of the United States Chamber of Commerce, and have access to the U.S. Chamber's resource library, reports, studies, magazines, and newsletter. NAWCC provides networking opportunities across the nation, a newsletter, annual conference, local and regional meetings, and recognition for professional accomplishments.

National Association of Women in Construction

327 South Adams Street
Fort Worth, TX 76104-1081
817-877-5551
http://www.nawic.org

NAWIC is an international association that promotes and supports the advancement and employment of women in the construction industry. NAWIC partners with other trades associations to offer training to women in the trades. It offers national scholarships and honors women working in the trades with the **Crystal Vision** and **Crystal Achievement Awards.** There are over 200 chapters in 47 states. Visit the Web site for membership information.

National Association of Women Judges

815 Fifteenth Street, Suite 601
Washington, DC 20005
202-393-0222

A professional organization for women judges.

National Association of Women Law Enforcement Executives

PO Box 2761
Sarasota, FL 34230-2761
http://nawlee.com

NAWLEE promotes the ideals and principals of women executives in law enforcement, conducts training seminars, and provides a forum for the exchange of information concerning law enforcement. It also provides mentoring opportunities for women in mid-management positions and those new to senior management positions.

National Association of Women Lawyers

750 North Lake Shore Drive
Chicago, IL 60611
312-988-6186
http://www.kentlaw.edu/nawl/

The National Association of Women Lawyers helps members who are seeking new employment, contemplating other career moves, or desiring legal career management advice. It holds regional meetings and two national meetings annually. Its mentoring program links law students or recently admitted attorneys with experienced attorneys for advice and assistance.

National Black Nurses Association

1511 K Street, NW, Suite 415
Washington, DC 20005
202-393-6870
http://www.nbna.org

The National Black Nurses Association works to increase the number of African American nurses in the nursing profession and support African American nursing professionals. NBNA and its chapters provide thousands of dollars in scholarships annually to students in undergraduate and graduate programs. It also sponsors institutes, conferences, and educational forums. Contact the national organization for local chapter information.

National Black Sisters Conference

3027 Fourth Street, NE
Washington, DC 20017
202-529-9250
http://www.bcimall.org/nbsc.htm

The National Black Sisters Conference is a group of black Catholic women networking to provide support through prayer, solidarity, and programs. The organization acts as a voice supporting women and confronting individual racism found in society and in the church. The group holds an annual convention.

National Center for Women and Policing

8105 West Third Street
Los Angeles, CA 90048
323-651-2532
http://www.feminist.org/police/ncwp.html

The Feminist Majority Foundation launched the National Center for Women and Policing to help increase the number of women police officers. It focuses on three areas: educational campaigns to raise awareness among decision makers and the general public; leadership training and advocacy programs; and promotion of specialized family violence protocols for more effective police response.

National Center for Women and Retirement Research

Southampton College
Long Island University
Southampton, NY 11968
800-426-7386

The National Center for Women and Retirement Research is a university-based center committed to educating women on how to live independent, secure, and satisfying lives as they grow older. It creates and distributes educational materials, such as handbooks, videos, audio, and conducts seminars. Members receive a newsletter.

Organizations

National Center for Women Health Care and Physician Executives

6518 80th Street
Cabin John, MD 20818
301-320-7861

This national membership organization supports and promotes women executives in the health care field with a newsletter, and networking and workshop opportunities.

National Chamber of Commerce for Women

10 Waterside Plaza, Suite 6H
New York, NY 10010
212-685-3454

The National Chamber of Commerce for Women helps women research, write, and reach their pay comparison goals, business plan goals, or career path goals.

National Child Care Association

1016 Rosser Street
Conyers, GA 30012
800-543-7161
http://www.nccanet.org

The NCCA serves the private, licensed childhood care and education community. Its Web site, NCCANet was developed to provide private, licensed child care center/preschool owners, administrators, and directors with up-to-date information and resources. NCCANet also serves parents looking for child care by providing information about member centers across the country.

National Child Care Information Center

243 Church Street, NW, Second Floor
Vienna, VA 22180
800-616-2242
http://nccic.org

The National Child Care Information Center was established to complement, enhance, and promote child care linkages and to serve as a mechanism for supporting quality, comprehensive services for children and families. Visit the Web site for links to national organizations, publications, and the Child Care Technical Assistance Network.

National Coalition of 100 Black Women

38 West 32nd Street, Suite 1610
New York, NY 10001-3816
212-947-2196
http://orgs.womenconnect.com/ncbw/index.html

NCBW is dedicated to community service, leadership development, and the enhancement of career opportunities through networking and programming. It offers a biennial conference, periodic leadership development seminars, conferences, and skills training. Women in Partnership: Young Women in Transition Career Exploration pairs role models with young women.

National Committee on Pay Equity

1126 16th Street, NW, Suite 411
Washington, DC 20036
202-331-7343
http://feminist.com/fairpay.htm

The National Committee on Pay Equity is a membership coalition of over 180 organizations and individuals working to eliminate sex- and race-based wage discrimination. It provides leadership, information, and technical assistance to pay equity advocates, public officials, employers, the media, and the public. It sponsors Equal Pay Day, a date symbolizing the point into a new year a woman must work to earn the wages paid to a man in the previous calendar year. Popular publications include the *Wage Gap Fact Sheet, Questions and Answers on Pay Equity,* and *Face the Facts About Wage Discrimination and Fair Pay.*

National Communication Association

Women's Caucus
5105 Backlick Road, Building E
Annandale, VA 22003
703-750-0533
http://www.natcom.org

Formerly the **Speech Communications Association**, the National Communication

Association promotes the study, criticism, research, teaching, and application of the artistic, humanistic, and scientific principles of communication. The Women's Caucus supports and promotes the interests of women working in the field of communications.

National Conference of State Legislatures

Women's Network
1560 Broadway, Suite 700
Denver, CO 80202
303-830-2200
http://www.ncsl.org

The **Women's Network of the National Conference of State Legislatures** supports women legislators and advocates for equal opportunity for state-level elective offices. The Web site lists the ratio of women to men for all state legislatures.

National Council for Research on Women

11 Hanover Square
New York, NY 10005
212-785-7335
http://www.ncrw.org

The NCRW is an alliance of over 75 women's research and policy centers and more than 3,000 affiliates. Its mission is to enhance the connections among research, policy analysis, advocacy, and innovative programming on behalf of women and girls. It publishes a directory of NCRW members (also available on the Web site) and issues many publications of interest to women.

National Council of Churches

Women in Ministry Group
475 Riverside Drive, Room 850
New York, NY 10115-0122
212-870-2227
http://www.nccusa.org

The National Council of Churches is an ecumenical coalition of several religious disciplines, such as Methodist, Baptist, and Presbyterian. The **Women in Ministry Group** is a forum for the discussion and support of women in the ministry profession.

National Council of Negro Women

633 Pennsylvania Avenue, NW
Washington, DC 20004
202-737-0120
http://www.ncnw.com

NCNW works at the international, national, state, and local levels to improve the quality of life for women, children, and families. Members include students and working professionals. NCNW has established the National Centers for African American Women to develop strategies for grassroots mobilization. The Economic and Entrepreneurial Development Center provides women with technical assistance to establish and maintain businesses. Other centers address social and community needs. The Dorothy I. Height Leadership Institute is a leadership development center for emerging and established African American women leaders in national and community organizations, on college campuses, and other public and private sector institutions.

National Council of Women's Organizations

1126 16th Street, NW, Suite 411
Washington, DC 20036
202-331-7343
http://www.womensorganizations.org

The National Council of Women's Organizations is a network of over one hundred women's organizations. Member organizations advocate change on issues of importance to women such as equal employment opportunity, economic equity, job training, and other areas. The Web site lists events and conferences and contact information for member organizations.

National Education Center for Women in Business

Seton Hill College
Seton Hill Drive
Greensburg, PA 15601
412-830-4625
http://www.necwb.setonhill.edu

Organizations

This center promotes women and business ownership on the national level by conducting research, providing educational programs, and serving as an information clearinghouse for women entrepreneurs. Articles available on the Web site include "Starting and Growing Your Business,"Reaching Out to Your Region," and "Profiles in Success."

National Federation of Black Women Business Owners

1500 Massachusetts Avenue, NW, Suite 34
Washington, DC 20005
202-833-3450

The federation provides networking, educational, and financial guidance to its members, which include women of diverse business backgrounds, including construction, manufacturing, professional services, and non-professional services. NFWBO especially focuses on access to credit and contracting opportunities for its members and women business owners overall. It offers workshops, seminars, a newsletter, and a scholarship program for needy children.

National Federation of Press Women

PO Box 5556
Arlington, VA 22205
800-780-2715
http://www.nfpw.org

NFPW is an organization of media professionals representing newspapers, magazines, television, radio, public relations, advertising, photography, and graphic design. It promotes professional excellence and high ethical standards, and equal opportunity in the field. Students may also join. It sponsors an annual high school journalism contest.

National Federation of Republican Women

124 North Alfred Street
Alexandria, VA 22314
http://www.nfrw.org

This national Republican organization supports Republican candidates and initiatives, but also offers program that encourage women to become involved in the political process and make politics a career. Through Campaign "Train the Trainers" seminars, NFRW teaches Republican women leaders skills to develop campaign schools in their local areas and run for office at the state and local level. NFRW also offers internships and scholarships to women interested in Republican politics.

National Foundation for Women Business Owners

1100 Wayne Avenue, Suite 830
Silver Spring, MD 20910-5603
301-495-4975
http://www.nfwbo.org

NFWBO supports the growth of women business owners by conducting research, sharing information, and increasing knowledge. Consulting and public relations services and customized seminars on how to reach the growing women's business market are offered. NFWBO's Gillian Rudd Leadership Institute helps women who own and lead established, growing businesses to gain visibility among women business owners. Visit the Web site for details or call for information.

National Golf Coaches Association

500 North Michigan, Suite 1530
Chicago, IL 60611
312-543-9225
http://www.ngca.com

NGCA promotes participation in women's golf. It works to encourage the professional education of women golf coaches and to encourage the playing of intercollegiate golf for women in correlation with a general objective of education. Members receive recognition through annual awards, and also receive a newsletter and participate in an annual convention.

National Head Start Community

1651 Prince Street
Alexandria, VA 22314
703-739-0875
http://www.nhsa.org

Members of NHSA are individuals who are involved with Head Start as directors, parents, volunteers, and staff members, as well as Head Start organizations. Professional members receive a subscription to *Children and Family* magazine; quarterly legislative reports; a quarterly newsletter, conference information, discounts on publications and products; and voting privileges.

National Hispana Leadership Institute

1901 North Moore Street, Suite 206
Arlington, VA 22209
703-527-6007
http://www.nhli.org

The National Hispana Leadership Institute offers a four-week intensive leadership training program that spans nine months and is implemented in four different cities in the U.S. Participants pay $3,000 toward the cost of $20,000. Additional partial scholarships may be provided to women in need. The curriculum focuses on building personal strengths and managing personal weaknesses to become better leaders.

National Institute for Leadership Development

1202 West Thomas Road
Phoenix, AZ 85013
602-285-7494
http://www.pc.maricopa.edu/community/nild/home.html

The National Institute for Leadership Development is designed to promote the success of women in roles of leadership. It was founded in the 1980s as a resource for women interested in succeeding in the male-dominated educational leadership climate. It offers training seminars and support to women at stages in their careers. The Leaders Program is for faculty and administrators who want to reach out for more responsibility. The Leaders for Change Program is geared for women whose next step could be chief executive officer. The Kaleidoscope Program gives special attention to minority female administrators in the college system. Retreats for women community college CEOs are also held periodically.

National Latinas' Council

1738 Park Road, NW, Suite B100
Washington, DC 20010
202-234-1904
http://www.incacorp.com/nlc

The National Latinas' Council promotes and supports the socioeconomic development of women of Latino background through programs that seek to fill gaps in professional, educational, economic, and social realms. NLC conducts seminars on leadership, employment, financial planning and investment, marketing, and networking. It publishes a quarterly newsletter and coordinates youth mentor programs.

National League for Nursing

61 Broadway
New York, NY 10006
800-669-9656
http://www.nln.org

The National League for Nursing advances quality nursing education through accreditation of nursing schools, testing services, and certification for specialty nursing groups. Over 10,000 individuals join nursing schools and health care agencies as members.

National League of American Pen Women

1300 17th Street, NW
Washington, DC 20036
202-785-1997

The National League of American Pen Women promotes development of the creative talents of professional women in the arts. The league offers its members assocation with creative professional women, workshops, discussion groups, and lectures. Art shows, and writing and poetry contests, are held at branch, state, and national levels. To qualify for Art membership, a woman may be an architect, cartoonist, choreographer, craftsman, designer, graphic artist, illustrator, painter, photographer, or sculptor. An applicant for Letters membership may be an author, compiler, dramatist, genealogist, writer, photojournalist, research worker, promotion writer, or script writer. An applicant for Music membership may be a composer, arranger, teacher, or performer. Applicants must submit samples of work for membership.

National League of Cities

Women in Municipal Government
1301 Pennsylvania Avenue, NW
Washington, DC 20004-1763
202-626-3000
http://www.nlc.org

Women in Municipal Government is a constituency group of the National League of Cities, which seeks to strengthen and promote cities as centers of opportunity, leadership, and governance.

National Museum for Women in the Arts

1250 New York Avenue, NW
Washington, DC 20005
202-783-7996
http://www.nmwa.org

The National Museum of Women in the Arts brings recognition to the achievements of women artists by exhibiting, preserving, acquiring, and researching art by women. The museum displays a permanent collection and offers special exhibitions. It offers education programs, maintains a library and research center, and supports a network of national chapters.

National Network of Commercial Real Estate Women

785-832-1808
http://www.nncrew.org

NNCREW seeks to promote the business of and provide educational opportunities for women in commercial real estate nationwide. It offers networking opportunities, a membership directory, quarterly newsletter, annual convention, road shows featuring topical seminars around the country, a job bank, and continuing education unit credits. There are over 40 independent chapters; visit the Web site for links and contact information.

National Nurses Society on Addictions

4101 Lake Boone Trail, Suite 201
Raleigh, NC 27607
919-783-5871
http://www.nnsa.org

The National Nurses Society on Addiction is a professional specialty organization for nurses committed to the prevention and treatment of addictive disorders. It offers members educational and research opportunities and assists in policy development.

National Order of Women Legislators

910 16th Street, NW, Suite 100
Washington, DC 20006
202-332-3565
http://www.womenlegislators.org

NOWL seeks to educate its members, women legislators, on critical issues and help them become more effective legislators through networking and honing political and communications skills. Its Campaign College program is a series of "nuts and bolts" sessions on getting re-elected. Members also participate in educational, professional, and social events throughout the year and receive a newsletter.

National Organization for Women

1000 16th Street, NW, Suite 700
Washington, DC 20036
202-331-0066
http://www.now.org

The National Organization for Women advocates for a broad range of women's rights. It campaigns for women-friendly workplaces and serves as an information resource on welfare, sexual harassment, Social Security, wage equity, and other issues.

National Osteopathic Women Physicians' Association

c/o West Virginia School of Osteopathic Medicine
400 North Lee Street
Lewisburg, WV 24901
304-645-6270

The National Osteopathic Women Physicians' Association supports and promotes women osteopaths.

National Panhellenic Conference

3901 West 18th Street, Suite 380
Indianapolis, IN 46268
317-872-3185
http://www.greeklife.org/npc/

The National Panhellenic Conference is an umbrella organization for 26 international/national women's fraternities and sororities. Each member group is autonomous as a social, Greek-letter society of college women and alumnae. The group's Web site lists awards and honoraries available to Greek women, including deadlines, criteria, application information, and information about sorority membership.

National Partnership for Women and Families

1875 Connecticut Avenue, NW, Suite 710
Washington, DC 20009
202-986-2600
http://www.nationalpartnership.org

The National Partnership for Women and Families is a nonprofit organization that uses public education and advocacy to promote fairness in the workplace, quality health care, and policies that help women meet the demands of work and families. It publishes fact sheets and pamphlets, offers online Q and A on employment laws, and offers internships. The partnership works with government, unions, nonprofit organizations, the media, and individuals as a force for change.

National Press Photographers Association

Women's Committee
3200 Croasdaile Drive, Suite 306
Durham, NC 27705
http://metalab.unc.edu/nppa/index.html

The NPPA Women's Committee organizes the annual Women in Photojournalism Conference, which provides opportunity for discussion with respected visual journalists and highlights women in the profession. Speakers come from television, newspaper, and new media backgrounds. Workshops range from location lighting to financial planning. Portfolio and tape reviews with people who do the hiring create job contacts.

National Student Nurses' Association

555 West 57th Street
New York, NY 10019
212-581-2211
http://www.nsna.org

NSNA is a membership organization representing students in AND, diploma, baccalaureate, generic master's and generic doctoral programs preparing students for registered nurse licensure, as well as RNs in BSN completion programs. Members receive access to educational publications, an annual conference/convention, awards, and discounts on products and services.

National Women Business Owners Corporation

1100 Wayne Avenue, Suite 830
Silver Spring, MD 20910
561-848-5066
http://www.wboc.org

NWBOC was established to increase competition for corporate and government contracts through implementation of a pioneering economic development strategy for women business owners. It has launched a national certification program for women-owned and controlled businesses as an alternative to the multiple state and local certifications required by many public and private sector agencies. NWBOC also seeks to provide more corporations with the opportunity to better their procurement practices and to women suppliers to compete.

National Women Coaches Association

800-668-0108
http://www.nwca org

The NWCA serves the 130,000 coaches of female athletes across the country. Its primary mission

Organizations

is to improve the professional opportunities and lives of coaches (both male and female) who coach female athletes. The Web site has a message and discussion board on topics such as motivating the female athlete, fundraising, and training tips. Members receive a newsletter and networking opportunities.

National Women Law Students Association

5515 82nd Street, SW, D306
Lakewood, WA 98499
http://nwlsa.org

NWLSA is a coalition of women law students across the country that works toward improving the status of women in the legal profession and in society. It holds an annual conference and publishes a newsletter. A membership application is available on the Web site.

National Women's Caucus for Art

PO Box 1498
Canal Street Station
New York, NY 10013
212-634-0007
http://nationalwca.com

The Women's Caucus for Art is a multidisciplinary membership of artists, art historians, students, educators, gallery and museum professionals, and others involved in the visual arts. It conducts research, holds exhibitions and conferences, and honors women in the field with awards. The Web site lists chapters and contact information.

National Women's History Project

7738 Bell Road
Windsor, CA 95492
707-838-6000
http://www.nwhp.org

The National Women's History Project may serve as a resource to women conducting research or with a general interest in the field of women's history. The organization provides a clearinghouse of women's history information and a seasonal catalog of women's history books and promotional items. It produces videos, guides, and supplies for schools and the workplace;

coordinates in-service training for schoolteachers; coordinates the Women's History Network; and provides consulting services for publishers, media producers, and journalists.

National Women's Political Caucus

1211 Connecticut Avenue, NW, Suite 425
Washington, DC 20036
202-785-1100
http://www.nwpc.org

The National Women's Political Caucus is a national organization dedicated to increasing the number of pro-choice women in office at all levels of government. It provides campaign training, campaign financial support, and publishes candidate lists and election reports. It publishes a quarterly newsletter for and about political women and offers an internship.

National Women's Studies Association

University of Maryland
7100 Baltimore Boulevard, Suite 500
College Park, MD 20740
301-403-0525
http://www.nwsa.org

NWSA supports and promotes feminist/womanist teaching, learning, research, and professional and community service. It publishes a newsletter and quarterly journal. Financial assistance in the form of scholarships and awards is available to women whose scholarship will help expand the boundaries and possibilities of women's studies programs. The NWSA annual conference provides an opportunity for teachers, students, scholars, and activists to share research findings and develop strategies for social change.

Native Women's Association of Canada

9 Melrose Avenue
Ottawa, ON K1Y 1T8
800-461-4043
http://www.careerplace.com

CareerPlace is a program of the Native Women's Association of Canada that assists aboriginal women in finding, keeping, and advancing their careers within the corporate and government sector. It matches candidates with companies for training and employment.

NCAA Women's Enhancement Program

6201 College Boulevard
Overland Park, KS 66211-2422
913-339-1906
http://www.ncaa.org

The NCAA Women's Enhancement Program was established to increase the pool of qualified women candidates in coaching, athletics administration, officiating, and support services. The program offers postgraduate scholarships, internships, and a vita bank for women interested in a career in intercollegiate athletics.

Network of Executive Women in Hospitality

800-593-NEWH
http://www.newh.org

NEWH brings together professionals from all facets of the hospitality industry and related fields, including management, design, architecture, education, manufacturing, production, purchasing, sales, and marketing. There are fourteen chapters nationwide that provide opportunities for education, networking, and professional development. NEWH awards scholarships to students and young women entering the hospitality industry and recognizes its members' achievements with awards.

New York Asian Women's Center

39 Bowery
Box 375
New York, NY 10002-0375
212-732-5230; also 888-888-7702

The New York Asian Women's Center provides a variety of services to Asian women of New York and the five boroughs. Information referral and job counseling are among services provided.

New York Coalition of Women in the Arts and Media

PO Box 2537
Times Square Station
New York, NY 10036
http://www.nycoalit.org

The coalition provides a centralized resource of information and talent, as well as a professional forum for the advancement of women in the arts and media industries. It works to bring together the unions, guilds, and profesional organizations of the arts and media communities.

New York Women Composers

http://metalab.unc.edu/nywc

New York Women Composers is a local group of women composers of serious concert music and women in musical occupations who support the composers in their efforts to be organized. NYWC seeks to improve conditions for all women composers. It publishes a catalog of concert music by NYWC members, which is also available on its Web site.

Newswomen's Club of New York

National Arts Club
15 Gramercy Park South
New York, NY 10003
212-777-1610
http://www.newswomensclub.com

The Newswomen's Club of New York is a professional organization for women journalists in the New York metropolitan (tri-state) area. Women who work in newspapers, magazines, radio, television, and new media are members. The club sponsors the annual Front Page Awards and awards scholarships to women students attending Columbia University Graduate School of Journalism. Networking events and programs are also club activities.

Organizations

9 to 5, National Association of Working Women

231 West Wisconsin Avenue, Suite 900
Milwaukee, WI 53204-2308
414-274-0925
http://www.9to5naww.qpg.com

9 to 5, National Association of Working Women is one of the largest organizations for working women, with nearly 15,000 members. The heart of the organization is secretaries, data processors, and office workers, but 9 to 5 works to be a voice for all working women. It advocates for women's rights in the workplace, taking on local causes of groups of workers. Counselors on its National Job Problem Hotline answer questions on the Family and Medical Leave Act, sexual harassment, discrimination, computer health and safety, pay equity, and other issues from callers in the U.S. and Canada. The hotline number is 800/522-0925. It conducts research and publishes pamphlets and fact sheets on women's workplace rights and issues.

Ninety-Nines

Box 965
7100 Terminal Drive
Oklahoma City, OK 73159-0965
800-994-1929
http://www.ninety-nines.org

Ninety-Nines is an international organization of licensed women pilots. The headquarters is home to a large collection of archival records, video oral histories, personal artifacts, collections, and memorabilia on thousands of women pilots around the world. This is also the site of the Ninety-Nines Museum of Women Pilots. Several scholarships and grants are offered for member and nonmember individuals and organizations. Educational workshops and training opportunities are available to members.

Nontraditional Employment for Women

243 West 20th Street
New York, NY 10011
212-627-6252
http://www.new-nyc.org

NEW is a regional organization that helps low-income women become economically self-suffi-cient through employment in jobs nontraditional for women. NEW focuses on skilled blue collar trades such as construction, carpentry, building maintenance, and machine repair. It provides training, support services, and job placement assistance and serves as an advocate for women's rights and a voice for low-income women in New York City.

North American Nursing Diagnosis Association

1211 Locust Street
Philadelphia, PA 19107
215-545-8105
http://www.nanda.org

NANDA works to increase the visibility of nursing's contribution to patient care by continuing to develop, refine, and classify phenomena of concern to nurses. It is a leader in developing standards for nursing diagnoses.

Northeast Women in Business Association

PO Box 603079
Providence, RI 02906
401-351-0080
http://www.womeninbusiness.org

Northeast Women in Business is a regional association for entrepreneurs, professionals, and corporate employees. It hosts an annual conference and publishes a newsletter.

Office of Federal Contract Compliance

202-219-9475
http://www.dol.gov/dol/esa/public/ofcp_org.htm

Call this federal agency to report sexual discrimination in any company that contracts with the federal government.

Oncology Nursing Society

501 Holiday Drive
Pittsburgh, PA 15220-2749
412-921-7373
http://www.ons.org

The Oncology Nursing Society is a national organization of over 27,000 registered nurses and other health care professionals working in the field of oncology. Membership benefits include educational opportunities, annual meetings, and access to research and reports.

Options, Inc.
225 South 15th Street, Suite 1635
Philadelphia, PA 19102
215-735-2202
http://www.optionscareers.org

Options, Inc. provides a range of career services for women in the Philadelphia area. Clients range from low-income to professional women and fees are adjusted on a sliding scale. Individual counseling, resume assistance, career development workshops, and job postings for clients are among services available.

Organization of American Historians
Committee on the Status of Women in the Historical Profession
112 North Bryan Street
Bloomington, IN 47408
812-855-9852
http://www.indianau.edu/~oah/

The **Committee on the Status of Women in the Historical Profession** supports the efforts of women historians and encourages leadership within the OAH and the field in general.

Organization of Chinese American Women
1300 N Street, NW, Suite 100
Washington, DC 20005
202-638-0330

The Organization of Chinese American Women advances the needs of Chinese and Asian Pacific American women by helping to improve their educational, economic, social, and political opportunities by recognizing their leadership.

Organization of Women in International Trade
http://www.owit.org

The Organization of Women in International Trade promotes women doing business in international trade through networking and educational opportunities. Its members include women and men doing business in all facets of international trade including finance, public relations, government, freight forwarding, international law, agriculture, logistics, and transportation. OWIT holds a national conference, seeks to establish global business contacts, and shares international trade information among members. There are chapters in 20 cities. The Web site has chapter contact information.

Outdoor Industry Women's Council
Membership OIWC
c/o Taum Sauk Wilderness, Inc.
PO Box 12048
Kansas City, MO 64152

The mission of the Outdoor Industry Women's Council is to promote the advancement and participation of women in the outdoor community and lead the industry to positive solutions for business, social, and environmental issues.

Partnership for Women Entrepreneurs
171 Main Street
Nyack, NY 10960
914-353-1250
http://www.partnershipforwomen.com

The partnership is a member service organization supporting the success and growth of women business owners in the New York City area. Monthly networking meetings are held in Manhattan, Orange, Westchester, Rockland, and Bergen/Hudson County. It offers seminars, workshops, a monthly newsletter, a membership directory, and discounts on a variety of insurance packages.

Pen and Brush Club
16 East 10th Street
New York, NY 10003
212-475-3669

Pen and Brush is an international organization for women artists of all disciplines. The organization publishes a monthly newsletter, works to raise awareness of art among youth, and holds an annual conference.

Philippine Nurses Association

http://www.pna-america.org

Members of the Philippine Nurses Association enjoy networking and educational opportunities, and scholarship eligibility.

Presbyterian Church of Canada

Women in Ministry
50 Wynford Drive
Toronto, Ontario M3C 1J7
http://www.presbycan.ca/wim/index.html

Women in Ministry is a national committee of the Ministry of Church Vocations of the Presbyterian Church of Canada. It supports women in ministry, with particular attention to those isolated by geography or function. The committee holds bimonthly meetings.

President's Interagency Committee on Women's Business Enterprise

202-205-6673

Women may call for information and assistance on women's entrepreneurial issues.

Professional Black Women's Enterprise

2425 West Loop South, Suite 200
Houston, TX 77027
http://www.pbwe.org

PBWE seeks to make an economic impact in women's and families' lives through business, education, and fellowship. Four main programs include the Young Eagles Entrepreneurship for youth and young adults, ages 6-21; Fresh Start Sisterhood, a welfare-to-work transition for single women; Sister-to-Sister Mentoring; and the Lena Gibbs Greenwood Scholarship Fund. Members include entrepreneurs, educators, students, corporate professionals, and women seeking business opportunities.

Professional Women of Color

PO Box 5196
New York, NY 10185
212-714-7190
http://www.pwconline.org

Professional Women of Color is a national organization dedicated to advancing the careers of professional women of color. PWC provides members with job postings, referral services, a newsletter, discounts on computer and Internet services, space on PWC's Web site for business cards, and workshops, seminars, and networking sessions. Members are eligible for awards.

Professional Women Photographers

212-726-8292

Professional Women Photographers holds regular monthly meetings in the New York area during the fall, winter, and spring. Guest speakers share their work and discuss issues in the field. Meetings are free for members and guests may attend for a small fee.

Professional Women Singers Association

P.O. Box 884, Planetarium Station
New York, NY 10024-0546
212-969-0590

Professional Women Singers Association is a networking organization that connects women singers with projects and employment.

Professional Women's Bowling Association

7117 Cherryvale Boulevard
Rockford, IL 61112
815-332-5756
http://www.pwba.com

Professional Women's Roundtable, California

909-679-8048
http://www.pwronline.org

PWR supports women in business in the Los Angeles and Southern California area with monthly meetings, quarterly seminars, mentoring opportunities, a speakers' bureau, and advocacy.

Puerto Rican Chamber of Commerce of Illinois

Hispanic Women's Business Conference
2436 West Division Street
Chicago, IL 60622
773-486-1331
http://prcci.com

The Puerto Rican Chamber of Commerce of Illinois organizes the annual **Hispanic Women's Business Conference**, in its sixth year in 1999. The conference is a day of recognition, workshops, resources, and networking opportunities for Hispanic women in the business community. Attendees range from business owners, potential entrepreneurs, and individuals wanting to excel in corporate America.

Reel Women

Austin, TX
512-280-8706
http://www.reelwomen.org

Reel Women serves as a permanent support system for women at all levels of experience in the film and video industries. It provides an information and resource pool that includes audition notices, employment referrals, and access to equipment. It is also a full service video and production firm that documents and preserves the stories of women in all fields overlooked by traditional history sources. It distributes a ten-part documentary series "Filmmakers on Film."

Roundtable for Women in Foodservice

1372 La Colina Drive B
Tustin, CA 92780
714-838-2749
http://www.rwf.org

The Roundtable for Women in Foodservice is a national trade association open to operators, suppliers, and service professionals who are committed to the development and enhancement of women's careers across all segments of the industry through education, mentoring, and networking. Members are eligible for scholarships and have access to a job listing, as well as various educational and networking events throughout the year. Membership information and links to eight chapters in major U.S. cities are available on the Web site.

Sigma Delta Epsilon

Graduate Women in Science
SDE/GWI Headquarters
PO Box 240726
Apple Valley, MN 55124
http://www.gac.edu/People/orgs/gwis

Sigma Delta Epsilon/**Graduate Women in Science** is a multidisciplinary professional organization of graduate students and scientists in academia, industry, and government. SDE/GWIS seeks to help women attain equality and honors in science and help them juggle the roles they play in society. Individual chapters hold seminars and workshops and offer financial assistance and mentoring programs. GWIS publishes a quarterly journal, *GWIS Bulletin* that includes job and research opportunities and articles about professional skills and juggling a career and family. For membership information, select the membership link on the Web site or write to the above address.

Small Business Administration

800-827-5722
http://www.gov.womeninbusiness

The SBA **Office of Women's Business Ownership** helps women start and build successful businesses through training, counseling, and loan assistance. SBA works at the local level through its regional offices. Call the 800 number listed to find an office in your region. It operates the Online Women's Business Center on the Internet (http://www.onlinewbc.org), which lists contact information for local organizations that help women build successful businesses. The Women's Network for Entrepreneurial Training is a network of more than 100 mentoring roundtables nationwide. The Women-Owned Small Business Procurement Program helps women-owned businesses initiate contracts with the federal government. Lending capital and venture programs are also available.

Organizations

The Small Business Administration's **Women's Network for Entrepreneurial Training** pairs experienced women business owners with women whose businesses are ready to grow. In the year-long, one-on-one program, mentors share their knowledge, skills, and support with proteges. Call the SBA for a regional office in your area that can get you started in the program.

Society for Music Theory

Committee on the Status of Women
School of Music
Western Michigan University
Kalamazoo, MI 49008-3831
616-387-4667
http://www.wmich.edu/mus-theo/scw_gen.h

The **Committee on the Status of Women** of the Society for Music Theory promotes gender equity and feminist scholarship in areas related to music theory and serves as a repository of information about women and music. The committee hosts sessions for women at annual SMT events. A membership application to join the committee is available online or contact the School of Music at Western Michigan University.

Society for Women in Philosophy

Department of Philosophy
FA 411E
University of Central Florida
Orlando, FL 32816
http://www.uh.edu/~cfreelan/SWIP/

The Society for Women in Philosophy promotes and supports women in philosophy through divisional meetings, meetings in conjunction with the American Philosophical Association, and the publication of newsletters. It also sponsors a listserv.

Society of Gastroenterology Nurses and Associates

800-245-7462
http://www.sgna.org

Membership benefits of the Society of Gastroenterology Nurses and Associates include subscriptions to its newsletter and professional journal; a membership directory; a national

employment network; continuing education credits through conferences; and opportunities for education, networking, and viewing new product developments.

Society of Urologic Nurses and Associates

http://www.suna.org

The Society of Urologic Nurses and Associates works for high quality urologic education for urologic nurses and allied health professionals through the study and discussion of urology, meetings, and cooperation with other organizations.

Society of Women Engineers

120 Wall Street, 11th Floor
New York, NY 10005-3902
212-509-9577
http://www.swe.org

The Society of Women Engineers encourages young women to enter careers in engineering and serves as a center of information for women engineers. SWE holds a combined convention and student conference annually and offers an extensive awards and recognition program, in addition to over 90 scholarships for women. SWE publishes *SWE Magazine* for its members and the engineering community at large. SWE also hosts a resume database and lists job listings on its Web site. Most members are women engineers or women engineering students, but anyone who supports SWE's objectives may apply for membership.

Society of Women Geographers

415 East Capitol Street, SE
Washington, DC 20003
202-546-9228

The Society of Women Geographers has chapters in Washington, DC, New York, Chicago, San Francisco, Los Angeles, and Florida. Meetings are held regularly throughout the academic year. Active members have carried out research and field activities in their particular disciplines and have developed specialized competence in some regional or topical aspect of the world.

Associate members include serious travelers who are dedicated to furthering geographical exploration and research. Membership is elective; proposals for new members must come from two active members. The society maintains a library and museum at its national headquarters. It also offers fellowships for women at selected institutions.

Sociologists for Women in Society

c/o American Sociological Association
1307 New York Avenue, NW
Washington, DC 20005
http://socsci.colorado.edu/sws/sws.html

Sociologists for Women in Society is an international organization for undergraduate and graduate students, faculty, researchers, and independent scholars. SWS meets twice a year, once with the American Sociological Association meetings in late summer. It publicizes job openings, oversees a mentoring program, testifies at legislative sessions, offers vita and interview assistance, sponsors an annual lecture published in *Gender and Society,* and recognizes achievements of women sociologists.

Soroptimist International of the Americas

2 Penn Center Plaza, Suite 1000
Philadelphia, PA 19102-1883
215-557-9300
http://www.siahq.com

SIA is a volunteer service organization for business and professional women. Clubs coordinate service projects at the local level. Members are women leaders across all professional disciplines. A major service project is the **Women's Opportunity Awards Program,** which provides cash grants for head-of-household women seeking to improve their economic situation through education and training.

South Asian American Women's Association

60 East Fourth Street
Corning, NY 14830
607-962-3277
http://www.umiacs.umd.edu/users/sawweb/
sawnet/saawa

SAAWA is a nonprofit, nonpolitical, international organization dedicated to education and leadership. It provides scholarship assistance nationally and internationally to assist students pursuing a higher education in America.

Southern Association for Women Historians

Department of History
Agnes Scott College
Decatur, GA 30030-3797
http://www.h-net.msu.edu/~sawh.html

SAWH supports the study of women's history and the work of women historians. It welcomes women and men who are interested in Southern history and/or women's history, as well as women historians in any field who live in the South. It meets annually in conjunction with the Southern Historical Association, publishes a newsletter, awards publication prizes, and sponsors the Southern Conference on Women's History every three years. A membership application is available on the Web site.

Stuntwomen's Association of Motion Pictures

13601 Ventura Boulevard, Suite 94
Sherman Oaks, CA 91423
http://www.stuntwomen.com

The Stuntwomen's Association serves as a resource for stuntwomen and the industry as a whole. It assists in job scouting via up-to-date production lists and additional stunt training.

Texas Women in Law Enforcement

PO Box 797784
Dallas, TX 78379-7784
http://www.twle.com

Texas Women in Law Enforcement is open to women and men in the criminal justice field, including border patrol agents. It offers training, public recognition of women as role models, communication links, and community service project opportunities.

Organizations

Today's Black Woman Foundation

954-341-7964
http://www.jktbw.com

Today's Black Woman is a national radio show, with a national newsletter, nonprofit teaching foundation, and chamber of commerce. The newsletter is free, and is distributed to 30,000 women across the United States. The foundation sponsors seminars, retreats, conferences, and workshops to empower and educate women in welfare-to-work training, domestic violence, entrepreneurship and career advancement, and life issues such as relationships, marriage, and motherhood. To subscribe to the newsletter, call or fill out the form on the Web site.

Tradeswomen Network

PO Box 86620
Portland, OR 97286
503-943-2771
http://tradeswomen.org

The Tradeswomen Network has chapters in Portland, Oregon, and Berkeley, California, to promote the success of women in the trades. It offers monthly meetings, support groups, a monthly newsletter, and the Women in the Trades Fair.

U.S. Department of Labor Women's Bureau

200 Constitution Avenue, NW, Room S3002
Washington, DC 20210
800-827-5335
http://www.dol.gov/dol/wb/

The Women's Bureau of the U.S. Department of Labor maintains the National Resource and Information Center. The NRIC has extensive information on business-to-business assistance, child care/elder care, equal pay, educational resources, regional job information, and nontraditional occupations. The Women's Bureau Clearinghouse is a computerized database and resource center on the rights of women workers. Call the clearinghouse at 202-219-4486 for a free database search on topics such as age, wage, and pregnancy discrimination, and equal pay.

Union Institute Center for Women

1710 Rhode Island Avenue, NW, Suite 1100
Washington, DC 20036
202-496-1630
http://www.tui.edu/~osr/

The Union Institute Center for Women is the only academic women's center linking scholars and grassroots activists. It sponsors the annual **Audre Lorde Legacy Awards**, the Women Organizing Documentation Project, and other projects.

United States Women's Curling Association

4114 North 53rd Street
Omaha, NE 68104
http://www.uswca.org

The USWCA works to promote and conserve the best interest of the game of curling throughout the United States. Each year it holds a USWCA National Bonspiel and USWCA Senior Bonspiel.

United Stuntwomen's Association

http://www.usastunt.com

USA is a small association of working professional stuntwomen, coordinators, and second unit directors.

USA Child Care

3606 Northeast Basswood Drive
Lee's Summit, MO 64064
800-484-9392
http://www.usachildcare.org

USA Child Care is an organization for providers of child care to low- to moderate-income families. It works to be a voice for local and state direct service providers at the state and national levels.

Webgrrls International

50 Broad Street, Suite 1614
New York, NY 10004
212-785-1276
http://www.webgrrls.com

Webgrrls provides a forum for women in or interested in new media and technology to network, exchange job and business leads, form strategic alliances, mentor and teach, intern, and learn the skills to help women succeed in an increasingly technical workplace and world. Communication is largely through the Internet, with job leads and promotional opportunities, community listserves, newsletters, and Web links. Local chapters offer meetings, classes, and events.

Wellesley Centers for Women

Women's Associates Program
106 Central Street
Wellesley, MA 02481
781-283-2500
http://www.wellesley.edu/WCW/index.html

Members support the work of the Center for Research on Women and the Stone Center, including research on child care, sexual harassment in schools, women and employment, and women's psychological development. They receive news of upcoming events and research initiatives, invitations to special gatherings, a discount on Wellesley Center publications, and a newsletter. Apply for membership online or write or call for an application.

Whirly Girls

Whirly Girls Executive Director
PO Box 7446
Menlo Park, CA 94026-7446
http://www.whirlygirls.org

Whirly Girls is an organization of women helicopter pilots that represent several backgrounds and interests, including civilian or military trained, flying for pleasure, business, industry, or defense. The organization seeks to promote helicopter aviation, safety through professionalism, and the advancement of women in helicopter aviation. It also offers scholarships to encourage further training of women in the helicopter field.

Wider Opportunities for Women (WOW)

815 15th Street, NW, Suite 916
Washington, DC 20005
202-638-3143
http://www.w-o-w.org

WOW works nationally and in Washington, DC, to help women and girls achieve economic independence and equality of opportunity. Programs emphasize literacy, technical and nontraditional skills, welfare-to-work transition, and career development. It leads the National Workforce Network, comprised of over 500 independent women's employment programs in every state.

Wired Woman Society—Canada

604-605-8825

The Wired Woman Society seeks to create an open environment that encourages women to explore opportunities in information technology and build successful careers that will allow them to play a positive role in the growth and development of the Information Age. With chapters in Vancouver, Toronto, and Winnipeg, it offers networking opportunities, career resources, community and academic presentations, role modeling, and mentoring for members.

Women and Mathematics Education

c/o Mount Holyoke College
302 Shattuck Hall
South Hadley, MA 010750-1441
413-538-2608

Women and Mathematics Education serves as a resource for anyone interested in furthering mathematics education for women and girls. The group publishes three newsletters a year and maintains a bibliography of resources for women in mathematics.

Women and Mathematics

Mathematical Association of America
Committee on the Participation of Women
1529 Eighteenth Street, NW
Washington, DC 20036-1385
800-741-9415
http://www.maa.org

Organizations

WAM is an advising and mentoring program that seeks to stimulate interest in mathematics among all students, regardless of career interest. The network provides professional development opportunities for program directors, forums for sharing ideas, and workshops for prospective directors. MAA also provides **MAA/Tensor Grants** to fund such outreach programs. WAM Network consultants work to build excitement for learning and inspire young women toward careers in mathematics, science, and technology. Visit the Web site for program details, or call.

Women Artists of the West
http://www.inland.net/~waow/index.htm

Women Artists of the West supports and promotes women artists throughout the world and embraces many different styles and diverse subject matter. WAOW offers marketing and promotion support and a regular newsletter. Membership includes group advertising at a discounted rate. No phone or address is provided because it changes periodically with appointment of new officers. Visit the Web site for information.

Women as Allies
http://www.womenasallies.org

The mission of Women as Allies is to increase sensitivity among women in organizations and in communities to the issues of discrimination and hate involving race, gender, sexism, class, disability, ethnicity, religion, culture, or sexual orientation. It offers workshops designed to teach women how to be more sensitive and effective in organizations and in the community.

Women Band Directors International, Inc.
2501 Madison Street
Waukesha, WI 54188
262-549-3227

Formerly Women Band Directors National Association, this organization supports women who direct professional and school bands at all levels, and encourages women to become involved in music and directing by offering workshops, networking, scholarships, and awards.

Women Basketball Coaches Association
WBCA
4646 Lawrenceville Highway
Lilburn, GA 30047-3620
770-279-8027
http://www.wbca.org

The WBCA is a national association that offers a coach's academy, national convention, summer camps for girls, recognition awards, and publications including an association newsletter (*At the Buzzer*, for high school coaches, and *Fast Break Alert*, a newsletter on NCAA legislation).

Women Business Owners of Canada
20 York Mills Road, Suite 100
North York, Ontario M2P 2C2
416-218-8801
http://www.wboc.ca

WBOC is a national organization for women entrepreneurs in Canada. WBOC provides a forum for members to interact and network through the Web site, newsletter, and other activities and is building a comprehensive database of information about Canadian women-owned businesses and resources available to women business owners.

Women Chefs and Restaurateurs
http://www.chefnet.com/WCR.html

The mission of the WCR is to promote the education and advancement of women in the restaurant industry and the betterment of the industry overall. It provides educational opportunities and facilitates communication among women in all sectors of the restaurant industry. Members are eligible for scholarships. Its online resource center includes advice on career options, freelance rate examples, and resume writing advice.

Women Construction Owners and Executives

4849 Connecticut Avenue, NW, Suite 702
Washington, DC 20008-5838
800-788-3458
http://www.wcoeusa.org

WCOE seeks to enhance the perception of women in construction through publicity, education, advocacy, and business services. It publishes the newsletter, *Turning Point,* for its members.

Women Contractors Association

PO Box 2074
Sugarland, TX 77478
281-835-8110
http://www.womencontractors.org

WCA is a regional organization that promotes the growth of women owners and executives in the construction industry. It seeks to enhance the perception of women in construction through publicity, education, advocacy, and business services.

Women Employed

22 West Monroe Street, Suite 1400
Chicago, IL 60603
312-782-3902
http://www.womenemployed.org

Women Employed is the membership arm of the Women Employed Institute, which conducts research on the status of working women and education. Women Employed offers career planning and placement services, and career and life planning assistance for teens. Special services include a job problems counseling service through a telephone hotline and Keys to Success, a program for displaced homemakers. Fact sheets on employment rights, pregnancy rights, sexual harassment prevention, the Family and Medical Leave Act, and the glass ceiling are available.

Women Executives in Public Relations

P.O. Box 609
Westport, CT 06881
203-226-4947
http://www.wepr.org

WEPR is a public relations organization for senior women in the field. Its mission is to support career advancement for female practitioners and foster the use of public relations to benefit business and society. It sponsors the Social Responsibility Awards for corporations with innovative social programs and provides scholarships to young women students majoring in public relations.

Women Executives in State Government

1225 New York Avenue, NW, Suite 350
Washington, DC 20005
202-628-9374
http://www.wesg.org

Peer-to-peer exchange is the cornerstone of WESG and its programs. Programs are designed to develop personal and professional skills and to provide insight into a broad range of state government, management, and leadership issues. WESG offers conferences, **Breaking the Glass Ceiling Awards** to organizations and officials, fellowships and scholarships for members, an executive search program, and issues briefings.

Women Grocers of America

1825 Samuel Morse Drive
Reston, VA 20190
703-437-5300

Women Grocers of America is an affiliate of the National Grocers Association. Members work in any aspect of the grocery industry, including retail, wholesale, manufacturers, or state associations. Women Grocers of America honors a woman in the grocery industry annually with a woman of the year award. It also sponsors a scholarship for men and women in the industry.

Organizations

Women in Advertising and Marketing of Metropolitan Washington

4200 Wisconsin Avenue, NW, Suite 106
Washington, DC 20016
301-369-7400
http://www.wamdc.org

WAM-DC is a regional organization where professional women gather to network for career and personal growth. Its programs address the marketing, advertising, and public relations fields, as well as personal issues related to growth as professionals. It provides a job bank for members and events throughout the year.

Women in Aerospace

PO Box 16721
Alexandria, VA 22302
202-547-9451
http://www.energialtd.com/wia/home.html

WIA seeks to expand women's opportunities for leadership and increase their visibility in the aerospace community. It recognizes the achievements of outstanding women in aerospace, holds monthly meetings, offers job postings, a newsletter, and aerospace and WIA chapter links on its Web site.

Women in Animation

PO Box 17706
Encino, CA 91416
818-759-9596
http://women.in.animation.org

Women in Animation offers networking opportunities, a newsletter, writer's group meetings and roundtables, and low-cost classes and study groups provided by local chapters.

Women in Aviation International

3647 S.R. 503 S
West Alexandria, OH 45381
937-839-4647
http://www.wiai.org

Women in Aviation International encourages women to seek opportunities and career advancement in aviation. Membership includes astronauts, corporate pilots, maintenance technicians, air traffic controllers, business owners, educators, journalists, flight attendants, students, airshow performers, airport managers, and others. WIAI offers an annual conference, educational outreach programs, and message boards on its Web site with job leads and career advice. WIAI publishes *Aviation for Women*, a bi-monthly magazine.

Women in Cable and Telecommunications

230 West Monroe, Suite 2630
Chicago, IL 60606
312-634-2330
http://www.wict.org

WICT is open to all women who are employed in a professional capacity in the cable and telecommunications industry or closely related field. Membership benefits include scholarships, local and national networking opportunities, conferences, and educational seminars. WICT also coordinates a speakers' bureau.

Women in Corporate Aviation

http://www.wca-intl.org

Women in Corporate Aviation seeks to promote the future of business aviation through education, public speaking, and scholarship programs. A mentoring program connects young women with questions to women with areas of expertise in the field, ranging from maintenance to flight training to public relations and editorial work. Visit the Web site for details.

Women in Defense

2111 Wilson Boulevard, Suite 400
Arlington, VA 22201-3061
703-247-2552
http://www.adpa.org/wid/default.html

Women in Defense is a national organization for women whose primary professional activities are related to the national defense or any aspect of national security. Members come from diverse backgrounds including computer science, engineering, law, and economics. Benefits of membership include networking, access to informational programs, and an online discussion group. WID's Horizons Foundation offers scholarships.

Women in Endocrinology
http://www.women-in-endo.org

Women in Endocrinology seeks to promote and facilitate the professional development and advancement of women in the field of endocrinology. Membership benefits include a newsletter, educational meetings, and the annual WE meeting, held in conjunction with the Endocrine Society meetings. It administers a Mentor Award to those who support women in their scientific careers.

Women in Engineering Programs and Advocate Network
1284 CIVL Building, Room G293
West Lafayette, IN 47907-1284
http://www.engr.washington.edu/
~wepan.member.html

WEPAN seeks to increase the pool of women engineers by improving engineering programs at U.S. institutions. It holds an annual conference, offers training seminars, and maintains a listserve. It also maintains three regional centers that evaluate engineering programs and provide technical assistance and conduct training programs for institutions desiring to initiate or expand Women in Engineering programs.

Women in Film and Video—New England
PO Box 342
Watertown, MA 02471-0342
617-924-9494
http://www.womeninfilmvideo.org

Women in Film and Video—New England promotes the work and advancement of women in the film, video, and television industry. Members include producers, directors, writers, animators, editors, designers, technicians, talent distributors, and attorneys in the northeastern United States.

Women in Film
6464 Sunset Boulevard, Suite 1080
Hollywood, CA 90028
323-463-6040
http://www.wif.org

Women in Film is a professional organization that seeks to recognize, develop, and promote women in the global communications industry. It offers special events, a job bank, and the opportunity to serve on committees that promote screenwriting workshops, directors, workshops, the business side of entertainment, and stuntwomen.

Women in Franchising
53 West Jackson Boulevard, Suite 205
Chicago, IL 60604
312-431-1467
http://www.infonews.com/franchise/wif

Women in Franchising is a national program that assists prospective women and minority entrepreneurs in all aspects of franchise business ownership. WIF educates individuals about franchising through seminars and workshops and trains franchisors in marketing to women and minorities. It offers self-study programs and tools for evaluating potential franchise purchases.

Women in French
http://www.fln.vcu.edu/WIF/wif.html

Women in French promotes the study of francophone women writers, and of women more generally in franchophone countries, and also supports the work of women teaching or studying French. It coordinates conferences and other events, sponsors an email list, and publishes a newsletter.

Women in German
Department of Foreign Languages
Indiana University, Purdue University
Fort Wayne, IN 46805-1499
http://www.bowdoin.edu/dept/german/wig/
home.html

Women in German provides a forum for all people interested in feminist approaches to

Organizations

German literature and culture or in the intersection of gender with other categories of analysis such as sexuality, class, and race. The organization seeks to make school and college curricula inclusive and eradicate discrimination in the classroom and teaching profession at all levels through special panels at national professional meetings and through the publication of the annual *Women in German Yearbook*. It also organizes an annual conference and publishes a newsletter.

Women in Government Relations

1029 Vermont Avenue, NW, Suite 510
Washington, DC 20005-3527
202-347-5432
http://www.wgr.org

Women in Government Relations provides members with educational programming and networking opportunities. Members represent corporations, trade associations, public interest groups, and federal, state, and local governments. Other benefits include a membership directory, annual job fair, job bank, and workshops with national policy makers. WGR also offers a fellowship for women studying in areas that will lead to a career in public policy. A membership application is available on the Web site.

Women in Government

2600 Virginia Avenue, NW, Suite 709
Washington, DC 20005
202-333-0825
http://www.womeningovernment.com

Women in Government is an issue-education association for elected and appointed women in state government. The Legislative Business Roundtable is a coalition of women in state government and members of the business and academic communities who meet periodically to address issues of mutual concern. The roundtables seek to help women look at impact consequences and to take the lead in offering fresh ideas to complex problem solving.

Women in Health Care Management

c/o Argosy
PO Box 273
Hanover, MA 02339
http://www.whcm.org

WHCM provides a forum for professional women to network, share information, meet their peers, and keep abreast of developments in the health care field. Members work in a variety of settings, including hospitals, HMOs, consulting firms, and long-term care facilities. Members receive a quarterly newsletter, and access to meetings, a job bank, mentoring, and networking opportunities.

Women in International Security

c/o Center for International Security Studies
University of Maryland
School of Public Affairs
College Park, MD 20742
301-405-7612
http://www.puaf.umd.edu/wiis/

Women in International Security works to enhance opportunities for women working in foreign and defense policy. It is open to women at all stages of their careers and seeks to inform the public about the contributions women are making in the international security community. WIIS maintains a computerized databank of women in the field of international security, organizes a seminar series highlighting women speakers on current issues, publishes a newsletter and JOBS HOTLINE, and distributes professional information in directories. WIIS conducts a summer symposium, a five-day intensive educational and networking program for thirty students. The program includes panel discussions, skill-building workshops, and simulations with senior policy makers and scholars in the field.

Women in Management

30 North Michigan Avenue
Chicago, IL 60602
http://www.opri.com/WIM/

WIM is a national organization of women managers, entrepreneurs, and professionals with a commitment to their families, the community, and their own personal growth. It is open in seven categories: corporate, academic, not-for-profit/social service, government, licensed professional, entrepreneur-product, and entrepreneur-service.

Women in Mining

1801 Broadway, Suite 760
Denver, CO 80202
303-298-1535
http://www.womeninmining.org

Women in Mining is a nationwide organization of engineers, geologists, land men, secretaries, lobbyists, mine workers, educators, and concerned citizens. It provides a forum for women and men working in the field to share information and learn from others. Its foundation develops educational material about mining and assists chapters with furthering members' education.

Women in Multimedia

PO Box 423777
San Francisco, CA 94142
415-263-0727
http://www.wim.org

WIM is a regional organization that provides support, advocacy, education, and resources to women involved in new media. WIM hosts monthly networking meetings, member showcases, and panel discussions. A mentoring program pairs established professionals with women in the beginning of their careers.

Women in Music National Network

31121 Mission Boulevard, Suite 300
Hayward, CA 94544
510-232-3897
http://www.womeninmusic.com

WIMNN is a national organization that identifies opportunities for women in the music industry by offering educational forums, mentoring programs, and by supporting community youth programs for music awareness and education. Members receive a bimonthly newsletter and a listing in the member directory.

Women in Neuroscience

WIN President Andrea Zardetto-Smith
Creighton University Department of Physical Therapy
2500 California Plaza
Omaha, NE 68178
402-280-5946
http://www.womenCONNECT.com/WIN/index.html

Women in Neuroscience promotes the professional and personal advancement of women neuroscientists, facilitates communication, and collaborates with the Society of Neuroscience in organizing activities for women at the annual meeting of the society. WIN gives travel awards to graduate students and postdoctoral fellows, publishes a newsletter, offers mentoring, and lists job announcements.

Women in New Media

Membership WINM
295 Greenwich Street, Suite 186
New York, NY 10007
http://www.winm.org

Women in New Media is a New York-based virtual organization for women in the new media industry. Women who are currently employed in the new media industry and have held a professional position in the business for at least two years are invited to apply. It hosts monthly gatherings to discuss industry trends and in-depth roundtable discussions on topics of interest to its membership. Members receive and are listed in the membership directory.

Women in Nontraditional Employment Roles

PO Box 905111
Long Beach, CA 90809-0511
310-590-2266

WINTER encourages and supports women's training, employment, and retention in high-wage, high-skill jobs. Programs include job rights and safety education, skill building, monthly support group meetings, a monthly newsletter, job counseling, job search assistance and referrals, and notice of job and apprenticeship openings.

Organizations

Women in Ornithology Resource Group

http://www-rci.rutgers.edu/~tsipoura/worg.html

The Women in Ornithology Resource Group seeks to bring together women and men interested in providing support to those women ornithologists who might need it. It holds conference receptions, offers a mentoring program, job listings, and a listserve discussion group.

Women in Periodical Publishing

Thea Selby
Computec Media
650 Townsend Street
San Francisco, CA 94103
650-632-4591
http://www.wipp.org

WIPP seeks to empower and educate women in the online and print periodical publishing industry. It provides opportunities for leadership, networking, and advocacy, a newsletter, and job bank. Membership applications are available online.

Women in Production

347 Fifth Avenue
New York, NY 10016
212-481-7793
http://www.wip.org

Women in Production is an educational organization from all areas of the graphic arts industry, including print production and publishing. The organization offers technical seminars, career advancement and job placement services, networking opportunities, educational programs and scholarships, and referrals and resources.

Women in Real Estate

WIRE Membership
c/o Real Estate Law Group
2330 Marinship Way, Suite 211
Sausalito, CA 94965
415-331-2555
http://www.womeninrealestate.org

WIRE is a San Francisco-based organization for women employed in the commercial real estate industry. It publishes a quarterly newsletter and membership directory. Members get networking opportunities at formal and informal meetings and luncheons.

Women in Sales Association

8 Madison Avenue
P.O. Box M
Valhalla, NY 10595
914-946-3802

The Women in Sales Association is a regional organization of women whose primary income is derived from sales in any field. WSA provides networking and professional development and training.

Women in Science and Technology Alliance

1828 L Street, NW, Suite 625
Washington, DC 20036
202-737-1118
http://www.wistalliance.org

WISTA brings together policy makers, strategists, and leaders of a wide range of institutions and federations interested in promoting women in science and technology. Public and private institutions, corporations, and individuals are invited to join. Members co-sponsor activities and events and have access to a variety of databases and other educational information materials.

Women in Sports and Events

244 Fifth Avenue, Suite 2087
New York, NY 10001
212-726-8282
http://www.womeninsportsandevents.com

WISE is a professional organization that connects women in the business of sports and special events. Through regular meetings, workshops, and special events, women hear speakers who discuss career-related topics. Mentor matches are arranged and members also have access to a job bank, membership directory, and newsletter. Women representing professional sports teams, and women who work in marketing, public relations, and media are represented.

Women in Sports Careers Foundation

409 Utica, Suite D-36
Huntington Beach, CA 92648
714-960-0411
http://www.womensportswire.com

The WISC Foundation is an affiliate organization of Women'Sports Services. It is an educational and service organization and industry resource. It offers the Women'Sports Career Package for a fee. The package includes resume review and evaluation, one 40-minute career consultation, resume preparation, and a six-month subscription to *Women'Sports Job Wire*.

Women in Technology International Foundation

14622 Ventura Boulevard, Suite 1022
Sherman Oaks, CA 91403
818-990-6705
http://www.witi.com

The WITI Foundation seeks to increase the number of women in executive roles in technology-based companies; help women become more financially independent and technology-literate; and encourage young women to choose careers in science and technology. WITI helps women develop the core competencies in demand by technology corporations. It conducts research and maintains statistics, hosts conferences, and works closely with industry leaders to further its goals.

Women in the Arts Foundation

1175 York Avenue, Apartment 2G
New York, NY 10021
212-751-1915

The Women in the Arts Foundation supports women artists of all skill levels in the New York area.

Women in the Director's Chair

941 West Lawrence, Suite 500
Chicago, IL 60640
773-907-0610
http://www.widc.org

Women in the Director's Chair is a media arts organization that promotes visibility for women artists and supports works that defy demeaning stereotypes of women. Membership benefits include discount on admission to WIDC events, such as the film festival and film festival entry fees; subscription to publications; fiscal sponsorship opportunities; and a forum for sharing ideas, skills, and opportunities.

Women in the Fire Service Inc.

P.O. Box 5446
Madison, WI 53705
608-233-4768

Women in Fire Service is a networking forum for women firefighters and provides information to the fire service on women's issues. The Web site features job postings, and information on issues affecting women firefighters such as pregnancy and reproductive safety, sexual harassment, protective gear, and station facilities. Members receive the monthly newsletter *Firework*. *WFS Quarterly* is published for departments.

Women in Trades and Technology National Network

10 Douglas Court, Unit 2
London, Ontario N5W 4A7
800-895-WITT
http://www.wittnn.com

WITT National Network is an education and advocacy organization that promotes and assists in the recruitment, training, and retention of women in trades, technology, operations, and blue collar work across Canada. The Web site lists local chapter contact information.

Women in Wireless Communications

c/o Allen Telecom, Inc.
30500 Bruce Industrial Parkway
Solon, OH 44139
http://www.wiwc.org

Women in Wireless Communications is a national organization for women in the wireless communications marketplace. Meetings are held in conjunction with the major wireless conventions and regionally throughout the year.

Organizations

Women Incorporated

333 South Grand Avenue, Suite 2450
Los Angeles, CA 90071
http://www.womeninc.org

Women Incorporated is a national organization dedicated to improving the business environment for women. WI offers networking opportunities, holds an annual conference, and publishes *Women's Business Journal* for its members. Members also have access to a loan pool and a national technical assistance network.

Women Life Underwriters Confederation

Blendonview Office Park
5008-45 Pine Creek Drive
Westerville, OH 43081-4899
614-882-6934
http://www.wluc.org

WLUC-Women in Insurance and Financial Services provides training, support, and leadership development opportunities to women in the insurance and financial services industry. Members receive the national quarterly newsletter, are invited to the annual conference, and participate in educational and networking events at the chapter level, including mentoring and business planning. WLUC recognizes members who achieve significant income levels.

Women Make Movies

462 Broadway, Suite 500 R
New York, NY 10012
212-925-0606
http://www.wmm.com

Women Make Movies is a national, feminist media arts organization that provides resources for both users and producers of media by women. Its Production Assistance Program for women producers and directors offers fiscal sponsorship and technical assistance. It publishes a catalog of more than 400 films and videotapes by and about women.

Women Marines Association

9608 North May Avenue, Box 265
Oklahoma City, OK 73120-2798
http://www.womenmarines.org

The Women Marines Association is a veterans association of women who have served or are serving honorably in the United States Marine Corps, regular or reserve components. It grants scholarships and awards and works to assist hospitalized veterans. Each member receives a membership directory, a quarterly newsletter, and an invitation to the biennial convention.

Women of Color Resource Center

2288 Fulton Street, Suite 103
Berkeley, CA 94704-1449
510-848-9272
http://www.coloredgirls.org

WCRC was established in 1990 to develop a firm, institutional foundation for social change activism on behalf of women of color. The Women's Education in Global Economics program is a set of training materials on structural aid programs, unpaid and contingent work, cutbacks in social welfare, environmental impacts on women, and women organizing in response to global change. Materials are published as a workbook and are intended for use in community, religious, and women's organizations. The Women's Economic Literacy Collaborative is a project that seeks to place gender and race central to popular economic education. The project will create materials on women and the global economy and women's strategies for change. Visit the Web site or call for information on other projects.

Women of Los Angeles

PO Box 241682
Los Angeles, CA 90024
310-446-8057
http://www.womenof.org

Women of Los Angeles is a nonprofit, nonpartisan organization based in Los Angeles, California. WLA provides monthly forums for women to exchange ideas, support the community, learn from leaders, and help each other personally and professionally. Together with its affiliates, Women of Washington, DC, and Women of Orange County, it fosters communication and networking among women on both coasts.

Women of Orange County, Inc.

PO Box 4272
Irvine, CA 4272
949-548-6749
http://www.womenof.org

Women of Orange County is a nonprofit, non-partisan organization based in Orange County, California. WOC provides monthly forums for women to exchange ideas, support the community, learn from leaders, and help each other personally and professionally. Together with its affiliates, Women of Washington, DC, and Women of Los Angeles, it fosters communication and networking among women on both coasts.

Women of Washington, Inc.

1900 L Street, Suite 550
Washington, DC 20036
202-296-5922
http://www.womenof.org

Women of Washington, DC, is a nonprofit, non-partisan organization based in the nation's capital. WW provides monthly forums for women to exchange ideas, support the community, learn from leaders, and help each other personally and professionally. Together with its affiliates, Women of Orange County and Women of Los Angeles, it fosters communication and networking among women on both coasts.

Women Officers Professional Association

PO Box 1621
Arlington, VA 22210
703-697-0302
http://www.dittinc.com/wopa

WOPA supports the professional development of officers in the sea services (Navy, Marines, and Coast Guard) through career planning, educational materials, and networking opportunities. It is a national organization; for information on chapters outside the Washington, DC, area, call or email and give the name, address, and telephone number of your point of contact.

Women on the Fast Track

http://www.womenonthefasttrack.com

This networking organization originated in New York City. Chapters are now in several states. Membership benefits include business and professional contacts, ideas and resources for success, informational meetings, and annual summer and holiday networking events.

Women Outdoors

55 Talbot Avenue
Medford, MA 02155
http://www.women-outdoors.org

Women Outdoors is a national organization for women whose vocation or avocation is related to the outdoors. It offers day activities, weekend trips, and slide show meetings at the local level. Regional gatherings, skill building workshops, and leadership training is also offered. Members receive *Women Outdoors,* the quarterly magazine and become eligible for scholarships.

Women Peace Officers Association of California

39525 Los Alamos Road, Suite A
Murrieta, CA 92563

The WPOA-California provides networking opportunities, preparation for promotion, and training to its members. It also sponsors a scholarship for members and non-members.

Women Rainmakers

Law Practice Management Section
American Bar Association
750 North Lake Shore Drive
Chicago, IL 60611
800-285-2221
http://www.abanet.org/LPM/womenrainmakers/
application.html

The ABA Section of Law Practice Management maintains its commitment to the advancement of women in the profession through the Women Rainmakers. It offers training and mentoring, networking opportunities, a quarterly newsletter, and publications and education programs.

Organizations

Women Work!

1625 K Street, NW, Suite 300
Washington, DC 20006
202-467-6346
http://www.womenwork.org

Women Work! assists women from diverse backgrounds achieve economic self-sufficiency through job readiness, education, training, and employment through a network of 1,400 programs in every state. Call 800-235-2732 to receive a listing of programs in your state. The organization helps women train for and obtain the high paying jobs that traditionally go to men.

The Women's Campaign School at Yale University

PO Box 686
Westport, CT 06881-0686
800-353-2878
http://www.yale.edu/wcsyale/about.html

The Women's Campaign School provides campaign training in brief, intensive sessions. Classes are taught by seasoned campaign strategists, and students are offered personal on-camera training and a campaign manual. All classes are held on the Yale University campus in Connecticut. Housing is available in area hotels at discounted rates. Call for information about tuition and availability.

Women's Alliance for Theology, Ethics and Ritual

8035 13th Street
Silver Spring, MD 20910-4803
301-589-2509
http://www.his.com/~mhunt/

WATER is a feminist educational center and a network of justice-seeking people seeking theological, ethical, and liturgical development for and by women. Local and national programs, projects, publications, workshops, retreats, counseling, and liturgical planning are activities of the organization. A quarterly newsletter, *WATERwheel* is published. A Visiting Scholars Program allows women to use the resource center for a fee.

Women's American Organization for Educational Resources and Technological Training

315 Park Avenue South
New York, NY 10010
212-505-7700
http://www.waort.org

Women's American Organization for Educational Resources and Technological Training is a national Jewish organization that works to strengthen the worldwide Jewish community by empowering people to achieve economic sufficiency through technological and vocational education.

Women's Aquatic Network

P.O. Box 4993
Washington, DC 20008
http://www.womenCONNECT.com/WAN

The Women's Aquatic Network brings together women and men with interests in marine and aquatic research, policy, legislation, and other areas. Members are scientists, lawyers, public policy and natural resource managers, students, professors, and entrepreneurs. Activities include monthly Washington, DC-area luncheons or evening meetings with speakers on current topics of interest. WAN publishes a monthly newsletter which includes employment announcements, updates on legislation, and a membership directory.

Women's Army Corps Veterans Association

PO Box 5577
Fort McClellan, AL 36205
http://www.armywomen.org

WACVA is a veteran's support and advocacy membership organization for women who are current, former, or retired members of the Army, Army National Guard, Army Reserves, Women's Army Auxiliary Corps, or Women's Army Corps. Members receive *The Channel,* a newsletter that keeps members aware of national projects and pertinent veterans' information. The group holds an annual national convention and promotes recognition of women veterans.

Women's Bass Fishing Association

PO Box 538
Pelham, AL 35124
205-663-5243
http://www.wbfatour.com

The Women's Bass Fishing Association promotes bass fishing among women and youth. The WBFA Tour provides professional and amateur women a financially viable bass fishing tournament series in which to compete. Visit the Web site for tournament information, standings, regulations, and fishing links.

Women's Business Center

1001 Connecticut Avenue, NW, Suite 312
Washington, DC 20036
202-785-4WBC
http://www.womensbusinesscenter.org

The National Women's Business Center's focus is to train and educate women who want to start or expand their own business. The center's programs include comprehensive, long-term training programs, hands-on workshops, full-day seminars, and Internet training and counseling sessions. WBC's program also provides support to a training and counseling site for women on the Internet, which links women's business organizations throughout the country. The site can be found at http://www.onlinewbc.org.

Women's Business Enterprise National Council

1156 15th Street, NW, Suite 1015
Washington, DC 20005
202-862-4810
http://orgs.womenconnect.com/wbenc

WBENC provides access to a national standard of certification and provides information on certified businesses to purchasing managers interested in supporting women-owned businesses through an Internet database.

Women's Caucus for Art

c/o Moore College of Art
20th and the Parkway
Philadelphia, PA 19103
212-634-0007

This national network for women in the visual arts is organized by regions. Call for a contact number for your region.

Women's Caucus for Political Science

c/o Department of Political Science
Vassar College
Maildrop 455
Poughkeepsie, NY 12601
914-437-5562
http://www.apsanet.org/PS/organizations/
related/wcps.html

The Women's Caucus for Political Science publishes a newsletter and meets periodically.

Women's Caucus for the Modern Languages

c/o Elaine Ginsberg, Department of English
PO Box 6296
Morgantown, WV 26506-6296

The Women's Caucus for the Modern Languages provides a forum and support network for women in the Modern Language Association. It organizes sessions at each annual meeting that focus on professional issues of concern to women. It publishes articles in *Concerns,* its professional journal, and awards a scholarship and travel grant annually. Regional caucuses are in the Midwest, New England, and Rocky Mountain areas.

Women's Classical Caucus

http://weber.u.washington.edu/~wcc/WCC.html

The Women's Classical Caucus seeks to incorporate feminist and gender-informed perspectives in the study and teaching of all aspects of ancient Mediterranean cultures and advance equality and diversity within the profession. Activities include a panel at the annual meeting of the American Philological Association and American Institute of Archaeology, meetings at regional conferences, and a twice yearly newsletter. Members may apply for grants from the Equity Fund, established to promote equitable treatment in hiring and promotion in the classics profession. A free, one-year member-

Organizations

ship is offered to all first-year graduate students who request it.

Women's College Coalition

125 Michigan Avenue, NE
Washington, DC 20017
202-234-0443
http://www.womenscolleges.org

The Women's College Coalition represents 78 women's colleges in the United States and Canada. The WCC makes the case for single-sex education for women to the higher education community, to policy makers, to the media and to the general public. The Web site lists academic rankings of women's colleges and contact information for member colleges. Additionally, the WCC collects and disseminates information and sponsors research on gender equity in education.

Women's Council of Realtors

430 North Michigan Avenue
Chicago, IL 60611-4093
312-329-3290
http://www.wcr.org

WCR offers networking and referral opportunities for women realtors nationwide, including local, state, national, and regional meetings, workshops, and special events. Its most valued benefit is the *Referral Roster,* WCR's annual member directory, which links thousands of real estate professionals nationwide who can provide qualified referrals. Members also receive a newsletter and access to the online Members Only Conferencing Area.

Women's Economic Club

Detroit, MI
313-963-5088
http://www.womenseconomicclub.org

The Women's Economic Club seeks to create a vibrant force for the advancement of women by emphasizing the important role of women in the workplace. Members are male and female professionals from corporations, small businesses, government, education, health care, and nonprofit organizations in Detroit and the Midwest. Members participate in luncheon

forums with high-profile speakers, seminars, mentoring, and have access to an online job bank.

Women's Economic Network

870 Market Street, Suite 1257
San Francisco, CA 94102
415-281-3225

The Women's Economic Network is a regional organization that supports women in creating economic independence through their own efforts. It offers a newsletter, directory, member discounts, monthly networking meetings, and special interest group participation. It publishes a freelance guide for women in the Bay Area.

Women's Educational Equity Act Resource Center

WEEA-EDC-C99
PO Box 1020
Sewickley, PA 15143-1020
800-793-5076
http://www.edc.org/WomensEquity/index.html

Funded by the U.S. Department of Education, the WEEA Equity Resource Center offers publications, contact information, and other resources for parents, teachers, students, and counselors. It works with schools, organizations, businesses, and individuals to reduce the educational disparity between women and men by issuing grants, offering technical assistance, and publishing gender equity information.

Women's Enterprise Initiative

Women's Enterprise Society of British Columbia
14-2070 Harvey Avenue
Kelowna, BC V1Y 8P8
250-868-3454
http://www.wes.bc.ca

The Women's Enterprise Initiative encourages the establishment and growth of women-owned and controlled businesses in British Columbia through mentoring, business counseling, and workshops.

Women's Environmental and Development Organization

355 Lexington Avenue, 3rd Floor
New York, NY 10017
212-973-0325
http://www.wedo.org

WEDO is an international advocacy network working to achieve a healthy and peaceful planet, with social, political, economic, and environmental justice through the empowerment of women and their equal decision-making from grassroots to global arenas. It offers a newsletter, monitors and works with the United Nations, and conducts programs on women and the environment and women and the global economy.

Women's Foreign Policy Group

1825 Connecticut Avenue, NW, Suite 660
Washington, DC 20009
202-986-8862
http://www.wfpg.org

WFPG is open to women and men with experience in international affairs who are committed to promoting women in the field. Membership benefits include leadership development sessions, networking opportunities with women leaders and experts in small groups, expertise listing in the membership directory, publications, job and fellowship listings, and internship listings. Fifty to sixty in-depth programs are offered per year in New York, Washington, DC, and California, addressing issues such as women ambassadors, leadership development, and regions, such as the Mideast and Russia.

Women's Franchise Network

International Franchise Association
1350 New York Avenue, NW, Suite 900
Washington, DC 20005-4709
202-628-8000

WFN provides an international networking forum for the exchange of ideas, resources, and experiences among women seeking to enter the world of franchising and existing women franchisees, franchisors, and suppliers.

Women's Gateway Golf Network

7536 Forsyth, Suite 303
St. Louis, MO 63105
314-995-8687
http://www.wggn.com

The Women's Gateway Golf Network was formed to unite women who want to learn, enjoy, and advance in the game of golf. It seeks to provide networking opportunities, create an environment of acceptance of new players, and improve members' golfing skills and enjoyment of the game. The Web site features golf tips and information on courses.

Women's Global Business Alliance, Lic.

361 Post Road West, Suite 205
Westport, CT 06880
http://www.wgba-business.com

WGBA members are senior-level women corporate executives and business owners focused on expanding their careers, businesses, and presence in world economies. Members-only executive seminars and symposiums provide a forum for open communications among members and business experts. WGBA also helps its members find venture capital and assists in site selection for business expansion.

Women's Information Network

1800 R Street, NW
Unit C4, DuPont Circle
Washington, DC 20009
202-347-2827
http://www.winonline.org

The Women's Information Network is a Washington-area professional, political, and social network dedicated to empowering pro-choice women. It provides members with a job bank, monthly newsletter, and educational events and networking opportunities.

Women's Initiative on International Affairs in Asia

Program for International Studies in Asia
George Washington University
2013 G Street, NW
Washington, DC 20006-4205
202-994-4313

Organizations

WIIAA is an Asia-Pacific-wide network of women who work professionally in international affairs as scholars, representatives of non-governmental organizations, public servants, business leaders, or journalists. The organization shares information and resources to enable women's participation in decision-making on international issues. It sponsors training programs and comparative research, translation, and the exchange of documentation, as well as the use of information technology to further these projects. It holds an annual meeting, participates in international conferences, publishes a resource directory and maintains a members' listserve.

Women's Institute for a Secure Retirement

1201 Pennsylvania Avenue, NW, Suite 619
Washington, DC 20004
http://www.wiser.heinz.org

WISER was created by the Heinz Family Philanthropies to improve the long-term economic security of millions of American women and men. It works to expand retirement planning education and enable women to make informed decisions about their finances and to take advantage of plans offered by their employers. It publishes a quarterly newsletter, and sponsors a variety of educational programs, including panel discussions, workshops, and conferences.

Women's Institute for Financial Education

13569 Tiverton Road
San Diego, CA 92130
619-792-0524
http://www.wife.org

WIFE was founded by a certified financial planner and an independent investment adviser in 1988. It provides financial education and networking opportunities for women of all ages, publishes a quarterly newsletter filled with money management strategies, and sponsors seminars and workshops. Examples of workshop topics include "Second Saturday: What Women Need to Know About Divorce," and "Suddenly Alone," which offers legal, financial,

and family information to anyone who has lost a loved one.

Women's Institute for Freedom of the Press

3306 Ross Place
Washington, DC 20008
202-966-7783
http://www.igc.org/wifp/

WIFP is an organization of over 700 media women and media-concerned women networking to achieve communication among women through research, publishing, and education. The organization issues publications and offers internships for young women.

Women's Intercultural Network

1950 Hayes, Suite 2
San Francisco, CA 94117
http://www.win-cawa.org

WIN conducts a variety of projects in California, including coalition building across cultures, arts, online conferences, educational conferences and seminars, skills training, social events, professional exchanges across borders, and language and communications training. Quotes for training and travel programs are furnished by request for weekly and monthly packages including housing, meals, transportation, and educational programs.

Women's International Network of Utility Professionals

PO Box 335
Whites Creek, TN 37189
615-876-5444
http://www.winup.org

WINUP, formerly the Electrical Women's Round Table, provides a means for developing and recognizing professionals involved in business trends, issues, products, and services in the utility industry. WINUP offers two annual fellowships and networking and mentoring opportunities.

Women's International Racquetball Tour

11355 Affinity Court, Number 189
San Diego, CA 92131
619-536-2393
http://www.eos.net/irt-tour/welcome.html

Organized as the Women's Professional Racquetball Association in 1979, the tour originally consisted of five tournaments with a total of $50,000 in prize money. Ten years later, the tour competed for over $100,000 in ten major cities and continues to grow.

Women's International Shipping and Trading Association

WISTA-USA
c/o Rigos Chartering
25 Tudor City Place
New York, NY 10017
212-943-3980

WISTA is an international organization for women involved in shipping-related businesses. Women working in all areas of shipping and trading such as operations, finance, brokerage, chartering, freight forwarding, consulting, management, law, shop registration, and insurance are members. It conducts annual conferences which include workshops and tours of port and cargo terminals. Members receive mailings and a listing in the international membership directory.

Women's Jewelry Association

333 B. Route 46 West
Suite B201
Fairfield, NJ 07004
973-575-7190
http://www.womensjewelry.org

The Women's Jewelry Association fosters professional skills for women in the jewelry industry through programs and workshops, a triannual newsletter, and scholarship program. Visit the Web site for program and regional chapter information.

Women's Music Alliance

PO Box 505
Largo, FL 33779-0505
727-539-1348
http://inklein.com/wma

The Women's Music Alliance seeks to promote independent female creators of today's music and encourage women of all ages to write and perform tomorrow's music. WMA offers workshops and seminars, a quarterly newsletter, a venue directory, sponsorship of events, and a discounted promotional Web site.

Women's National Book Association

160 Fifth Avenue
New York, NY 10010
212-675-7805

The Women's National Book Association is open to women and men in all occupations allied to the publishing industry including publishers, authors, librarians, literary agents, illustrators, educators, critics, booksellers, and those engaged in book production, marketing, and personnel.

Women's Philharmonic

44 Page Street
San Francisco, CA 94102
415-437-0123

The Women's Philharmonic performs and promotes music of women conductors, composers, and performers. The organization has a local concert season in San Francisco, commissions and reconstructs historical works by women composers, and disseminates information about works by women composers to other orchestras and audiences. Its National Women Composers Resource Center is developing a database of orchestral works by women composers.

Women's Presses Library Project

1483 Laurel Avenue
St. Paul, MN 55104-6737
612-646-0097

The Women's Presses Library Project works to encourage librarians to stock titles from their presses and to create more visibility for women's presses titles. It exhibits as a group at American Library Assocation national and regional conferences, organizes author appearances, and creates catalogs and reference materials.

Women's Professional Billiards Association

5676 Summer Avenue
Memphis, TN 38134
901-380-1102
http://www.wpba.org

There are four types of membership into the WPBA: patron members, player members, semiprofessional members, and pros/touring pros. The organization sanctions tournaments, including the annual WPBA Amateur Nationals, and publishes a monthly newsletter.

Women's Professional Rodeo Association

1235 Lake Plaza Drive, Suite 134
Colorado Springs, CO 80906
719-576-0900

The Women's Professional Rodeo Association is a national network of over 2,000 women in professional rodeo. The WPRA sanctions competitions that pay out over $400,000 in prize money annually. It sponsors the Professional Women's Rodeo Association National Finals each year with payouts over $50,000.

Women's Project and Productions

55 West End Avenue
New York, NY 10023
212-765-1706
http://www.womensproject.org

Women's Project and Productions produces and develops new plays by women and is the oldest and largest women's theatre company in the nation. WPP fosters emerging playwrights and directors, offers internships, runs an arts education program, and honors women of exceptional achievement.

Women's Referral Service

818-995-6646
http://www.wypwrs.com

WRS membership includes the opportunity to network through any of 17 chapters and a networking seminar. Services geared toward women business owners and entrepreneurs and offered for a fee include Web site design and hosting, marketing assistance, and listing in the printed *Women's Yellow Page*s or online version.

Women's Research and Education Institute

1700 18th Street, NW, Suite 400
Washington, DC 20009
202-628-0444
http://www.wrei.org

WREI is a nonpartisan organization that provides information and analyses on issues of concern to women and policy makers. The organization prepares fact sheets, holds briefings on Capitol Hill, and responds to press inquiries. It offers a fellowship program and an internship program to provide practical policymaking experience to women. For information about any of its programs, send a SASE with your request to WREI or visit the Web site.

Women's Soccer Foundation

PO Box 2097
Norton, MA 02766-0993
508-285-5699
http://www.womensoccer.org

The Women's Soccer Foundation seeks to strengthen the voice of girls and women in soccer throughout the world. It publishes *Network* a quarterly publication with articles on the value of sports, health, and psychology for women, strategies for making changes, and other topics of interest to girl and women athletes.

Women's Sports Foundation

Eisenhower Park
East Meadow, NY 11554
800-227-3988
http://www.womenssportsfoundation.org

The Women's Sports Foundation seeks to increase opportunities for girls and women in sports and fitness through education, advocacy, recognition, and grants. Anyone with an interest in women's sports is eligible for membership. Members receive the newsletter, The *Women's Sports Experience,* six times a year and access to conferences, publications, research, and video tapes. Members and nonmembers may apply for grants to assist individuals and women's teams in athletic pursuits.

Women's Studies in Religion Program
Harvard Divinity School
45 Francis Avenue
Cambridge, MA 02138
617-495-5705
http://www.wsrp.harvard.edu

The Women's Studies in Religion Program fosters critical inquiry into the interaction between religion and gender. Each year, the program appoints five research associates to spend a year at the Harvard Divinity School pursuing a book-length project on women and religion. Each scholar is appointed to the faculty as a member of one of the Divinity School's departments. Positions are open to candidates with doctorates in religion or with primary competence in other fields of the humanities or social sciences. Generally, the group includes an international scholar, a scholar working in a non-Western tradition, a scholar of Judaism, and a minority scholar.

Women's Studio Workshop
Women's Studio Workshop
PO Box 489
Rosendale, NY 12472
914-658-9133
http://www.wsworkshop.org

The Women's Studio Workshop offers an alternative space for artists to create new work and come together to share skills. WSW offers studios for rent with Intaglio, papermaking, screenprinting, print shop, darkroom, and clay/pottery equipment. It publishes *Binnewater Tides,* an arts journal, and offers exhibitions and a summer arts institute. Visit the Web site to learn about WSW's many programs.

Women's Tennis Association Tour
1266 East Main Street, 4th Floor
Stamford, CT 06902-3546
203-978-1740
http://www.wtatour.com

The WTA is the worldwide governing body of women's tennis.

Women's Theological Center
PO Box 1200
Boston, MA 02117-1200
617-536-8782
http://world.std.com/~wtc/

The Women's Theological Center works to nourish women's spiritual leadership and communities for liberation movements. Programs include retreats, gatherings, and discussions for African-American women; evening and weekend workshops on a variety of topics; and an annual conference on spirituality and ending racism. WTC services offered include consultations, workshops, and speeches that explore the connection between spirituality/theology and social justice.

Women's Transportation Seminar
One Walnut Street
Boston, MA 02108-3616
617-367-3273
http://www.wtsnational.org

WTS seeks to encourage women to enter careers in the transporation field and supports women who currently work in various aspects of transportation. WTS offers an annual conference and monthly local programs, a membership directory, national and local newsletters, career development seminars and roundtable discussions, an online job bank, and scholarships.

Women's Western Golf Association
PO Box 85
Golf, IL 60029
800-753-WWGA
http://www.mcs.net/~wwga/

The WWGA seeks to advance women in scholastic achievement and intercollegiate golf. It is the umbrella organization for over 500 clubs in 43 states and holds three major tournaments: the WWGA Amateur Championship, Junior Championship, and Senior Championship. The Women's Western Golf Foundation offers scholarships for female high school seniors who golf, who plan to attend college, and are involved in the sport of golf. A GPA of 3.5 or higher is required; level of skill in golf is not a criterion. Contact the WWGA in writing for an application.

Women'Sports Services

409 Utica, Suite D-36
Huntington Beach, CA 92648
714-960-0411
http://www.womensportswire.com

Women'Sports Services serves as a commercial resource for women in sports. It offers publishing, marketing/consulting, career services, event/special projects assistance, and athlete representation. Womens' Sports Career Seminars were designed to meet the growing needs of women interested in sports-related careers. Seminars include resume preparation, interview and presentation skills, networking, and salary negotiating. It also publishes *Women'Sports Wire*, a national clearinghouse for women's sports news and information.

Wound, Ostomy and Continence Nurses Society

http://www.wocn.org

WOCN is a professional nursing society that promotes educational, clinical, and research opportunities for its members. It hosts an annual conference, meetings, and seminars, and offers scholarships and educational programs.

Young Women/Students Caucus

Women's Caucus for Art
PO Box 1498
Canal Street Station
New York, NY 10013
212-634-0007
http://www.geocities.com/SoHo/Square/9106/

YSWC is a sub-caucus of the national organization Women's Caucus for Art. Its membership consists of young women artists, art profession-

als, students, and returning students pursuing an art career.

SBA Women's Business Centers

The federal government's Small Business Administration coordinates a network of more than 60 Women's Business Centers in 36 states, the District of Columbia, and Puerto Rico. These centers provide a wide range of services to women entrepreneurs at all levels of business development. WBCs teach women the principles of finance, management, and marketing, as well as specialized topics such as how to get a government contract or how to start a home-based business. The SBA Web site also offers online information, such as articles on starting and growing a business, technology, and procurement.

American Women's Economic Development Corporation

71 Vanderbilt Avenue, Suite 320
New York, NY 10169
212-692-9100

AWED is a national organization that offers formal course instruction, counseling, seminars, special events, and peer group support to help women start and grow their own businesses.

Career Training Institute and Women's Business Center

347 North Last Chance Gulch
Helena, MT 59601
406-443-0800

The Career Training Institute provides job training, welfare-to-work, displaced homemakers, and nontraditional careers services to women in Montana.

Center for Economic Options, Inc.

601 Delaware Avenue
Charleston, WV 25302
304-345-1298
http://www.centerforeconoptions.org

The Center for Economic Options is a statewide organization that works to develop the economic capacity of West Virginia's rural citizens, particularly women. It seeks alternative approaches to economic development, such as networks of home-based businesses.

Center for Women Entrepreneurs— Columbia College of South Carolina

1301 Columbia College Drive
Columbia, SC 29203
803-786-3582
http://www.colacoll.edu

The center seeks to expand economic opportunities for women by advancing entrepreneurship and providing resources to assist in successful business startups and maintenance of growth.

Enterprise Center/Women's Business Center

Ohio State University
1864 Shyville Road
Piketon, OH 45661
614-289-3727
http://www.ag.ohio-state.edu/~prec

The Women's Business Center focuses on rural transition issues and alternative income sources, and is an international trade assistance center.

Grand Rapids Opportunities for Women

25 Sheldon Street, SE, Suite 210
Grand Rapids, MI 49503
616-458-3404

GROW provides women from diverse backgrounds with opportunities to develop the skills

and acquire the knowledge to achieve financial independence. Its three program components are Small Business Readiness and Entrepreneurial Training; Business Support Services; and Economic Literacy Training.

Greater Columbus Women's Business Development Center

37 North High Street
Columbus, OH 43215-3065
614-225-6081
http://www.columbus.org/busi/sbdc/index.html

The Women's Business Initiative offers training for start-ups and existing women business owners, specializing in procurement and international trade issues.

Massachusetts Center for Women and Enterprise

45 Bromfield Street, Sixth Floor
Boston, MA 02108
617-423-3001

The center seeks to empower women to become economically self-sufficient through entrepreneurship, providing courses, workshops, roundtables, counseling, and loan packaging assistance.

Mi Casa Resource Center for Women

571 Galapago Street
Denver, CO 80204
303-573-0333
http://www.micasadenver.org

Mi Casa provides employment and education services that promote economic independence for Hispanic women and youth. An entrepreneurial training program is offered with microloans available to graduates. Job readiness, job search training, and nontraditional and computer skills training are provided.

Micro-Business Assistance Pyramid Career Services

2400 Cleveland Avenue North
Canton, OH 44709
330-453-3767

Organizations

The Micro-Business Assistance Program offers business plan development and counseling for new and existing small businesses, including computer and Internet training.

Mississippi Women's Economic Entrepreneurial Project
106 West Green Street
Mound Bayou, MS 38762
601-741-3342

The NCNW established economic entrepreneurial centers in Mound Bayou and Ruleville in Bolivar County, Mississippi. This area has been designated as a Rural Enterprise Zone by the government, and NCNW works with officials to administer this revitalization effort.

Montana Community Development Corporation
127 North Higgins
Missoula, MT 59802
406-543-2550

MCDC provides training using real-world information, featuring local business owners as speakers. Trainers emphasize problem-solving that business owners can carry out independently.

National Association for Women Business Owners—Nashville
PO Box 101024
Nashville, TN 37224
615-248-3474

The NAWBO—Nashville Women's Business Center offers on-site business counseling services, training programs, and technical assistance to women business owners in middle Tennessee, which includes 21 counties, and statewide through video conferences.

National Association of Women Business Owners—St. Louis
7165 Delmar, Suite 204
St. Louis, MO 63130
314-863-0046
http://www.stlmo.com/nawbo

NAWBO—St. Louis offers counseling, mentoring, and monthly educational meetings. It operates Successavvy, a series of classes to help women start and grow successful businesses.

National Council of Negro Women
633 Pennsylvania Avenue, NW
Washington, DC 20004
202-737-0120
http://www.ncnw.com

The NCNW established economic entrepreneurial centers in Mound Bayou and Ruleville in Bolivar County, Mississippi. This area has been designated as a Rural Enterprise Zone by the government, and NCNW works with officials to administer this revitalization effort.

National Women's Business Center
1250 24th Street, NW, Suite 350
Washington, DC 20037
202-466-0544
http://www.womenconnect.com/womensbusinesscenter

The National Women's Business Center offers programs for women at all stages of business development, such as Introduction to Business Ownership, Federal Procurement, The Business Laboratory, and The Bottom Line.

Nevada Microenterprise Initiative
1600 East Desert Inn Road, Suite 209E
Las Vegas, NV 89109
702-734-3555

Nevada Micro-Enterprise Initiative provides entrepreneurial training, business technical assistance, and loans for low- to moderate-income individuals throughout the state of Nevada. The Carson City office phone number is 702-841-1420.

New Jersey National Association of Women Business Owners
225 Hamilton Street
Bound Brook, NJ 08805-2042
732-560-2042
http://www.njawbo.org

New Jersey NAWBO manages the Excel Training and Counseling Program. The program is offered in three stages of planning, creating, and growing a business.

New Mexico Women's Economic Self-Sufficiency Team

414 Silver Southwest
Albuquerque, NM 87102
505-241-4760

WESST assists low-income and minority women throughout New Mexico. It is a micro-lender for the Small Business Administration and offers counseling and mentoring through professional volunteers. There are offices throughout the state: Farmington, 505-325-0678; Las Cruces, 505-522-3707; Roswell, 505-622-4196; Santa Fe, 505-988-5284; and Taos, 505-751-1575.

North Texas Women's Business Development Center, Inc.

Priest Institute for Economic Development
1402 Corinth Street, Suite 1536
Dallas, TX 75125-2111
214-428-1777

NTWBDC is a collective effort of several Texas organizations, focusing on women's government contracting opportunities, long-term training, counseling, and mentoring.

Ohio Women's Business Resource Network

77 South High Street, 28th Floor
PO Box 1001
Columbus, OH 43215-1001
614-466-2682
http://www.ohiobiz.com

The OWBRN is a statewide effort to assist women business owners. It promotes information sharing, technical assistance, and education among member businesses.

Onaben—A Native American Business Network

3201 Broadway, Suite C
Everett, WA 98201
425-339-6226
http://www.onaben.org

ONABEN offers training, individual counseling, assisted access to markets, and faciliated access to capital for its Native American clients.

Onaben—Native American Business Network

520 Southwest Sixth Avenue, Suite 930
Portland, OR 97204
503-243-5015
http://www.onaben.org

ONABEN was created to increase the number and profitability of private enterprises owned by Native Americans, offering training, counseling, and assistance in access to markets and capital.

Self-Employment Loan Fund

201 North Central Avenue, Suite CC10
Phoenix, AZ 85073-1000
602-340-8834

SELF provides training, technical assistance, and loan access to low-income individuals, primarily women and minorities.

Southeast Louisiana Black Chamber of Commerce Women's Business Center

2245 Peters Road, Suite 200
Harvey, LA 70058
504-365-3866
http://www.gnofn.org/~slbcc/wbc

The Women's Business Center assists women in ten parishes in southeast Louisiana, providing training, counseling, and mentoring to encourage the growth of businesses owned by women.

Organizations

Southern Oregon Women's Access to Credit

33 North Central, Suite 209
Medford, OR 97501
541-779-3992
http://www.sowac.org

SOWAC provides business training, mentoring, and financing services for women and men with barriers, including low-income Hispanics, rural entrepreneurs, and others.

Texas Center for Women's Business Enterprise

2 Commodore Plaza, 13th Floor
206 East Ninth Street, Suite 13.140
Austin, TX 78734-0219
512-261-8525
http://www.onr.com/CWE

TxCWBE assists women who are starting or expanding a business in Texas, offering certification information, Internet training, business plans, and loan assistance referrals.

Watertown Area Career Learning Center—The Entrepreneur Network for Women

100 South Maple
PO Box 81
Watertown, SD 57201-0081
605-882-5080
http://www.network4women.com

ENW is a statewide program serving South Dakota entrepreneurs with toll-free telephone counseling and training seminars in management, marketing, financing, government contracting, and entrepreneurial confidence.

West Company—Ukiah Office

367 North State Street, Suite 201
Ukiah, CA 95482
707-468-3553

West Company serves micro-enterprise owners in rural northern California, targeting low-income women and minorities. It provides business planning and management assistance at any stage of business ownership, and access to capital through peer loans.

Western Reserve Business Center for Women

University of Akron Community and Technical College
M/185V Polski Building, Room 185
Akron, OH 44325-6002
330-972-5592
http://www.wrbcw.org

The business center provides information and support to help women's businesses flourish, including home-based business assistance, referrals, networking, mentoring, and financing sources.

Wisconsin Women's Business Initiative Corporation

1915 North Dr. Martin Luther King Jr. Drive
Milwaukee, WI 53212
414-263-5450
http://www.wwbic.com

WWBIC is an economic development corporation providing business education, access to capital, and technical assistance. It is the state's largest Small Business Administration microlender. The Madison office can be reached at 608-257-7409.

Women Entrepreneurs for Economic Development

1683 North Claiborne Avenue, Suite 101
New Orleans, LA 70116
504-947-8522

WEED has assisted hundreds of women in the Orleans Parish area of New Orleans become economically self-sufficient.

Women Entrepreneurs of Baltimore

28 East Ostend Street
Baltimore, MD 21230
410-727-4921

WEB is an entrepreneurial training program designed to help economically disadvantaged women become self-sufficient through business development.

Women Entrepreneurs, Inc.

Bartlett Building
36 East Fourth Street, Suite 925
Cincinnati, OH 45202
513-684-0700

Women Entrepreneurs Inc. is a networking and membership organization for women business owners that offers seminars. It is a Small Business Administration micro-loan technical assistance recipient.

Women in New Development

Bi-County Community Action Programs
2715 15th Street, NW
PO Box 579
Bemidji, MN 56601
218-751-4631

WIND serves the small business communities in rural northwestern Minnesota, providing technical assistance and an annual regional women's business conference.

Women$ Fund, A Program of the YWCA of Anchorage

245 West Fifth Avenue
PO Box 102059
Anchorage, AK 99510-2059
907-274-1524

The Women$ Fund is a microenterprise training and microlending program for women entrepreneurs in Anchorage. It provides training, mentoring, and seed money for women's businesses.

Women's Business Assistance Center

1301 Azalea Road, Suite 201A
Mobile, AL 36693
800-378-7461
http://ceebic.org/~wbac

WBAC is a business incubator and training center for the South Alabama and Northwest Florida area.

Women's Business Center at the Chamber

Salt Lake Area Chamber of Commerce
175 East 400 South, Suite 600
Salt Lake City, UT 84111
801-328-5051
http://www.slachamber.com

The Women's Business Center at the Chamber supports women business owners throughout Utah with counseling, training, and loan packaging assistance. There is a modest fee for some services, but scholarships are available for socially or economically disadvantaged women.

Women's Business Center

150 Greenleaf Avenue, Unit 4
Portsmouth, NH 03801
603-430-2892
http://www.womensbusinesscenter.org

The Women's Business Center encourages and supports women in all phases of business development by providing access to educational programs, financing alternatives, technical assistance, and a network of mentors.

Women's Business Development Center

1315 Walnut Street, Suite 1116
Philadelphia, PA 19107-4711
215-790-9232

WBDC enables women to launch new businesses and improve existing businesses, through courses and business consulting in management, marketing, and finances.

Women's Business Development Center

10555 West Flagler Street, Room 2612
Miami, FL 33174
305-348-3951

The center provides business education, technical assistance, and access to capital for women, minorities, and low- to moderate-income individuals who are starting or growing their own business. The center is an intermediary for the Small Business Administration Women's Prequalification Loan Program.

Organizations

Women's Business Development Center

8 South Michigan Avenue, Suite 400
Chicago, IL 60603
312-853-3477

The WBDC serves women business owners in the greater Chicagoland area, providing entrepreneurial training courses, counseling, financial assistance, and loan packaging for microloans. It is an intermediary for the Small Business Administration Women's Prequalification Loan Program.

Women's Business Development Program

Coastal Enterprises, Inc.
PO Box 268
Wiscasset, ME 04578
207-882-7552
http://www.ceimaine.rog

CEI is a non-profit community development corporation. The Women's Business Development Project assesses women business owners' needs and provides training, technical assistance, financing, and advocacy. Participants have access to capital through its Small Business Administration Micro-Loan Program and Women's Prequalification Loan Program.

Women's Business Development Program

Coastal Enterprises, Inc.
7 North Chestnut Street
Augusta, ME 04330
207-621-0245
http://www.ceimaine.rog

CEI is a non-profit community development corporation. The Women's Business Development Project assesses women business owners' needs and provides training, technical assistance, financing, and advocacy. Participants have access to capital through its Small Business Administration Micro-Loan Program and Women's Prequalification Loan Program.

Women's Business Institute

320 North Fifth Street, Suite 203
PO Box 2043
Fargo, ND 58107-2043
701-235-6488
http://www.rrtrade.org/women/wbi

The WBI serves women statewide with business information and counseling. Training seminars focus on management, marketing, financing, government contracting, and entrepreneurial self-confidence.

Women's Business Institute

University of the Sacred Heart
PO Box 12383
San Juan, Puerto Rico 00914-0383
787-728-1515
http://www.rrtrade.org/women/wbi

The Women's Business Institute offers technical assistance to women interested in establishing a business.

Women's Business Resource Program of Southeastern Ohio

Ohio University
20 East Circle Drive, Suite 155
Technology and Enterprise Building
Athens, OH 45701
614-593-1797

The Women's Business Resource Program of Southeastern Ohio supports women-owned businesses through services that focus on expanding networking opportunities, including support groups, monthly networking luncheons, business classes, and an annual trade fair.

Women's Development Center

42101 Griswold Road
Elyria, OH 44035
216-324-3688

The Women's Development Center provides a long-term training program, focusing first on personal development and then on entrepreneurship for low-income women.

Women's Economic Development Agency

675 Ponce de Leon Avenue
Atlanta, GA 30308
404-853-7680

The WEDA program is for individuals who are planning, expanding, or strengthening a business. It is a 21-seminar series for women business owners, lasting two and a half hours per week. The majority of clients are African-American women.

Women's Enterprise Development Corporation

100 West Broadway, Suite 500
Long Beach, CA 90802
562-983-3747

WEDC's core programs consist of two long-term training modules: Starting Your Own Business for beginning business and Managing Your Own Business for women who have been in business at least one year.

Women's Initiative for Self-Employment

Center for Empowerment and Economic Development
2002 Hogback Road, Suite 12
Ann Arbor, MI 48105
313-677-1400

The WISE program provides low-income women with the tools to begin and expand businesses, including business training, credit counseling, startup and expansion financing, and mentoring.

Women's Initiative for Self-Employment

450 Mission Street, Suite 402
San Francisco, CA 94105
415-247-9473

WISE provides business training and technical assistance in English and Spanish to women in the San Francisco Bay Area. Programs include workshops on business assessment and writing a business plan, and peer networking and support groups.

Women's Organization for Mentoring, Entrepreneurship and Networking

526 South Main Street, Suite 235
Akron, OH 44311-1058
330-379-9280
http://www.womennet.org

WOMEN provides training and counseling for startup and existing small businesses and provides mentoring opportunities for expanding businesses.

Women's Venture Fund

155 East 42nd Street, Suite 316
New York, NY 10017
212-972-1146

The Women's Venture Fund makes micro-loans to entrepreneurial women who cannot get funding through conventional sources and helps address their credit and training needs.

Working Women's Money University

234 Quadrum Drive
Oklahoma City, OK 73108
405-232-8257

The WWMU women's business center is an entrepreneurial training camp where a team of small business supporters help those who want to help themselves and their businesses through training and access to capital.

Sororities

Greek-letter societies, including sororities, honorary societies, and service organizations, offer social, philanthropic, and personal development opportunities to

Organizations

women. Contact information only is listed for sororities and service organizations. Although there are sororities in specific career fields, most list sisterhood and service in general as their main objectives. This list is certainly not a comprehensive list of all sororities in the United States. Rather, the national offices of large sororities and service organizations with a presence on several campuses are listed here. Honorary societies for professionals and college alumnae are also listed here.

Alpha Chi Omega
5939 Castle Creek Parkway, North Drive
Indianapolis, IN 46250
317-579-5050
http://www.alphachiomega.org

Alpha Delta Kappa International Honorary Society for Women Educators
1615 West 92nd Street
Kansas City, MO 64114
http://www.alphadeltakappa.org

Alpha Delta Pi
1386 Ponce de Leon Avenue, NE
Atlanta, GA 30307
404-378-3164
http://www.alphadeltapi.org

Alpha Epsilon Iota
100 South Main Street
Ann Arbor, MI 48104

Alpha Epsilon Phi
http://www.aephi.org

Alpha Gamma Delta
8701 Founders Road
Indianapolis, IN 46268
317-872-2655
http://www.alphagammadelta.org

Alpha Kappa Alpha
5656 South Stony Island Avenue
Chicago, IL 60637
312-684-1282
http://www.aka1908.com

Alpha Kappa Delta Phi
http://www.akdphi.org

Alpha Omicron Pi
9025 Overlook Boulevard
Brentwood, TN 37027
615-370-0920
http://www.alphaomicronpi.org

Alpha Phi
1930 Sherman Avenue
Evanston, IL 60201
847-475-0663
http://www.alphaphi.org

Alpha Sigma Alpha
9001 Wesleyan Road, Suite 200
Indianapolis, IN 46268-1176
http://www.alphasigmaalpha.org

Alpha Sigma Kappa
http://www.alpha-sigma-kappa.org

Alpha Sigma Tau
http://www.alphasigmatau.org

Alpha Xi Delta
8702 Founders Road
Indianapolis, IN 46268
317-872-3500
http://www.alphaxidelta.org

Beta Pi Sigma
PO Box 9112
Inglewood, CA 90305
http://members.aol.com/bpssi/index.html

Chi Omega
3395 Players Club Parkway
Memphis, TN 38125
http://www.chiomega.org

Chi Upsilon Sigma
Grand Chapter Board
99 Park Avenue, 278A
New York, NY 10016
212-969-0793

Delta Delta Delta
P.O. Box 5987
2331 Brookhollow Plaza Drive
Arlington, TX 76005
817-633-8001
http://www.tridelta.org

Delta Gamma
3250 Riverside Drive
PO Box 21397
Columbus, OH 43221-0397
614-481-8169
http://www.deltagamma.org

Delta Kappa Gamma Society International
PO Box 1589
Austin, TX 78767-1589

Delta Phi Epsilon
734 West Port Plaza, Suite 271
St. Louis, MO 63146
314-275-2626
http://www.dphie.org

Delta Sigma Theta
1707 New Hampshire Avenue, NW
Washington, DC 20009
202-483-5460
http://www.dsi1913.org

Delta Zeta
202 East Church Street
Oxford, OH 45056
513-523-7597
http://www.deltazeta.org

Epsilon Sigma Alpha
Drake Office Center
363 West Drake Road
Fort Collins, CO 80526
970-223-2824
http://www.esaintl.com

Gamma Phi Beta
12737 East Euclid Drive
Englewood, CO 80111-6445
303-799-1874
http://www.gammaphibeta.org

Gamma Phi Delta
2657 West Grand Boulevard
Detroit, MI 48208
313-872-8597
http://www.gphid.org

Iota Phi Lambda
Chicago, IL
800-982-IOTA
http://www.iota1929.org

Iota Sigma Pi
http://chem-faculty.ucsd.edu/
sawrey/ISP/awards.html

National honorary society for women in chemistry. No centralized contact information available. Contact your campus' chemistry department for information on local chapters.

Kappa Alpha Theta
8740 Founders Road
Indianapolis, IN 46268
317-876-1870
http://www.kappaalphatheta.org

Kappa Delta
2211 South Josephine Street
Denver, CO 80210
303-777-4900
http://www.kappadelta.org

Kappa Kappa Gamma
530 East Town Street
PO Box 38
Columbus, OH 43215-0038
614-228-6515
http://www.kappakappagamma.org

Kappa Omicron Nu Honor Society
4990 Northwind Drive, Suite 140
East Lansing, MI 48823
517-351-8335

Organizations

Phi Mu
3558 Habersham at Northlake
Tucker, GA 30084-4015
770-496-5582
http://www.phimu.org

Phi Sigma Sigma
23123 State Road 7, Suite 250
Boca Raton, FL 33428
561-451-4415
http://www.phisigmasigma.org

Pi Beta Phi
7730 Carondelet, Suite 333
St. Louis, MO 63105
314-727-7338
http://www.pibetaphi.org

Sigma Alpha Iota
34 Wall Street, Suite 515
Asheville, NC 28801-2710
828-251-0606
http://www.sai-nationa.org

Sigma Gamma Rho
8800 South Stony Island Avenue
Chicago, IL 60617
773-873-9000

Sigma Kappa
8733 Founders Road
Indianapolis, IN 46268-1338
317-872-3275
http://www.sigmakappa.org

Sigma Sigma Sigma
225 North Muhlenberg Street
Woodstock, VA 22664
540-459-4212
http://www.trisigma.org

Sigma Theta Tau International Honor Society of Nursing
550 West North Street
Indianapolis, IN 46202
317-634-8171
http://www.nursingsociety.org

Tau Beta Sigma
PO Box 849
Stillwater, OK 74076-0849
800-543-6505
http://www.kkytbs.org

Theta Phi Alpha
27025 Knickerbocker Road
Bay Village, OH 44140
440-899-9282
http://members.aol.com/TPAweb

Zeta Phi Beta
1734 New Hampshire Avenue, NW
Washington, DC 20009
202-387-3103
http://zpb1920.org

Zeta Tau Alpha
3450 Founders Road
Indianapolis, IN 46268
317-872-0540
http://www.zetataualpha.org

Women's Colleges

The following section lists most, if not all, of the nation's women's colleges (83 in all) and gives a brief description of each. As you browse through this listing, keep in mind the following:

Most of the colleges listed are exclusively for women. Some have recently started admitting men, but their students are still predominantly women.

The colleges with graduate schools and evening and weekend schools generally admit men to those programs as well as women. (The undergraduate schools tend to be for women only.)

Little detail about financial aid is given. Nearly every school offers some sort of financial aid, usually a combination of grants, loans, scholarships, and work-study programs. Just because a school isn't listed as having financial aid doesn't mean it isn't available.

Degrees awarded by the colleges are coded as follows: A = associate degree, B = bachelor's degree, M = master's degree, and D = doctoral degree.

The majors and program areas listed are selected from broader lists, most of which include standard subjects like biology, chemistry, computer science, English, history, mathematics, political science, psychology, and sociology. Most of the colleges also offer programs in one or more foreign languages as well as in women's studies. This listing cites the more unusual programs to give prospective students an idea of the focus of each college.

Most of the colleges have athletic programs (inter-collegiate and/or intramural) and some offer athletic scholarships.

Most of the colleges offer study-abroad programs.

The figures for enrollment are not exact; in some cases, they have been rounded off to the nearest ten, in others, the nearest hundred. Also, the figures reflect the enrollment for the entire institution, including graduate students and in the case of the larger universities, the other colleges within that university.

Some of the telephone area codes may have changed since this directory was printed. The Web sites listed for each college should have the most up-to-date contact numbers and information.

Agnes Scott College (B, M) Enrollment: 750+

141 East College Avenue
Atlanta/Decatur, GA 30030
404-471-6285 or 800-868-8602
http://www.agnesscott.edu

Agnes Scott is an independent liberal arts college affiliated with the Presbyterian Church. Located in the heart of metropolitan Atlanta and Decatur, the college is home to the Atlanta Science Center for Women and offers 28 bachelor's degree programs, a master's program in teaching secondary English, a post-baccalaureate pre-medical program, and a professional program in teacher education.

Alverno College (A, B) Enrollment: 2,000+

3401 South 39th Street
P.O. Box 343922
Milwaukee, WI 53234-3922
414-382-6100 or 800-933-3401
http://www.alverno.edu

Affiliated with the Catholic Church, this undergraduate liberal arts college is located in a residential neighborhood of Milwaukee. The college offers majors, minors, and associate degrees in seven academic divisions, including business and management, fine arts, and nursing. The college offers several of its own scholarships, including the **Ellen Harcourt Scholarship,** for students pursuing liberal arts or nursing programs, and the **Peck Scholarship,** recognizing a first-year student with a strong commitment to community service.

Aquinas College (A) Enrollment: 200

303 Adams Street
Milton, MA 02186
617-696-3100
http://www.aquinas-college.net

Aquinas is a small, Catholic commuter college with campuses in Milton and Newton, Massachusetts. Its students are women of all ages, backgrounds, and origins from the greater Boston area. Students may earn a two-year associate degree or one-year college certificate, or they may prepare for transfer to a four-year college. Associate degree programs are business management, criminal justice, early childhood education, executive assistant, international trade, legal office management, legal secretarial, medical assisting, medical office administration, and tourism and hospitality. Day care teacher training is among the certificate programs offered.

Organizations

Barnard College (B) Enrollment: 2,300

3009 Broadway
New York, NY 10027
212-854-2154
http://www.barnard.edu

Barnard is one of four undergraduate schools at New York's Columbia University. It offers a quality liberal arts education in an intimate setting with easy access to the resources of a world-class research university. Academic departments include ancient studies, architecture, Asian and Middle Eastern cultures, biopyschology, environmental science, linguistics, Pan-African studies, quantitative reasoning, Slavic, statistics, and urban affairs. Several special programs are offered in writing, music, theology, and other areas. Barnard's Center for Research on Women houses an extensive collection of materials on women. Prospective students have access to a large number of scholarships, both directly through the school and through other sources.

Bay Path College (A, B) Enrollment: 600+

588 Longmeadow Street
Longmeadow, MA 01106
413-565-1000 or 800-782-7284
http://www.baypath.edu

Bay Path is a four-year private college located in historic western Massachusetts. The school's activities and curriculum are aimed at the development of leadership, communication, and technological skills for women. Baccalaureate degree programs are business, criminal justice, information technology, legal studies, liberal studies, occupational therapy, psychology, and teacher preparation. Associate degrees are also available, including one in travel and hospitality. The college offers a range of scholarships and provides financial aid to 75 percent of its student body.

Bennett College (A, B) Enrollment: 650

900 East Washington Street
Greensboro, NC 27401-3239
336-370-8725
http://www.bennett.edu

Bennett College is a private liberal arts institution affiliated with the United Methodist Church and set in urban Greensboro, North Carolina. Traditionally, Bennett students have been mostly of African-American descent, but the college welcomes women of all races. Bachelor's degrees are granted in divisions of humanities, professional studies, and sciences. A dual-degree program in engineering is available through North Carolina A&T State University. An associate degree is offered in secretarial administration. Bennett College is home to an active Women's Leadership Institute.

Blue Mountain College (B) Enrollment: 400

P.O. Box 338
Blue Mountain, MS 38610
601-685-4771

Located in a rural environment, Blue Mountain is a private Protestant college affiliated with the Southern Baptist Church. Students work toward bachelor's degrees in a range of areas, some of which include agriculture sciences; conservation and natural resources; construction trades; engineering; library science; military technologies; parks, recreation, leisure, and fitness; public administration and services; theological studies; and transportation.

Brenau University, Women's College (B, M) Enrollment: 2,500

One Centennial Circle
Gainesville, GA 30501
770-534-6299

Located 50 miles from Atlanta, Brenau has three divisions: the Women's College, the Evening and Weekend College, and the Academy (a college preparatory school for girls grades 9-12). The Women's College, which serves both residential and commuter students, specializes in fine arts and leadership development programs. Among the 30 majors offered are art/art management, business administration, environmental science/studies, fashion merchandising, interior design, international studies, mass communications, and occupational therapy (one of two programs in the state offering both bachelor's and master's degrees).

Bryn Mawr College (B, M, D)
Enrollment: 1,750

101 North Merion Avenue
Bryn Mawr, PA 19010
610-526-5000
http://www.brynmawr.edu

Built on a strong academic tradition of education for women, Bryn Mawr offers a challenging curriculum covering everything from chemistry to theater. The college features a Graduate School of Arts and Sciences and a Graduate School of Social Work and Social Research. The school has close ties with neighboring Haverford College, Swarthmore College, and the University of Pennsylvania, giving students access to broader extracurricular activities. Some scholarships are available; about half of undergraduates receive grants from the college.

Cedar Crest College (B) Enrollment: 1,550

100 College Drive
Allentown, PA 18104
610-437-4471

Sciences, nutrition wellness, and the arts are the specialties of this college, which draws the largest number of students for its health science and allied health programs. Genetic engineering—said to be the first program of its kind at a women's college—nuclear medicine, and nursing are just some of the academic options. In all, the college offers 35 majors and pre-professional programs. Scholarships are available.

Chatham College (B, M) Enrollment: 750

Woodland Road
Pittsburgh, PA 15232
412-365-1290 or 800-837-1290
http://www.chatham.edu

Many students at this college are adults starting a degree program or returning to school. The course schedules and curriculum are flexible to allow for students to enroll in evening programs, earn graduate degrees part-time, and attend workshops and seminars aimed at personal and professional enrichment.
Baccalaureate programs include arts manage-

ment, behavioral neuroscience, entrepreneurial management, environmental science, global communications, media arts, modern European cultures, and student development. Teacher certificates and several master's programs are also offered. The college is home to the Rachel Carson Institute, which provides a forum for education and discussion on environmental issues.

Chestnut Hill College (A, B, M)
Enrollment: 730

9601 Germantown Avenue
Philadelphia, PA 19118
215-248-7000

A Catholic liberal arts institution, Chestnut Hill offers both undergraduate and advanced degree programs. The graduate division awards degrees in applied technology, counseling psychology and human services, education, holistic spirituality, and professional psychology. Through what is called the Accelerated Program, students work toward undergraduate degrees in a flexible format: six eight-week sessions a year, with classes during the week as well as at night and on weekends. A number of scholarships are offered, including two for biology students.

College of New Rochelle (B, M)
Enrollment: 6,500

29 Castle Place
New Rochelle, NY 10805
914-632-5300 or 800-211-7077
http://www.cnr.edu

Located 16 miles north of Manhattan, this Catholic college has both a small-town feel and proximity to big-city resources. The college consists of four schools: the School of Arts and Sciences (the only all-women's school), the School of Nursing (including a graduate program), the School of New Resources (for adult learners), and the Graduate School. Arts and sciences majors include American studies, art education, classics, communication arts, environmental studies, modern foreign languages, social work, and visual communication design. Art therapy, law, and physical therapy are among the pre-professional offerings. Professional programs are also offered, including two five-year bachelor-master's programs—in community school psychology and therapeutic education. Merit-based scholarships are available.

College of Notre Dame of Maryland (B, M) Enrollment: 2,100

4701 North Charles Street
Baltimore, MD 21210-2476
410-532-5330 or 800-435-0200 (within Maryland) or 800-435-0300 (outside Maryland)

A four-year Catholic college primarily for women, this school is located in suburban Baltimore. Besides its undergraduate programs, the college features a continuing education program (for women 25 and older who are working toward undergraduate degrees), a weekend college, and a graduate studies program (offering programs in five fields plus a certificate program). The college has cooperative arrangements with several coed institutions, giving students exposure to additional resources and curricula. Undergraduates choose from 22 majors and dual-degree programs in engineering (with Johns Hopkins University or the University of Maryland) and nursing (with Johns Hopkins). Various scholarships are available.

College of St. Benedict (B) Enrollment: 1,950+

37 South College Avenue
St. Joseph, MN 56374
320-363-5011 or 800-544-1489
http://www.csbsju.edu

Affiliated with the Catholic Church but open to students of all faiths, the College of St. Benedict houses a Benedictine monastery, which infuses a sense of community and spirituality into campus life. Partnered with St. John's University (for men), the college is just for women but offers a number of coed activities. Students have a choice of nearly 50 majors, including athletic training, dietetics, medieval studies, music, peace studies, pre-divinity, pre-forestry, and pre-pharmacy.

College of St. Catherine (B, M) Enrollment: 2,700

2004 Randolph Avenue
St. Paul, MN 55104
651-690-6000 or 800-945-4599

Commonly called St. Kate's, this college is a Catholic institution with two campuses—the main campus in St. Paul, offering undergraduate liberal arts and pre-professional programs for women only, and a campus in Minneapolis, offering associate degrees and certificate programs in health care and human services for both men and women. Coeducational graduate programs are offered on both campuses. Undergraduates may enroll in day or weekend programs and choose from 30 majors. St. Catherine's is home to an Institute for Leadership and Continuing Education, which supports continuing education and community outreach programs.

College of St. Elizabeth (B, M) Enrollment: 1,500

2 Convent Road
Morristown, NJ 07960
201-605-7000
http://www.st-elizabeth.edu

A Catholic liberal arts college about an hour's drive from New York City, this school encompasses a women's college, an adult undergraduate weekend college, and a graduate school. Twenty-six bachelor of arts and bachelor of science degrees are awarded, some of which are American studies, chemistry, clinical laboratory science (joint degree with another school), communication, computer science, elementary education, foods and nutrition, international studies, philosophy, pre-law, pre-medicine, pre-veterinary, and sociology. Seven master's degrees are awarded, including health care management and theology. A number of endowed scholarships are available.

College of St. Mary (A, B) Enrollment: 1,200

1901 South 72nd Street
Omaha, NE 68124
402-399-2416

The only small, private Catholic institution in a five-state region, the College of St. Mary offers baccalaureate degree programs as well as an evening and weekend college and classes on a campus in Lincoln. The college has recently introduced a new academic program called Sixty Saturdays, which leads to a bachelor's degree in business leadership through classes on 60 Saturdays. Undergraduate program offerings include health information management, nursing, occupational therapy, paralegal studies, special education, telecommunications systems management, and more. Need-based grants are available.

Columbia College (B, M) Enrollment: L, 300

1301 Columbia College Drive
Columbia, SC 29203
803-786-3012
http://www.colacoll.edu

Affiliated with the United Methodist Church, Columbia College offers an undergraduate curriculum of 37 majors, five pre-professional programs (including pharmacy), three master's programs (in conflict resolution, divergent learning, and elementary education), and an evening college. Bachelor of arts, science, fine arts, and music degrees are offered in business administration, chemistry, Christian education, dance performance and choreography, piano pedagogy, public affairs, sacred music, sociology (three different emphases), speech language pathology, and more. About 10 merit-based scholarships are available.

Converse College (B, M) Enrollment: 1,150

Spartanburg, SC 29302
864-596-9040 or 800-766-1125
http://www.converse.edu

This college is nationally recognized for its School of Music and offers a range of majors in the arts and sciences. Some of these are art therapy, interior design, and special education. Career and pre-professional programs include arts management, pre-ministry, pre-pharmacy, and urban planning. Converse College also features an adult undergraduate program for women ages 24 and older. Graduate degrees offered are a master of liberal arts and a master of education. A number of specialized scholarships are available, including several for music students.

Cottey College (A) Enrollment: 410

1000 West Austin Avenue
Nevada, MO 64772
417-667-8181 or 888-5-COTTEY

Located about 100 miles south of Kansas City, Cottey is an independent two-year college offering associate degrees in arts and science. Course offerings include art, astronomy, business, drama, economics, German, journalism, music, philosophy, and speech. More than 95 percent of the school's graduates transfer to four-year colleges. Approximately 97 percent of students receive some form of need- or merit-based financial aid.

Douglass College at Rutgers University (B) Enrollment: 3,000

New Brunswick, NJ 09903
908-932-7755
http://www.rci.rutgers.edu/~dougcoll

Douglass calls itself the nation's largest women's college. Located on the New Brunswick campus of New Jersey's Rutgers University, the college gives students access to all the resources of a large coed university in a close-knit community environment. Students may choose from 70 major programs of study toward a bachelor of arts or bachelor of science degree. Some of the college's draws are its nationally recognized Douglass Project for Rutgers Women in Math and Science, its Emerging Leaders Program, and its Institute for Women's Leadership. More than 70 percent of Douglass students receive some form of financial aid.

Elms College (B, M) Enrollment: 1,200

291 Springfield Street
Chicopee, MA 01013-2839
413-592-3189 or 800-255-ELMS
http://www.elms.edu

Organizations

Elms is a Catholic college in western Massachusetts offering more than 30 undergraduate majors in both liberal arts and professional disciplines. Nursing, social work, and biology are some of the college's strongest offerings. The graduate school awards master of arts degrees in applied theology and social work. A range of scholarships are available to first-year and transfer students.

Emmanuel College (A, B, M)
Enrollment: 1,400
400 The Fenway
Boston, MA 02115
617-735-9825

Said to be New England's first Catholic college for women, Emmanuel is a liberal arts college offering baccalaureate degrees in the arts and sciences. Undergraduate, graduate, and professional degree programs are open to both men and women through the school's Center for Adult Studies. These include: BSN for registered nurses, BS in health care administration, BS in business administration, MA in teaching, MA in human resource management, and MS in management. Emmanuel is one of the five Colleges of the Fenway, a collaboration of Boston colleges giving students access to greater resources and course offerings. Several scholarships are available for incoming students.

Endicott College (B) Enrollment: 1,100
376 Hale Street
Beverly, MA 01915
978-927-0585 or 800-325-1114

Located on an oceanfront campus north of Boston, this four-year college offers bachelor of arts and bachelor of science degrees, as well as a master of education and an associate of science degree. Arts and Sciences Division majors often participate in internships for hands-on experience. Certificate programs are available in graphic design, landscape design, and other areas. A **Presidential Merit Scholarship** and several college-funded grants are available to bachelor degree candidates.

Georgian Court College (B, M)
Enrollment: 2,500
900 Lakewood Avenue
Lakewood, NJ 08701
732-364-2200
http://www.georgian.edu

Georgian Court is a four-year, Catholic liberal arts college open to women of all faiths. The campus is situated halfway between New York and Philadelphia, minutes from the Atlantic Ocean. Undergraduate degrees offered are bachelor of arts, bachelor of fine arts, bachelor of science, and bachelor of social work. In addition to pre-professional programs, students may choose from majors in 21 fields, including biochemistry, elementary education, fine arts, physical education and health, physics, theology and religions studies, and social work. Certificate programs are in gerontology, international management, and holistic health. Graduate degrees offered: nine master of arts, a master of science, and a master of business administration. Scholarships are available.

Harcum College (A) Enrollment: 650
750 Montgomery Avenue
Bryn Mawr, PA 19010-3476
610-525-4100 or 800-345-2600
http://www.harcum.edu

Harcum is a private, two-year residential and commuter college located just west of Philadelphia. It offers associate degrees in art and science, including animal center management, business administration, dental hygiene, early childhood education, fashion design, graphic design, hospitality and tourism, physical and occupational therapist assistant, retail merchandising, and veterinary technology. Several certificate and special programs are also offered. The school's English Language Academy draws students from around the world. Specialized scholarships and other aid are available.

Hartford College for Women at the University of Hartford (A, B) Enrollment: 210

1265 Asylum Avenue
Hartford, CT 06105
203-236-1215
http://www.hartford.edu

Hartford College is the undergraduate college for women at the University of Hartford. The college offers three academic tracks: liberal arts, preparing students for bachelor's degrees in more than 50 areas (including the college's own BA in women's studies); legal studies, offering associate and bachelor's degrees; and math, science, engineering, and technology, designed for students interested in these fields who wish to begin their studies in an all-female environment. Also offered is Academic Express, a special concentrated program that gives working women the chance to earn an associate degree in two years or a bachelor's in four years. Need-based awards and merit scholarships are available.

Hollins University (B, M) Enrollment: 1,100

P.O. Box 9657
Roanoke, VA 24020-1657
540-362-6451

Virginia's first chartered women's college, Hollins is a liberal arts institution with nationally acclaimed programs in creative writing, art, and psychology. Classical studies, film and photography, and physical education are some of the other undergraduate study areas. Graduate programs focus on children's literature, liberal studies, teaching, and screenwriting and film studies. Women over the age of 25 can return to college and earn a degree through the university's Horizon program. Special resources include the university's internships program and its Women's Center, offering workshops, career counseling, and other support. More than 100 endowed scholarships are available.

Hood College (B, M) Enrollment: 1,800

401 Rosemont Avenue
Frederick, MD 21701-8575
301-663-3131
http://www.hood.edu

Hood is a private, liberal arts, residential college for women that also enrolls men as undergraduate commuters and graduate students. The campus, an hour's drive from Washington, DC, features a center located near a Metro rail station—convenient for older students returning to school. Bachelor of arts and bachelor of science degrees are offered in 25 fields and master's degrees in seven fields. Five-year bachelor-master's degree programs are offered in biology, environmental science, and computer and information technology sciences. One in five Hood students receives an honors scholarship.

Immaculata College (A, B, M, D) Enrollment: 2,300

Immaculata, PA 19345
610-647-4400
http://www.immaculata.edu

Located in suburban Philadelphia, Immaculata College is a private, Catholic liberal arts institution. The college offers a range of BA, BS, and associate degrees. Specialized programs are in nursing and music, including certification in music therapy. Other course offerings: allied health sciences, criminal justice, dietetics, fashion marketing, home economics, intercultural communication, institutional food service management, liturgical studies, pre-law, and urban studies.

Judson College (B) Enrollment: 300

P.O. Box 120
Marion, AL 36756-0120
334-683-5157 or 800-447-9472
http://www.home.judson.edu

Founded by Baptists in the 1800s, this independent liberal arts college in west central Alabama remains affiliated with the Alabama Baptist Convention. It is the state's only women's college. In addition to liberal arts majors, students may choose from a range of pre-professional programs, including dentistry, engineering, law, medicine, pharmacy, and physical therapy. The Judson campus is home to the Alabama Women's Hall of Fame, which honors accomplished women from throughout the state's history. A number of scholarships are available through the Baptist Foundation of Alabama.

Lasell College (A) Enrollment: 490

1844 Commonwealth Avenue
Newton, MA 02466
617-243-2111

Lasell was an all-women's college until it voted in 1997 to admit men. The school is known for its cutting-edge programs like Camp Colors, a day camp for children with HIV/AIDS, and PACT (Parent and Child Together), designed to help single mothers break the cycle of poverty. The college's early childhood and elementary education program is enhanced by the Holway Child Study Centers, a nursing school and day care center which serve as laboratory schools for students. Other Lasell programs include exercise physiology, fashion design and production, hotel and travel administration, legal studies, and nonprofit management.

Lesley College (A, B, M, D) Enrollment: 6,000+

29 Everett Street
Cambridge, MA 02138-2790
617-349-8500
http://www.lesley.edu

A mid-sized coeducational institution with a graduate school, Lesley also includes an undergraduate women's college with more than 500 students. Students at the women's college choose majors in the areas of education, human services, management, and liberal arts. All programs lead to bachelor of science degrees and combine study with field experience. Dual-degree (bachelor-master's) programs also are offered, mostly in education and psychology. Merit scholarships are available.

Marian Court College (A) Enrollment: 190

35 Little's Point Road
Swampscott, MA 01907
617-595-6768
http://www.mariancourt.edu

A small college situated on the Massachusetts coastline, Marian Court offers associate degree and certificate programs in the following areas: accounting assistant; business management; human resource management; office administration; travel, tourism, and hospitality; and general studies. The general studies program is ideal for students who need extra preparation before entering a four-year university. Grants and scholarships are available.

Mary Baldwin College (B, M) Enrollment: 1,300

Staunton, VA 24401
540-887-7022

Mary Baldwin features the Virginia Women's Institute for Leadership, a special program that combines baccalaureate degree requirements with leadership and community activities, physical education courses, and military practices. Carpenter Quest is another degree enhancement program. Undergraduates may choose from 34 majors, including Asian studies, health care administration, and theater. Ministry is offered as a pre-professional program, and the graduate school awards an MA in teaching. More than 90 percent of students receive some form of financial aid.

Marymount College (B) Enrollment: 1,000+

100 Marymount Avenue
Tarrytown, NY 10591
914-631-3200
http://www.marymt.edu

Located 25 miles north of New York City, Marymount is an independent, liberal arts institution affiliated with the Catholic Church. The college features the Marymount Institute for Women and Girls, which supports teacher training, conferences, and educational programs for women and girls, as well as the Marymount

Weekend College, which offers an alternative education option for working adults. Students choose from programs in American studies, art therapy, clothing design, corporate training and development, English as a second language, journalism, peace studies, philosophy, and more.

Marymount Manhattan College (B) Enrollment: 2,200+

221 East 71st Street
New York, NY 10021
212-517-0555
http://www.marymount.mmm.edu

Originally established as the city campus of Marymount College in Tarrytown, New York, Marymount Manhattan is an independent, undergraduate liberal arts college. Programs range from arts and sciences to pre-profession-al. Some of these are communication information management, international studies, speech language pathology and audiology, and theatre arts. Also available is a special five-year program combining a BA in business management with an MBA in executive management from St. John's University. Financial aid options are diverse, including benefits for orphans of veterans and grants for mothers and daughters both enrolled at Marymount Manhattan.

Meredith College (B, M) Enrollment: 2,300+

3800 Hillsborough Street
Raleigh, NC 27607-5298
919-829-8600
http://www.meredith.edu

Undergraduates at this Christian women's college may choose from 35 majors—or create their own program—to earn a bachelor of arts, science, or music degree. The varied curriculum includes courses in child development, criminal justice studies, family and consumer sciences, foods and nutrition, interior design, medical technology, and studio art. The graduate school, also for women only, awards master's degrees in business administration, education, health administration, and music.

Midway College (A, B) Enrollment: 810

512 East Stephens Street
Midway, KY 40347
606-846-5310

Located in the heart of central Kentucky's blue-grass region, Midway classifies itself as a contemporary women's college. Students work toward bachelor's degrees in biology, business administration, early childhood education, equine studies, liberal studies, nursing, and other areas. Associate degrees are also offered. The college's School for Career Development gives adults an opportunity to complete their college degrees through evening programs in organizational management, computer information systems, and other fields. Academic and athletic scholarships are available.

Mills College (B, M) Enrollment: 1,110

5000 MacArthur Boulevard
Oakland, CA 94613-1301
510-430-2255
http://www.mills.edu

A private liberal arts college located in the San Francisco Bay Area, Mills offers 33 undergraduate majors, including ethnic and women's studies and creative writing. Pre-professional programs include business, education, law, and medicine and health sciences. Master of arts and master of fine arts degrees are offered in several disciplines, including art, dance, literature, and music. More than 75 percent of Mills students receive some form of financial aid.

Mississippi University for Women (A, B, M) Enrollment: 3,300

PO Box W-1614
Columbus, MS 39701
601-329-7114
http://www.muw.edu

Originally called the Industrial Institute and College, Mississippi University for Women is said to have been the first public college for women in the U.S. Primarily an undergraduate institution offering associate and bachelor's degrees, the university also awards master's degrees in gifted studies, instructional management, health education, nursing, and speech language pathology. The school features a

Organizations

Culinary Arts Institute, offering a bachelor of science degree in culinary arts and a culinary certificate. A number of general and specialized scholarships are available.

Moore College of Art and Design (B)
Enrollment: 420

20th Street and The Parkway
Philadelphia, PA 19103
215-568-4515

Moore was the first visual arts college in the U.S. open just to women. Located in the heart of Philadelphia, the college offers a range of BFA and continuing education courses in art education, communication arts (including graphic design), fashion design, fine arts (including ceramics, drawing, metals, painting, printmaking, and sculpture), interior design, studio art, and textile design. The college also offers certificate programs, open to men as well as women.

Mount Holyoke College (B, M)
Enrollment: 2,000

50 College Street
South Hadley, MA 01075
413-538-2000
http://www.mtholyoke.edu

This liberal arts college calls itself the nation's oldest continuing institution of higher education for women. Its historic strengths are in the sciences, international and interdisciplinary studies, and innovative curricula. Students today choose from 44 majors, including critical social thought, Latin American studies, neuroscience and behavior, and theater arts. Special programs include the Center for Environmental Literacy; the Center for Leadership and Public Interest Advocacy; and Speaking, Arguing, and Writing. Mount Holyoke is part of the Twelve Colleges Exchange program and the Five Colleges consortium (including Amherst, Hampshire, Smith, and the University of Massachusetts), giving students access to more extensive resources.

Mount Mary College (B, M)
Enrollment: 1,500+

2900 North Menomonee River Parkway
Milwaukee, WI 53222-4545
414-258-4810
http://www.mtmary.edu

Mount Mary College is nationally known for its pioneering program in art therapy, offering undergraduate, post-baccalaureate, and master's degrees in the field. All of the college's programs are built from a core curriculum centered around theology, philosophy, and human relationships. Majors include behavioral science, consumer science, hotel and restaurant management, music, and social work. Master's programs are in art therapy, education, dietetics, and occupational therapy.

Mount Saint Mary's College (A, B, M)
Enrollment: 1,600+

12001 Chalon Road
Los Angeles, CA 90049
310-471-9505
http://www.msmary.edu

Mount Saint Mary's is a Catholic institution dedicated to liberal learning and the affirmation of values and beliefs central to the Catholic social vision. The undergraduate curriculum offers courses in international studies, philosophy, rhetoric and communications, sociology, theology, and visual and performing arts.

Mount Vernon College at The George Washington University (A, B)
Enrollment: 400

2100 Foxhall Road, NW
Washington, DC 20007
202-625-0400
http://www.mvc.gwu.edu

Mount Vernon, with programming just for women, is one of two campuses at The George Washington University; the other, Foggy Bottom, is coeducational. This gives Mount Vernon students the benefits of a women's college within a larger, university setting. Located next to historic Georgetown, Mount Vernon offers undergraduate-level courses in business, communications, engineering, interior design, international affairs, liberal arts, performing arts, and sciences. All programs emphasize leadership development and professional mentoring. The campus is home to the Elizabeth J. Somers Center, which provides resources and programs that promote women's education and leadership. First-year students participate in Women and Power Leadership programs, a group learning experience in which students take classes together, join in symposiums, and live in the same residence hall.

Newcomb College of Tulane University (B)

New Orleans, LA 70118-5683
504-865-5731

Newcomb claims it was the first degree-granting women's college to be established as a coordinate division of a men's university. Newcomb is part of Tulane University and shares a curriculum and faculty with Tulane College for men. Newcomb students earn BA, BFA, and BS degrees in 30 majors. The college is home to a prominent Center for Research on Women, as well as the Newcomb Children's Center, which provides students with the opportunity to observe children's social, physical, and cognitive development.

Notre Dame College of Ohio (A, B, M) Enrollment: 650

4545 College Road
South Euclid, OH 44121
216-381-1680 or 800-NDC-1680
http://www.ndc.edu

One of two women's colleges in Ohio, Notre Dame is a four-year, Catholic liberal arts school dedicated to "empowering women leaders." The college awards four degrees: bachelor of arts, bachelor of science, associate of arts (including environmental technology and pastoral ministry), and master of education. Majors include accounting, education, financial services management, marketing, nutrition/dietetics, paralegal studies, and theology. Many students design their own majors; for example, in graphic design. The school's Center for Excellence in Education provides development opportunities for elementary and secondary teachers. The

Tolerance Resource Center provides research, outreach, and education on the Holocaust, anti-bias issues, and diversity. Financial aid is available.

O'More College of Design (A, B) Enrollment: 120

Franklin, TN 37065
615-794-4254

This unique, intimate school was fashioned after a small, European college and is designed to enhance creativity within an educational setting. Programs are offered in fashion, graphic design and advertising, and interior design.

Peace College (A) Enrollment: 600

15 East Peace Street
Raleigh, NC 27604-1194
919-508-2000; 800-PEACE-47
http://www.peace.edu

Located in the heart of Research Triangle Park in Raleigh, North Carolina, Peace College is a small liberal arts and sciences college. It is one of two women's colleges in the southeastern United States to award both associate and baccalaureate degrees. Baccalaureate programs are in biology, business administration, communication, English, human resources, liberal studies, music performance, psychology, and visual communications. The school awards associate of arts, fine arts in music, and science degrees.

Pine Manor College (A, B, M) Enrollment: 340

400 Heath Street
Chestnut Hill, MA 02467
617-731-7000

Pine Manor is a four-year liberal arts college dedicated to preparing women for "roles of inclusive leadership and social responsibility in their workplaces, families, and communities." The college employs a team approach to teaching and advising, involving staff, faculty, alumni, and peers in each student's educational experience. Students are required to participate in an internship before graduating. Majors include American studies, art history, biology, business administration, communication, English, psychology, social and political studies, and visual arts. Baby-sitting and other special services are offered for reentry women.

Radcliffe College (B, M, D) Enrollment: 4,500

10 Garden Street
Cambridge, MA 02138
617-495-8601
http://www.radcliffe.edu

Radcliffe is the undergraduate women's college at Harvard University. It classifies itself as "a comprehensive center for advancing society by advancing women" and is composed of two branches: its Educational Programs, which serve undergraduate and post-baccalaureate students, and its Institutes for Advanced Study, the college's four flagship research and policy programs. Besides a wide range of quality undergraduate programs, Radcliffe offers graduate and professional certificate programs, as well as lectures, seminars, and workshops for non-students. The Graduate Consortium in Women's Studies joins Radcliffe faculty with their counterparts at six degree-granting institutions to advance women's studies scholarship. A range of specialized prizes, fellowships, and grants are available.

Randolph-Macon Woman's College (B) Enrollment: 730

2500 Rivermont Avenue
Lynchburg, VA 24503
804-947-8128

An independent, liberal arts and sciences institution, this college is situated in the foothills of the Blue Ridge Mountains. BA and BS degrees are awarded in art, chemistry, communication, French, international relations, philosophy, political sciences, Russian studies, sociology/anthropology, and other fields. Students also may choose from an interesting array of emphases and concentrations or design their own major. Dual-degree programs are offered in nursing and public health. The college is a member of the International 50, a group of liberal arts colleges noted for their international programs. A handful of scholarships are available, including a special award in the name of distinguished alumna Pearl S. Buck.

Regis College (B, M) Enrollment: 1,300+

235 Wellesley Street
Weston, MA 02493-1571
781-768-7000 or 800-456-1820
http://www.regiscollege.edu

Regis is a Catholic liberal arts and sciences college located 12 miles from downtown Boston. Undergraduates may choose from 18 majors, including art, biochemistry, classical studies, history, management, political science, and social work. Special programs are offered in legal studies, nursing (associate, bachelor's, master's), and education (master of arts in teaching). Several need- and merit-based scholarships are available.

Rosemont College (B, M) Enrollment: 500

1400 Montgomery Avenue
Rosemont, PA 19010
610-527-0200
http://www.rosemont.edu

With a strong focus on personal growth, this Catholic college offers a liberal arts education as well as opportunities for pre-professional study. Among the 22 majors are American studies, chemistry, Italian studies, psychology, sociology, and studio art. Students also may earn teaching certificates. Rosemont's graduate school awards master of arts degrees in counseling psychology, English, and English and publishing; a master of science degree in management; and master of education degrees in middle school education and technology in education. Scholarships and grants are available, including one for students whose mothers graduated from Rosemont.

Russell Sage College (B, M) Enrollment: 2,300+

65 First Street
Troy, NY 12180
518-270-2341
http://www.sage.edu

Russell Sage is one of the four Sage Colleges located in Troy and Albany, New York. (The others—all coed—are Sage Junior College, Sage Evening College, and Sage Graduate School.) Students can earn bachelor's degrees in athletic training, business administration, computer science, computer network administration, creative arts in therapy, criminal justice, elementary education, global and community studies, nursing, nutrition, and sociology. Joint BA-BS degrees are offered with other schools in law and mathematics/engineering. Five-year BS-MS programs are offered in occupational and physical therapy. Scholarships are available.

Saint Mary's College (B) Enrollment: 1,350

Highway 31/33
Notre Dame, IN 46556
219-284-4000
http://www.saintmarys.edu

Saint Mary's is the women's college affiliated with the nationally known University of Notre Dame, both Catholic institutions. Saint Mary's students earn BA and BS degrees in biology, communication, cytotechnology, elementary education, humanistic studies, medical technology, nursing, philosophy, religious studies, social work, and other subjects. Also awarded are bachelor of business administration, bachelor of music, and bachelor of fine arts degrees. Other options are a cooperative engineering program with the University of Notre Dame and pre-medical, pre-dental, and pre-health programs. A handful of scholarships and grants are available.

Salem College (B, M) Enrollment: 1,000+

P.O. Box 10548
Winston-Salem, NC 27108
800-32-SALEM
http://www.salem.edu

Reportedly the 13th oldest college in the nation, Salem is a liberal arts institution offering both undergraduate and graduate degrees. Undergraduates may earn a bachelor of arts, bachelor of science, or bachelor of music degree, but all students are required to partici-

pate in the Salem Signature, a leadership development program. The college also emphasizes the importance of writing skills, offering both a creative writing minor and the Center for Women Writers, which helps students to develop their creativity, hone their writing techniques, and learn about the publication process. Graduate degrees awarded are an MA in teaching and a master of education. A handful of merit-based scholarships and need-based grants are available.

Samuel Merritt College (B, M) Enrollment 500+

370 Hawthorne Avenue
Oakland, CA 94609
510-869-6511 or 800-607-6377
http://www.samuelmerritt.edu

Originally founded as a hospital school of nursing, Samuel Merritt College now offers baccalaureate and graduate degree programs in a variety of health science fields. For undergraduates, there's a bachelor of science in nursing program—offered in cooperation with a nearby college—and a bachelor of science in health and human sciences program. Master's degrees are awarded in nursing, occupational and physical therapy, and physician assistant. Eighty-five percent of students receive some financial aid.

Scripps College (B) Enrollment: 750

1030 Columbia Avenue
Claremont, CA 91711-3948
909-621-8149 or 800-770-1333
http://www.scrippscol.edu

Scripps is the women's college of Southern California's Claremont Colleges group. Students primarily earn bachelor's degrees, but the school also offers a post-baccalaureate pre-medical program, which involves 15 months of prerequisite science and math courses. The school's academic departments include anthropology, art and art history, classics, Hispanic studies, politics and international relations, languages and literature, music, and religion. Special programs are featured in humanities, women's studies, and writing. Financial aid is provided to about 60 percent of the student body.

Organizations

Seton Hill College (B) Enrollment: 1,100

Seton Hill Drive
Greensburg, PA 15601-1599
724-838-4255 or 800-826-6234
http://www.setonhill.edu

Affiliated with the Catholic Church, Seton Hill has recently widened and diversified its scope. The college now admits men, has opened a National Catholic Center for Holocaust Education, and has launched a special project focusing on the contributions of women during the Industrial Age. Undergraduates may choose from programs in art therapy, corporate and instructional communications, engineering, family and consumer sciences, medical technology, physics, pre-physician assistant, social work, and more. Seton Hill also offers graduate programs. Financial aid, including athletic scholarships, is available.

Simmons College (B, M, D) Enrollment: 3,500+

300 The Fenway
Boston, MA 02115-5898
617-521-2051
http://www.simmons.edu

One of Boston's five Colleges of the Fenway, Simmons is a liberal arts and career-preparation institution for both undergraduate and graduate students. Twenty percent of undergraduates undertake dual majors—one in the liberal arts and one in a professional field. Programs include African American studies, environmental science, graphic design, international management, marketing, psychobiology, and retail management. Graduate study is in liberal arts, health studies, library and information science, management, and social work. The school's Dorothea Lynde Dix Scholars program provides educational opportunities for women beyond the age of traditional college students. Financial aid is available.

Smith College (B, M, D) Enrollment: 3,000+

Northampton, MA 01063
413-585-2176
http://www.smith.edu

Smith is a liberal arts college offering opportunities for both undergraduate and graduate study. Undergraduates focus on ancient studies, astronomy, comparative literature, education and child study, ethics, film studies, German culture studies, government, Jewish studies, Latin, logic, marine sciences, neuroscience, peninsular Spanish literature, Portuguese-Brazilian studies, and other areas. Graduate programs are offered in a range of disciplines and at the college's School for Social Work. The Ada Comstock Scholars program is designed for women over the age of 23 who did not finish college and wish to earn a bachelor's degree. Smith is a member of the prestigious Five Colleges consortium. Grants and loans are available.

Southern Virginia College for Women (A) Enrollment: 300+

Buena Vista, VA 24416
540-261-8400
http://www.southernviginia.edu

Affiliated with the Church of Jesus Christ of Latter-day Saints, this college awards bachelor of arts degrees in liberal studies and associate of arts degrees in liberal studies and equine studies. Majors are American legal studies, business administration, computer-assisted design, English, fine arts, general studies/pre-medicine, performing arts, and recreational management. Southern Virginia's campus features a full range of horsemanship facilities. Academic, athletic, and talent scholarships are available, as well as a scholarship for incoming students honorably released from Latter-day Saints missions.

Spelman College (B) Enrollment: 1,950+

350 Spelman Lane, Southwest
Atlanta, GA 30314-4399
404-681-3643
http://www.spelman.edu

Students at this urban college are predominantly African American. The school aims to enrich women academically, socially, and spiritually, offering a number of special programs in addition to its course work. An International Affairs Center, a Writing Center, and other resources enhance students' overall development. Students choose from majors in art, biology, child development, computer and information sciences, foreign languages, health and physical education, music, physics, sociology, and others. A dual-degree program in engineering is also available.

St. Joseph College (B, M) Enrollment: 1,800

1678 Asylum Avenue
West Hartford, CT 06117-2700
860-232-4571
http://www.sjc.edu

More than 90 percent of the students at this liberal arts college are involved in community service. Academically, they work toward BA and BS degrees in a range of areas, including American studies, child study, environmental science, family studies, nursing, social work, and special education. There's also a teacher certification program and pre-professional programs in law and medicine. MA, MBA, and MS degrees are awarded as well. Facilities include two laboratory schools, one for young children and one for special needs students. Eighty percent of students receive financial aid.

St. Mary of the Woods College (A, B, M) Enrollment: 1,250

Saint Mary of the Woods, IN 47876
812-535-5108 or 800-926-SMWC
http://www.smwc.edu

Said to be the nation's oldest Catholic liberal arts college for women, Saint Mary of the Woods has baccalaureate, associate, and certificate programs as well as two graduate programs. A unique feature is the Women's External Degree (WED) program, a distance learning program that caters to the needs of professionals, homemakers, and parents. Roughly three-fourths of the college's undergraduates take advantage of this independent study program, while the other fourth live on campus. Course offerings include accounting, gerontology, human resource management, journalism, paralegal studies, and special education. Graduate students can earn a master's degree in pastoral theology or a master of arts degree in earth literacy.

Approximately 87 percent of students receive financial aid.

Stephens College (A, B) Enrollment: 550

1200 East Broadway
Columbia, MO 65215
800-876-7207
http://www.stephens.edu

Stephens is a comprehensive private college, offering 23 majors in three schools of study: the School of Business and Professional Studies, the School of the Arts, and the School of Liberal Arts and Sciences. Some of the majors are creative writing, environmental biology, equestrian business management, fashion design and product development, fashion marketing and management, marketing/public relations and advertising, mass communication, and theatre arts. Pre-professional choices include dentistry, engineering, and veterinary medicine. The college also has an external degree program, an evening college, and a graduate school, offering an MBA and two master of education degrees. More than 70 percent of students receive financial aid.

Stern College at Yeshiva University (B) Enrollment: 900

http://www.yu.edu/stern/

Yeshiva University is the nation's oldest educational institution under Jewish auspices and a top research university. Stern is the university's undergraduate college of arts and sciences for women at Yeshiva. Infused with the values of Judaism, the college's curriculum features majors in 19 arts and sciences disciplines, all leading to the bachelor of arts degree. Also available is an associate of arts degree in Hebrew language, literature, and culture. Joint degree programs with Yeshiva graduate schools and other universities are offered in engineering, dentistry, optometry, podiatry, social work, nursing, and psychology. A broad range of Jewish studies courses are also available.

Organizations

Sweet Briar College (B) Enrollment: 600

Sweet Briar, VA 24595-9989
804-381-6100
http://www.sbc.edu

Math, engineering, sciences, and pre-law are this college's strongest offerings. The four-year liberal arts and sciences institution also offers two junior year abroad programs—in France and Spain—and an honors program. Students may major in anthropology, classical civilization, dance, economics-computer science, international affairs, mathematical physics, pre-engineering studies, Spanish-business, and theater arts. Special programs are arts management, business management, and public administration. Through the Seven College Exchange and the Tri-College Exchange, students may take courses or spend a term at another school. More than 80 percent of Sweet Briar students receive financial aid.

Texas Woman's University (B, M, D) Enrollment: 10,000+

P.O. Box 23925
Denton, TX 76204
940-898-3201
http://www.twu.edu

Texas Woman's University offers more than 100 majors leading to bachelor's, master's, and doctoral degrees in the College of Arts and Sciences, College of Education and Human Ecology, School of Library and Information Studies, College of Health Sciences, College of Nursing, School of Physical Therapy, School of Occupational Therapy (the largest in the U.S.), and the Graduate School. Some of the more unusual academic departments include fashion and textiles, reading and bilingual education, communication sciences and disorders, kinesiology, and nutrition and food sciences. On campus is the Center for Research on Women's Health and The Woman's Collection, an extensive collection of research material on women. Founded for women, the university now admits men to all of its programs. Students have access to a large number of scholarships.

Trinity College (B, M) Enrollment: 1,500

125 Michigan Avenue, NE
Washington, DC 20017-1094
202-884-9400 or 800-492-6882
http://www.trinitydc.edu

A Catholic liberal arts college located in residential Washington, DC, Trinity offers an undergraduate weekday program (bachelor of arts, bachelor of science), an undergraduate weekend program, and a graduate program (master of arts in counseling, master of arts in teaching, master of education, and master of science in administration). Trinity students have access to Washington's many other colleges and universities as well as diverse non-degree and affiliated programs offered by Trinity. The college also features a child care center and the Women's College Coalition offices. Among undergraduate majors are children, family, and public policy; engineering; environmental science; language and cultural studies; physical science; and public affairs.

Trinity College of Vermont (A, B, M) Enrollment: 970

208 Colchester Avenue
Burlington, VT 05401
802-846-7000

Fifteen percent of the students of this Catholic liberal arts college are men, and 40 percent are non-traditional students over the age of 22. Twenty-five undergraduate majors are offered in five departments: basic and applied social sciences (including majors in sociology/criminal justice, and gerontology), business and economics (which offers a women's small business program), education, humanities, and natural sciences and mathematics. The college runs a Peace and Justice program and an Institute for Program Development, which aims to promote exemplary education and community mental health practices regionally and nationally. Scholarships are available through Trinity and other sources.

Ursuline College (B, M) Enrollment: 1,560

2550 Lander Road
Pepper Pike, OH 44124
440-449-4203 or 888-URSULINE
http://www.ursuline.edu

One of the oldest Catholic women's colleges in the U.S., Ursuline is located just outside Cleveland. It offers liberal arts, pre-professional, and certificate programs, and awards undergraduate bachelor of arts and bachelor of science in nursing degrees. Graduate degrees offered are master of arts in art therapy, education, educational administration, and pastoral ministry. Among undergraduate majors are allied health science, business information technology, cytology, fashion merchandising, historic preservation, interior design, long-term care administration, and travel and tourism. The Ursuline College Accelerated Program provides adults with an opportunity to earn a degree while working. A number of scholarships are available, including one for students from Catholic high schools in Cleveland and one for a daughter of an Ursuline alumna.

Wellesley College (B) Enrollment: 2,200

106 Central Street
Wellesley, MA 02481
781-283-1000

A leading four-year liberal arts institution, Wellesley also offers the Davis Degree Program for women beyond college age—many with families—who wish to earn an undergraduate degree. A varied curriculum offers courses in biological chemistry, Chinese studies, classical studies, cognitive science, Japanese studies, Jewish studies, Latin American studies, peace and justice studies, psychobiology, and Russian area studies. Special programs are in quantitative reasoning and writing. Taking advantage of courses at nearby MIT, many students design their own majors in subjects like urban planning and engineering. Students also can spend their junior year at one of 11 other schools in the Twelve College Exchange program. The Wellesley Centers for Women support research, outreach, and other activities aimed at advancing the role of women in society.

More than 50 percent of students receive financial aid.

Wells College (B) Enrollment: 400+

Aurora, NY 13026
315-364-3370 or 800-952-9355
http://www.wells.edu

Wells is an undergraduate liberal arts school centrally located near Cornell University and several other well-known New York schools. With a curriculum aimed at preparing women for leadership roles in all areas of life, the school offers majors in American studies; environmental policy; science and values; foreign languages, literatures, and cultures; international studies; public affairs; religious studies and human values; and visual arts. Pre-professional programs include dentistry, educational studies, law, medicine, and veterinary, as well as a military officer education program (ROTC). Several dual-degree (BA-BS) programs are also available, mostly in engineering and science. Scholarships include one that covers a first-year internship for academically qualified students as well as awards for daughters and granddaughters of Wells alumnae.

Wesleyan College (B) Enrollment: 400+

4760 Forsyth Road
Macon, GA 31210-4462
912-477-1110
http://www.wesleyan-college.edu

Affiliated with the United Methodist Church, Wesleyan provides a quality liberal arts education. Students may earn a BA degree in 24 areas of study or an MA degree in middle-level math and science education. Majors include American studies, anthropology, business and economics, computer science, German, Japanese, and theater. Pre-professional programs, including engineering, are also available. An undergraduate evening school, with flexible scheduling, child care, and other features, allows mothers and other non-traditional students to earn a degree. Wesleyan also offers Spectacles, a math and science camp for middle school girls. A large number of scholarships is available.

Organizations

Westhampton College at the University of Richmond (B)

The Deanery
28 Westhampton Way
University of Richmond, VA 23173
804-289-8468
http://www.richmond.edu/~wcollege

Westhampton is the residential college for women at the University of Richmond who are enrolled in the School of Arts and Sciences, the School of Business, or the School of Leadership Studies (the university's three undergraduate schools). Like its male counterpart, Richmond College, Westhampton is deemed a "community within a community." It focuses on the special developmental needs of women while giving its residents the chance to take classes, share dining halls, and interact socially with men. Westhampton has its own residence halls, programs, academic advisers, student government, and student-faculty committees. Its biggest program is WILL (Women Involved in Living and Learning), which enhances women's collegiate experiences through course work in women's studies, gender-related events outside the classroom, and leadership development activities.

Wheelock College (B, M) Enrollment: 1,300

200 The Riverway
Boston, MA 02215
617-734-5200
http://www.wheelock.edu

Education and social work are the historic strengths of this undergraduate and graduate institution, located on Boston's Riverway. Undergraduates receive more than academic training; students in all programs are placed in schools, hospitals, and community agencies for a well-rounded learning experience. Baccalaureate degrees awarded are a BS in human development or mathematics/science, a BA in arts or humanities, and a bachelor of social work. MS programs are in departments of care and education; human development and family studies; and leadership, policy, and administration. Dual BS-MS degrees are also available, as well as a new dual degree combining a master of social work with a master of

education. The college has several dozen endowed scholarships.

William Smith College (B) Enrollment: 900

Geneva, NY 14456
315-781-3000
http://www.hws.edu

A four-year liberal arts college with a diverse curriculum, William Smith College (for women) is paired with Hobart College (for men). The two share a campus, facilities, curriculum, and faculty, while maintaining separate programming, activities, athletics, and residences. Majors include such unusual choices as African studies; architectural studies; critical social studies dialogues; European studies; geoscience; Greek; lesbian, gay, and bisexual studies; media and society; peer education in human relations; public policy studies; urban studies; and writing and rhetoric. Special programs include Writing Colleagues, a peer-oriented writing development program; the Fisher Center for Men and Women, which looks at cross-gender relationships; and a summer youth institute for environmental studies. Among financial awards offered is an arts scholarship.

William Woods University (A, B, M) Enrollment: 1,000

200 West 12th Street
Fulton, MO 65251-1098
314-642-2251 or 800-995-3159
http://www.wmwoods.edu

William Woods, located halfway between St. Louis and Kansas City, describes itself as a professions-oriented, liberal arts university. It offers majors and minors in more than 80 programs of study. Undergraduate students may work toward a BA, BFA, or BS degree. Graduate degrees are also available, including a master of business administration, a master of education in administration, a master of education in curriculum and instruction, and a master of education in equestrian studies. An Adult Studies program gives working adults the chance to complete a baccalaureate degree or earn an advanced degree in a flexible, group-oriented format. Approximately 85 percent of students receive financial aid.

Wilson College (A, B) Enrollment: 200+

1015 Philadelphia Avenue
Chambersburg, PA 17201-1285
717-264-4141
http://www.wilson.edu

This liberal arts college offers 21 bachelor's degree programs, eight associate degree programs, three certificate programs, and a post-baccalaureate teacher intern program. The college is also known for its personal enrichment and business and job retraining programs. Bachelor's degree majors: behavioral sciences, environmental studies, equestrian studies, equine facilitated therapeutics, legal studies, physical education and dance, psychobiology, and veterinary medical technology. Pre-professional offerings are in health science, law, medicine, and veterinary medicine. A joint BS-MS degree is awarded in computer science. Need- and merit-based scholarships are provided, one with a community or church volunteer service requirement.

Section C
Additional Information

A variety of career aids can be found in this section, including publications, online resources, internships, work-at-home resources, women's history and research programs, and programs especially for girls.

Girls' Programs

There are a number of excellent academic and career programs to help girls get interested in and explore science, math, technology, and other careers. Girls' programs such as weekend workshops, academic camps, career workshops, mentoring arrangements, and competitions are also listed. Of course, many programs operate on a small scale at the local level. Included here are programs that are nationally available or duplicated locally.

All Girls/All Math
University of Nebraska-Lincoln
Center for Science, Math and Computer Education
126 Morrill Hall
Lincoln, NE 68588-0350
402-472-3731

Nebraska high school girls are invited to apply for a week of All Girls/All Math summer mathematics camp at the university. Girls in grades nine through twelve attend courses and work with women professors and graduate students. They stay in a UNL residence hall and are chap-eroned by a female mathematics graduate student. The 1999 camp cost was $100; scholarships are available.

Autodesk Design Your Future Project
San Rafael, CA
http://www.autodesk.com/compinfo/dyf/dyfmain.html

The Design Your Future Web site is a place for girls, parents, and educators to learn about career possibilities, internships, and links to organizations and opportunities in technology. The site is designed and maintained by female student interns. Young women, ages 14-19, are offered internships and Autodesk, a software company, endows a scholarship for its interns.

Belvoir Terrace Summer Programs
Belvoir Terrace
Lenox, MA 01240
413-637-0555
http://www.belvoirterrace.com

Belvoir Terrace is an educational camp for girls devoted to the fine and performing arts. Girls in grades six through eleven are housed in age-specific dorms. Programs in art, dance, music, theater, and sports are offered.

Additional Information

Camp Startup

12 Merrill Street
Newburyport, MA 01950
800-350-2978

Camp Startup is a business and entrepreneurial camp for girls age 13-19.

Chateau Fleuri—France

Hambeau du Villers Poz Colombier
France 70000
00333-84-75-93-31

This one-week international study camp in France is open to girls ages 12-17. Maximum camp size is twelve. Cost for one week in 1999 was $4,000.

Douglass Project for Rutgers Women in Math, Science, and Engineering

Rutgers, The State University of New Jersey
50 Bishop Street
New Brunswick, NJ 08901-8530
732-932-9197

DSI is a four-week summer residential program for young women entering ninth grade who want to explore a variety of areas including biology, chemistry, computers, environmental and marine sciences, engineering, physics, and mathematics. It offers hands-on labs, workshops, and field trips. Students must attend a high school in one of nine surrounding counties and apply during their eighth grade year. Also offered are a weekend academy and science career exploration day. Call for eligiblity information.

Explorathon AZ

8776 East Shea Boulevard
PMB B3A-442
Scottsdale, AZ 85260
602-735-3950
http://www.explorathon.com

Explorathon AZ is a career day that allows girls to meet professional women working in the fields of technology, science, engineering, and mathematics. The program reaches hundreds of girls in the Phoenix area annually. Participants attend workshops and visit with employers to learn about career opportunities.

Girls Basketball Camps Directory

131 Berkshire Court
Piscataway, NJ 08854
732-699-1678
http://www.girlsbasketballcamps.com

Girls Basketball Camps is a directory on the Internet of girls basketball camps held in the United States. The site includes a list and contact information of girls camps across the country, links to individual camps, and registration forms.

Girls' Domain Project

http://www.myowndomain.com/girlsdomain

The Girls' Domain Project is working to change the view that computers are just for boys by teaming up with women who work in Internet technology in California. The project, a partnership with the American Association of University Women, primarily benefits girls in California, but the Web site offers guidance and support for any girls interested in computing and any other nontraditional fields. For example, recent online articles offered first-hand information from women in nontraditional fields, a pediatrician and a professional basketball player.

Girls Incorporated

Girls Inc. National Resource Center
441 West Michigan Street
Indianapolis, IN 46202
http://www.girlsinc.org

Girls Incorporated is a national network of programs that serves 350,000 girls between the ages of 6-18 at over 1,000 states nationwide. The Web site lists contact information by state for Girls Incorporated sites. Operation SMART, which operates in 35 states, encourages girls to follow natural curiosity in math, science, and technology and in preparation for nontraditional careers such as automechanic, astronaut, and microsurgeon.

Integrating Gender Equity and Reform

Center for Education Integrating Science,
Mathematics, and Computing
500 Tech Parkway
Georgia Institute of Technology
Atlanta, GA 30332-0282
404-894-0777
http://www.ceismc.gatech.edu

INGEAR is a program of CEISMC, which seeks to expand students' interest in mathematics, science, and engineering. An example of an INGEAR program is the Saturday Workshop series for middle and high school girls to interact with professional women in science and engineering and participate in hands-on activities.

Math and Science Network

c/o Mills College
5000 MacArthur Boulevard
Oakland, CA 94613-1301
510-430-2222
http://www.elstad.com/msnprog.html

The Math/Science Network is a nonprofit membership organization of educators, scientists, mathematicians, parents, community leaders, and government and corporate representatives who promote the continuing advancement in mathematics education of all people, with a particular emphasis on women and girls. On a national level, MSN coordinates the one-day Expanding Your Horizons in Science and Mathematics conferences for sixth through twelfth grade girls, conducted annually in over 130 locales. A typical conference takes place on a Saturday at a local college or university and is attended by 200 to 500 girls with workshops and keynote speakers. MSN also sponsors periodic national conferences for adults at the career decision-making level and the mid-career level to examine the personal, historical, social, philosophical, and political context in which women work in science.

Michelet NCSY—Jerusalem

333 Seventh Avenue
New York, NY 10001
212-613-8324

Michelet NCSY is an international study camp in Jerusalem for girls age 14-18. Cost for the six-week program in 1999 was $3,300.

One-Week Summer in Engineering for High School Women

University of Maryland
1106 Engineering Classroom Building
College Park, MD 20742
301-405-0315

This one-week summer program is for girls age 15-18. Maximum camp size is 30.

Precollege Program in Animal Behavior

Chatham College
Dean of Continuing Education
Pittsburgh, PA 15232
412-365-1155

This camp is for girls only, age 14-16, at Chatham College. Maximum camp size is 25.

The Role Model Project for Girls

Womens Work
PO Box 299
Palo Alto, CA 94302-0299
http://womenswork.org/girls/about.html

The Role Model Project for Girls is a project of the professional organization, Womens Work. It is geared toward girls age nine to sixteen. The project consists of two parts: a CD-ROM and a supporting Web site of examples of women professionals in a wide range of nontraditional careers. The CD-ROM is a database of basic information introducing between 100 and 200 careers, viewed in a short form (one to three minutes) of the woman professional answering questions about herself and her career.

Saint Mary's College Paula Program

Saint Mary's College
Notre Dame, IN 46556
219-284-4778

The Paula Program is a one-week computer camp for girls age 12-15. Cost for one week in 1999 was $525.

Additional Information

Science Institute for High School Women in Math, Sciences, and Engineering

Douglass College
P.O. Box 270
New Brunswick, NJ 08903-0270
908-932-9197

A three-week summer study course is offered at the Douglass College of Rutgers University for young women interested in a career in science, math, and/or engineering. The program includes hands-on laboratory activities, workshops, and field trips to corporate and natural scientific sites. Individuals work on a research project and participate in a math and science fair. Juniors in high school are eligible to apply.

Science Quest

Seton Hill College
Science Quest Director
Greensburg, PA 15601-1599
724-830-4611

Science Quest (for grades 7-9) and Science Quest II (for grades 10-12) are summer programs for young women interested in exploring the possibilities of science. Admission is limited to 15 girls for each one-week camp. There is no regional residency requirement. Students live on the Seton Hill college campus for a week and participate in hands-on laboratory projects guided by professors and women science, math, and computer professionals. Need-based scholarships are available to assist with the cost.

Spectacles Math and Science Camp

4760 Forsyth Road
Macon, GA 31210-4462
912-757-5228

Spectacles Math and Science Camp is a two-week camp for girls age 10-13. Cost in 1999 for two weeks was $995.

Star Camp for Girls

Science and Technology at Rensselaer
Rensselaer Polytechnic Institute
Troy, NY 12180
518-276-6216

STAR Camp is a math, science, and technology camp for girls age 12-15 at Rensselaer Polytechnic Institute. Maximum camp size is seventy; cost for one week is $350.

Summer Engineering Exploration

Society of Women Engineers
1226 EECS
Ann Arbor, MI 48109-2166
734-763-5027

The Summer Engineering Exploration is for girls age 16-18. Maximum camp size is sixty.

Summer in Engineering Program for High School Women

University of Maryland at College Park
Women in Engineering, James Clark School of Engineering
1106 Engineering Classroom Building
College Park, MD 20742-3000
301-405-3931

This one-week program exposes young women to engineering through hands-on activities, professional engineer speaker series, field trips, and informational sessions.

Summer Science and Math Workshop

Marymount College Math/Computer Science Department
100 Marymount Avenue
Tarrytown, NY 10591-3796
914-332-8235

The Summer Science and Math Workshop is for girls age 15-17. Maximum camp size is twenty.

Summer Science Program

Smith College
Tilly Hall
Northampton, MA 01063
413-585-3879

Summer Science at Smith College is a camp for girls age 13-18. Maximum camp size is ninety. Cost for two weeks in 1999 was $1,575; four weeks was $3,150.

Summer Youth Programs

Michigan Technological University
1400 Townsend Drive
Houghton, MI 49931-1295
906-487-2219
http://www.yth.mtu.edu/syp/

A one-week Women in Engineering Program is sponsored by the university to help female high school students evaluate their interest in engineering and to aid in decision making regarding college study. Some financial aid is available.

SummerMath

Mount Holyoke College
50 College Street
South Hadley, MA 01075-1441
http://www.mtholyoke.edu/proj/summermath/appinfo.htm

SummerMath is for young women in grades eight through twelve. The $3,900 tuition in 1999 included instruction, trips, tickets, meals, room, and activities.

Tomorrow's Girl

PO Box 254
Strasburg, PA 17579-0254
http://www.tomorrows-girl.com

Tomorrow's Girl publishes a fictional book series that features young girls using science and technology to help solve mysteries or problems. The girl is helped in the story by a woman in a science or technology field. The Web site is geared toward school-age girls and offers interaction, information, and activities.

Young Women in Science

Mary Baldwin College
Staunton, VA 24401
800-822-2460

Young Women in Science is a summer program for girls age 16-18 at Mary Baldwin College, a Presbyterian-affiliated college. Maximum camp size is thirty-six. Cost for three weeks in 1999 was $750.

Young Women's Institute for Leadership

Mary Baldwin College
Staunton, VA 24401
800-822-2460

The Young Women's Insitute for Leadership is a one-week program for girls age 15-18. Maximum camp size is thirty-six. Cost for one week in 1999 was $495.

Internships

Internships are a great way to gain valuable work experience and develop contacts that may help you find a job later. Many internships are unpaid; others offer assistance with lodging. Most will work with the schools to allow the intern to receive college credit. The internships listed in this section are geared toward women. Many state that they are women-only; others are for organizations that generally attract women, such as feminist, reproductive health, and women's research organizations.

Artists in Residence (A.I.R.) Gallery

40 Wooster Street, Second Floor
New York, NY 10013
212-966-0799

The gallery exhibits women's visual artwork. Send a self-addressed, stamped envelope for a prospectus. The gallery also offers an internship for women to assist in the daily operation of the gallery. Send a resume and letter of interest.

Asian Immigrant Women Advocates

310 Eighth Street, Suite 301
Oakland, CA 94604
510-268-0192

Additional Information

This organization seeks to empower low-income Asian immigrant women. It offers unpaid internships throughout the year. Hours and length of internship are flexible.

Association for Women in Science

1200 New York Avenue, NW, Suite 650
Washington, DC 20005
202-326-8940
http://www.awis.org

AWIS is a national, professional organization for women in all scientific disciplines. Paid internships lasting two to four months are available year-round at the national office. Interns represent AWIS at events, assist with proposal writing, provide editorial assistance, help develop and analyze surveys, conduct research, and review legislation. To apply send a resume and cover letter stating the time of year for which you are applying. Further internship information is available on the Web site.

Association for Women in Sports Media

PO Box 17536
Fort Worth, TX 76102
612-228-5509
http://users.southeast.net/~awsm

AWSM, an organization that supports women employed in sports writing, editing, broadcast and production, public relations, and sports information offers eight to 12 summer internships. In the past, internships in writing, copy editing, public relations, and radio have been offered at *Sports Illustrated, Cleveland Plain Dealer,* U.S. Olympic Committee, Nike, and ESPN. Visit the Web site for updates on AWSM internships.

Association of Flight Attendants— AFL-CIO

1625 Massachusetts Avenue, NW
Washington, DC 20036
202-328-5400

The AFA is a labor union representing flight attendants; 86 percent of members are women.

It offers paid and unpaid internships throughout the year. Call for information.

AT&T Undergraduate Research Program

AT&T Labs Undergrad Research Administrator
Room D302-A04
200 Laurel Avenue
Middletown, NJ 07748
http://www.research.att.com/academic/urp.html

The AT&T Undergraduate Research Program seeks to assist women and minority U.S. citizens in electrical engineering, mathematics, statistics, computer science, and related fields. Candidates should be available 10 weeks during the summer for work on individual projects that are part of ongoing research in the lab. They are paid a salary commensurate with other AT&T employees of similar education and experience. Travel expenses are paid and living arrangements are made at a nearby college campus.

Aunt Lute Books

PO Box 410687
San Francisco, CA 94141
800-949-LUTE
http://www.auntlute.com

Aunt Lute Books is a nonprofit, multicultural women's press. Aunt Lute Books seeks part-time, unpaid interns to assist in all phases of book production, including order fulfillment, marketing, Web research, grants, and book production. Interns work a minimum of 10 hours a week for six months or one semester. Academic credit may be arranged; a number of informal classes on publishing are given.

Autodesk Design Your Future Project

San Rafael, CA
http://www.autodesk.com/compinfo/dyf/dyfmain.html

Autodesk, a software developer, offers internship opportunities for young women ages 14-19 at its corporate headquarters. Interns work together with women employees of Autodesk to develop and maintain the Design Your Future Web site (technology career information for girls). Autodesk endows a college scholarship for female interns. In a recent year, there were eight interns.

Bell Labs—Lucent Technologies
Summer Research Program for Minorities and Women
Special Programs Manager-SRP
Room B1-D29, 283 King George Road
Warren, NJ 07059
http://www.bell-labs.com/employment/srp

The Summer Research Program offers women and minorities the opportunity for technical employment experience at Bell Labs research and development laboratories. Eligible students are second- or third-year undergraduates in ceramic engineering, chemical engineering, chemistry, communications science, computer science, electrical engineering, information science, materials science, mathematics, mechanical engineering, operations research, physics, or statistics. Students must be available for at least 10 weeks beginning in early June. Salaries will be commensurate with those of regular Bell Laboratories employees with comparable education. Living accommodations and local transportation will be arranged. Visit the Web site or write for further information.

Center for the American Woman and Politics
191 Ryders Lane
Rutgers University
New Brunswick, NJ 08901
732-932-9384
http://www.rci.rutgers.edu/~cawp/

Through its Young Women's Leadership Initiative, CAWP offers paid and unpaid internships at its office at Rutgers University. Applicants need not be Rutgers students. There is a paid internship from May to June to assist with the NEW Leadership program. Interns help with program logistics and contracting speakers. Non-paid internships are also offered in other programs for women with an interest in politics. To apply, submit a cover letter, resume, three references, and a three- to five-page writing sample. Call or write for details.

The Center for the Education of Women
University of Michigan
330 East Liberty
Ann Arbor, MI 48104
734-998-7080
http://www.umich.edu/~cew/intern.html

The center offers administrative internships for women who have been out of the workforce for some time, or who are making a significant change in career and need experience. Internships are paid, short-term project-oriented work experiences sponsored by units at the University of Michigan, selected community agencies, and businesses. All placements pay a stipend of $1,680 for 240 hours of work (20 hours per week for 12 weeks). The applicant must have a bachelor's degree.

Center for Women Policy Studies
1211 Connecticut Avenue, NW, Suite 312
Washington, DC 20036
http://www.centerwomenpolicy.org

The center implements its commitment to intergenerational partnerships among women through its internship program, bringing young women into the policy process, encouraging their leadership, and inspiring them to work for institutional change. Interns assist in administrative tasks, as well as researching and reporting on issues, helping develop and write new publications, and helping develop new projects.

Colorado Women's Agenda
Internship Program
1420 Ogden Street
Denver, CO 80218-1910
http://www.womensagenda.org

The Colorado Women's Agenda has several internship positions available for women who seek experience working in a grassroots, political, nonprofit setting, including skills development in issue-based research, policy analysis, grassroots organizing, media outreach, and fundraising, marketing, and membership. Course credit and a stipend are negotiable. Interns should be available to work 15-20 hours per week for six to nine months. The Colorado

Additional Information

Women's Network is a statewide network of women working for social justice, political power, and economic security for all women in Colorado.

DC Commission for Women

Internships
2000 14th Street, NW, Suite 354
Washington, DC 20009
202-939-8083

The DC Commission for Women is an advocacy organization for women and their families in the Washington, DC area. It offers unpaid internship experience with flexible dates and hours.

Democratic National Committee

Office of Women's Research
430 Capitol Street, SE
Washington, DC 20003
202-488-5017

The DNC Office of Women's Research seeks to mobilize more women to vote Democratic. It offers an unpaid internship for a minimum of six weeks.

EMILY's List

Internship Program
805 15th Street, NW, Suite 400
Washington, DC 20005
202-326-1400

EMILY's List is a political network that seeks to raise money for Democratic, pro-choice women candidates and mobilize female voter turnout. It offers paid internships year-round in the areas of communications, development, election law compliance, events, political, and research. Stipend is $500 a month.

The Empower Program

6925 Willow Street, NW, Suite 228
Washington, DC 20012
202-882-2800

The Empower Program is an educational organization that works with youth to end gender-based violence and sexual violence. Unpaid internships with flexible hours and dates are available.

Feminist Health Center

PO Box 456
Freeland, NH 03849
202-939-8083

The Feminist Health Center provides well-woman gynecology and abortions and provides education for women about their bodies and reproductive health. Unpaid internships with flexible dates and hours are available.

Feminist Majority

Internship Program in Feminism and Public Policy
1600 Wilson Boulevard, Suite 801
Arlington, VA 22209
703-522-2214
http://www.feminist.org

Undergraduate, graduate, and professional school students who are interested in working in the women's movement may apply. Some expenses and local transportation are reimbursed. A small stipend is paid for work from September through May. Apply any time; internships begin in September, January, and June of each year.

Feminist Women's Health Center

580 14th Street, NW
Atlanta, GA 30318
404-875-7115

The Feminist Women's Health Center advocates, provides, and protects reproductive choices for all women. Unpaid internships with flexible dates and times are available.

Financial Women's Association of New York

Wall Street Exchange/FWA
215 Park Avenue South, Suite 1713
New York, NY 10003
212-533-2141
http://www.fwa.org

Wall Street Exchange is a summer program open to students between their junior and senior years in college who are interested in pursuing careers in business and finance, and who will be working for a financial services company in New York City during the summer. The Wall Street Exchange offers seminars, mentoring, and social networking events with leaders in the financial industry. Visit the Web site for application information, or call.

Fort Wayne Women's Bureau

303 East Washington Boulevard
Fort Wayne, IN 46802
219-424-7977

The Fort Wayne Women's Bureau provides advocacy for women, training for women on welfare, drug addiction counseling, and crisis counseling. Paid and unpaid internships throughout the year with flexible hours are available.

Fund for the Feminist Majority

Internship Program in Feminism and Public Policy
1600 Wilson Boulevard, Suite 801
Arlington, VA 22209
703-522-2214
http://www.feminist.org

Applicants must be undergraduate, graduate, or professional school students who aspire to become leaders in the feminist movement; especially sought are women of color. Internships are available on either a full- or part-time basis and are served in the Feminist Majority's Washington, DC, Boston, or Los Angeles offices. Contact: Los Angeles office at 8105 West Third Street, Suite 1, Los Angeles, CA 90048, 213-651-0495; Boston office at 675 Massachusetts Avenue, Cambridge, MA 02139, 617-864-0130.

General Federation of Women's Clubs

Internship for Communications Majors
1734 N Street, NW
Washington, DC 20036-2990
202-347-3168
http://www.gfwc.org

The Public Relations Department of the GFWC offers college juniors and seniors majoring in some area of mass communications an opportunity to get hands-on experience working with federation members and the media. Students earn a small stipend and course credit, if applicable. Internship is offered during fall, winter, and summer semesters.

Illinois Institute of Technology

Office of Admission
3300 South Federal Street
Chicago, IL 60616-3793
312-567-3000

The Women in Science and Engineering Program offers high school females in grades 10 through 12 a two-week opportunity to explore career options in science and engineering. The program includes laboratory investigations, hands-on projects developed and taught by women undergraduate students, and tours of Chicago-area engineering companies, as well as mentoring opportunities.

Institute for Women's Policy Research

Research Internships/Fellowships
1400 20th Street, NW, Suite 104
Washington, DC 20036
202-785-5100
http://www.iwpr.org

The Women's Institute for Policy Research provides policy-relevant research on women's lives and issues fact sheets and publications. Visit the Web site for information about internship and job opportunities at the institute.

International Paper Math and Science Scholars

International Paper Math and Science Scholars
Marymount College Summer Workshop
Box 1173, 100 Marymount Avenue
Tarrytown, NY 10591-3796
http://www.marymt.edu/~summersci/

This two-week workshop is designed as an educational experience to inspire young women entering grades 10-12 to continue their study of math and science and consider careers in these areas. Thirty girls from the New York metropoli-

Additional Information

tan area are chosen to participate. Participants and families are urged to attend an information session before applying. Visit the Web site or write for session dates and further information.

Ipas
Boston, MA
http://www.ipas.org

Ipas is an international non-governmental organization dedicated to improving abortion and postabortion care services. A paid internship in the Boston area is available for a graduate student. The intern will have the opportunity to be the co-author of publications related to the internship work.

Jewish Women International
1828 L Street, NW, Suite 250
Washington, DC 20036
202-857-1300

Jewish Women International works for the rights of women and children, and Jewish values such as social justice, community, and caring. It offers unpaid internships with flexible dates and hours.

Los Alamos National Laboratory
Underrepresented Minority and Female Program
Student Programs
MS P290
Los Alamos, NM
http://hrntserverl.lanl.gov/Students/
application.html

The program was established to assist underrepresented minorities and females from the southwest to achieve parity representation in science, mathematics, engineering, and technology. Applicants must be enrolled in an undergraduate degree program or have a bachelor's degree and intend to continue with graduate studies. An application is available online or by writing.

MANA, A Latina Organization
Scholarships
1725 K Street, NW, Suite 501
Washington, DC 20006
202-833-0060
http://www.hermana.org

MANA seeks to empower Hispanic women through leadership development and community action. In addition to several scholarships, the Tensia Alvirez Internship offers Hispanic women the opportunity to gain valuable educational and work experience at the national headquarters in Washington, DC

Massachusetts Coalition on New Office Technology
1 Summer Street
Somerville, MA 02143
617-776-2777

The Massachusetts Coalition organizes women office workers for improved workplace health, safety, and rights. Unpaid internships with flexible hours are offered throughout the year.

MCP Hahnemann University Women's Health Education Program
Summer Internship
Fax: 215-843-0253

This unpaid summer internship is ideal for a pre-med student interested in women's health. Projects include case review, review of current journal articles, development of teaching modules on domestic violence, reproductive options, eating disorders, and more. Fax resume to above number.

Media Watch
PO Box 618
Santa Cruz, CA 95061-0618
408-423-6355
http://www.mediawatch.com

Media Watch challenges sexism and violence in the media through education and action. Unpaid internships of 10-20 hours per week are available.

Melpomene Institute for Women's Health Research

1010 University Avenue
St. Paul, MN 55104
612-642-1951

The Melpomene Institute researches the link between physical activity and women's health concerns. Paid internships with flexible dates and hours are available.

Mothers' Voices United to End AIDS

65 West 46th Street, Suite 701
New York, NY 10036
212-730-2777

Mothers' Voices is a national organization that mobilizes mothers as AIDS educators and advocates. It offers an unpaid internship to assist in maintaining its Web site. Interns should have familiarity with the Internet, and be available electronically or in NYC headquarters for 4-12 hours per week. Academic credit may be arranged.

National Abortion and Reproductive Rights Action League

1156 15th Street, Suite 700
Washington, DC 20005
202-973-3000

NARAL seeks to secure and protect reproductive choice and women's rights. It offers paid and unpaid internships of 30-40 hours per week. Internships are available year-round.

National Abortion and Reproductive Rights Action League—Maryland

817 Silver Spring Avenue, Suite 409
Silver Spring, MD 20910
301-565-4154

NARAL-Maryland seeks to guarantee every woman the right to make personal decisions regarding the full range of reproductive choices. Unpaid internships with flexible dates and times are available.

National Abortion and Reproductive Rights Action League—Ohio

760 East Broad Street
Columbus, OH 43205
614-221-2594

NARAL-Ohio works to maintain a full range of reproductive rights for women in Ohio. It offers unpaid internships with flexible dates and hours.

National Abortion and Reproductive Rights Action League—Virginia

PO Box 489
Falls Church, VA 22040
703-532-3448

NARAL-Virginia promotes reproductive choice, including bearing healthy children, preventing unintended pregnancies, and choosing legal abortion. Unpaid internships of 12 weeks with flexible hours are available.

National Center for Lesbian Rights

870 Market Street, Suite 570
San Francisco, CA 94102
415-392-6257

The center provides a legal resource center to end discrimination against all lesbians and their families. Unpaid internships with flexible dates and times are available.

National Chamber of Commerce for Women

10 Waterside Plaza, Suite 6H
New York, NY 10010
212-685-3454

The National Chamber of Commerce for Women assists professionals in writing business and career plans and provides support services for women business owners. It offers paid internships. Length of internship is determined by the scope of the project the intern undertakes. Interns work an average of 20 hours per week.

Additional Information

National Clearinghouse on Marital and Date Rape

2325 Oak Street
Berkeley, CA 94708
510-524-1582

The clearinghouse provides information on marital/date rape. Unpaid internships with flexible dates and times are available.

National Council for Research on Women

11 Hanover Square
New York, NY 10005
212-785-7335
http://www.ncrw.org

The National Council for Research on Women provides information about women's research, policy, and activism. Unpaid internships of 10-15 hours a week are available throughout the year.

National Council of Jewish Women

1707 L Street, Suite 950, NW
Washington, DC 20036
202-296-2588

The National Council of Jewish Women is a prochoice women's organization that seeks to effect legislation concerning work and family, child care, economic justice, civil rights and liberties, reproductive rights, and international affairs. Unpaid internships of 20 hours per week are available throughout the year.

National Family Planning and Reproductive Health Association

122 C Street, NW, Suite 380
Washington, DC 20001
202-628-3535

The association maintains and expands access to publicly funded family planning and reproductive health services. Unpaid internships with flexible dates and times are available.

National Federation of Republican Women

Attn: Internships
124 North Alfred Street
Alexandria, VA 22314
http://www.nfrw.org

To involve more women in the political process, the NFRW offers the Dorothy Andrews Kabis Memorial Internship. Four undergraduate women each year are offered a one-month experience at NFRW headquarters and housed at George Washington University. No monetary allowance is given, but round trip airfare is provided. Applications are available on the Web site or send a letter of interest. Applicants must be at least a junior or 21 or older, with a knowledge of government, a keen interest in Republican politics, campaign experience, and clerical office skills. State federations also offer internships for Republican women. Visit the Web site for contact information on state federations.

National Foundation for Women Legislators

910 16th Street, NW, Suite 100
Washington, DC 20006
202-337-3565

NFWL is an arm of the professional organization, the National Order of Women Legislators. Unpaid internships with flexible dates and hours are available.

National Museum of Women in the Arts

1250 New York Avenue, NW
Washington, DC 20005
202-783-7996
http://www.nmwa.org

The National Museum of Women in the Arts is dedicated to recognizing and encouraging women artists' efforts. NMWA offers paid and unpaid internships ranging from 10 to 12 weeks to undergraduate (sophomore and above) and graduate students. Fall, winter, and summer internships are available in the following departments: accounting, administration, corporate relations, curatorial, education, exhibition design and production, library and research center, membership, national programs, public relations, publications, registrar, retail operations and special events.

The **Clara Hoffberger Lebovitz Internship** is offered each fall. The Coca-Cola Endowed Internship is offered every fall, winter, and summer. The North Carolina Internship is offered each summer for a student enrolled in a North Carolina university with an arts-related major. Each is a full-time, 12-week internship that pays $1,500. General, unpaid internships are also available. Visit the Web site for complete details or call to request information.

National Organization for Women Legal Defense and Education Fund
395 Hudson Street
New York, NY 10014
212-925-6635
http://www.nowldef.org

The NOW Legal Defense Fund pursues equal rights for women and girls in the workplace, schools, and the courts through litigation, advocacy, and public education. It offers 20 internships per year, some paid and some unpaid. Sixteen of the 20 are for second- and third-year law students.

National Organization for Women
1000 16th Street, NW, Suite 700
Washington, DC 20036
202-331-0066
http://www.now.org

NOW offers unpaid internships throughout the year. College credit may be arranged. Interns will work with one of the following team:, Government Relations/Public Policy, Field Organizing, Direct Mail/Fundraising/Membership, Communications, or Political Action Committee.

National Partnership for Women and Families
1875 Connecticut Avenue, NW, Suite 710
Washington, DC 20009
202-986-2600
http://www.nationalpartnership.org

The National Partnership for Women and Families is a nonprofit organization that promotes fairness in the workplace, quality health care, and policies that help women balance the demands of family and career. It offers internships throughout the year; internships are not specified women only, but the work is women's issues-oriented and most interns have been women. All internships are unpaid, but college credit is available. The Undergraduate Internship Program is offered in spring, summer, and fall.

Internships are offered in the Workplace Fairness, Communications, Action Council/Membership, and Annual Luncheon sections, with different duties in each. Law students may apply to the Law Clerk Internship Program, in the Workplace Fairness, and Health Care sections. Summer interns are generally full-time; spring and fall may work part-time.

National Women's Health Network
514 10th Street, NW, Suite 400
Washington, DC 20004
202-347-1140

The National Women's Health Network works to give women a greater voice in the U.S. health care system. Unpaid internships of at least three months are available with flexible hours and dates.

National Women's History Project
7738 Bell Road
Windsor, CA 95492
707-838-6000
http://www.nwhp.org

The National Women's History Project promotes gender equity through multicultural women's history. Unpaid internships of 20 hours per week for three to six months are available.

National Women's Law Center
1 Dupont Circle, NW, Suite 800
Washington, DC 20036
202-588-5180

Additional Information

The Communications Department of the National Women's Law Center seeks undergraduate or graduate journalism, communications, and public relations majors for an unpaid internship. English, political science, or pre-law majors may also qualify. The center works on issues affecting women including employment, health, education, dependent care, and income security.

National Women's Political Caucus

1211 Connecticut Avenue, NW, Suite 425
Washington, DC 20036
202-785-1100
http://www.nwpc.org

The National Women's Political Caucus is a national organization dedicated to increasing the number of pro-choice women in office at all levels of government. It offers a one-semester, unpaid internship at its Washington, DC, office. Interns assist with daily office operations and provide editorial and organizing assistance.

NCAA Women's Enhancement Program

Internships
6201 College Boulevard
Overland Park, KS 66211-2422
913-339-1906
http://www.ncaa.org

The NCAA Women's Enhancement Program was established to increase the pool of qualified women candidates in coaching, athletics administration, officiating, and support services. One-year internships at the NCAA national office allow on-the-job learning experiences for female college graduates who express an interest in pursuing a career in intercollegiate athletics.

Network of East-West Women

1601 Connecticut Avenue, Suite 302
Washington, DC 20009
202-265-3585

The Network of East-West Women provides a communications and resource network for women in the former Soviet Union and in Central and Eastern Europe. Unpaid internships of a minimum of ten hours per week with flexible dates are available.

New Moon Publishing

PO Box 3620
Duluth, MN 55803
218-728-5507
http://www.newmoon.org

New Moon publishes *New Moon: The Magazine for Girls and Their Dreams,* exploring the passage of girl to woman and helping girls build a healthy resistance to gender stereotypes. Internships are unpaid. Editorial interns work with adult and girl editors. New Moon works with interns to secure high school or college credit for 16 to 40 hours of work per week.

Office of Educational Research and Improvement

555 New Jersey Avenue, NW
Washington, DC 20208-5643
202-219-2038

The Office of Educational Research and Improvement establishes gender equity standards. Unpaid internships with flexible dates and times are available.

Older Women's League

666 11th Street, NW, Suite 700
Washington, DC 20001
202-783-6686

The Older Women's League addresses the special concerns of women as they age. Paid internships are available with varying hours per week for two- to three-month periods throughout the year.

Planned Parenthood Federation of America

1120 Connecticut Avenue, NW, Suite 461
Washington, DC 20036
202-785-3351

Planned Parenthood is an advocate of reproductive rights for everyone. Paid internships with a stipend of $500 per month are available. Interns work 20-25 hours per week for three to four months.

Planned Parenthood of Western Pennsylvania
209 Ninth Street, Suite 400
Pittsburgh, PA 15222
412-434-8957

Planned Parenthood of Western Pennsylvania offers a public affairs/education internship. Interns should be available to work 10 to 15 hours throughout the school year, have transportation to downtown Pittsburgh, and be computer literate. Internships are unpaid, but credit hours are available.

Planned Parenthood—Connecticut
129 Whitney Avenue
New Haven, CT 06510
203-865-5158

Planned Parenthood supports and educates on reproductive health care. Unpaid internships with flexible dates and hours are available.

Planned Parenthood—Los Angeles
1920 Morengo Street
Los Angeles, CA 90033
213-223-4462

Unpaid internships are available in the spring and summer with flexible hours and dates.

Preparing to Lead: The College Women's Guide to Internships and Other Public Policy Learning Opportunities in Washington, DC
Public Leadership Education Network
Book Orders
1001 Connecticut Avenue, NW, Suite 900
Washington, DC 20036
202-872-1585

Preparing to Lead was written by women students for women students. It provides descriptions of over 125 internships, seminars, fellowships, and other resources for women interested in public leadership. The book is available to students at a discounted price.

Pro-Choice Resource Center
16 Willett Avenue
Port Chester, NY 10573-4326
914-690-0938

The Pro-Choice Resource Center trains pro-choice grassroots organizations. Paid internships are available part-time during the fall and spring and full-time during winter and summer months. Academic credit can also be arranged.

Seventeen Magazine
Awards
850 Third Avenue
New York, NY 10022
212-407-9700
http://www.seventeen.com

Seventeen magazine and Cover Girl offer the Volunteerism Awards for females ages 13 to 21 who have done something amazing in the field of volunteerism and whose accomplishments have benefited others in a major way. In a recent year, three top prize winners received $20,000 scholarships; second-prize winners received $10,000 scholarships and 24 more winners received a U.S. savings bond. Details of the competition are listed in an issue of *Seventeen* magazine, usually in early fall, or can be obtained by calling.

College students interested in working on a women's magazine are eligible to apply for internships. Interns receive a weekly stipend. Call or write for details.

Sisterhood Is Global Institute
4343 Montgomery Avenue, Suite 201
Bethesda, MD 20814
301-657-4355

Sisterhood Is Global seeks to improve women's rights on the local, national, regional, and global levels. Unpaid internships with flexible dates and times are available.

Additional Information

Sojourner, The Women's Forum

42 Seaverns Avenue
Boston, MA 02130
http://www.sojourner.org

Sojourner is a monthly national feminist news-paper based in Boston. It seeks feminist writers and women of color to write local, national, and international news briefs as part of its intern-ship program. Internships are unpaid but offer an excellent opportunity to build a clip file.

Wider Opportunities for Women

815 15th Street, NW, Suite 916
Washington, DC 20005
202-638-3143
http://www.w-o-w.org

WOW works nationally and in Washington, DC to help women and girls achieve economic independence and equality of opportunity. Interns may be undergraduates in public policy, women's studies, political science, economics, social work, journalism, marketing, counseling, psychology, or education. Stipend is a $10 per day reimbursement for lunch and travel costs.

Womanist Studies Consortium/Rockefeller Foundation Humanities Fellowship

Womanist Theory and Research Institute for African-American Studies
164 Psychology Building
University of Georgia
Athens, GA 30602-3012
706-542-5197
http://www.uga.edu/~womanist/fellowship.html

The Womanist Studies Consortium seeks to sup-port "womanists" (black feminists or feminists of color). The Graduate Summer Internship pro-vides a stipend of $1,000 to allow one out-of-state graduate student working in any field to reside for one month at the University of Georgia at Athens. The student participates in the WSC Summer Seminar and assists with editorial and technological projects. Write or call for information.

Women Express

316 Huntington Avenue
Boston, MA 02115
617-262-2434

Women Express seeks to provide an alternative positive image for teenage women through *Teen Voices* magazine. Unpaid internships of 12-15 hours a week are available throughout the year.

Women's Campaign Fund

734 15th Street, NW, Suite 500
Washington, DC 20005
202-393-8164

The Women's Campaign fund provides cash and technical support to pro-choice women running for office at all levels of government. A paid 40-hour per week internship is offered from March to May.

The Women's Center

133 Park Street, NE
Vienna, VA 22180
703-281-4928

The center provides affordable mental health services to women and families in the greater Washington metropolitan area. A research intern is needed to assist the Development Department in researching new foundation and corporate support for the center.

Women's Foreign Policy Group

1825 Connecticut Avenue, NW, Suite 660
Washington, DC 20009
202-986-8862
http://www.wfpg.org

WFPG is a national organization for women and men with experience in international affairs. Its members are experts in a range of areas, such as agriculture, economics, environment, health, arts, law, trade, and women's and children's issues. Unpaid internships are offered during the fall, spring, and summer terms. One-month internships are available in January, May, and August. College credit is available. Interns per-form general office work, public relations assis-tance, and attend foreign policy programs and enjoy exposure to mid- and senior-level professionals from across the international affairs field.

Women's Institute for Freedom of the Press

3306 Ross Place
Washington, DC 20008
202-966-7783
http://www.igc.org/wifp/

WIFP is a support network for media-concerned women. Internships at WIFP are unpaid, but the organization cooperates for college credit and helps meet academic requirements. Internships can be for any length of time and any time of year. Interns work 30 to 40 hours a week, with half of the time spent on a project mutually agreed upon by the intern and the institute that will advance the studies and career of the intern and be published by WIFP. To apply, write, telling about yourself, why you have chosen WIFP, and your career goals.

Women's Interart Center

549 West 52nd Street
New York, NY 10019
212-246-1050

The center offers work experience to women who are interested in careers in business management in the arts. High school and college students as well as persons of higher ages are eligible. Modest stipends are paid.

Women's International League for Peace and Freedom

1213 Race Street
Philadelphia, PA 19107-1691
215-563-7110

The league works with the UN Center for Human Rights to push the parameters of what are usually considered human rights. Paid internships of at least 15 hours per week are available.

Women's Policy, Inc.

409 12th Street, SW, Suite 705
Washington, DC 20024
202-554-2323

Women's Policy, Inc. tracks legislation of importance to women and families. Unpaid internships of 20-40 hours per week are available throughout the year.

Women's Project and Productions

55 West End Avenue
New York, NY 10023
212-765-1706
http://www.womensproject.org

Women's Project and Productions produces new plays by women. WPP offers internships in six areas, administration, development, education, marketing/publicity, literary management, and production. Interns have the opportunity to work with theatre professionals and receive tickets to all WPP productions. To request a complete internship packet, visit the Web site for an email connection or write for information.

Women's Research and Education Institute

Internships/WREI
1750 New York Avenue, NW, Suite 350
Washington, DC 20006
202-628-0444
http://www.wrei.org

WREI, a nonpartisan organization that provides information and policy analyses on issues of concern to women and policy makers, offers unpaid internships throughout the year. The internships are designed to give participants practical policymaking experience on Capitol Hill. Interns help organize briefings and conferences, do research and provide editorial assistance in fact sheet preparation, and represent WREI at Washington-area events. Participants must have completed at least one year of college for the 10-12 week internship, which generally requires 30-hour work weeks. Send a brief letter of interest along with your resume, college transcripts, two writing samples, and two letters of recommendation to the address above, or call for further assistance.

Additional Information

Women's Sports Foundation

Internships
Eisenhower Park
East Meadow, NY 11554
800-227-3988
http://www.womenssportsfoundation.org

See WSF's Web site for internship details.

Women's Studio Workshop

WSW Internships
Women's Studio Workshop
PO Box 489
New York, NY 12472
914-658-9133
http://www.wsworkshop.org

Women's Studio Workshop, an alternative space for artists to create new work and come together to share skills, offers internship opportunities for young women art students and recent college graduates. Interns work alongside staff, learning about papermaking, print media, book arts, and arts administration. Interns have access to WSW's studios during non-working hours. Internships are available during the Summer Institute, as well as spring and fall. See WSW's Web site for details.

Young Women's Project

923 F Street, NW, Third Floor
Washington, DC 20004
202-393-0461

The Young Women's Project supports teens and young women as community problem solvers. Paid internships of 20-40 hours per week are available throughout the year.

Online Resources

The Internet provides a wealth of information for working women and students, all free! The Web sites listed in this section vary from informal discussion forums for women in a particular field to detailed articles with professional advice from women who have experience working in a certain area. Web sites compiled as free information resources by organizations are included here, as well as some Web sites compiled by individuals. Please note that the information found on Web sites created by an individual may not be as reliable as that posted by an organization. Every effort has been taken to include only Web sites with reliable, accurate information, but readers will be well-served to consider the source of any information they find on the Internet.

The Ada Project

http://www.cs.yale.edu/~tap/tap.html

The Ada Project is a project of the Association of Computing Machinery Committee on the Status of Women in Computing. TAP is designed to serve as a clearinghouse of information and resources on women and computing. It includes extensive information on women/technology organizations, conferences, projects, discussions groups, and funding resources.

Advancing Women.Com

http://www.advancingwomen.com

Advancing Women.com seeks to create a network for women to share career strategies and to provide cutting edge resources that power women's successes. Its site features an international network, a network for Hispanic women, online digital business tools, and directories and resources for entrepreneurs, small/home office owners, and women-owned businesses. It offers the online publication *Advancing Women in Leadership* quarterly, with manuscripts that report, synthesize, review, or analyze scholarly inquiry that focuses on women's issues in all professional fields.

American Statistical Association
Meeting Today's Challenges: Women in Statistics
http://www.amstat.org

The online publication *Meeting Today's Challenges: Women in Statistics* offers information on becoming a statistician and using statistics in your career with separate sections for high school and college students. It is several pages long and offers helpful first-hand accounts, links to career and college information, and specific examples of what statisticians do.

Asian Women in Business
1 West 34th Street, Suite 200
New York, NY 10001
http://www.awib.org

Asian Women in Business seeks to assist Asian women in realizing their entrepreneurial potential. Its Web site contains a business reference library for those starting a small busines, with topics such as Legal Considerations, How to Write A Business Plan, Designing Your Own Web Site, and Evaluating Your Employees.

AT&T Women in Business Online
http://www.att.com/wib/

AT&T's Women in Business provides a place for women in diverse fields to network. The site does include some plugs for AT&T communications products, but provides valuable information about communications options, as well as the networking section, "Business Women's Exchange."

Autodesk Design Your Future Project
San Rafael, CA
http://www.autodesk.com/compinfo/dyf/
dyfmain.html

The Design Your Future Web site is a place for girls, parents, and educators to learn about career possibilities, internships, and links to organizations and opportunities in technology. The site is designed and maintained by female student interns. Young women, ages 14-19, are offered internships, and Autodesk, a software company, endows a scholarship for its interns.

The Backyard Project
Executive Coordinator Backyard Project
Garnett Foundation, c/o CrossWorlds
577 Airport Boulevard, Suite 800
Burlingame, CA 94010
http://www.backyard.org

The Backyard Project is a Web site designed to help girls find out about a computer science career. It also offers computer science camps in the San Francisco Bay Area. It is named because even in the "backyard" of the Silicon Valley, high school girls have little access to information about what it means to work in the computer science field. The site describes the variety of creative and well-paid work available in the field and the skill sets and requirements needed to major in computer science in college.

Business Women's Network Interactive
http://www.bwni.com

BWNi.com offers resources and news to help women in business improve their careers, learn more about the skills they need, and find help in the issues they face. Procurement opportunities in both the government and private sector and access to e-commerce tools are available for women business owners. BWNi.com is a partnership of the Business Women's Network in Washington, DC, a division of the woman-owned Public Affairs Group and One Family Inc.

Canadian Women's Internet Association
http://www.women.ca

This Web site serves as a resource center and meeting place for Canadian women. Its Information Center has hundreds of links to sites relevant to women. The site also hosts a job board and a section on Internet help for women.

Additional Information

Career Women
http://www.careerwomen.com

Career Women offers an extensive list of A-Z links of organizations, publications, and government agencies for girls and women. The site also features a job bank, resume bank, corporate profiles, and career advice.

Catholic Information Center on Internet (CICI)
http://www.catholic.net

The Catholic Information Center on Internet lists links to women's religious orders. Follow the link under Vocations on the main page.

Center for the Child Care Workforce
202-737-7700
http://www.ccw.org

CCW is a membership organization for child care providers. Available free from its Web site for members and nonmembers is a several page article "Rights in the Workplace: A Guide for Child Care Teachers."

College Board Online Scholarship Handbook
http://www.collegeboard.org

The College Board Online Scholarship Search offers users a free search of scholarships, loans, internships, and other financial aid programs from noncollege sources from a database of 3,400 programs.

Committee on the Status of Women in Computing Research
Mentoring Workshops for Women in Computing Research
1100 17th Street, NW, Suite 507
Washington, DC 20036-4632
202-234-2111
http://cra.org/Activities/craw/

The CRA-W, an effort of the Computing Research Association, sponsors a series of workshops of practical information and advice to women in computing research at the annual CRA conference. Summaries and complete transcripts and slides of past workshops are available online. The transcripts provide practical advice that is still valuable to computer science students and young professionals. Past topics have included "Building a Research Career: Going Beyond Your Thesis," "Strategies for Success in Industry and the National Laboratories," and "Networking and Professional Social Interaction."

Digital Women
http://www.digital-women.com

Digital Women was created for women in business and women around the globe looking for a place to gather resources, free business, sales and marketing tips, home business ideas, and a place to network with other business women. Other resources include classifieds, a section on bartering, promotional ideas, and travel information.

Disabled Women on the Web
http://www.disabilityhistory.org/women/aboutdw.html

Disabled Women on the Web was established to provide information, resources, and support for women with disabilities. The site is new, but intentions are to include a directory of women working on disability issues, announcements of conferences and forums, bibliographies, links to organizations, and information on artists with disabilities.

Essence Online
http://www.essence.com

The online version of this African-American women's magazine offers helpful information in its Careers section, including "@ work," a monthly profile of African-American women, the jobs they do, requirements, and salary.

Exploring Your Future in Math and Science: Encouraging Women in the Sciences

http://www.cs.wisc.edu/~karavan/afl/home.html

This page was produced as a project by three University of Wisconsin-Madison students, Andrew Frank-Loron, Jennifer Handrich, and Chia-Chen Wu. Based on their research, the site answers and asks questions as well, such as how much money scientists make and how girls are treated in science and math classrooms.

Familyfriendly.Com

http://www.familyfriendly.com

This Web site contains a variety of information to help working parents balance the demands of work and family. Sections include the Job Chooser, with job descriptions and salary ranges to help those considering a career change; Women and Opportunity—What Women Need to Know; and Family Friendly Programs, see what programs are available and what companies offer them.

Fastweb

http://www.fastweb.com

FastWeb is a free searchable database of college admission, financial aid, and scholarship information.

Feminist.Com

http://www.feminist.com

Feminist.com provides links and online resources on a range of topics related to women. Sections include the Feminist.com bookstore, articles and speeches by and about women, activism, women-owned businesses, and links to women's organizations.

FinAid

http://finaid.org

FinAid: The Smart Student Guide to Financial Aid offers free information on loans, scholar-ships, military aid, application assistance, and financial aid calculators.

Gender-Related Electronic Forums

http://www.umbc.edu/wmst/forums.html

Hosted by the University of Maryland-Baltimore County, this Web site is a directory of hundreds of gender-related, publicly accessible electronic forums in categories such as activists, business/finance, health, motherhood, science/technology, and sports/recreation.

Girls' Domain Project

http://www.myowndomain.com/girlsdomain

The Girls' Domain Project is working to change the view that computers are just for boys by teaming up with women who work in Internet technology in California. The project, a partnership with the American Association of University Women, primarily benefits girls in California, but the Web site offers guidance and support for any girls interested in computing and any other non-traditional fields. For example, recent online articles offered first-hand information from women in non-traditional fields, a pediatrician and a professional basketball player.

The Glass Ceiling Website

http://www.theglassceiling.com

The Glass Ceiling Website was created as a home for *Shatter the Glass Ceiling,* a working woman's magazine. The magazine is now online with over 2,000 pages on business and how to succeed, health issues, family issues, glass ceiling issues, a resource center, and a business directory.

Grantsnet

http://www.grantsnet.org

GrantsNet is a free, searchable database of biomedical funding options from nonprofit organizations and federal agencies. GrantsNet was created by the American Association for the

267

Additional Information

Advancement of Science and the Howard
Hughes Medical Institute.

Institute of Electrical and Electronic Engineering

445 Hoes Lane
PO Box 459
Piscataway, NJ 08855-0459
800-678-IEEE
http://www.ieee.org

The IEEE organization Web site offers an excellent online mentoring guidebook for mentors and mentees. Topics discussed include "Questions for Your Mentor," "Expectations and Benefits of the Relationship," "Tips on Networking," and "Mentoring Women."

Links to Your State Government

All 50 states use the same URL (web address) format for their main menu page. The format is: http://www.state.(substitute your state postal code here).us. For example, http://www.state.il.us is a link to all state agencies and offices in Illinois. When beginning a search for funding, your state government is a good place to start. Many have commissions on women, economic development assistance, and governor's scholarships, to name a few examples. Most also provide a directory of state colleges and universities.

Mentornet

http://www.mentornet.net

MentorNet is the National Electronic Industrial Mentoring Network for Women in Engineering and Science. It pairs women who are studying science or engineering at one of its participating universities with professional scientists and engineers working in industry, and helps them form email-based mentoring relationships. Corporations such as Intel support the program and often recruit participants for employment. Fifteen universities participated in a recent year. The goal is to link 5,000 mentor pairs by the fifth year of the program.

Military Woman Home Page

http://www.militarywoman.org

This site provides a meeting place for military women to exchange information unique to their military experience and to offer firsthand information to women thinking about a military career. A sampling of discussions and articles include "Military Family Life and Children," "Tell Us About Your Military Job," "Women Who Served in Hot Zones," and "Health Issues," featuring the Veteran's Health Care-Women Update Newsletter.

MLM Woman Newsletter

http://www.mlmwoman.com

MLM Woman is an online newsletter for women in network marketing. The site includes tips and resources for women networkers marketing on and off the Internet.

Moms Network

http://www.momsnetwork.com

The Moms Network offers practical information on working at home, promoting your business, and home ideas. Services include banner creation, Web hosting, and Web design. The site features Business Tip of the Week, online classified for women to advertise their businesses, and links to business tools and resources.

National Academy of Engineering Celebration of Women in Engineering

http://www.nae.edu

The Celebration of Women in Engineering is a project of the National Academy of Engineering to bring national attention to the opportunities, creativity, and potential that engineering represents to women and to people of all ages. Its Gallery of Women Engineers offers biographies of successful women in different areas of engineering, and serves as a directory of mentoring programs, educational resources, funding and financial aid, and career information.

National Partnership for Women and Families
202-986-2600
http://www.nationalpartnership.org

The National Partnership for Women is a non-profit organization that promotes fairness in the workplace, quality health care, and policies that help women balance the demands of family and career. It offers an online guide to the Health Insurance Portability and Accountability Act, useful for women who are changing jobs, having a baby, or getting divorced. An online Q and A about the Family and Medical Leave Act is also informative.

Nurse Recruiter
http://www.nurserecruiter.com

Nurse Recruiter seeks to bring health care employers and the nursing community together on the World Wide Web. Features include free resume services (an online form and email and faxing), information on nursing scholarships, and links to nursing sites.

Nursing Net
http://www.nursingnet.org

Nursing Net provides a forum for nursing professionals and nursing students. It offers an online newsletter, chatrooms, and online mentoring.

Outdoor Women, The (Online) Magazine
Outdoors Online, Inc.
4008 Southwest Walker Street, Suite 300
Seattle, WA 98116-2043
800-789-9797
http://www.ool.com/women/menu.shtml

The women's section of the magazine *Outdoors Online* includes articles for women who work in outdoors-oriented professions, as well as those who pursue outdoor interests in a recreational sense.

Pleiades Network
http://www.pleiades-net.com

The Pleiades Network lists hundreds of women's arts, entertainment, business, and professional organizations under the Connections section of its Web site. The Web site also provides a guide to the Internet, a calendar of events of interest to women, and discussion forums.

Resources for Women Computing Professionals
http://www.geocities.com/SiliconValley/Park/9417/

This site was designed to provide resources and establish an Internet community for women in information technology. It is maintained privately, not by an institution or organization, so it may not always be updated or available.

RN Central
http://www.rncentral.com

RN Central offers a list of links for nursing professional and nursing students, hosts Web forums, and posts educational articles and career information.

Smartbiz.Com/Women and Minority Issues
http://www.smartbiz.com

Smartbiz.com is a series of resources for small business, including a page devoted to women and minority issues. The page features information on discrimination, harassment, equal pay opportunities, organizations, and regulations. Go to smartbiz.com, select "Browse SBS" and select Women and Minority Issues from the drop-down menu.

South Asian Women's Network
http://www.umiacs.umd.edu/users/sawweb/sawnet

The SAWNet Web site is an outgrowth of a subscription list of over 700 South Asian women. The Web site lists resources, including contact information and links, for South Asian women's

Additional Information

organizations, books by and for South Asian women, careers, grants, funding, and electronic resources.

Spiderwoman

http://www.spiderwoman.org

Spiderwoman on the Web is an online mailing list for women Web designers to meet and share information online. It offers Web conferencing, plus SpiderwomanBiz, for women who run Web-based businesses. Recent topics included graphics, promotion, databases, HTML, Java, and multimedia.

Springboard 2000

Women's Venture Capital Forum
http://www.springboard200.org

Springboard 2000 is the first-ever venture capital forum to showcase women entrepreneurs. The forum is a joint project of the National Women's Business Council and the Forum for Women Entrepreneurs. The forum will bring together over 350 investors and key service providers with women seeking seed or later-round investments of $1 million to $15 million. Forums are planned for California early in 2000, for Washington, DC in April, and for Boston in the fall; additional forums may be held after 2000. Contact the Web site, or call the National Women's Business Council at 202-205-3850 or the Forum for Women Entrepreneurs at 650-357-0222.

Systers

http://www.systers.org

Systers is an informal, online organization for technical women in computing that began as a small mailing list in 1987 and has grown with the proliferation of computers and the Internet. The main service is a private forum and database system.

U.S. Department of Education

Financial Aid Online
http://www.ed.gov/offices/OPE/Students/index.html

This federal government site offers information about the Free Application for Student Aid (FAFSA) used as the application for many scholarships and other types of financial aid. The Student Guide to Financial Aid provides information about federal assistance and is also available in its entirety. Students seeking school codes to complete the FAFSA will also find them here on the Federal School Code Search Page.

The Varo Registry of Women Artists

http://www.netdreams.com/registry/

The Varo Registry is an electronic registry of artwork by contemporary international women artists. The registry is designed to provide all women artists an opportunity to become part of today's electronic community. Each artist is provided with her own personal Web page of images, background information, and artist's statement. The Varo Registry also sponsors two art listservs. Visit the Web site or call Untitled Productions, 617-243-9888, 132 Adams Street, Newton, MA 02158.

Voices of Women Online

http://www.voiceofwomen.com

Voices of Women is a journal and resource guide with articles on a variety of topics, a calendar of events, directory of women-friendly businesses, and links to other organizations. Recent articles included "Caring, Nurturing, and Cooperating: A Woman's Way to Deal with Conflict in the Workplace," and "Home Office Design."

Volleyball.Org

http://www.volleyball.org/college/finaid

This site offers information about NCAA divisions, scholarship limits for volleyball, and Title IX.

Woman Owned Workplaces
http://www.womanowned.com

This site has a directory of over 8,000 women-owned businesses from all over the world. It highlights a member's business every month, compiles resources, and offers guidelines on getting government contracts. Recent online articles included "Deciding What to Charge," "Getting Money for Your Business," and "Saving on Hidden Expenses."

Women Chef's Resource Center
http://www.chefnet.com/womenchefs

The Women Chef's Resource Center is an online home for women chefs and students. Its goal is to provide a networking environment, practical advice, and spotlights on women chefs and their careers.

Women in Aviation Resource Center
http://www.women-in-aviation.com

The Women in Aviation Resource Center seeks to provide an educational link for the worldwide network of women in all aspects of aviation. Categories include books, education and training, employment opportunities, organizations, an online forum, and others.

Women in Computer Visual Arts
http://www.animation.org

This online mentoring resource links women at all levels of experience working in computer visual arts, graphics, effects, and animation.

Women in Computing Academic Resource List
http://www.womenswork.org/wcar/

The WCAR list is a compilation of colleges and universities that have formal or informal programs for encouraging and retaining women in computer science. It is an officially sponsored activity of the American Computing Machinery Committee on the Status of Women. Fifty-six "women-friendly" computer science programs were listed recently.

Women in Cyberspace Field of Dreams
http://www.fodreams.com

This site was designed for and by women in business. It offers discussion forums, a message board, Web hosting, mentoring training, and timely articles on e-commerce and tips for women in business. A Webring links member businesses.

Women in Sports
http://www.makeithappen.com/wis

Women in Sports is dedicated to providing role models of women athletes who validate women's accomplishments and perpetuate a vision of women's abilities, autonomy, and self-determination. The Web site's "reading list" is an extensive list of links of interest to women in sports, including organizations, funding, and publications.

Women in the Engineering Industry, By Kaitlin Duck Sherwood
http://www.webfoot.com/advice/women.in.eng.html

This Web site consists of an article based on a speech given by Kaitlin Duck Sherwood, a professional engineer, to the Society of Women Engineers in Illinois. It contains practical information not found elsewhere on the Internet, such as physiology differences, myths, and other interesting firsthand observations.

Women in Weather
http://www.nssl.gov/nws/women/career.html

The Women in Weather site is maintained by a woman employee of the National Weather Service. It offers helpful information in several areas, with question forms on weather careers in academia, the military, and the private sector. Women professionals working in those areas will answer questions via email. Career informa-

Additional Information

tion and biographies are provided for women meteorologists, hydrologists, and technicians. Links to information on scholarships in meteorology and related organizations are provided.

Women in Wilderness
http://www.onelist.com/subscribe/
womeninwilderness

This free email community provides a forum for discussion of careers for women in the field of natural science, such as game warden, conservation officer, and biologist. The forum is also for women who enjoy outdoor recreation such as mountain climbing, backpacking, and scuba diving.

Women International Publishing
PMB 327
91-590 Farrington Highway, Suite 210
Kapolei, HI 96707-2002
http://www.womentakecontrol.com

Women International Publishing is an independent publishing company that publishes and promotes books and information that improve women's economic and personal well-being. It offers online articles of interest to women, as well as information on its titles. Available online is Starting a Home Business: Startup Checklist and Guide to Smart Living and Investing for Women. It also offers a scholarship to high school senior women who are U.S. citizens.

Women of NASA
http://quest.arc.nasa.gov/women

The Women of NASA resource was developed to encourage more young women to pursue careers in math, science, and technology. The interactive project showcases outstanding women who are enjoying successful careers and how these women balance personal and professional responsibilities. The main components of the project are profiles and weekly Web chats. Participants have the opportunity to ask questions of the mentor during the chats. Visit the Web site to subscribe to the mail list, which notifies participants of chat times and personalities.

Women's International Electronic University
PO Box 4236
Star City, WV 26504-4236
http://www.wvu.edu/~womensu/more.htm

WIEU seeks to facilitate the connection and collaboration between learners and mentors. It is an international, non-profit corporation. WIEU does not grant degrees. Rather, it seeks to promote the empowerment of women through training in information technology, health promotion and living skills, academic and professional training, and continuing education.

Women's Internet Council—Resource Clearinghouse
http://www.rain.org/wic.html

WIC seeks to establish a point of presence for women working with the Internet. It is hosted by GAIA WEB, a Public Internet Broadcasting Service. The Resource Clearinghouse offers hundreds of links to World Wide Web sites of interest to women.

Women's Outdoor Sports Resources
http://secure.adventuresports.com/shops/
outresor.htm

The equipment supplier Totally Outdoors offers this online database of women-friendly organizations dedicated to helping women enjoy the outdoors. Resources are arranged geographically with contact information, and links, where available.

Women's Studies List (WMST-L)
http://research.umbc.edu/~korenman/
wmst-l_index.html

WMST-L is an international email forum for discussion of women's studies, teaching, research, and program administration. Helpful user guides and a database of more than 500 women's studies, syllabi are available.

Womenbiz.Net

23230 Greater Mack
St. Clair Shores, MI 48080
888-830-6040
http://www.womenbiz.net

This online resource features articles of general interest to women in business and working women in general. A sampling of articles includes "Email Tips for Business Use," "The Name (of your business) Game," and "Gainfully Goofing Off: How Employees Share Knowledge."

WomenConnect

http://www.womenconnect.com

WomenConnect offers thousands of pages of content relevant to business and professional women, including daily women-related news; searchable job listings; a directory of women-owned businesses and women's organizations; information centers on business, personal finance, career, health, and politics, and message boards and chats.

WomenConnect—Asia

http://www.women-connect-asia.com

WomenConnect-Asia is an online resource center for Asian American women and women living and working in Asia. The site features a directory of professional women, news, a traveler's assistance network, a list of organizations, an events calendar, and discussion board.

WOMUNSCI—Women Undergraduates in Science

WOMUNSCI is a mailing list for discussion concerning the topic of increasing participation of undergraduate women in science. This list is devoted to answering the question, "What can be done to attract and retain women in the sciences?" at the undergraduate level. Membership is open to college science educators and administrators, and women undergraduates interested in science. To subscribe, send an email to majordomo@cs.umass.edu with "subscribe womunsci your-email-address (your name)" in the body of the message.

Working Women

http://www.wwork.com

This site offers business and career resources for the professional woman running a business. Resources offered include free items to enhance your Web site, free investment products, free business listings, and JobNet, SwapNet, and an events calendar. A recent article targeted work-at-home scams.

WWWomen

http://wwwomen.com

WWWomen is a good starting point for a wide variety of topics of interest to women. Its Women in Business section includes a large list of career links. Also helpful are the Women and Computers, Science and Technology, and Education of Women sections.

Publications

There are many publications offered free or for a nominal fee that contain career-specific information not found elsewhere. Professional journals keep women up to date on developments in the field and provide an outlet for research conducted by and about women. Newsletters that are membership benefits of an organization are listed under organizational entries in Section B. Publications listed in this section are available to the general public upon request or by subscription. Membership in an organization is not necessary.

Additional Information

African-American Women Business Owners Association

3363 Alden Place, NE
Washington, DC 20019
202-399-3645
http://www.angelfire.com/biz2/aawboa.html

AAWBOA has many in-house publications available to both members and nonmembers. Publications are free to members and cost a nominal fee for non-members. Publications are of interest to African-American and other minority women who own, operate, or plan to start a business. Titles include *Small Business Startup Guide, AAWBOA Guide to Effective Customer Service,* and government publications of interest, such as *Women's Investment and Savings Equity Act,* and *Women's Right to Know Act of 1999.* An order form is available on the Web site.

American Bar Association

Commission on Women in the Profession
750 North Lake Shore Drive
Chicago, IL 60611
312-988-6500
http://www.abanet.org/women/activities.html

The commission promotes gender equity in the profession and in law schools. It publishes *Don't Just Hear It Through the Grapevine,* a guidebook for law school leaders to evaluate their institutional atmosphere for women; *Directory of Associations for Women Lawyers,* and other publications on women in law. The ABA also publishes a list of accredited schools that offer paralegal training, a profession dominated by women.

American Federation of Teachers

Women's Rights Committee
555 New Jersey Avenue, NW
Washington, DC 20001-2079
202-879-4400
http://www.aft.org/human/women/

The Women's Rights Committee of the AFT's Human Rights and Community Relations Department offers free single copies of *How to Get Started on Women's Rights,* a guide to organizing a women's rights committee in your union;

and *How to Celebrate National Women's History Month,* a guide for teachers.

American Film Institute

Independent Film and Video Maker Program
2021 North Western Avenue
Los Angeles, CA 90027
213-856-7628

The institute publishes *Guide to College Courses in Film and Television.*

American Philosophical Association

Committee on the Status of Women
University of Delaware
Newark, DE 19716
302-831-1112
http://www.udel.edu/apa

The Committee on the Status of Women is concerned with gender equity and discrimination, teaching, research, and feminist theories. It publishes the *Newsletter on Feminism and Philosophy.*

American Physical Society

1 Physics Ellipse
College Park, MD 20740-3844
301-209-3232
http://www.aps.org

The Committee on the Status of Women in Physics offers the brochure, *Physics in Your Future,* profiling seven women physicists and encouraging middle school girls to explore the diverse career options related to statistics.

American Psychological Association

Women's Programs Office
750 First Street, NE
Washington, DC 20002
http://www.apa.org/pi/wpo/homepage.html

The APA Women's Program Office develops reports, pamphlets, and other materials on professional and consumer issues. Two free publications offered are *Surviving and Thriving in Academia: A Guide for Women and Ethnic Minorities,* and *The Directory of Financial*

Opportunities for Women and Ethnic Minorities in Psychology and Related Fields.

American Statistical Association
1429 Duke Street
Alexandria, VA 22314-3402
703-684-1221
http://www.amstat.org

The ASA offers the free publication *Women and Statistics* on careers for women in statistics.

American Woman Motorscene
2424 Coolidge Road, Suite 203
Troy, MI 48084
http://www.americanwomanmag.com

American Woman Motorscene is about cars from a woman's point of view and women who work in the automotive industry. Articles include road test reviews, travel and safety for women, career opportunities in the auto industry, and everything a woman needs to know about buying and maintaining a vehicle. The Web site offers a women's workshop on everyday do's and don'ts of maintaining a vehicle and travel and safety tips.

Angles: Women Working in Film and Video
PO Box 11916
Milwaukee, WI 53211
414-963-8951

Angle recognizes the contribution women have made in the field of film and video with news and reviews. Call or send a SASE for subscription or manuscript information.

Ask Women Success Guide
93 Fruehauf Avenue
Buffalo, NY 14226
716-839-0855

Call or write for more information about this publication.

Association for Women Geoscientists
PO Box 280
Broomfield, CO 80038-0280
http://www.awg.org

AWG encourages the participation of women in the geosciences. It is the publisher of *Resume Writing for Geoscientists: A Guide to Preparing and Using Your Resume.* The journal of the association, *Gaea* profiles the successes of women geoscientists and addresses the issues that concern women in geoscience careers. *Career Profiles,* a booklet of short biographies of women geoscientists, is also available.

Association for Women in Science
1200 New York Avenue, NW, Suite 650
Washington, DC 20005
202-326-8940
http://www.awis.org

AWIS is a national, professional organization for women in all scientific disciplines. It offers a number of publications, available to members and non-members for a fee. *AWIS Magazine* is published bimonthly. Other publications include *Mentoring Means Future Scientists,* a summary of AWIS first mentoring programs; *Cultivating Academic Careers: AWIS Project on Academic Climate; A Hand Up: Women Mentoring Women in Science;* and *Creating Tomorrow's Scientists: Models of Community Mentoring.*

Association of American Colleges
1818 R Street, NW
Washington, DC 20009
800-297-3775
http://www.aacu-edu.org

The association publishes a number of reports each year on the campus climate for female teachers and administrators, such as *On Campus With Women,* on women's leadership, the campus climate and the newest research about women. Order online or call for a brochure.

Additional Information

Association of American Colleges and Universities

Program on the Status and Education of Women
1818 R Street, NW
Washington, DC 20009-1604
202-387-3760
http://www.aacu-edu.org/initiatives/psew.html

The PSEW office of the AACU supports and disseminates research on women in higher education. Its series on women of color in postsecondary education includes *Asian Pacific American Women in Higher Education: Claiming Visibility and Voice; Black Women in Academe: Issues and Strategies;* and *Hispanic Women: Making Their Presence on Campus Less Tenuous.*

Association of American Medical Colleges

Women in Medicine Program
2450 N Street, NW
Washington, DC 20037-1126
202-828-0521
http://www.aamc.org

AAMC's Women in Medicine program compiles information on women working in medicine, especially in the academic realm. In addition to its newsletter, *Women in Medicine Update,* it publishes *Enhancing the Environment for Women in Academic Medicine: Resources and Pathways,* based on periodic surveys, and the annual *Women in Medicine Statistics.*

Association of Women in Math

4114 Computer and Space Sciences Building
University of Maryland
College Park, MD 20742-2461
301-405-7892
http://www.awm-math.org

AWM publishes *Careers That Count: Opportunities in Mathematical Sciences.* Copies are available for $1.50 by mail or in its entirety on the Web site.

Aviation for Women

Women in Aviation International
3647 S.R. 503 S
West Alexandria, OH 45381
937-839-4647
http://www.wiai.org

Aviation for Women is a bimonthly magazine published by Women in Aviation International. It is the official publication of the organization, which encourages women to seek careers in aviation, but is available to non-members as well.

Business and Professional Women

BPW Foundation
Publications Order
2012 Massachusetts Avenue, NW
Washington, DC 20036
202-293-1200
http://www.bpwusa.org

BPW, one of the largest national organizations for working women, has several publications available. An order form is available on the Web site, or by calling the organization.

Chicago Women in Trades

220 South Ashland Avenue, Suite 101
Chicago, IL 60607-1805
312-942-1444

Chicago Women in Trades publishes *Tools for Success,* a manual for tradeswomen, plumbers, carpenters, electricians, ironworkers, laborers, and other women working in nontraditional fields. It provides practical suggestions to help women survive and thrive as they go about their daily work. There are chapters on working in a traditionally male environment, sexual harassment, and getting hired in the trades.

Colorado Women's Business Directory

6860 South Yosemite Court, Suite 200
Englewood, CO 80112
303-221-4929

Call or write for more information on this publication.

Committee on the Status of Women in Physics

American Physical Society
1 Physics Ellipse
College Park, MD 20740-3844
http://www.aps.org/educ/cswp/gazette.htm

The *Gazette* is the newsletter of the APS Committee on the Status of Women in Physics and is distributed free to members, physics department chairs, and others on request. Items featured include updates on CSWP activities, book reviews, statistical reports, and articles on increasing the participation of women and girls in science.

Corporate Woman Online

http://www.corporatewoman.com

Corporate Woman is an online magazine for female executives. A sampling of recent articles includes "Metro Atlanta Female Entrepreneurs Share Their Stories," "Financial Resources for Aspiring Female Entrepreneurs," and "Savvy Accounting Strategies: Buying vs. Leasing an Automobile."

Empowering Women in Sports

Feminist Majority Foundation—Publications Department
1600 Wilson Boulevard, Suite 801
Arlington, VA 22209
703-522-2214

Empowering Women in Sports is a report on inequities in athletic funding that also features profiles of women in sports and strategies for change. The book is geared toward parents, teachers, college students, and anyone interested in seeing women break through stereotypes.

Enterprising Women

I.E. Publishers, Inc.
3932 Via Valmonte
Palos Verdes, CA 90274
310-791-1020

Enterprising Women is written exclusively for women business owners. It reports on trends and statistics on women in business and features success profile interviews.

The Greater Philadelphia Women's Yellow Pages

PO Box 1002
Havertown, PA 19086
610-446-4747

The Greater Pittsburgh Women's Yellow Pages

1516 Fifth Avenue
Pittsburgh, PA 15219-5106
412-391-8208

International Alliance for Women in Music

IAWM Administrative Office
Department of Music
422 South 11th Street, Room 209
Indiana, PA 15705-7918
724-357-7918
http://music.acu.edu/www.iawm/home.html

The International Alliance of Women in Music publishes the *IAWM Journal,* and *Women and Music: A Journal of Gender and Culture.* Both publications are available for subscription or purchase by nonmembers. Visit the IAWM Web site or call to subscribe.

International Association of Women Police

IAWP Administrative Assistant
Rural Route 1, Box 149
Deer Isle, ME 04627
http://www.iawp.org

IAWP publishes *Women Police,* which includes information on law enforcement issues from around the world, as well as articles on issues specific to women officers.

International Women Pilots

The Ninety-Nines
4300 Amelia Earhart Road
Oklahoma City, OK 73159
800-994-1929
http://www.ninety-nines.org

International Women Pilots is the official publication of the Ninety-Nines and is published bi-monthly. The price of a yearly subscription is

Additional Information

included in membership dues. Non-members may subscribe for a fee.

Introduction to Non-Traditional Employment for Women

Project for Homemakers in Arizona Seeking Employment
1230 North Park Avenue
Tucson, AZ 85721
520-621-3902

This manual is published as a project of PHASE for those interested in incorporating non-traditional information into their programs, work settings, etc. The manual focuses on recruitment, assessment, training, and retention. Call or write for information.

Leadership Conference on Women Religious

8808 Cameron Street
Silver Spring, MD 20910-4113
301-588-4955
http://www.lcwr.org

LCWR is an organization of Catholic sisters who are leaders of their religious institutes (orders) in the United States. Several books and periodicals concerning women's involvement in the church, spiritually and professionally, are available for purchase.

Linguistic Society of America

Committee on the Status of Women in Linguistics
1325 18th Street, NW, Suite 211
Washington, DC 20036

COSWL seeks to help monitor and improve the status of women in linguistics. Its publications include *The Cornell Lectures: Women in the Linguistics Profession* and *The COSWL Collection of Language and Gender Syllabi.*

Minerva Center

20 Granada Road
Pasadena, MD 21122-2708
410-437-5379
http://www.minervacenter.com

The Minerva Center is an educational and research corporation for the study of women in war and the military. The center publishes two periodicals. *MINERVA: Quarterly Report on Women and the Military* carries articles by historians, sociologists, and political scientists, as well as autobiographies and bibliographies. *Minerva's Bulletin Board* is a news magazine focusing on American servicewomen and women veterans, but including news relating to women and the military from all parts of the world.

National Association for Female Executives

135 West 50th Street, Suite 16
New York, NY 10020-1201
800-634-6233
http://www.nafe.org

NAFE is among the nation's largest business-women's organizations, with more than 150,000 members. The monthly *Executive Female* is free to members and available by subscription. Regular features include Capitol Report and tips on business, money, technology, and management, and updates on NAFE events.

National Association of Girls and Women in Sport

1900 Association Drive
Reston, VA 20191-1599
703-476-3450
http://www.aahperd.org/nagws/nagws-main.html

The association issues several publications useful to women working in sports and student athletes, including titles such as *Going Forth: Women's Leadership Issues in Higher Education and Physical Education, The NAGWS Internship Guide, Maximize Your Performance Now: Pre-Event Meals,* and rulebooks and scorebooks for various sports. To order by phone, call 800-321-0789 or order from the Web site.

National Association of Women in Education

1325 18th Street, NW, Suite 210
Washington, DC 20036
202-659-9330
http://www.nawe.org

NAWE seeks to advance and support women working in higher education professions. NAWE publications are available at a discount to members. *Initiatives-The Journal of NAWE* is devoted to research and scholarship about women. *About Women on Campus* reports on issues and legislation that impact women in higher education. *Women in Higher Education* is a monthly newsletter with news about the higher education field as it relates to women.

National Center for Women and Retirement Research

Southampton College
Long Island University
Southampton, NY 11968
800-426-7386

The National Center for Women and Retirement Research is a university-based life planning center for women. It publishes handbooks, videos, and audiotapes aimed at helping women live independent and secure lives as they grow older. Titles available include *Looking Ahead to Your Financial Future; Women and Divorce: Turning Your Life Around; Employment and Retirement Issues for Women;* and *Social and Emotional Issues for Midlife Women.*

National Council for Research on Women

11 Hanover Square
New York, NY 10005
212-785-7335
http://www.ncrw.org

NCRW is an alliance of women's research centers. It issues books, periodicals, and reports of interest to women. *IQ: Women and Girls in Science, Math and Engineering* considers the experience of women in the sciences today with an overview of recent debates, funding, and opportunities and obstacles. *IQ* is a periodic publication that considers different career

issues. Its directory series includes *Opportunities for Research and Study,* a list of grants, fellowships, and internships offered by NCRW members; *International Research Centers for Women; A Directory of Women's Guides to Federal Funding Opportunities;* and *A Directory of Women's Media.* An order form is available online.

National Directory of College Athletics, Women's Edition

Collegiate Directories, Inc.
P.O. Box 450640
Cleveland, OH 44145-0611
440-835-1172
http://www.collegiatedirectories.com

This directory lists all senior and junior colleges that compete in intercollegiate athletics, with contact information, administrators, coaches, assistants, affiliation, conference, enrollment, and facility information also listed.

National Directory of Women of Color Organizations and Projects

Women of Color Resource Center
2288 Fulton Street, Suite 103
Berkeley, CA 94704-1449
510-848-9272
http://www.coloredgirls.org

The Women of Color Resource Center publishes *The National Directory of Women of Color Organizations and Projects.* The directory is available for purchase as a book, on disk, or as mailing labels. More than 250 organizations and contact information are included. Visit the Web site for an index of organizations, and an order form.

National Organization for Women Legal Defense and Education Fund

395 Hudson Street
New York, NY 10014
212-925-6635
http://www.nowldef.org

The National Organization for Women Legal Defense Fund is largely a social advocacy organization, but also offers some career-oriented

Additional Information

resources. One publication on workplace issues is the *Manual for Survival for Women in Nontraditional Employment,* which provides information on legal issues, securing apprenticeships, and resolving problems.

National Partnership for Women and Families

1875 Connecticut Avenue, NW, Suite 710
Washington, DC 20009
202-986-2600
http://www.nationalpartnership.org

The National Partnership for Women and Families is a nonprofit organization that promotes fairness in the workplace, quality health care, and policies that help women balance the demands of family and career. It issues several pamphlets and fact sheets on workplace issues, such as *Guide to the Family and Medical Leave Act: Questions and Answers; Infertility and Adoption: How the Family and Medical Leave Act Can Help;* and *Guide to HIPAA: What the Health Insurance Reform Law Means to Women and Their Families.* Many publications are downloadable from the Web site. Single copies are generally free by mail request.

National Women's Studies Association

University of Maryland
7100 Baltimore Boulevard, Suite 500
College Park, MD 20740
301-403-0525
http://www.nwsa.org

NWSA supports and promotes feminist/womanist teaching, learning, research, and professional and community service. It offers publications such as the *Guide to Graduate Work in Women's Studies* and *National Report on the Women's Studies Major.*

New Ways to Work

785 Market Street, Suite 950
San Francisco, CA 94103
http://www.nww.org

New Ways to Work offers seminars and publications that help workers reshape the workplace.

Some of the titles offered for purchase include *Flexible Work Arrangements: Guidelines for Managers and Employees, Creating a Flexible Workplace: How to Select and Manage Alternative Work Options,* and *Flexibility: Compelling Strategies for a Competitive Workplace.*

9 to 5, National Association of Working Women

231 West Wisconsin Avenue, Suite 900
Milwaukee, WI 53203-2308
414-274-0925
http://www.9to5naww.qpg.com

This national organization publishes a number of fact sheets and pamphlets of interest to working women, especially office workers. *High Performance Office Work: Improving Jobs and Productivity* is an overview with case studies of clerical job redesign. *The 9 to 5 Guide to Combating Sexual Harassment* gives step-by-step advice on what to do if you are harassed, and information for companies. *9 to 5 Fact Sheets on Office Health and Safety* is a series of seven fact sheets on preventing office injuries. There is a fee for most publications.

Onyx Woman

Jackson Publishing
2301 Fairlawn Street
Pittsburgh, PA 15221
http://www.littleafrica.com/onyxwoman/
business.html

Onyx Woman is a business and career development magazine for women of color. Some articles are posted online, but the complete product is a quarterly, hard-copy publication. A sampling of articles includes "Successful Entrepreneurs," "Black Business Resources," and "Can Temping Work for You?"

Packaging Horizons

Kennesaw, GA
770-924-3563
http://www2.packaginghorizonsmag.com

Packaging Horizons is the official publication of Women in Packaging and is also available by subscription to non-members. It seeks to change stereotypes and raise awareness and visibility of women and minorities in the packaging industry and industry in general.

Preparing to Lead: The College Women's Guide to Internships and Other Public Policy Learning Opportunities in Washington, DC

Public Leadership Education Network
Book Orders
1001 Connecticut Avenue, NW, Suite 900
Washington, DC 20036
202-872-1585

Preparing to Lead was written by women students for women students. It provides descriptions of over 125 internships, seminars, fellowships, and other resources for women interested in public leadership. The book is available to students at a discounted price.

Project on the Status and Education of Women Mentoring Report

Association of American Colleges
1818 R Street, NW
Washington, DC 20009
800-297-3775

Academic Mentoring for Women Students and Faculty: A New Look at an Old Way to Get Ahead is a project on the AACU's Status and Education of Women.

The Real Deal on Telecommuting

Sienna Publishing
PMB 121
L 3350 San Pablo Avenue, A1
San Pablo, CA 94806

The Real Deal on Telecommuting was written by Rosalind Mays, a mother who grew frustrated at all of the work-at-home and telecommuting scams she encountered when looking for a work-at-home job. She offers a list of work-at-home scams, tips on detecting scams, four ways to find a telecommuting job, and information on freelance contract jobs.

SWE Magazine

Society of Women Engineers
120 Wall Street, 11th Floor
New York, NY 10005-3902
212-509-9577
http://www.swe.org

SWE, the magazine of the Society of Women Engineers, is published six times a year. Articles cover issues of interest to women engineers including career development, guidance for students, SWE activities, and technical themes. Subscriptions are included in membership or are available for $30 a year for non-members. Circulation is 15,000.

Today's Florida Business Women

PO Box 7223
St. Petersburg, FL 33734-7223
813-825-0018

Tools of the Trade: A Woman's Guide to the International Union of Operating Engineers

Wider Opportunities for Women
215-545-3700
http://www.workplacesolutions.org/about/pubs.htm

Tools of the Trade is a guide designed to assist current and potential female IUOE members to understand and address workplace issues as they relate to tasks performed by operating engineers.

U.S. Department of Labor Women's Bureau

200 Constitution Avenue, SW, Room S-3311
Washington, DC 20210
202-219-6652
http://www.dol.gov/dol/wb/

The Department of Labor's Women's Bureau issues several publications on working women's rights and workplace statistics. Single copies are free. Fact sheets offered include *Women Who Maintain Families, Nontraditional Occupations for Women, Hot Jobs for the 21st Century,* and others. *Don't Work in the Dark* is a series of brochures on topics such as pregnancy discrimination, Family and Medical Leave Act, and age

Additional Information

discrimination. *Office Automation Impact on Women* discusses quality of work, training, retraining, and home-based work for clerical workers.

Wellesley Centers for Women

Publications Office
106 Central Street
Wellesley, MA 02481
781-283-2500
http://www.wellesley.edu/WCW/index.html

The Wellesley Centers for Women (Center for Research on Women and Stone Center) publish research annually in a variety of areas of interest to women, including careers, employment, and leadership. Examples of publications available are *Women in Corporate Leadership: Reviewing the Current Research, Women in Management Today,* and *Corporate Policy and Women at the Top.* An order form is available online or call to request a catalog.

Woman Engineer

Equal Opportunity Publications
1160 East Jericho Turnpike, Suite 200
Huntingon, NY 11743
http://www.eop.com/mag-we.html

Woman Engineer is a career guidance and recruitment magazine for women engineering, computer science, and information technology students and professionals. Subscriptions are free to qualified women engineers and students.

Woman Pilot

http://www.womanpilot.com

Woman Pilot magazine is a print magazine with highlights of the current and past issues on the Web site. The Web site also lists aviation resources and offers an online subscription form.

Womanet

643 West Crosstown
Kalamazoo, MI 49008
616-388-8831
http://www.womanbusiness.com/womanet.html

Women and Music: A Journal of Gender and Culture

Editor, Women in Music
Department of Music
B144 Academic Center, George Washington University
Washington, DC 20052
http://music.acu.edu/www/iawm/home.html

Women and Music, a publication of the International Alliance for Women in Music, is a journal of scholarship about women, gender, and music of varied disciplines and approaches.

Women and Politics

c/o Haworth Press, Inc.
Political Science Department
State University of West Georgia
Carrollton, GA 30118
770-836-6504

Women and Politics is an academic journal that emphasizes women's place in the political spectrum. The journal encourages research and the development of theory on women's political participation and the impact of public policy on women's lives.

Women Basketball Coaches Association

WBCA
4646 Lawrenceville Highway
Lilburn, GA 30047-3620
770-279-8027
http://www.wbca.org

WBCA, a national association for women basketball coaches and players, has three regular publications. *Coaching Women's Basketball* is a coaching magazine devoted to girls' and women's basketball, with features, commentary, and advice. *At the Buzzer* is written by high school coaches for high school coaches. *Fast Break Alert* is a quarterly newsletter on NCAA legislation, including rule additions and changes.

Women Entrepreneurs' Directory of Northern California
PO Box 2246
McKinleyville, CA 99519
707-442-3115

Women in Engineering Programs and Advocate Network
1284 CIVL Building, Room G293
West Lafayette, IN 47907-1284
http://www.engr.washington.edu/
~wepan.member.html

WEPAN seeks to increase the pool of women engineers by improving engineering programs at U.S. institutions. It publishes *The WEPAN Data Book of Women in Engineering Programs,* with information on women's engineering programs throughout the country. The publication is geared toward teachers and counselors, and undergraduate and graduate students.

Women in Franchising
53 West Jackson Boulevard, Suite 205
Chicago, IL 60604
312-431-1467
http://www.infonews.com/franchise/wif

Women in Franchising is a national program that assists prospective women and minority entrepreneuers in all aspects of franchise business ownership. Self-study programs, such as the audio seminars, *Buying a Franchise: How to Make the Right Choice* and *Growing Your Business: The Franchise Option* are available. *The Business Review of a Franchise Offering Circular—the UFOC Review,* is an in-depth written evaluation tool.

Women in Higher Education
1934 Monroe Street
Madison, WI 53711-2027
608-251-3232
http://www.wihe.com

Women in Higher Education is a monthly source of news and views on issues affecting women on campus. Its circulation is over 12,000.

Women in International Security
c/o Center for International Security Studies
School of Public Affairs
University of Maryland-College Park
College Park, MD 20742
301-405-7612
http://www.puaf.umd.edu/wiis/

Women in International Security publishes directories to assist women, and men, seeking and currently working in international security. Available for purchase are *Internships in Foreign and Defense Policy* and *Fellowships in International Affairs: A Guide to Opportunities in the United States and Abroad.* Orders may be placed on the Web site.

Women in Medicine
FPIC Publishing, Inc.
ATTN: Amy Ryan, Publisher
1000 Riverside Avenue, Suite 800
Jacksonville, FL 32204
800-741-3742
http://www.womeninmedicine.com

Women in Medicine magazine features respected women physicians who practice as individuals, in multi-physician facilities, or in special hospital programs. Subscriptions are free to women physicians, hospital administrators, medical group and IPA physician administrators, and managed care organizations throughout the Southeast.

Women in Natural Resources
WINR
PO Box 3577
Moscow, ID 83843
208-885-6754
http://www.ets.uidaho.edu/winr/

Women in Natural Resources is a journal written by women at all levels in forestry, fisheries, wildlife, range, recreation, soils, and the environmental and social sciences as they relate to natural resources. Contributing authors are women in management, in federal and state agencies, on faculties, in labs, and in the business world.

Additional Information

Women in the Arts

National Museum of Women in the Arts
1250 New York Avenue, NW
Washington, DC 20005
800-222-7270
http://www.nmwa.org

Women in the Arts is a quarterly magazine
devoted to promoting the achievements of
women in the visual arts, as well as in music,
theater, dance, film, and literature. Membership
in the museum includes a subscription. Sample
issues are available online.

Women in the Fire Service, Inc.

PO Box 5446
Madison, WI 53705
608-233-4768
http://www.wfsi.org

Women in the Fire Service is an information
resource for women firefighters and the departments that employ them. Publications include
packets on recruitment and orientation for
women considering a career in fire service,
reproductive safety for fire personnel, and an
EMS information packet, for firefighters who
serve the dual role of firefighter/EMS.

Women Incorporated

333 South Grand Avenue, Suite 2450
Los Angeles, CA 90071
http://www.womeninc.org

Women Incorporated offers the following publications to assist women employed in business
and women business owners: *The Busy Woman's
Guide to Successful Business Plans* helps entrepreneurs create successful business plans; *The
Busy Woman's Guide to Self-Employment* is a
step-by-step guide to the entrepreneurial alternative; *The Busy Woman's Guide to Successful
Marketing Plans* is for women who need to create a comprehensive marketing strategy. All
publications may be purchased through the
Web site or by writing for a publications order
form and information.

Women of Note Quarterly

Vivace Press
PO Box 157
Readfield, WI 54969
800-543-5429
http://www.vivacepress.com/

Women of Note Quarterly is a journal of historical and contemporary women composers. The
audience includes libraries, musical scholars
and performers, those interested in women's
social and political issues, and all who enjoy
classical music.

Women Rainmakers' 101+ Best Marketing Tips

Law Practice Management Section
American Bar Association
750 North Lake Shore Drive
Chicago, IL 60611
800-285-2221
http://www.abanet.org/LPM/womenrainmakers.
html

Women Rainmakers' 101+ Best Marketing Tips
includes over 130 tips from women rainmakers
from diverse geographic locations and law practices, including corporate counsel, family law,
general practice, and litigation. Advice is on
developing a professional image, writing an
effective press release, advertising selec-
tively, lining up speaking engagements,
and other topics.

Women's Alliance for Theology, Ethics and Ritual

8035 13th Street
Silver Spring, MD 20910-4803
301-589-2509
http://www.his.com/~mhunt/

WATER is a feminist educational center and
national network for people seeking theological,
ethical, and liturgical development for and by
women. It publishes *The Woman-Church
Sourcebook,* a directory of women's church
groups, sample liturgies, and a how-to guide for
organizing local groups, and several other relevant publications.

Women's Business Directory

416 Oakmears Crescent
Virginia Beach, VA 23462
757-499-3543

Women's College Coalition

125 Michigan Avenue, NE
Washington, DC 20017
202-234-0443
http://www.womenscolleges.org

The Women's College Coalition offers publications that may assist women considering a woman's college. *Advantages of Women's Colleges: A Compilation of Facts* and *Women's College Coalition Membership Directory* are available for purchase. The Web site also provides information on the benefits of women's colleges.

Women's Economic Network

870 Market Street, Suite 1257
San Francisco, CA 94102
415-281-3225

The Women's Economic Network, a regional organization that supports women's economic independence, publishes *Freelancing in the San Francisco Bay Area: A Resource Guide for Artist, Writers, and Photographers.*

Women's Exchange

PO Box 660824
Birmingham, AL 35266-0824
205-967-0085

Women's Exchange publishes a regional women's yellow pages.

Women's History Review

Triangle Journals, Ltd.
PO Box 65
Wallingford, Oxford, UK OX10 0YG
44-1491-838-052
http://www.triangle.co.uk/whr/index.htm

Women's History Review is a major international journal that aims to provide a forum for the publication of new scholarly articles in the rapidly expanding field of women's history. The journal publishes contributions from a range of disciplines that further feminist knowledge and debate about women and/or gender relations in history. The journal is published quarterly.

Women's Information Directory

Gale Research Company
27500 Drake Road
Farmington, MI 48331
248-699-4253
http://www.gale.com

Women's Information Directory guides users to a range of information sources for and about women. Information is arranged under chapter headings such as women's centers, national associations, government agencies, publications, and more. Gale also publishes other women-focused books, such as *Notable Black American Women, Notable Hispanic American Women, Notable Women Scientists,* and *Women of Achievement.*

Women's Institute for a Secure Retirement

1201 Pennsylvania Avenue, NW, Suite 619
Washington, DC 20004
http://www.wiser.heinz.org

WISER works to expand retirement planning education and enable women to make informed decisions about their finances. Publications include a newsletter, on topics such as social security, long-term care, and divorce, available to those who join. Other publications are also available to the general public, such as *What Every Woman Needs to Know About Money and Retirement.*

Women's Institute for Financial Education

13569 Tiverton Road
San Diego, CA 92130
619-792-0524
http://www.wife.org

WIFE informs women about investing, money management, and retirement through seminars, workshops, and publications. Books available for purchase include *Our Money, Our Selves: Money Management for Each Stage of A Woman's*

Additional Information

Life, Your Next Fifty Years: A Completely New Way to Look at How, When, and If You Should Retire, and *The Way to Save: A 10-Step Blueprint for Lifetime Security.*

Women's Resource and Business Directory

10310 Main Street, Suite 110
Fairfax, VA 22030
703-764-0303

Women's Resource and Yellow Pages

3104 O Street, Suite 255
Sacramento, CA 95816
916-452-3264
http://www.workingwoman.com

Women's Resource Directory/Women's Yellow Pages

The Women's Resource Directory
PO Box 66796
Houston, TX 77266
281-242-0908
http://www.ghgcorp.com/wordweb

The Yellow Pages is an international directory of women in business. The Women's Online Resource Directory (WORD) seeks to promote the economic health of women, with a motto of "Buy it from a woman, for a change." It provides links and contacts for information on starting your own business, and Business Digest, an online publication.

Women's Sports Foundation

Publications
Eisenhower Park
East Meadow, NY 11554
800-227-3988
http://www.womenssportsfoundation.org

Many publications of interest to young women athletes, parents, program administrators, and coaches of women's sports are available from the Women's Sports Foundation. Guides available for a minimal charge include *A Parent's Guide to Girls' Sports, The Women's Sports Foundation College Athletic Scholarship Guide, Sports in the Lives of Urban Girls: A Resource Manual, Playing Fair: A Guide to Title IX, Sports*

Injury Concerns and the Female Athlete, The Balancing Act: A Woman's Guide to Sports and Fitness, and *Go Get Fit: A Woman's Guide to Finding the Right Sport.* Expert packets include an overview, articles, references, and resources. Packets available for a minimal charge include Businesswomen and Golf, Creating Gender Neutral Coaches' Employment and Compensation, Drug Use, General Fitness, Images and Words in Women's Sports, and Sport Psychology. Videotapes on careers for women in sports are also available. Contact the foundation for cost and ordering information.

Women's Studies Quarterly

Feminist Press
365 Fifth Avenue, Fifth Floor
New York, NY 10016
212-817-7915
http://www.feministpress.org

Women's Studies Quarterly is an educational project of the Feminist Press. It is geared for teachers of women's studies and program administrators with classroom aids such as course syllabi, discussions of strategies for teaching, and bibliographies.

Women's Yellow Pages of Greater St. Louis

222 South Meramec, Suite 203
St. Louis, MO 63103
314-725-1452
http://www.wypstlouis.com

Women's Yellow Pages of the Gulf Coast

PO Box 6021
Mobile, AL 36660
334-660-2725
http://www.gulfcoastwomen.com

Women'Sports Wire

409 Utica, Suite D-36
Huntington Beach, CA 92648
714-960-0411
http://www.womensportswire.com

Women'Sports Wire serves as a national clearinghouse for women's sports news and information. It publishes a business edition and an employment edition. Information is compiled from women's sports organizations, corporations, public relations, and marketing firms. The business edition covers areas such as corporate sponsorship, new business development, and marketing opportunities. The employment edition covers funding and job opportunities, and professional development information.

Working Mother

135 West 50th Street
New York, NY 10020
800-234-9675
http://www.workingmother.com

Working Mother and *Working Woman* are published by MacDonald Communications. Articles cover a range of topics including child care, work flexibility, school issues, and innovative approaches to the challenges of work and motherhood. The 800 number is for subscriptions. To contact the offices, call 212-445-6100

Yellow Pages of Metro Chicago and Springfield

Women in Business Yellow Pages
47 West Division Street, Suite 260
Chicago, IL 60610
312-294-6300

Women's Research/Studies

Many U.S. colleges and other institutions now offer Women's History/Research programs and resources. Umbrella organizations such the National Women's History Project, National Council for Research on Women, and National Women's Studies Association maintain lists of member organizations across the country and can direct you to resources in your area; there are women's history/research resources in all 50 states. Contact information for members programs are listed in this section.

Adirondack Women in History

5 Middle Road, PO Box 565
Willsboro, NY 12996
518-963-7504

Agnes Scott College

Women's Studies Program
141 East College Avenue
Decatur, GA 30030
404-471-5039
http://www.agnesscott.edu

Albion College

Anna Howard Shaw Center for Women's Studies
611 East Porter Street
Albion, MI 49224
517-629-0535
http://www.albion.edu/fac/womn

Alfred University

Women's Studies Program
Saxon Drive
Alfred, NY 14802
607-871-2215

American Historical Association

Women and Minorities
400 A Street, SE
Washington, DC 20003
202-544-2422
http://www.theaha.org

Additional Information

Anne Arundel Community College
Women's Studies Program
101 College Parkway
Arnold, MD 21012
410-541-2808

Appalachian State University
Women's Studies Program
B-2 East Hall
Boone, NC 28608
828-262-7603

Arizona State University
Women's Studies Program
PO Box 873404
Tempe, AZ 85287-3404
602-965-2358

Arizona State University West
Women's Studies Department
4701 West Thunderbird Road
Glendale, AZ 85306
602-543-3300

Atlanta-Fulton Public Library
Auburn Avenue Research Library
101 Auburn Avenue, NE
Atlanta, GA 30303-2502

Augsburg College
Women's Studies
2211 Riverside Avenue
Minneapolis, MN 55454
612-330-1193

Augustana College
Women's Studies Program
639 38th Street
Rock Island, IL 61201
309-794-7362

Avila College
Women's Studies Program
11901 Wornall Road
Kansas City, MO 64145
816-942-8400

Barnard College
Barnard Center for Research on Women
3309 Broadway
Room 101, Barnard Hall
New York, NY 10027-6598
212-854-2067
http://www.barnard.columbia.edu/learning.html

Bates College
Women's Studies
111 Bardwell Street
Lewiston, ME 04240
207-784-8317

Beloit College
Women's Studies Program
700 College Street
Beloit, WI 53511
608-363-2680
http://www.beloit.edu/~academic/majors/ws/l
ws.html

Benzie Area Women's History Project
737 Hill Street
Beulah, MI 49176
616-882-4389

Binghamton University
Women's Studies Program
LN-1105, PO Box 6000
Binghamton, NY 13902-6000
607-777-2815

Boston University
Women's Studies Program
226 Bay State Road
Boston, MA 02215
617-353-3308
http://www.bu.edu/womenstudies

Boston Women's Health Book Collective
240 A Elm Street
Somerville, MA 02144-0192
617-625-0277

Bowdoin College
Women's Studies Program
7100 College Station
Brunswick, ME 04011-8471
207-725-3834

Bridgewater State College
Women's Studies
Hart Hall
Bridgewater, MA 02325
508-697-1389

Broward County Women's History Coalition
1350 East Sunrise Boulevard, 114
Fort Lauderdale, FL 33304
954-467-2999

Brown University
Pembroke Center for Teaching and Research on Women
Box 1958
Providence, RI 02912
401-863-2643

Butte Women's Labor History Project
Butte Silver Bow Public Archives
Box 81
Butte, MT 59703

California Polytechnic State University
Women's Studies
San Luis Obispo, CA 93407
805-756-1525

California State University, Dominguez Hills
Women's Studies
SBS B232
1000 Victor Street
Carson, CA 90747
310-243-3037

California State University, Fresno
Women's Studies
5340 North Campus Drive
m/s 5578
Fresno, CA 93740-8019
559-278-2958

California State University, Long Beach
Women's Studies Program
1250 Bellflower Road
Long Beach, CA 90840-1603
562-985-4839
http://www.sculb.edu/depts/womens-studies/

California State University, Northridge
Women's Studies Department
Northridge, CA 91330-8251
818-677-3110

California State University, San Marcos
Women's Studies Program
San Marcos, CA 92096
760-750-4114

California State University, Stanislaus
Women's Studies
801 West Monte Vista Avenue
Turlock, CA 95382
209-667-3682
http://www.csustan.edu/ppa/jjpolitics

Casper College
Women's Studies Program
125 College Drive
Casper, WY 82601

Center for Advanced Feminist Studies
496 Ford Hall
Minneapolis, MN 55406
612-624-6310
http://www.cla.umn.edu/cafs

Center for Policy Alternatives
Women's Policy and Programs
1875 Connecticut Avenue, NW, Suite 710
Washington, DC 20009
202-387-6030
http://www.cpfa.org

Center for Women Policy Studies
1211 Connecticut Avenue, NW, Suite 312
Washington, DC 20036
202-872-1770
http://www.centerwomenpolicy.org

Additional Information

Center for Women's Studies and Gender Research
PO Box 117352
Gainesville, FL 32611-7352
352-392-3365
http://web.wst.ufl.edu

Central Connecticut State University
Women's Studies Program
New Britain, CT 06050-4010
860-832-2809

Central Washington University
Women's Studies Program
400 East Eighth
Ellensburg, WA 98296
509-963-1134

Century College
Women's Studies Program
3300 Century Avenue, N
White Bear Lake, MN 55110
651-779-3425

Chatham College
Woodland Road
Pittsburgh, PA 15232

Chicago Area Women's History Conference
400 East Randolph, 3910
Chicago, IL 60601
312-938-0990

City Colleges of Chicago
30 East Lake Street
Chicago, IL 60601

City University of New York
Center for the Study of Women and Society
365 Fifth Avenue
New York, NY 10016
212-642-2295

City University of New York Graduate School and University Center
Center for the Study of Women and Society
25 West 43rd Street, Room 410
New York, NY 10036-8099
212-642-2954

Claremont Graduate School
Women's Studies in Religion
Claremont, CA 91761
909-607-3214

Clark University
Women's Studies
950 Main Street
Worcester, MA 01610
508-793-7358

Cleveland State University
Women's Comprehensive Program
2121 Euclid Avenue
363 University Center
Cleveland, OH 44115
216-687-4674

Colby College
Women's Studies Program
4720 Mayflower Hill
Waterville, ME 04901-8847
207-872-3416
http://www.colby.edu/womens.studies/

College of New Jersey
Women and Gender Studies
PO Box 7718
Ewing, NJ 08628-0718
609-771-2539
http://www.tcnj.edu/~wgst/index.html

College of St. Catherine
Abigail Quigley McCarthy Center for Women
2004 Randolph Avenue
St. Paul, MN 55105
651-690-6783

College of St. Mary Library
1901 South 72nd Street
Omaha, NE 68124-2301

College of the Holy Cross
Women's Studies Program
1 College Street, POB 63A
Worcester, MA 01610
508-793-2703

College of William and Mary
Women's Studies Program
PO Box 8795
Williamsborg, VA 23187-8795
757-221-2453
http://www.wm.edu/fas/ws

Colorado Coalition for Women's History
PO Box 673
1200 Madison
Denver, CO 80206
303-377-6315

Colorado College
14 E. Cache La Poudre Street
Colorado Springs, CO

Colorado State University
Women's Studies Graduate Program
112 Student Services
Fort Collins, CO 80523-8200
970-491-6384
http://www.colostate.edu/Depts/Grad/wmpr.html

Columbia University
Institute for Research on Women and Gender
736 Schermerhorn Extension
New York, NY 10027
212-854-3277
http://www.stanford.edu/group/IRWG/

Community Coalition for Women's History
351 NW Fifth Street
Miami, FL 33128-1615
305-377-9922

Cornell University
Institute on Women and Work
New York School of Industrial and Labor Relations
16 East 34th Street, Fourth Floor
New York, NY 10016
212-340-2800

Dartmouth College
Women's Studies Program
6038 Carpenter Hall, Room 2
Hanover, NH 03755-3570
603-646-2722

Daughters of Hawaii
2913 Pali Highway
Honolulu, HI 96817

Denison University
Women's Studies Program
Granville, OH 43023
740-587-6536

DePaul University
Women's Studies
2320 North Kenmore Avenue
Chicago, IL 60614-3250
773-325-4500

DePauw University
Women's Studies
109 Asbury Hall
Greencastle, IN 46135
765-658-4505

Dickinson College
Women's Studies
Carlisle, PA 17013
717-245-1869

Drake University
Women's Studies Program
2507 University Avenue
Des Moines, IA 50311
515-271-3563

Duke University
Women's Center
126 Few Fed, Box 90920
Durham, NC 27708-0920
919-684-3897
http://www.wc.stuaff.duke.edu

East Stroudsburg University
Women's Studies
Stroudsburg, PA 18301
717-422-3472

Additional Information

East Tennessee State University
Women's Studies
Department of Sociology and Anthropology
Johnson City, TN 37614-0644
423-439-7056

Eastern Connecticut State University
Women's Studies Program
Willimantic, CT 06226
860-465-4522

Edgewood College
855 Woodrow Street
Madison, WI 53711

Elizabeth Cady Stanton Foundation
PO Box 603
Seneca Falls, NY 13148

Elon College
Women's Studies/Gender Studies Program
2172 Campus Box
Elon College, NC 27244
336-584-2358

Emory University
Institute for Women's Studies
S301 Callaway Center
537 Kilgo Circle
Atlanta, GA 30322
404-727-0096
http://www.emory.edu/womens_studies/

Emporia State University
Ethnic/Gender Studies Program
1200 Commercial
Emporia, KS 66801
316-341-5661

Equity Policy Center
2759 NW Pettygrove Street
Portland, OR 97219
503-228-9486
http://www.netcome/~gsummer/epoch.html

Feminist Majority Foundation
1600 Wilson Boulevard, Suite 801
Arlington, VA 22209
703-522-2214
http://www.feminist.org

The Feminist Press at City University of New York
Convent Avenue at 138th Street
New York, NY 10031
212-650-8890
http://www.feministpress.org

Five College Women's Studies Research Center
Mount Holyoke College
Dickinson House
South Hadley, MA 01075-1485
413-538-2527
http://www.persephone.hampshire.edu/~fcwsrc/

Florida Atlantic University
The Women's Center
777 Glades Road
Boca Raton, FL 33431
561-297-3865

Florida State University
Women's Studies Program, 2205
Tallahassee, FL 32306-2205

Fordham College at Lincoln Center
Women's Studies Program
New York, NY 10023-7472
212-636-6394

Foundation for Women's Resources
3500 Jefferson Street, Suite 210
Austin, TX 76102
512-459-1167

George Mason University
4400 University Drive
MSN 3136
Fairfax, VA 22030
703-993-2896

George Washington University
Women's Studies Program
2201 G Street, NW
Funger 5061
Washington, DC 20052
202-994-6942
http://www.gwu.edu/~wstu/

Georgetown University
Women's Studies Program
Box 571038
Washington, DC 20057-1038
202-687-3117

Georgia College and State University
Women's Studies
Campus Box 44
Milledgeville, GA 31061
912-445-4581

Georgia State University
Women's Studies Institute
University Plaza
Atlanta, GA 30303-3083
404-651-4633

Gettysburg College
Campus Box 2450
Gettysburg, PA 17325
717-337-6788

Girls Incorporated National Resource Center
441 West Michigan Street
Indianapolis, IN 46202-3233
317-634-7546
http://www.girlsinc.org

Goucher College
Women's Studies
1021 Dulaney Valley Road
Towson, MD 21204
410-337-6125

Greater Grand Rapids Women's History Council
143 Bostwick, NE, Room 57-G2
Grand Rapids, MI 49503-3295
616-234-3603

Gustavus Adolphus College
Women's Studies
800 West College Avenue
St. Peter, MN 56082

Hamline University
Upper Midwest Women's History Center
1536 Hewitt Avenue
St. Louis Park, MN 55104-1284
612-644-1727

Hofstra University
History Department
104 Hager Hall
Hempstead, NY 11549
516-463-5604

Holley House Museum
PO Box 553
Salisbury, CT 06068
860-453-2878

Hope College
Women's Studies Program
Holland, MI 49423
616-395-7724

Howard University
African-American Women's Institute
Department of Sociology/Anthropology
PO Box 987
Washington, DC 20059
202-806-6853

Humboldt State University
Women's Studies Program
Arcata, CA 95521
707-826-4925

Hunter College
Center for the Study of Family Policy
Room E1209 C-East
695 Park Avenue
New York, NY 10021
212-772-4450

Illinois Wesleyan University
Women's Studies Program
Bloomington, IL 61702-2900
309-556-3677

Additional Information

Immaculate Heart College Center
425 Shatto Place, Suite 401
Los Angeles, CA 90020-1712
213-386-3116
http://www.ihcc.edu

Indiana Purdue
Women's Studies Program
IPFW, 2101 East Coliseum Boulevard
Fort Wayne, IN 46805

Indiana University, South Bend
Women's Studies Program
PO Box 7111
South Bend, IN 46634
219-237-4308

International Center for Research on Women
1717 Massachusetts Avenue, NW, Suite 302
Washington, DC 20036
202-797-0007
http://www.icrw.org

International Museum of Women
PO Box 642370
San Francisco, CA 94164-2370
415-775-1366

International Women's Air and Space Museum
Room 165, Burke Lakefront Airport
Cleveland, OH 44114
212-623-1111
http://www.iwasm.org

Iowa State University
Women's Studies Program
349 Catt Hall
Ames, IA 50011-5104
515-294-9733
http://www.public.iastate.edu/~womenstu/
wsprogram.htm

Italian-American Women's History Project
3531 Kutztown Road
Laureldale, PA 19605
610-929-4463

Ithaca College
Women's Studies Program
Ithaca, NY 14850
607-274-1212

Jewish Women's Archive
68 Harvard Street
Brookline, MA 02143
617-232-2258
http://www.jwa.org

Jewish Women's Resource Center
9 East 69th Street
New York, NY 10021
212-535-5900

Kansas State University
Women's Studies Program
3 Leasure Hall
Manhattan, KS 66506-3505
785-532-5738

Kent State University
Project on the Study of Gender and Education
College of Education
405 White Hall
Kent, OH 44242
330-672-2178

Kenyon College
Women's and Gender Studies
Gambier, OH 43022
740-427-5289
http://www.kenyon.edu/depts/wmns/welcom.htm

Lafayette College
English Department
Women's Studies Coordinator
Easton, PA 18042
610-330-5238

Lehigh University
Women's Studies Program
9 West Packer Avenue
Bethlehem, PA 18105
610-758-3776

Lehman College Library
Acquisition Division, Serials Section
250 Bedford Park, Boulevard W
Bronx, NY 10468-1589

Louisiana State University
Women's and Gender Studies
238 Himes
Baton Rouge, LA 70803
225-488-4807
http://www2.artsci.lsu.edu/wgs

Loyola University
Women's Studies Program
6525 North Sheridan Road
Chicago, IL 60626
773-508-2934
http://www.luc.edu/dpets/women_stu

Loyola University at Chicago
Gannon Center for Women and Leadership
Sullivan 200
6525 North Sheridan Road
Chicago, IL 60626
773-508-8430
http://www.luc.edu/orgs/gannon

Loyola University Library
Serials Department, Box 198
6363 St. Charles Avenue
New Orleans, LA 70118

Mansfield University
Women's Studies Program
Belknap Hall
Mansfield, PA 16933
570-662-4581

Massachusetts College of Liberal Arts
Susan B. Anthony Women's Center
North Adams, MA 01247
413-662-5497

Massachusetts Institute of Technology
Women's Studies
14E-216
77 Massachusetts Avenue
Cambridge, MA 02139

Mercer University
College of Liberal Arts and Sciences
Department of Interdisciplinary Studies
Women's and Gender Studies
Macon, GA 31207
912-752-2359

Metropolitan State College
Institute for Women's Studies and Services
Campus Box 36
PO Box 173362
Denver, CO 173362
303-556-8441
http://www.clem.mscd.edu/~wms/

Metropolitan State University
730 Hennepin Avenue
Minneapolis, MN 55403-1897
612-341-7254

Miami University
The Women's Center
30 MacMillan Hall
Oxford, OH 45056
513-529-1510

Michigan State University
Women's Studies Program
301 Linton Hall
East Lansing, MI 48824-1044
517-432-1858

Michigan Women's History Center
213 West Main Street
Lansing, MI 48933
517-484-1990

Middle Tennesse State University
Women's Studies Program
PO Box 498 MTSU
Murfreesboro, TN 37132
615-898-5910
http://www.mtsu.edu/~womenstu

Middleburg College
Women's Resource Center
May Belle Chellis House
Middleburg, VT 05753
802-443-5937

Additional Information

Millersville University
Women's Studies Program
Millersville, PA 17551

Mills College
Women's Studies
5000 MacArthur Boulevard
Oakland, CA 94613
510-430-2233

Minneapolis Community and Technical College
Women's Studies
1501 Hennepin Avenue
Minneapolis, MN 55403
612-341-7045

Minnesota State University, Mankato
Women's Studies
Morris Hall 109
Mankato, MN 56001
507-389-2077

Mohawk Valley Women's History Project
20 Upper Woods Road
New Hartford, NY 13413
315-735-3742

Monmouth University
Gender Studies Department
West Long Branch, NJ 07764
732-571-3524

Moravian College
Women's Studies
Bethlehem, PA 18108
610-861-1563

Mount Holyoke College
Women's Studies Program
South Hadley, MA 01075

National Center on Women and Aging
Brandeis University
The Heller School
Mailstop 035
Waltham, MA 02454-9110
http://www.brandeis.edu/heller/national/ind.html

National Cowgirl Museum and Hall of Fame
111 West Fourth Street, 300
Fort Worth, TX 76102
817-336-4475

National Museum of Women's History
303 West Glendale Avenue
Alexandria, VA 22308
703-299-0552
http://www.nmwh.org

National Women's Hall of Fame
PO Box 335
Seneca Falls, NY 13148
315-568-2936

National Women's Studies Association
University of Maryland, College Park
7100 Baltimore Avenue, Suite 301
College Park, MD 20740
301-403-0525
http://www.nwsa.org

NAWE: Advancing Women in Higher Education
1325 18th Street, NW, Suite 210
Washington, DC 20036-6511
202-659-9330
http://www.nawe.org

Nevada Women's History Project
201 West Liberty Street, Suite 201
PO Box 50428
Reno, NV 89513
775-786-2335

New Jersey City University
2039 Kennedy Boulevard
Jersey City, NJ 07305
201-200-2221
http://ellserver3.njcu.edu/
courses.fisch.default.htm

Newcomb College Center for Research on Women
Tulane University
New Orleans, LA 70118-5683
504-865-5238
http://www.tulane.edu/~wc

North Carolina State University
2806 Hillsborough Street
Raleigh, NC 27695-7107
919-515-7995

Northern Arizona University
Women's Studies
Box 5695
Flagstaff, AZ 86011
520-523-3330

Northern Illinois University
Women's Studies
Reavis 103
DeKalb, IL 60115
815-753-1038

Northern Kentucky University
Women's Studies
Highland Heights, KY 41099
513-572-5550
http://www.nky.edu/~wms/

NOW Legal Defense and Education Fund
395 Hudson Street, 12th Floor
New York, NY 10014
212-925-6635

Oberlin College
Women's Studies
Rice 116
Oberlin, OH 44704
440-775-8907
http://www.oberlin/~wstudies/

Ohio State University
Center on Education and Training for Employment Sex Equity Library
1908 Kenny Road
Columbus, OH 43210
614-292-4353

Ohio State University
Department of Women's Studies
286 University Hall
230 North Oval Mall
Columbus, OH 43210-1311
614-292-1021
http://www.cohums.ohio-state.edu/wost/

Ohio Wesleyan University
Women's Studies
Sturges Hall
Delaware, OH 43015
740-368-3871

Old Dominion
Women's Studies
1 EHW 5101
Norfolk, VA 23823
757-683-3823

Pace University
Women's and Gender Studies
41 Park Row, 15th Floor
New York, NY 10038
212-346-1642

Pacific Lutheran University
Women's Studies
Tacoma, WA 98447
253-756-3173

Pacific University
Feminist Studies Program
Forest Grove, OR 97116-0669
503-359-2886

Penn State University
Women's Studies
12 Sparks Building
University Park, PA 16802
814-863-4025
http://www.psu.edu/womensstudies/

Penn State, Hazelton
Honors Program
Highacres
Hazelton, PA 18201-1291
717-450-3188

Additional Information

Pioneer Woman Museum
701 Monument Road
Ponca City, OK 74604
405-765-6108

Purdue University, Calumet
Women's Studies
Hammond, IN 46323
219-989-2256

Purdue University
Women's Studies Program
1361 LAEB
West Lafayette, IN 47907-1361
765-494-6295
http://www.sla.purdue.edu/womens-studies/

Quilters Hall of Fame
PO Box 681
Marion, IN 46952
765-496-6864

Quinnipiac
Women's Studies
Hamden, CT 06518
203-281-8703

Quinsigamond Community College
670 West Boylston Street
Worcester, MA 01606-2092
508-854-4290

Radcliffe College
Arthur and Elizabeth Schlesinger Library on the
History of Women in America
10 Garden Street
Cambridge, MA 02138
617-495-8647
http://www.radcliffe.edu/schles/index.html

Radcliffe College
Henry A. Murray Research Center
10 Garden Street
Cambridge, MA 02138
617-495-8140

Radcliffe College
Graduate Consortium in Women's Studies
6 Ash Street
Cambridge, MA 02138
617-496-3022

Radcliffe College
Mary Ingraham Bunting Institute
34 Concord Avenue
Cambridge, MA 02138
617-495-8212
http://www.radcliffe.edu/bunting/index.html

Regis College
235 Wellesley Street, Box 1068
Weston, MA 02193
781-768-7459

Richard Stockton College of New Jersey
Women's Studies
PO Box 195
Pomona, NJ 08240
609-652-4273
http://www.stockton.edu/~women/

Rider University
Women's Studies Program
2083 Lawrenceville Road
Lawrenceville, NJ 08648
609-895-5570

Rock County Women's History Committee
3205 North Crystal Springs Road
Janesville, WI 53545
608-756-2045

Rogue Valley Women's History Project
PO Box 674
Ashland, OR 97520

Russell Sage College
Helen Upton Women's Center
45 Ferry Street
Troy, NY 12180
518-244-2306

Rutgers University
Women's Studies Program
162 Riders Lane
New Brunswick, NJ 08901
732-932-9331

Rutgers University
Center for the American Woman and Politics
Eagleton Institute of Politics
191 Ryders Lane
New Brunswick, NJ 08901
732-932-9384
http://www.rci.rutgers.edu/~cawp/

Rutgers University
Center for Women's Global Leadership
Douglass College
160 Ryders Lane
New Brunswick, NJ 08901-8555
732-932-8782
http://www.rci.rutgers.edu/~cwgl/humanrights

St. Ambrose University
Women's Studies Program
Davenport, IA 52803
319-333-6100

St. Olaf College
Women's Studies Program
Northfield, MN 55057
507-646-3264

San Diego State University
Women's Studies Department
5500 Campanile Drive
San Diego, CA 92182-8138
619-594-2952
http://www.rohan.sdsu.edu/dept/wsweb/

Sarah Lawrence College
Women's History Program
Bronxville, NY 10708
518-244-2306

Scripps College
Intercollegiate Women's Studies Teaching and
Research Center
1030 Columbia Avenue
Claremont, CA 91711
909-621-8274

Seton Hall
Women's Studies Program
South Orange, NJ 07079

Seton Hill College
Women's Studies
Greensburg, PA 15601
724-830-1054

Shippensburg University
1871 Old Main Drive
Shippensburg, PA 17257
717-532-1264

Simmons College
African-American Women's Studies
300 The Fenway
Boston, MA 02115

Smith College
Women's Studies
Seelye Hall 412
Northampton, MA 01063

Smith College
Project on Women and Social Change
Seelye Hall, Room 210
Northampton, MA 01063
413-585-3591

Smith College
Sophia Smith Collection
Northampton, MA 01063
413-585-2978
http://www.smithcollege.edu/libraries/ssc

Sonoma State University
Women's and Gender Studies
1801 East Cotati Avenue
Rohnert Park, CA 94928
707-664-2840
http://www.sonoma.edu/WomenStudies

South Carolina State University
Association of Black Women Historians
c/o Department of History
Orangeburg, SC 29117
803-536-8672

Additional Information

South Dakota State University
Women's Studies Program
325 SCO Box 504
Brookings, SD 57007
605-688-4919

Southern Association of Women Historians
COE College, Department of History
Cedar Rapids, IA 52402
319-399-8572

Southern Connecticut State University
Women's Studies Program
501 Crescent Street
Morrill B-10
New Haven, CT 06515
203-392-2166

Southern Illinois University
Women's Studies Program
MC 6518
Carbondale, IL 62901
618-453-5141
http://www.siu.edu/women

Southern Illinois University at Edwardsville
Women's Studies
WMST Box 1350
Edwardsville, IL 62026
618-650-2185

Southern Methodist University
Women's Studies Program
317 Clements Hall
Dallas, TX 75275
214-768-3612

Southern Oregon University
Women's Studies Program
1250 Siskiyou Boulevard
Ashland, OR 97520
541-552-6750

Southwestern University
Women's Studies
Georgetown, TX 78626
512-863-1492

Spelman College
Women's Resource and Research Center
350 Spelman Lane, Box 115
Atlanta, GA 30314-4399

Stanford University
Institute for Research on Women and Gender
Serra House
Stanford, CA 94305-6905
650-723-1994
http://www.stanford.edu/group/IRWG/

State University College
Women's Studies
Ravine Parkway
Oneonta, NY 13820

State University of New York at Albany
Center for Women in Government
13 Western Avenue
Draper Hall, Room 302
Albany, NY 12222
518-442-3896

State University of New York at Albany
Institute for Research on Women
1400 Washington Avenue
Ten Broock 105
Albany, NY 12222
518-442-4995
http://irw.rutgers.edu

State University of New York at Brockport
Women's Studies
350 New Campus Drive
Brockport, NY 14420
716-395-5700

State University of New York at Buffalo
Institute for Research and Education on Women and Gender
Harriman Student Center, Room 102, Box M
Buffalo, NY 14214-3702
716-829-3451

State University of New York at Buffalo

Women's Studies Program
1010 Clemens Hall
Buffalo, NY 14260
716-645-2546

State University of New York at Fredonia

Women's Studies
E249 Thompson Hall
Fredonia, NY 14063
716-673-3158
http://www.fredonia.edu/womanstudies

State University of New York at New Paltz

Women's Studies Program
Southside 75-S Manheim Boulevard
New Paltz, NY 12561
914-257-7975
http://www.newpaltz.edu/wmnstudies

State University of New York at Plattsburgh

Women's Studies Program
Hawkins Hall, PSU
101 Broad Street
Plattsburgh, NY 12901
518-564-3002

State University of New York at Potsdam

Women's Studies Program
44 Pierreport Avenue
Potsdam, NY 13676
315-267-2026

Swarthmore College

Women's Studies Program
500 College Avenue
Swarthmore, PA 19081
610-328-7750
http://www.swarthmore.edu/humanities/women/

Temple University

Women's Studies Program
811 Anderson Hall
1114 West Berks Street
Philadelphia, PA 19122-6090
215-204-6954

Tennessee Women's Network

5632 Meadowcrest Lane
Nashville, TN 37209
615-356-3136

Texas A&M

Women's Studies Program
Mail Stop 4351
College Station, TX 77843-4351
409-845-7994

Texas Tech University

Women's Studies
PO Box 41162
Lubbock, TX 79409-1162
806-742-3001
http://www.hs.ttu.edu/womensstudies

Texas Woman's University

Library-Serials
Box 425528 TWU Station
Denton, TX 76204-5528

Towson State University

Institute for Teaching and Research on Women
8000 York Road
Towson, MD 21252
410-830-2334
http://www.towson.edu/itrow

Towson University

Women's Studies Program
Towson, MD 21252
410-830-2862
http://www.towson.edu/~pilardi/wmsthome.htm

Triangle Multicultural Women's History Project

605 Germaine Street
Apex, NC 27502
919-362-4436

Trinity College

Women's Studies Program
300 Summit Street
Hartford, CT 06106
860-297-2373

Additional Information

Tufts University
Women's Studies Program
111 Eaton Hall
Medford, MA 02155
617-627-2955
http://ase.tufts.edu/womenstudies

Tulane University
Center for Research on Women
200 Caroline Richardson
New Orleans, LA 70118
504-865-5238
http://www.tulane.edu/~wc

The Union Institute Center for Women
1710 Rhode Island Avenue, NW, Suite 1100
Washington, DC 20009-1146
202-496-1630
http://www.tui.edu/OSR/cfw.htm

University at Albany, State University of New York
Department of Women's Studies, SS341
Albany, NY 12222
518-442-4220

University of Akron
Women's Studies Program
204 Leigh Hall
Akron, OH 44325-6218
330-972-7008

University of Alabama—Birmingham
Women's Studies Program
1212 University Boulevard
Birmingham, AL
205-934-8685

University of Alaska—Anchorage
Women's Studies Program
3211 Providence Drive
Anchorage, AK 99508
907-786-4392

University of Arizona
Women's Studies
Communication 108
Tucson, AZ 85721
520-621-7338

University of Arizona
Southwest Institute for Research on Women
Communication 108
PO Box 210025
Tucson, AZ 85721
520-621-7338
http://w3.arizona.edu/~ws/newweb/sirow.html

University of California, Berkeley
Beatrice M. Bain Research Group
2539 Channing Way, Room 21
Berkeley, CA 94708
510-643-7172

University of California, Davis
University Library
Serial Records Section
Davis, CA 95616-5292

University of California, Davis
Consortium for Women and Research
1 Shields Avenue
Davis, CA 95616-8731
530-754-8851
http://www.aes.ucdavis.edu/outreach/profem/index.htm

University of California, Irvine
Women's Studies Program
212 Humanities Instructional Building
Irvine, CA 92697-2655
949-824-4234
http://www.hnet.uci.edu/WomenStudies

University of California, Los Angeles
Center for the Study of Women
405 Hilgard Avenue, 288 Kinsey Hall
Los Angeles, CA 90095-1504
310-825-0590
http://www.csw.ucla.edu/csw/webfro~1.htm

University of California, San Diego
Women's Studies/Critical Gender Studies
Mail Code 0106 UCSD
La Jolla, CA 92093-0106
619-534-3589

University of California, Santa Cruz
Women's Studies
180 Kresge College
Santa Cruz, CA 95064
831-459-4324
http://www.ucsc.edu/wst/index.html

University of Central Florida
Women's Studies Program
HFA 201H
Orlando, FL 32816
407-823-2269
http://pegasus.cc.ucf.edu/~womenst/

University of Cincinnati
Center for Women's Studies
Research and Resources Institute
PO Box 210164
Cincinnati, OH 45221-0164
513-556-6776

University of Colorado, Boulder
Women's Resource Center
Campus Box 207
Boulder, CO 80309-0207
303-492-1929

University of Connecticut
The Women's Center
Storrs, CT 06269-1118
860-486-4738

University of Dayton
Women's Studies Program
303 Zehler Hall
Dayton, OH 45469-1492
937-229-4285

University of Detroit Mercy
Women's Studies
PO Box 19900
Detroit, MI 48219-0900
313-993-3387

University of Houston
Women's Study Program
Houston, TX 77204-3784
713-743-3214

University of Illinois
Women's Studies
911 South Sixth
Champaign, IL 61820
217-333-2990

University of Illinois at Chicago
Women's Studies
MC 360
1007 West Harrison
Chicago, IL 60607

University of Illinois at Chicago
Center for Research on Women and Gender
MC 980
1640 West Roosevelt Road, Room 503
Chicago, IL 60608-6900
312-413-1924

University of Illinois at Springfield
Women's Studies Program
Shepherd Road, PO Box 19243
Springfield, IL 62794-9243

University of Illinois at Urbana-Champaign
Office of Women in International Development
320 International Studies Building, MC-480
910 South Fifth Street
Champaign, IL 61820
217-333-1994
http://www.uiuc.edu/providers/ips/wid.html

University of Kentucky
Women's Studies Program
915 Patterson Office Tower
Lexington, KY 40506-0027
606-257-1388

University of Louisville
Women's Studies Program
Louisville, KY 40292
502-852-8160

University of Maine
Women in the Curriculum
5728 Fernald Hall
Orono, ME 04469-5728
207-581-1228

Additional Information

University of Maine at Farmington
Women's Studies Program
37 High Street
Farmington, ME 04360
207-778-7387

University of Maryland, Baltimore County
Women's Studies
1000 Hilltop Circle
Baltimore, MD 21250
410-455-2001
http://www.umbc.edu/wmst/

University of Maryland, College Park
Women's Studies Program
2101 Woods Hall
College Park, MD 20742

University of Massachusetts, Amherst
Women's Studies Program
208 Bartlett Hall
Amherst, MA 02003-0530
413-545-1922
http://www.umass.edu/wost

University of Massachusetts, Dartmouth
Women's Studies
285 Old Westport Road
North Dartmouth, MA 02747-2300

University of Memphis
Center for Research on Women
Campus Box 526105
Memphis, TN 38152-6105
901-678-2770
http://www.people.memphis.edu/~intprogs/crow

University of Michigan
Women's Studies Program
234 West Hall
Ann Arbor, MI 48109-1092
734-763-2047

University of Michigan
Center for the Education of Women
330 East Liberty
Ann Arbor, MI 48104-2289
313-998-7240
http://www.umich.edu/~cew

University of Michigan
Institute for Research on Women and Gender
460 West Hall
Ann Arbor, MI 48109-1092
313-764-9537
http://www.stanford.edu/group/IRWG/

University of Michigan, Dearborn
Women's Studies
4901 Evergreen Road
Dearborn, MI 48128
313-593-1183

University of Minnesota
Hubert H. Humphrey Institute Center on Women and Public Policy
301 19th Avenue South, 130 Humphrey Center
Minneapolis, MN 55455
612-625-6351

University of Minnesota, Duluth
Women's Studies Program
10 University Drive
Duluth, MN 55812-2496

University of Minnesota Libraries
170 Wilson Library
309 19th Avenue South
Minneapolis, MN 55455-0414

University of Missouri, Columbia
309 Switzler Hall
Columbia, MO 65211
573-882-2703

University of Missouri, St. Louis
Institute for Women and Gender Studies
8001 Natural Bridge Road
St. Louis, MO 63121-4499
314-516-5581
http://www.umsl.edu/divisions/artscience/iwgs.html

University of Montana
Women's Studies Program
LA 138A
Missoula, MT 59812-1045
406-243-2584

University of Montana
Montana Women's History Project
University Center
Missoula, MT 59812

University of Nebraska, Lincoln
Women's Studies Program
Avery Hall 307
Lincoln, NE 68588-0136
402-472-9392
http://www.unl.edu/women22p/

University of Nebraska, Omaha
Women's Studies Program
Ash 200
Omaha, NE 68182
402-554-3833

University of Nevada Las Vegas
Women's Studies
4505 Maryland Parkway, Box 455055
Las Vegas, NV 89154-5055
702-895-0838

University of North Carolina at Asheville
Women's Studies Program
KH 126, 1 University Heights
Asheville, NC 28804-8509

University of North Florida
Women's Center
4567 St. Johns Bluff Road South
Jacksonville, FL 32224
904-620-2528

University of North Texas
Women's Studies Program
PO Box 305189
Denton, TX 76203
940-565-2098
http://www.smst.unt.edu

University of Oregon
Center for the Study of Women in Society
340 Hendricks Hall
Eugene, OR 97403-1201
541-346-5015
http://darkwing.uoregon.edu/~csws/

University of Pennsylvania
Women's Studies Program
411 Logan Hall
Philadelphia, PA 19104-6304
215-898-8740
http://www.sas.upenn.edu/wstudies

University of Pennsylvania
Alice Paul Center for the Study of Women
340 Market Street
Philadelphia, PA 19104-6403
215-898-8740
http://www.sas.upenn.edu/wstudies/
AlicePaulResearchCenter

University of Pittsburgh
Women's Studies Program
2632 Cathedral of Learning
Pittsburgh, PA 15260

University of Puget Sound
Women's Studies Program
Tacoma, WA 98413
253-756-3173

University of Redlands
Women's Studies
1200 East Colton Avenue
Redlands, CA 92373-0999
909-793-2121

University of Rhode Island
Women's Studies Program
315 Eleanor Roosevelt Hall
Kingston, RI 02881
401-874-5150

University of Richmond
Women's Studies Program
2309 Park Avenue
Richmond, VA 23226
804-289-8965

Additional Information

University of Rochester
Susan B. Anthony Institute for Gender and
Women's Studies
RC Box 270434
Rochester, NY 14627-0434
716-275-8318
http://www.rochester.edu/college/wst

University of Scranton
Women's Studies
Scranton, PA 18510-4507
http://academic.uofs.edu/department/wstudies

University of Southern California
Center for Feminist Research
Safety and Systems Management, Suite 116
Los Angeles, CA 90089-0022
213-740-1739
http://www.usc.edu/dpet/cfr/

University of Southern Colorado
Women's Studies Program
Pueblo, CO 81001
719-549-2348

University of Southern Maine
Women's Studies Program
94 Bedford Street
Portland, ME 04103
207-780-4289

University of Texas, Austin
Center for Women's Studies
401 West 25th Street, Suite 401
Austin, TX 78705
512-471-5765
http://www.utexas.edu/depts/wstudies

University of Utah
Women's Resource Center
Higher Education Resource Services, West
200 South Campus Drive, Room 293
Salt Lake City, UT 84112
801-581-8030
http://www.saff.utah.edu/women/wrc

University of Vermont
Women's Studies
Old Mill, PO Box 54260
Burlington, VT 05405
802-656-4282
http://www.uvm.edu/women/

University of Washington
Northwest Center for Research on Women
Imogen Cunningham Hall, Box 351380
Seattle, WA 98195-1380
206-543-9531
http://www.weber.u.washington.edu/~nwcrow/

University of Western Ontario
DB Weldon Library
Serials Acquisition Unit
London, Ontario N6A 3K7

University of Wisconsin, Eau Claire
Women's Studies
Eau Claire, WI 54702-4004
715-836-5717

University of Wisconsin, La Crosse
1725 State Street
La Crosse, WI 54601
608-785-8357

University of Wisconsin, Madison
Women's Studies Research Center
1155 Orchard Drive
Madison, WI 53706
608-263-2053

University of Wisconsin, Milwaukee
PO Box 413
Milwaukee, WI 53201
414-229-5918
http://www.uwm.edu/dept/cws/

University of Wisconsin, Oshkosh
Women's Studies
800 Algoma Boulevard
A/C 314
Oshkosh, WI 54901
920-424-0892

University of Wisconsin, Platteville
Women's Studies Program
449 Gardner Hall
Platteville, WI 53818
608-342-1750

University of Wisconsin System
Women's Studies Consortium
1664 Van Hise Hall
1220 Linden Drive
Madison, WI 53706
608-262-3056

University of Wyoming
Women's Studies Program
PO Box 4297
Laramie, WY 82071
307-766-2733

Upstate New York Women's History Conference
1202 East State Street
Ithaca, NY 14850

Utah State University
Women's Studies Program
Department of Communication
Logan, UT 84322-4605
435-797-3253

Utah State University
Women and Gender Research Institute
310 Taggart Student Center, UM 0186
Logan, UT 84322-0186
801-797-1396

Virginia Commonwealth University
Women's Studies
Box 843060
Richmond, VA 23284-3060
804-828-6710
http://www.has.vcu.edu/wst

Virginia Tech
Women's Center
Price House
Blacksburg, VA 24060-0270
540-231-7806

Wake Forest University
Women's Studies
PO Box 7365
Winston-Salem, NC 27109
336-758-5193

Washington State University
Women's Studies Program
PO Box 644007
Pullman, WA 99164-4007
509-335-1794

Washington State University
Women's Resource Center
Pullman, WA 99164-7204
509-335-6830
http://www.saff.utah.edu/women/wrc

Washington University
Women's Studies Program
1 Brookings Drive, 1078
St. Louis, MO 63130
314-935-5102
http://ascc.artsci.wustl.edu/~women/

Washington Women Historians
1668 Wainwright Drive
Reston, VA 20190
703-742-0578

Weber State University
Women's Studies
1217 University Circle
Ogden, UT 84408
801-626-7632

Webster University
Women's Studies Program
470 East Lockwood
St. Louis, MO 63119
314-968-7067

Wellesley College
Wellesley Centers for Women
106 Central Street
Wellesley, MA 02181
617-283-2503
http://www.wellesley.edu/WCW/index.html

Additional Information

Wellesley College
Women's Studies Department
Founders Hall
Wellesley, MA 02481
781-283-2538

Wellesley College
Higher Education Resource Services, New England
Waban House
828 Washington Street
Wellesley, MA 02181
617-283-2529

Wells College
Women's Studies
105 MacMillan Hall
Aurora, NY 13026
315-364-3224

Wesleyan University
Women's Studies Program
Middletown, CT 06459
860-685-3453

West Valley College
Women's Studies Program
14000 Fruitvale Avenue
Saratoga, CA 95070
408-741-2507

Western Association of Women Historians
23250 Mariano Street
Woodland Hills, CA 91367

Western Kentucky University
Women's Studies Program
1532 State Street
Bowling Green, KY 42101
502-745-6477

Western New York Women's History Committee and Hall of Fame
153 Lancaster Avenue
Buffalo, NY 14222
716-878-6820

Westfield State College
Women's Studies Program
Westfield, MA 01086
413-572-5623

Wheaton College
Women's Studies Program
Norton, MA 02766
508-286-3671

Wichita State University
Center for Women's Studies
1848 North Fairmount, Campus Box 82
Wichita, KS 62760-0082
316-689-3358
http://www.twsu.edu/~wmstudy/welcomes

Widener University
Women's Studies Program
Chester, PA 19103
610-499-4374

William Paterson University
Student Center
300 Pompton Road
Wayne, NJ 07420

Williams College
Women's and Gender Studies
Williamstown, MA 01267
413-597-2305

Wittenberg University
Women's Studies Program
PO Box 720
Springfield, OH 45501
937-327-6130

Women and Labor History Project
5320 North Sheridan Road, 1902
Chicago, IL 60640
773-769-2665

Women Historians of Greater Cleveland
3391 Tiellamore
Cleveland Heights, OH 44118

Women Historians of the Midwest

c/o Minnesota Women's Consortium
550 Rice Street, 101
St. Paul, MN 55103
612-373-0984

Women in Military Service for America

5510 Columbia Pike, Suite 302
Arlington, VA 22204
703-533-1555

Women Who Lead

Sophia Smith Foundation
PO Box 991
Groton, MA 01450
978-448-3212
http://www.womenwholead.org

Women's History and Resource Center

General Federation of Women's Clubs
1734 N Street, NW
Washington, DC 20036-2990
202-347-3168

Women's History Coalition of Kentucky

c/o Karen McDaniel
Kentucky State University
Blazer Library
Frankfort, KY 40601
502-227-6854

Women's History Museum

Box 209
108 Walnut Street
West Liberty, WV 26704
304-336-7159

Women's History Project of Akron

PO Box 72077
Akron, OH 44372-2077
216-366-2578

Women's History Project of Greene County

1475 President Street
Yellow Springs, OH 45387

Women's History Reclamation Project

2323 Broadway, Suite 107
San Diego, CA 92102
619-233-7963

Women's History Research Center

c/o American Heritage Center
University of Wyoming
Box 3924
Laramie, WY 82071-3924
307-766-4114

Women's Interart Center

549 West 52nd Street
New York, NY 10019
212-246-1050

Women's Research and Education Institute

1750 New York Avenue, Suite 350
Washington, DC 20009
202-628-0444
http://www.wrei.org

Women's Rights National Historical Park

National Park Service
136 Fall Street
Seneca Falls, NY 13148
315-568-2991

Worcester Women's History Project

c/o YWCA
1 Salem Square
Worcester, MA 01608
508-767-1852

Wright State University

Women's Studies Program
401 Millett Hall, 3640
Colonel Glenn Highway
Dayton, OH 45435
937-775-7008

Yale University

Women's and Gender Studies Program
PO Box 208319
New Haven, CT 06520-8319
203-432-0845

Young Women's Christian Association

350 Fifth Avenue, Suite 301
New York, NY 10118
212-273-7800

Youngstown State University

Center for Women's Studies
1 University Plaza
Youngstown, OH 44559

Work at Home

Work-at-home resources are included in this directory because working at home or other alternative work arrangements are attractive options for many women trying to balance professional and family responsibilities. Many of the organizations listed in this section are not expressly for women.

African American Women Entrepreneurs at Home

c/o Virtual Support Services
PMB 190, 1401 Pulaski Highway, Suite U
Edgewood, MD 21040
http://www.wix.com/vss/aaweh_m.htm

How to Start and Manage a Home-Based Business is available for purchase from the African American Women Entrepreneurs at Home Web site. The site also lists resources for freelancers, telecommuters, and small businesses, and links to sites of interest to African American women.

American Association of Home-Based Businesses

PO Box 10023
Rockville, MD 20849
800-447-9710
http://www.aahbb.org

THE AAHBB is a non-profit organization for those who run a business from their homes. It was founded to provide support, networking, and legislative monitoring. Members include accountants, writers, contractors, lawyers, crafters, artists, caterers, and others. It advocates for issues such as tax reform, issues a newsletter, provides links to members, Web sites, provides tips on getting started, and offers discounts on office products.

Black Educated At-Home Moms

http://members.aol.com/DADAWCPD/beams.html

BEAMS is a Web-based forum geared toward the African American at-home mother. Tips and resources are offered on topics from child-rearing to finding ways to work at home.

Business Opportunities Classifieds Online

http://www.boconline.com

BOC Online is a Web resource for small and home business startup information. Most of its services are free, including a listing on the BOC Classifieds Network. Recent featured articles included "What Is Franchising?" "Do You Need a License or Permit for Your Home-Based Business?" and "Incorporating Your New Business."

The Entrepreneurial Parent

PO Box 370722
Fairfield, CT 06432
203-371-6212
http://www.en-parent.com

The Entrepreneurial Parent is a work/family resource for home office entrepreneurs and career professionals who are seeking alternative work options. Membership is free. Benefits include resource centers, articles, forums, member listings, career counseling, products and services, and mentoring.

Formerly Employed Mothers at the Leading Edge
P.O. Box 31
Elmhurst, IL 60126
630-941-3553
http://www.femalehome.org

FEMALE is an international organization that supports women who have altered their career paths in order to care for their children at home. There are over 170 chapters in the United States, Canada, and the U.K. It advocates for public and employment policies that make it easier to keep family a priority. Members receive a newsletter. Local chapters provide support through playgroups, discussion groups, and babysitting co-ops, and offer committee experience in writing, desktop publishing, fundraising, and marketing. The Web site lists chapter contacts.

Home Business Magazine
9582 Hamilton Avenue, Suite 368
Huntington Beach, CA 92646
714-968-0331
http://www.homebusinessmag.com

Home Business Magazine is available in hard copy or electronically. A recent sampling of articles included "Lighting Your Home Office," "What You Should Know About Patents," "Seven Tips for Entrepreneurs Seeking Equity Capital," and "Strategic Alliances." Web channels include Business Startup, Home Office Equipment, Webmastery, and Network Marketing.

Home Office Association of America
10 Gracie Station
Box 806
New York, NY 10028-0082
800-809-4622
http://www.hoaa.com

The Home Office Association of America is a national organization for home-based and small businesses. It offers health insurance packages, shipping rate discounts, access to a national

collection agency, travel discounts, and a newsletter.

Home Office Magazine
Entrepreneur Media
2392 Morse Avenue
Irvine, CA 92614
949-261-2325
http://www.homeofficemag.com

Home Office Magazine offers news and advice for home-based business entrepreneurs. Recent special reports included "A How-To Guide to E-commerce," "Computer Upgrades," and "Independent Contractors."

Home-Based Working Moms
PO Box 500164
Austin, TX 78750
512-266-0900

Home-Based Working Moms is a national association for parents who work at home or those who would like to. HBWM provides members with support, networking, information, a monthly (print) newsletter, tips for avoiding scams, members' listserve, panel of experts, publicity opportunities, and membership directory.

International Society for Work Options
c/o New Ways to Work
785 Market Street, Suite 950
San Francisco, CA 94103
415-995-9860
http://www.nww.org/iswo/

The ISWO works to improve communication among members of different disciplines, including human resource personnel, organizational consultants, academics, policy makers, and people who work at home. ISWO advocates for flextime, annual hours, compressed workweeks, job sharing, telecommuting, temporary employment, at-home, and contract work.

Additional Information

Mothers' Access to Careers at Home

PO Box 123
Annandale, VA 22003
703-205-9664
http://www.freestate.net/match/about.net

MATCH is a regional organization for women in Maryland and Virginia who are balancing careers and families by working from home. Membership benefits include attendance at meetings in Virginia or Maryland, a bi-monthly newsletter, member directory, a resource guide, and seasonal events.

Mothers At Home

8310-A Old Courthouse Road
Vienna, VA 22182
703-827-5903
http://www.mah.org

Mothers At Home is a national organization supporting at-home mothers, including mothers who work from home. It publishes the advertisement-free monthly journal "Welcome Home," and periodically publishes books on the topic. The Web site and journal offer advice and creative solutions to the challenges all mothers face. Call 1-800-783-4666 for a free information packet or to subscribe.

Mothers' Home Business Network

P.O. Box 423
East Meadow, NY 11554
516-997-7394
http://www.homeworkingmom.com

Mothers' Home Business Network supports mothers who work at home and those who would like to. It offers information on flexible work options, and resources on at-home business assistance and opportunities. The Web site is updated regularly with at-home business topics such as how to telecommute and accepting credit card orders for your home-based business.

National Home Office Association

3412 Woolsey Drive
Chevy Chase, MD 20815
301-652-1667
http://www.nhoa.org

The National Home Office Association offers free membership to people who work in a home office environment. Members receive discounts on products and services related to the home office, insurance options, time-saving and money-making hints, and advocacy at the state and federal, state, and local levels.

New Ways to Work

785 Market Street, Suite 950
San Francisco, CA 94103
http://www.nww.org

New Ways to Work offers seminars and publications that help workers reshape the workplace. Some of the titles offered for purchase include *Flexible Work Arrangements: Guidelines for Managers and Employees, Creating a Flexible Workplace: How to Select and Manage Alternative Work Options,* and *Flexibility: Compelling Strategies for a Competitive Workplace.*

A New Workplace at Home

http://www.newworkplace.com

A New Workplace is an online resource for those who dream of working at home. It offers home business ideas, articles, and resources to help start a home-based business.

The Real Deal on Telecommuting

Sienna Publishing
PMB 121
L 3350 San Pablo Avenue, A1
San Pablo, CA 94806

The Real Deal on Telecommuting was written by Rosalind Mays, a mother who grew frustrated at all of the work-at-home and telecommuting scams she encountered when looking for a work-at-home job. She offers a list of work-at-home scams, tips on detecting scams, four ways to find a telecommuting job, and information on freelance contract jobs.

Service Corps of Retired Executives

409 Third Street, SW, Sixth Floor
Washington, DC 20024
800-634-0245
http://www.score.org

SCORE is a group of working and retired executives and business owners who donate their time and expertise as volunteer business counselors. Local chapters provide free counseling and low-cost workshops to entrepreneurs. Free email counseling is available for those without a local SCORE chapter. Free workbooks available include *How to Secure Financing* and *How to Choose the Best Bank for Your Business*.

United States Postal Inspection Service

http://www.usps.gov/Web
sites/depart/inspect/emplmenu.htm

The United States Postal Inspection Service maintains current information on work-at-home employment schemes. The Web site alerts consumers about distributorship and franchise frauds, phony job opportunities, multi-level marketing scams, postal job scams, and work-at-home schemes.

Women International Publishing

PMB 327
91-590 Farrington Highway, Suite 210
Kapolei, HI 96707-2002
http://www.womentakecontrol.com

Women International Publishing is an independent publishing company that publishes and promotes books and information that improve women's economic and personal well-being. One of the articles offered on its Web site is "Starting a Home Business: Startup Checklist."

Work-at-Home Mom.com

http://www.wahm.com

Work-At-Home Mom.com is an online magazine for mothers who work at home, providing job listings, advice, and frequently asked questions about working at home, message boards, and a business opportunity page. Recent articles included "Scams and How to Avoid Them," and "Single WAHMs and Self Esteem."

WorkOptions.Com

808-531-9939
http://www.workoptions.com

WorkOptions.com bills itself as the "working mother's guide to negotiating flexible work." Tips on telecommuting, job sharing, and flex-time arrangements are offered, including a guide to convincing your employer to allow telecommuting or other flexible arrangements for working mothers. Mothers who need a completed proposal to present to their employer can check out the free online workbook, *Flex Success: A Proposal Blueprint for Getting a Family-Friendly Work Schedule*.

Institution and Financial Aid Name Index

This index lists the names of all the institutions, organizations, publications, Web sites, and financial aid (fellowships, grants, scholarships, awards, loans, internships) that appear in this directory.

Index

Index

Index

Index

Index

Index

M

Index

Index

Index

Index

Index

Index

Index

State Index

This index lists financial aid (fellowships, grants, scholarships, awards, loans, internships) by state.

Index

Colorado

Connecticut

District of Columbia

Internships

Loans

Scholarships

Women's Colleges

Florida

Awards

Fellowships

Georgia

Awards

Internships

Index

Loans

P.E.O. Sisterhood, 94, 96, 114

Scholarships

National Federation of the Blind, 111
P.E.O. Sisterhood, 94, 96, 114

Kansas

Internships

NCAA Women's Enhancement Program, 112

Scholarships

NCAA Women's Enhancement Program, 112

Kentucky

Grants

Kentucky Foundation for Women, 93

Women's Colleges

Midway College, 235

Louisiana

Women's Colleges

Newcomb College of Tulane University, 237

Maryland

Awards

American Congress on Surveying and Mapping, 70, 98
American Physical Society, 70
Association for Women in Communications, 71, 100
Association for Women in Mathematics, 71, 91
Biophysical Society, 72
National Women's Studies Association, 77, 112

Grants

Association for Women in Mathematics, 71, 91

Internships

Sisterhood Is Global Institute, 261

Scholarships

American Congress on Surveying and Mapping, 70, 98
National Women's Studies Association, 77, 112
Society of Daughters of the United States Army, 115

Women's Colleges

College of Notre Dame of Maryland, 230
Hood College, 233

Massachusetts

Fellowships

M. A. Cartland Schackford Medical Fellowship, 84
Radcliffe College, 86

Internships

Ipas, 256
Massachusetts Coalition on New Office Technology, 256
Sojourner, The Women's Forum, 262
Women Express, 262

Scholarships

Hitchcock Scholarship Fund, 107
Wellesley College, 84, 103, 118
Women's Transportation Seminar, 121

Women's Colleges

Aquinas College, 227
Bay Path College, 228
Elms College, 231
Emmanuel College, 232
Endicott College, 232
Lasell College, 234

Index

Index

Index

Washington

Scholarships

Wisconsin

Scholarships

Women's Colleges

Academic Index

This index lists financial aid (fellowships, grants, scholarships, awards, loans, internships) by academic subject.

Agriculture/Consumer Science

Awards

American Association of Family and Consumer Sciences, 69, 80, 90
Women's World Summit Foundation, 79

Fellowships

American Agricultural Economics Association, 80
American Association of Family and Consumer Sciences, 69, 80, 90
Kappa Omicron Nu Honor Society, 84
Women's National Farm and Garden Association, 89

Grants

American Association of Family and Consumer Sciences, 69, 80, 90
Webber Educational Grants Committee, 100

Scholarships

Canadian Home Economics Association, 103
Family, Career, and Community Leaders of America, 105
Odwalla, Inc., 113
Oregon State Scholarship Commission, 113
Van Wert County Foundation, 117
Washington Fashion Group, 118

Any subject/general

Awards

Avon Latina Model of the Year, 72
Hobart and William Smith Colleges, 74
Independent Means, 75
National Hispana Leadership Institute, 76
National Women's Studies Association, 77, 112
Professional Women of Color, 77
Soroptimist International of the Americas, 78

Fellowships

American Association of University Women Educational Foundation, 81
Asian Pacific American Women's Leadership Institute, 81
Business and Professional Women's Clubs of New York State, 83
International Women's Forum, 84
National Science Foundation, 85, 91-92
New Jersey Federation of Women's Clubs, 86
World-Wide Fellows Program, 87

Grants

Altrusa International, 90
P.E.O. Sisterhood, 94, 96, 114
Thanks Be To Grandmother Winifred Foundation, 94
Woodrow Wilson Dissertation Grants in Women's Studies, 95

Index

Internships

Loans

Scholarships

Athletics

Awards

Grants

Internships

Scholarships

Business/Finance

Grants

Internships

Loans

Scholarships

Business/Finance, Social Science

Scholarships

Computer Science

Awards

Index

Fellowships

National Physical Sciences Consortium, 85

Grants

Conference Experiences for Women, 92

Internships

AT&T Undergraduate Research Program, 252
Autodesk Design Your Future Project, 247, 252, 265

Scholarships

Microsoft Corporation, 109
Society of Women Engineers, 115
Women in Wireless Communications, 119

Computer Science, Engineering, Science

Fellowships

Luce Foundation, 83

Education

Awards

National Association of Women in Education, 76
National Council of Administrative Women in Education, 76

Fellowships

Canadian Federation of University Women, 83

Grants

Alpha Delta Kappa, 90, 97

Scholarships

Alpha Delta Kappa International Honorary Society for Women Educators, 97
Association of Black Women in Higher Education, 101

Business and Professional Women's Foundation, 96, 102
United Methodist Church, 117
Zeta Phi Beta Sorority, 89, 122

Engineering

Awards

American Congress on Surveying and Mapping, 70, 98
Association of Universities and Colleges of Canada, 101

Fellowships

American Water Works Association, 81
Women's International Network of Utility Professionals, 88
Zonta International Foundation, 80, 89, 122

Grants

American Chemical Society, 69, 91

Loans

Business and Professional Women's Foundation, 96, 102

Scholarships

American Congress on Surveying and Mapping, 70, 98
American Society of Landscape Architects, 99
Intel Foundation Women in Science and Engineering Scholarships, 107
National Research Council of Canada, 111
National Society of Professional Engineers, 111
New Mexico Educational Assistance Foundation, 113
Sons of Norway Foundation, 116
Transportation Clubs International, 117
Women's Transportation Seminar, 121

Index